Twelve Infallible Men

Twelve Infallible Men

The Imams and the Making of Shiʿism

MATTHEW PIERCE

Harvard University Press
Cambridge, Massachusetts ▪ London, England
2016

Printed in the United States of America

Second printing

Library of Congress Cataloging-in-Publication Data

Names: Pierce, Matthew, author.
Title: Twelve infallible men : the imams and the making of shiʿism / Matthew Pierce.
Description: Cambridge, Massachusetts : Harvard University Press, 2016. |
Includes bibliographical references and index.
Identifiers: LCCN 2015040452 | ISBN 9780674737075 (cloth)
Subjects: LCSH: Islamic hagiography. | Imams (Shiites)—Biography—History
and criticism. | Shiʿah. | Identification (Religion)
Classification: LCC BP189.43 .P54 2016 | DDC 297.8/20922—dc23
LC record available at http://lccn.loc.gov/2015040452

For Ramona and Mae

Contents

Note on Dates and Transliteration

Following standard practice in Islamic Studies, I provide the death dates of individuals in both the Islamic (*hijri*) and Gregorian calendars in parentheses after their names. All other dates are simply given in the Gregorian calendar. In further efforts to remove unnecessary distractions to nonspecialist readers, I have refrained from using any diacritical marks in transliteration of Arabic or Persian words in the body of the book. I kept only the standard symbols for *ʿayn* and *hamza*. However, in the appendixes, bibliography, and endnotes, which I assume will be of greater interest to specialists, I have used the system of transliteration adopted by the American Library Association and the Library of Congress (ALA-LC). Words that have now become common in English, such as *Islam* or *Sunni*, are not given diacritical marks. My sole departure from the ALA-LC system is that I only render the *ta barbuta* into English when it is in the construct state (in which case it is a "t"). I have also used *Shiʿa* consistently in the nominative grammatical form rather than shifting it to *Shiʿi* to reflect Arabic usage. Where English translations exist, I have sought to quote from those translations (most notably I. K. A. Howard's translation of *The Book of Guidance*), as indicated in the notes. Otherwise, all translations are my own.

Twelve Infallible Men

Prologue

In 2003 I took up residence in the shrine city of Qum, Iran, a center of Shiʿa learning rivaled only by Najaf.[1] One of the most striking aspects of the popular religious life I encountered was the love people expressed for the imams—the twelve pure and infallible figures believed to have inherited the knowledge and wisdom of the Prophet Muhammad. Teachers, friends, and neighbors recounted stories of the imams' remarkable achievements and tales of the suffering and oppression they endured. Many of these stories were set in the distant past, drawn from books about the imams' lives or recalled from preachers' sermons. More striking, however, were the stories of the imams as actors in our present-day world, as arbiters of divine favor in the daily lives of believers. Some people encountered imams in their dreams; others were blessed during pilgrimages to shrines. I came away from these encounters with a profound sense that the imams who walked the earth over a thousand years ago remain present to the faithful who love them, who mourn their suffering, and who seek their guidance with confidence and devotion. Interestingly, the stories that I heard were not exclusively, or even primarily, focused on the most famous imams, like ʿAli or al-Husayn. Several of the imams about whom I knew little at the time, and whose historical roles seemed insignificant to outsiders, also appeared regularly in inspirational accounts.

Alongside the contemporary oral culture of stories of the imams, countless books on the holy figures' lives are found in Shiʿa shrines, mosques, and bookstores. Ranging from small leaflets to multivolume compendiums, these texts help sustain and authenticate popular conceptions of the nature of the imams and their role in the history of Islam. But oral and written accounts propagated today do much more than document the historical lives of the imams; they also provide a framework for meaningful devotion and a system of piety rooted in the communal remembrance of the Prophet Muhammad and his progeny. This system of piety is the subject of this book. Rather than seeking to recover the historical Shiʿa imams, though that may also be an important task, this study explores how those imams have been remembered by the Shiʿa communities who love them. More specifically, *Twelve Infallible Men* is an analysis of a subgenre of Islamic hagiography: works containing the life stories of all twelve Shiʿa imams. These collective biographies played a significant role in the formation of Twelver Shiʿa identity and religious orientation from the tenth to today. The earliest collective biographies, and the later works that followed their example, are connected not only by a common subject matter, but by recurring themes and motifs that can help increase our understanding of the development of Shiʿism.

Stories of saints offer us a window through which we can view the cultures in which the narratives are meaningful. Such stories help illuminate the concerns and perspectives of the religious communities in which they have been composed and transmitted, revealing the deep desires of those who tell them. As Elizabeth Castelli shows in her study of early Christian martyrdom accounts, these narratives reflected and shaped broader Christian notions of martyrdom and its meaning in late antiquity, providing a platform through which early Christian identity was articulated. Drawing upon studies of social memory, she illustrates how these accounts functioned as loci of communal reflection from antiquity until today.[2] Though my project focuses on Shiʿa rather than Christian martyrdom accounts, Castelli's research has shaped my own reading of early Muslim narratives, pointing as it does to the ways that Shiʿa communities made sense of their past through vivid narratives of the suffering of revered members of Muhammad's family. The insights of another scholar of early Christianity, Averil Cameron, have also sharpened my perspective. As she points out, Christianity was able to "create its own intellectual and imaginative universe" in the context of a changing Roman Empire in part by telling the stories of the lives and deaths of Christian saints. Such stories were central to the development of a "totalizing discourse" resilient enough to create an enduring universe of Christian myth.[3] Though the early Christian context is significantly different from the ʿAbbasid-era Islamic setting, Shiʿa Muslims also formulated an understanding of their community on the basis of a shared memory of former suffering.

The theme of suffering in Shiʿa stories of the imams has been explored,[4] but analyses of the significance of martyrdom have largely been focused on the most famous instance: the death of al-Husayn at Karbala. As I explain later, a loose consensus gradually developed among the Shiʿa that all of the deceased imams (the twelfth is considered still living, though in hiding) died a martyr's death. But this view took time to coalesce, and questions about this narrative of history remain. Why did the Shiʿa come to the conclusion that all the imams were martyrs? What made that version of history compelling and convincing? Pursuing these questions, it becomes clear that martyrdom is only one of many experiences the imams are portrayed as having in common. Though the biographers of the imams are remarkably (though never completely) consistent in the signs, symbols, and themes they use to portray their infallible leaders, suffering and martyrdom cannot be understood in isolation from other themes that appear across the biographies. By analyzing these narrative patterns,[5] while keeping in mind other saintly stories in different contexts, the significance of the stories of the imams for Shiʿa communities in the late ʿAbbasid Empire becomes clearer.

The Stories of the Imams

Many forms of Shiʿa ritual, art, and literature played a role in shaping and transmitting the stories of the imams, but my study focuses on the subgenre mentioned above: collective biographies of the imams. Beginning in the tenth century, Shiʿa writers began compiling these works, collating historical anecdotes and compelling narratives into single works that bound together the lives of all twelve imams. Over the course of subsequent centuries, this type of Shiʿa literature expanded and developed immensely, and works of this kind continue to be written today.[6] The present study focuses on five of the earliest extant examples: five texts, which I believe constitute the formative stage of this genre, that were written in Arabic from the tenth to twelfth centuries. Additional historiographical information on these works is included in the first chapter, but I will introduce them briefly here.

The earliest collective biography of any substantial length that survived the trials of history is *Establishment of the Inheritance* (*Ithbat al-wasiya*), a fascinating work completed in the year 943. Shiʿa sources have traditionally ascribed this book to the well-known Shiʿa historian al-Masʿudi (d. 345/956), but there are good reasons to doubt this attribution. Another early surviving example, *Proofs of the Imamate* (*Dalaʾil al-imama*), is of equally questionable authorship. It has traditionally been ascribed to an early tenth century author, but some of its content clearly dates to the early eleventh century. We are on firmer historical ground with the other three works. The *Book of Guidance* (*Kitab al-irshad*), a profoundly influential biography of the imams, was written around the turn of the eleventh century by a towering figure in classical Shiʿism, al-Shaykh al-Mufid (d. 413/1022), who lived in the tumultuous political context of the ʿAbbasid capital of Baghdad. The fourth work in the genre, *Informing Humanity* (*Iʿlam al-waraʾ*), was written just over a century later by al-Fadl b. al-Hasan al-Tabrisi (d. 548/1154), who lived near Mashhad in the small town of Sabzevar. Al-Tabrisi most likely wrote this book between the years of 1130 and 1140. One of his students during that time, Ibn Shahrashub (d. 588/1192), went on to write the last of the five works at the heart of this study. Ibn Shahrashub completed the expansive *Virtues of the Descendants of Abu Talib* (*Manaqib al Abi Talib*) while in Baghdad around 1150. These five works are intertextually entwined with one another, and they provide a unique window into the development of a distinctly Shiʿa narrative of history of the imams.[7]

These texts are relatively well known in Western academic contexts (with one, al-Mufid's *Book of Guidance*, being available in English translation), and numerous scholars have mentioned their importance in passing;[8] but overall, the collective biographies have received little scholarly analysis. Although they defy easy classification, they have been variously conceptualized as works of hadith, history, or hagiography.[9]

Like works of hadith, they contain sayings and teachings of the imams that have been referenced in attempts to understand Shiʿa theology and law.[10] As historical accounts, they have been read alongside other works in attempts to construct a historical narrative of the early Islamic period.[11] Less frequently, these works have been treated as hagiography,[12] for they contain praises of the imams that reappear in Shiʿa shrine visitation rituals (*ziyara*), dramatic commemorations (*taʿziya*), and public retellings of the stories of the imams (*rawza khwani*).

For scholars of religious studies, the biographies of the imams may most naturally be seen as works of hagiography. This categorization provides a helpful point of orientation from which to examine the literature, but it is not unproblematic. The modern academic study of hagiography (or hagiology) is rooted in European scholarship on Christian saints, and even in that context scholars have debated the usefulness of conceptualizing hagiography as a genre.[13] Hagiography, after all, is a modern construct that has no premodern equivalent—writers in the late antique and early medieval period did not conceive of hagiography as a category. Debate over the usefulness of hagiography as a conceptual tool has not led to a full abandonment of the term, but it has led to more nuanced discussions of subgenres of the literature and how different texts functioned in specific contexts.[14] Approaches to hagiography, as Felice Lifshitz argues, must "consciously take into account changing political contexts."[15]

Applying the concept of hagiography to non-Christian traditions comes with its own set of problems. Casting a text as Islamic hagiography can lead us to assume that what we know about Christian saints and Christian hagiography is applicable to a vastly different religious and historical context. Despite the methodological risks, however, recent research on hagiography is helpful when it comes to examining the biographies of the imams. The questions and methods used to read hagiography in other religious contexts illuminate the dynamics at play in the imams' biographies, which, as I will show, have much in common with other forms of hagiography. But even when applying the methods and insights of those studies, I have attempted to remain open to arriving at different answers. Literary analyses of texts from non-Christian traditions must take into account key differences in sociopolitical and religious contexts. Doing so not only sheds light on key developments within Islam, but also enriches the study of hagiography by demonstrating how stories of revered figures developed and operated in Muslim contexts.

The study of hagiography in Islam has been slow to develop. John Renard has made significant recent contributions to this underdeveloped field of studies with his *Friends of God: Islamic Images of Piety, Commitment, and Servanthood.* This compendium is accompanied by an anthology of stories he edited entitled *Tales of God's Friends: Islamic Hagiography in Translation.* The bulk of Renard's work, however, as well as that of others who have written on Muslim saints, is focused primarily on either Sufi saints or the prophets. The stories of the imams also deserve attention, in part because they give us information about the communities that received and transmitted them. *Twelve Infallible Men* is the first study to take a broad approach to this literature in an attempt to understand how it reflected and shaped the concerns of early medieval Shiʿa communities.

Approaching the Texts

In his frequently cited article, "The Rise and Function of the Holy Man in Late Antiquity," Peter Brown notes that stories of saints often function "like a mirror." He writes, "In studying both the most admired and the most detested figures in any society, we can see, as seldom through other evidence, the nature of the average man's expectations and hopes for himself."[16] This is equally true of the biographies of the imams, who are, among other things, aspirational paragons of humanity. But the portrayals of the imams are complex. At every turn, the biographies reveal layers of legal, theological, and devotional concern. The authors' assumptions about the ideal man, a just society, and bonds of loyalty are interwoven throughout the texts. Understanding the function of the biographies in the communities therefore requires looking at the texts from multiple angles, including through the lenses of literary theory and gender studies.[17] Using a multidisciplinary approach risks overgeneralization, and specialists in any number of subfields will likely find deficiencies in my analysis in certain areas. I hope, however, that my study will spark further research into the biographies of the imams and offer a new way to engage the biographies as well as the communities that are devoted to these imams.

The questions at the center of this study are related to conceptions of the imams that solidified in the first few centuries in which their collective stories were told and retold. As such, my research is less concerned with the origin of specific accounts than with the way those stories contribute to the metanarrative constructed in the biographies. The emergence and endurance of the themes and motifs considered in this book reveals a great deal about the concerns of the communities that found them meaningful. The question I have asked throughout, then, is what made these stories meaningful? Above all others, the theoretical apparatus that best helped me grapple with this question has been collective memory studies.[18]

The historical events around which a community coalesces often have less influence on the development of that community than how those events are remembered. Human memories of events or experiences are always at odds, to some degree, with the occurrences themselves. Moreover, individuals do not remember in isolation. All memory is so cially mediated and occurs within community. The preservation of a memory is contingent upon there being meaningful reasons to retain some details and not others, and meaning is supplied by an individual's relationship to a social context.[19] In this study, when I speak of social memory, I mean the general process of remembering certain accounts (and not others) from the near and distant past and preserving and transmitting those accounts to future generations. This process takes place in a social environment—it occurs in the context of the relationship between the individual and the community to which he or she is connected. Viewing the historical record through the lens of social memory provides a way of putting the collective and communal nature of historical writing in the foreground. It understands the individual author of each text in relationship to a community for which he or she writes and, perhaps most importantly, through the needs of that community.[20]

This study makes use of the discourse on social memory in an effort to more fully understand the classical Shiʿa biographies of the imams. Doing so helps us better assess the relationship between the Shiʿa memories of the imams and the development of Shiʿa identity. By analyzing the themes of the collective biographies with an eye on the social memory being produced and reproduced through them, we can ask different questions of the texts. Throughout this study, I have attempted to be mindful of questions such as: Why is a given account memorable rather than forgettable? What purpose does this memory serve? What was it that made these accounts sensible? What are the assumptions about community, personhood, gender, power, authority, and suffering that undergird these stories? What feelings are evoked through this literature? What was the anticipated response from the reader/audience? How do the stories express the concerns of this community of memory?[21]

I have not attempted to verify whether the events described in the stories actually occurred. I make no claims about the historical imams. Instead, I am concerned with what this literature tells us about the community for which the works were written and by which the works have been transmitted. The issue of historicity is moot, for the facticity of the literature has little bearing on the community's ultimate judgment of its truth. Religion is not determined solely by the facts of history. It is created through interpretations that are molded into memorable, shareable narratives in relationship to the needs of a community. This is not to say that the stories of the imams are fictional. Some of them likely are; others likely are not. We cannot presume a clear division between myth and history, as if texts can be categorized according to their relationship to facts. As Castelli persuasively argues, memory making can include history, and neither genre can be protected from the interests of those who tell these stories.[22] With this in mind, it may be better to steer away from categorizing the accounts of the imams as hagiographies, which, as Thomas Heffernan rightly notes, conjures up ideas of "pious fictions." Instead, the collective biographies may be better understood as what Heffernan calls "sacred biography."[23]

The process of constructing a story that makes sense—one that is both memorable and shareable—is timeless, and it transcends the distinctions between fiction and nonfiction and between rationality and emotion.[24] To understand these concepts as mutually exclusive binaries is to misapprehend the power of stories. Even today we tell stories that help us comprehend the barrage of information that science and technology bring to us.[25] The biographers of the imams were storytellers. By calling them such I do not mean that they were unconcerned with historical facts and accurate information. Nor do I mean that they were the professional "storytellers" (*qussas*)[26] of classical Arabic contexts.[27] Rather, I am connecting these works to storytelling in its broadest and deepest sense, storytelling as a fundamental and indispensable means of making sense of one's own life and identity.

Charting the Path

I have organized this book into five chapters. The first chapter provides a few notes on the historical context from which this genre of collective biographies of the imams emerged. I provide some historiographical notes about each of the five works on which this study is focused, and I attempt to make clear why I have chosen to focus on these particular collective biographies. Readers with less interest in the specifics of each author may prefer to skip over that section; doing so will not jeopardize a reading of the subsequent chapters. Other readers may wish to return to the first chapter after the substance of my arguments becomes clearer. The remaining chapters are thematic and topical analyses of the works themselves. Each subsection of these chapters explores a particular topic using the stories of a single imam/infallible. Limiting the scope of the subsections to accounts about a single figure serves the purposes of coherence and brevity, but the observations within each section generally apply to the other imams as well, and I have included numerous cross-references in the notes. The appendixes at the end of this work are intended to help readers navigate the many names and honorifics of the imams and to identify biographies beyond those I include in this study.

Chapter 2 begins my analysis of the biographies by exploring the deaths of the imams and the manner in which the authors negotiated a particular understanding of, and response to, those deaths. I show how the memories of a community were shaped and maintained by these works. This relationship between the narratives and their meaning for the community helps frame the remaining chapters.

In Chapter 3, I address the most famous aspect of the imams' lives: their suffering. Specifically, I probe the nature and significance of their suffering through the notion of betrayal, a concept that suffuses the biographies. The ways the imams' betrayals are remembered reveal the broad social implications of their sufferings, and the examples used demonstrate the pervasiveness and importance of the notion of betrayal in this literature.

Chapter 4 focuses on the imams as embodied beings in a physical world. Descriptions of the imams' bodies and their physical actions tell us much about the authors' conceptions of the ideal human as an individual and social being. Accounts about the imams not only reveal assumptions about masculinity, but also the gendered nature of authority and corporeality. The three case studies in this chapter point to how the imams' idealized bodies attest to communal hopes and concerns.

Chapter 5 returns to the beginnings of the imams' lives, to their birth narratives. These compelling stories indicate how the imams fit into a larger narrative of sacred history. The birth accounts contain an array of religious symbols that emphasize the cosmic and personal significance of the imams' lives. This chapter shows how the biographers employ myriad symbols and motifs to demonstrate the uniqueness of the imams and the rightfulness of their authority.

CHAPTER ONE

Setting the Stage

> If poetry is the "archive of the Arabs," biography is the archive of the Muslims.
>
> —*Michael Cooperson*[1]

ONE THOUSAND YEARS AGO, Baghdad was embroiled in a sectarian controversy that polarized the city and contributed to the destabilization of a fractured empire. During the years 1003, 1008, and 1018, large riots and massive street brawls led to politically sanctioned executions, and entire quarters of the city were burned to the ground. Religious celebrations and parades staged by one group and opposed by another were often flashpoints for violent clashes. Historians have long framed the Baghdad riots as Sunni-Shiʿa conflicts, and it is tempting to see them as early manifestations of the same sectarian disputes that plague Baghdad today. But there are reasons to revisit these assumptions. Hidden layers of history need to be uncovered and considered.

To describe the riots in Baghdad a thousand years ago as Sunni-Shiʿa debates is not an anachronism. The sources closest to the period describe them as such.[2] The problem is that the definition and attribution of "Sunni" and "Shiʿa" have shifted over time. The disputes in Baghdad occurred in a turn-of-the-millennium context in which sectarian identities were still unsettled. Participants in the street brawls of late tenth and early eleventh century were unlikely to have considered themselves "Sunni" as opposed to "Shiʿa." At that time "Sunni" meant something akin to "orthodox,"[3] and the typical form of the term, *ahl al-sunna,* was championed by traditionalist circles that discouraged speculative readings of texts and philosophically based hermeneutics. The term “traditionalist,” as I am using it, is not to refer to someone who collected hadith traditions (a “traditionist”), but denotes a person who adopted a scripturalist approach to interpretive questions rather than the methods outlined by various theological and philosophical schools. The groups that used “Sunni” as a self-appellation were spearheaded by a traditionalist group in Baghdad, namely the Hanbalis, and their opponents were all those they considered heretical (no small number of people). These included not only the Shiʿa in their various forms, but also members of prominent theological schools, like the ʿAsharis and Muʿtazilis. Many people who came to be included in the fold of Sunni Islam, including most Shafiʿi and Hanafi Muslims, would not have been considered Sunni by the groups who championed this term. Even the so-called “Sunni revival” of the tenth to twelfth centuries was really a traditionalist resurgence opposed to a wide array of other interpretive communities.[4] Islamic orthodoxy was only beginning to coalesce, and using the term “Sunni” for a group was not so much a description as it was an assertion.

Likewise, the communities that might be called “Shiʿa” in the tenth century had a mix of loyalties that did not always align with how the term would be defined in subsequent centuries. The biological descendants of ʿAli b. Abi Talib (known as ʿAlids) were often categorized along with the various forms of Shiʿism.[5] Moreover, traditionalists often saw any sympathy for Shiʿism as evidence of conspiracy with the Ismaʿili Shiʿa dynasty that threatened western ʿAbbasid lands. The Twelver Shiʿism that would later rise to prominence was still in its nascent form, occupying a small but expanding portion of a nebulous Shiʿa landscape. The core concepts and rituals that later bound Twelver Shiʿa Muslims together were not yet fully developed, nor was it clear what relationship Shiʿism had to traditionalist orthodoxy. Tellingly, Shiʿa literatures did not typically use the term “Sunni” as a description for any particular group.

Members of the educated urban classes in this period were connected to one another by a complex web of political, familial, and scholastic loyalties. These communal bonds were animated by competing ritual practices and interpretations of the Qurʾan, but the differences cannot always be reduced to the paradigm of religious sectarian identity. Several more centuries would pass before the Sunni-Shiʿa divide commonly functioned as a binary. Many scholars of the period whom later generations of Shiʿa considered one of their own did not publicly identify as such during their lifetimes. To identify as Shiʿa prior to the tenth century was tantamount to declaring political rebellion. Being a "Shiʿa" (literally, "partisan") of someone other than the caliph—whether that someone was a living imam or the long-dead ʿAli—was synonymous with denying loyalty to the caliph. Making such a claim was generally done in secret or on the fringes of the empire where the caliph had tenuous control.

A vast borderland existed between explicit Shiʿism (adherence to an identified imam and the secret or public rebellion that entailed) and the (subsequently described as) Sunni default position of coming to terms with the powers that were. Numerous scholars of the period did not fit either category, and some may best be described as both.[6] For example, Abu ʿAbd al-Rahman al-Nasaʾi (d. 830/915), author of one of the six semicanonical collections of Sunni hadith, was believed to have been killed precisely for his ʿAlid sympathies.[7] Such instances are common in the historical record. Many prominent figures that were criticized for their Shiʿa proclivities would come to be seen by later historians as unquestionably Sunni, based on later uses of the term. And even as late as the twelfth century, some Sunni communities participated in the commemorations of ʿAshuraʾ.[8] Thus trying to determine whether a particular figure from this period is better understood as Sunni or Shiʿa becomes an anachronistic exercise borne out of assumptions about religious commitments that were not fully formed until later centuries.[9] In the early eleventh century, the conception of an Islam comprised of two divergent—and irreconcilable—branches had simply not coalesced. In fact, we should keep in mind that the absolute separation between Sunni and Shiʿa Muslims has never been comprehensively actualized (either socially or religiously), and some Muslims have attempted, especially in the modern period, to try to harmonize the two categories.[10]

And yet most Muslims were divided. The centuries-long process of separation into conceptually and socially distinct Sunni and Shiʿa communities had begun.[11] Numerous scholars have explored how and why this process occurred. Some have focused on legal differences between the two groups, while others have examined theological arguments or political confrontations. No single angle provides a comprehensive explanation of this development, but each area of focus gives us additional insight into one of the most complex and enduring disputes of Islamic history. How Shiʿa groups would tell their own story of origin undoubtedly has relevance to this conversation.

A new form of religious literature emerged in the tenth century. Scholars within Shiʿa circles began to record the life stories of their twelve imams, collating the biographies of their community's most holy figures into single works. By the twelfth century, the collective biographies of the imams, as I call it, had come to look like a subgenre of its own. The parameters had been set, and works within the genre utilized a common religious vocabulary and drew upon an established canon of themes and motifs.[12]

The stories of the imams were not written in a vacuum, and our study of this literature must begin with an understanding of the religious, political, and literary contexts in which it was written. This chapter provides a brief sketch of key events leading up to the tenth century and a review of the religious and literary culture of the central ʿAbbasid lands. This background information gives us a sense of some of the implications of writing about the imams, and it enables us to discern the issues at stake for those who wrote the five works at the heart of this study.

History and the Literatures of Memory

In the year 945, just four years after the twelfth imam was said to have gone into the semipermanent period of hiding known as the "greater occultation," the city of Baghdad fell under the control of a powerful family known as the Buyids, inhabitants of a mountainous region called the Daylam located on the southern shores of the Caspian Sea. The occupiers were ethnically and culturally foreign to most residents of Baghdad, but the Buyids justified their actions by questioning the legitimacy of ʿAbbasid rule, a sentiment shared by many.

Political authority was a matter of legitimacy as well as strength. Leadership by the descendants of the Prophet's family had long held widespread appeal, especially in times of political and institutional corruption and mismanagement. For many Muslims, the *ahl al-bayt* (a ubiquitous term referring to the Prophet's family) was a powerful symbol of justice, resistance to oppression, and hope for a reorganized society.[13] This wasn't limited to the Shiʿa.

The seventh, eighth, and ninth centuries saw a slew of uprisings against central powers, most of them carried out by—or at least in the name of—a member of the Prophet's family. The ʿAbbasids themselves had risen to power on the slogan of "The Chosen from the Family" (*al-rida min ahl al-bayt*), a promise many took to mean that the revolution would put political rule in the hands of the Prophet's progeny.[14] The first caliph of the ʿAbbasid dynasty, Abu al-ʿAbbas al-Saffah, was in fact connected to the Prophet's family (he was descended from ʿAbbas, the Prophet's uncle), though his ascension to political power was a surprise and disappointment to many in the movement.

The sentiments that helped bring the ʿAbbasids to power returned to plague the dynasty in the ninth and tenth centuries. The dynasty's claim to legitimacy had appeased some who desired the leadership of *ahl al-bayt,* but many Shiʿa were less than thrilled, and some felt deeply deceived. This was particularly the case for the "Imamis" in their various forms (a term typically reserved for a variety of followers of the imams that descended from one of the Prophet's grandsons, al-Hasan or al-Husayn). The ʿAlid and ʿAbbasid families had a rocky relationship throughout the classical period, and some of those tensions came out in the biographies, as I discuss in Chapter 3. Anti-ʿAbbasid uprisings were carried out in the name of various ʿAlids who could claim closer kinship ties to the Prophet than could the caliphs. Even the infamous Zanj uprising in southern Iraq, a massive slave revolt that lasted from 868 to 883, was led by an ʿAlid claimant.

The ʿAbbasid caliphs gradually lost control of their empire due to a combination of incompetent leadership, mismanagement of revenue, and military exhaustion. By the early tenth century it was only a matter of time before an outside force came in to fill the power vacuum. When a Buyid prince assumed control of Baghdad in 945, he did so with the support of many Shiʿa-inclined groups. The Shiʿa of Baghdad were disparate, and many were awaiting the return of a hidden imam. Without an ʿAlid imam present to compete for authority, there was space for a degree of political quietism that facilitated a Shiʿa transition away from the cycle of uprisings. It also factored into the Buyid power play. The Buyids had no claim to ʿAlid lineage, and they lacked the legitimacy to take on the caliphal role. Rather than toppling the ʿAbbasids, the Buyids decided to "protect" them until the imam returned. This effectively put the reins of power in ʿAlid-friendly hands. The Buyids patronized Shiʿa scholars extensively and gave the Twelver Shiʿa of Baghdad the voice they had previously lacked.

The period leading up to the tenth century was more than a succession of conflicts. Major intellectual and artistic advancements took place throughout the ʿAbbasid caliphate in the eighth and ninth centuries. Scholarly communities across the Near East were undergoing major changes, and modern historians have often called this the "classical age" of Islam. This was the period in which political and scholarly elites from Andalusia to the Indus Valley established Arabic as the primary language for intellectual discourse. The linguistic shift affected non-Muslim communities as well. The renowned Gaonic rabbi and scholar Saadia ben Joseph (d. 942) began writing in Arabic at this time (albeit using Hebrew characters), and his work became the model for a Judeo-Arabic literary tradition that flourished for centuries among Jews living in Muslim-controlled lands. The dramatic socioreligious developments of this period were accompanied by a proliferation of many new genres of Arabic literature that treated historical, scientific, and philosophical themes, among many others. A culture of book production and book collecting emerged among the urban educated classes, perhaps nowhere more prominently than in Baghdad. The insatiable appetite for books of all sorts and the willingness of elites to financially support their production were fueled by (and in turn further enabled) the immense translation movement of the eighth to tenth centuries, which made the great works of Greek philosophers, scientists, and doctors available in Arabic. Dimitri Gutas's *Greek Thought, Arabic Culture* is an excellent history of this social phenomenon, which "cut across all lines of religious, sectarian, ethnic, tribal, and linguistic demarcation."[15] As Gutas notes, "Patrons were Arabs and non-Arabs, Muslims and non-Muslims, Sunnis and Shiʿites, generals and civilians, merchants and land-owners, etc."[16]

The biographies of the Shiʿa imams emerged out of this context. In order to understand the significance of those biographies, we need to consider the literary options available to their authors. This will help us to discern how the biographies were originally received and to avoid the risk of imposing modern expectations of the genre of biography onto these medieval works. This is not to suggest that the analytical tools of the twenty-first century are useless when reading premodern biographies; it is merely to emphasize the necessity of incorporating into our analysis what knowledge we have of the literary horizons of the authors. This information gives us a sense of the religious and political implications of the biographies in their historical contexts. It also brings into relief the unique qualities of these writings and the ways they overlapped with or differed from similar writings with which their authors were likely familiar.

Arabic literature was just beginning to take shape in the ʿAbbasid period. Oral poetry had long been considered the pinnacle of the language and the standard of eloquence, but in the early Islamic context, it ceded its place to the Qurʾan, which became the bedrock not only of Islam but of Arabic literature. The production of religious texts and the massive influx of works translated into Arabic from different religious and cultural traditions inspired scholars to experiment with new ways of organizing their writings. By the tenth century, several biographical genres had begun to develop that may have informed Shiʿa writings on the imams. These genres included biographies of the Prophet, stories of the pre-Islamic prophets, and various forms of hagiography.

As one might expect, the earliest stages of Islamic literary output included writings on the life of the Prophet Muhammad. Two terms typically used for these early Arabic biographies were *maghazi* and *sira*.[17] The earliest writings on Muhammad's life were often referred to as *maghazi* ("raids") and focused on his military leadership.[18] But they chronicled a variety of Muhammad's nonmilitary activities as well. They often included events from shortly before his life and proceeded past his lifetime to the period of the first four caliphs who followed him.[19] By the middle of the eighth century, *maghazi* writings were beginning to be called *sira* ("way of going," or "conduct").[20] One key difference between *maghazi/sira* works and collections of hadith was that hadith collections were typically organized around topics, especially legal issues. In contrast, *maghazi/sira* works followed a relatively chronological approach that centered on the person of Muhammad. These two early (overlapping) forms of biography endured into the modern period (especially the *sira*),[21] and they significantly influenced other forms of Islamicate historiography.

The Prophet was not the only figure whose life was chronicled. Simultaneous to the emergence of *maghazi* and *sira,* shorter pieces were composed that detail the actions and attributes of other notable persons, especially the Prophet's companions.[22] These biographical endeavors were often connected to efforts to defend the legitimacy of a caliph over and against any competitors.[23] The concern with piety and moral excellence found further expression in a variety of hagiographical forms, especially in "virtue" literature (*manaqib* or *fada'il* literature).[24] Virtue writings played a prominent role in political discourse, and they helped bolster the credentials of new leaders, particularly after the ʿAbbasid revolution. The format was also utilized for transmitting accounts of scholars, warriors, and Sufis of all sorts. These writings were biographical in nature,[25] and, like many European biographical accounts dating to the same period, they often emphasized miracles or other extraordinary events.

By the early ninth century, scholars had begun collecting short biographical notices (*tarajim*)[26] and collating them into single-themed works.[27] These collective biographies, often voluminous in scope, were one of the most significant and distinctive literary contributions of classical Arabic.[28] Biographical dictionaries, which tended to be organized alphabetically by name and themed around a particular guild or profession, are particularly noteworthy, but *tabaqat* literature,[29] which was organized by generation or time period and often incorporated into larger historical annals,[30] was important as well. These collective biographies do not fit neatly into the Western literary category of *biographia,* and they have often been considered prosopography rather than biography.[31]

A final relevant genre of literature was known simply as the *qissa* ("story," pl- *qisas*).[32] The *qissa* emerged from a professional, court-employed class of preachers in the Umayyad period known as the *qusas.* The *qisas* were often little more than distillations of Qur'anic commentary (*tafsir*), *sira/maghazi,* and other historical literatures, but the genre had a unique role in the development of early Islamic biographical writings.[33] Collections of stories about pre-Islamic prophets were circulated under this term by the early eighth century.[34] "Tales of the Prophets" (*qisas al-anbiya*) became a literary category in its own right, combining serious stories intended for devotional purposes with light-hearted stories that entertained.[35]

Significant portions of this literature were often included in larger historical works like al-Tabari's (d. 310/923) grand *History of the Prophets and Kings* (*Ta'rikh al-rusul wa-al-muluk*) and Ibn Kathir's (d. 774/1373) *Beginning and End* (*al-Bidaya wa-al-nihaya*). Some of the accounts of the prophets in this literature are extensive enough to be considered full biographical treatments and are related to Qur'anic exegetical questions. Many Muslim scholars, perhaps most influentially Ibn Taymiya (d. 728/1328), have attacked the historical reliability of these accounts, yet they remained important in popular culture.[36]

By the end of the ninth century, the literary conventions of each of the aforementioned types of Arabic biographical writing had solidified.[37] The types were overlapping in some respects, but each had its own subject matter, stylistic conventions, and social functions. *Sira* and *manaqib* literatures met the devotional needs of the community and played key roles in political/sectarian controversies.[38] Collections of shorter biographical notices were compiled into biographical dictionaries. *Tabaqat* works addressed the needs of individual disciplines (particularly hadith scholarship) and other social networks.[39] *Qisas* were performed orally as entertainment and exhortation. They were usually relegated to stories of pre-Islamic prophets and other legendary figures.[40] These classical Arabic genres represent the literary context out of which biographies of the imams were conceived and assembled.

The Collective Biographies of the Imams

Like the authors of works in the abovementioned genres, Shiʿa writers were concerned with the life stories of their communities' most significant figures. Collections of the sayings and teachings of the imams were assembled that mirrored hadith literature on the Prophet Muhammad, and biographers drew from such accounts, rearranging them into a birth-to-death chronology that removed them from legal questions and placed them in the realm of history. After the occultation of the twelfth imam began gaining wider acceptance, the writers started collecting biographies of all twelve imams into a single book. These collective biographies had some similarities with stories of the pre-Islamic prophets, biographies of Muhammad, and other hagiographies. Indeed, the collective biographies of the imams adopted the themes and motifs of many of those literatures. But the biographies of the imams also had unique aspects. They functioned in different ways and have endured as a distinct scholarly genre among the Shiʿa to this day.[41] Hundreds, if not thousands, of these works have been written, though many have been lost to history.[42]

It may not be surprising that the stories of the twelve Shiʿa imams were recorded and preserved by their followers, but the importance of these narratives was in no way predetermined. Even less predictable was the general style, tone, and themes that came to characterize these writings. Those details originated in the needs of specific communities that occupied different periods but were united by the confidence that the lives of the imams were profoundly meaningful. And thus we approach the biographies of the imams with an eye for what we can learn about the communities for whom they were written.

I have used a simple, twofold standard for categorizing a work as a collective biography of the imams. First, the work must have devoted at least half of its length specifically to the lives of the twelve imams. Second, the structure of the book must be around the lives of each of the imams (thus excluding thematically organized hadith collections). These books were not the only type of literature that contained biographical information about the imams, but the collective biographies are an identifiable genre with its own assumptions, expectations, and conventions.

Five key works that fit these criteria were composed in the tenth to twelfth centuries, and these works are the central focus of my analysis. They represent the formative stage of this genre's literary development. These are:

1. *Establishment of the Inheritance (Ithbat al-wasiya),* attributed to al-Masʿudi
2. *Proofs of the Imamate (Dalaʾil al-imama),* attributed to Ibn Jarir
3. *Book of Guidance (Kitab al-irshad),* by al-Mufid
4. *Informing Humanity (Iʿlam al-wara),* by al-Tabrisi
5. *Virtues of the Descendants of Abu Talib (Manaqib al Abi Talib),* by Ibn Shahrashub

There are good reasons to focus on these five works. First, they have been well received among the Shiʿa. They are among the most regularly cited works in biographies of the imams composed after the twelfth century, and teachers, scholars, and preachers across the centuries have considered them helpful and valuable. Second, they are the earliest extant examples of this genre of sufficient length to be useful objects of study. And third, they contain most of the content that was recycled (often in creative and new ways) in similar works in subsequent centuries. After Ibn Shahrashub, very few narratives appear in Shiʿa literature on the imams that are not found in some form in these works.[43]

These collective biographies are known to scholars of medieval Islamic thought, but they are underutilized. They are occasionally mined for historical tidbits about the imams, but their uneven reliability makes the historian look at them askance. A fresh look at these texts is warranted—one that asks new questions. I am less interested in what these narratives tell us about the imams than in the light they shed on the social memory of medieval Shiʿa communities. Reading historical texts through the lens of social memory puts the collective and communal nature of historical writing in the foreground. It allows authors to be understood in relationship to the communities for which they write. It illuminates the needs of that community. But before proceeding to an analysis of the works themselves, it is necessary to provide background information on the environments in which they emerged. Context helps make sense of content. The following sections provide a general introduction to the authors and their historical circumstances, putting them in relationship to the historical development of Twelver Shiʿism.

Canonizing the Infallibles: *Establishment of the Inheritance* and *Proofs of the Imamate*

Two of the earliest extant collective biographies of the twelve imams of any length are *Establishment of the Inheritance* and *Proofs of the Imamate,* both of uncertain origins. Though the significance of the two works lies in the features they share with later biographies, their distinctive aspects are worth noting. The authorship of each work is in question, but mainstream Twelver Shiʿa scholars have generally accepted the books as part of their literary tradition. It is possible that either of them could be a composite work, and thus determining a precise temporal or geographical context for their composition is unlikely at this point. That said, the core content of each appears to have been assembled around the end of the lesser occultation in the early tenth century. Such collections would not have made sense prior to this time.

These two works signal an important shift in Imami Shiʿa circles. Those coping with the prolonged absence of the twelfth imam found solace in the belief that the imamate was limited to twelve men and that no further imams would ever exist. The first clear Shiʿa teachings about twelve imams appeared around 900.[44] The group of Shiʿa among whom these teachings emerged came to believe that the canon of imams was officially closed, and the time span of the imams' public lives came to be seen as a defined era of human history that ended with the occultation. A new epoch had begun in which the Shiʿa must faithfully await the return of the twelfth imam, an event that would usher in the final era of human civilization. *Establishment* and *Proofs* were part of a community's transition from one era to another. Each work reflects an attempt to come to terms with the past and to incorporate that past into meaningful conceptions of the community's present and future trajectory.

Traditional accounts give us some possibilities for the authorship of both works. *Establishment* has conventionally been attributed to the famed historian and belle-lettrist al-Masʿudi (d. 345/956),[45] an author remembered primarily for *Meadows of Gold* (*Muruj al-dhahab*), a history of impressive breadth and literary skill.[46] Al-Masʿudi penned at least thirty-six separate works,[47] but only one other surviving text—a general history entitled *The Book of Notification and Review* (*Kitab al-tanbih wa-al-ishraf*)—can safely be attributed to him.

Al-Masʿudi's authorship of *Establishment of the Inheritance* has been considered doubtful by recent scholars like Tarif Khalidi and Charles Pellat.[48] The reasons for such doubt include the work not being mentioned by any Sunni biographers of al-Masʿudi. Moreover, it is not mentioned by al-Masʿudi in *Meadows* or *Notification,* and there are stylistic discrepancies between *Establishment* and al-Masʿudi's histories. Other modern scholars, like Agha Buzurg al-Tihrani (1876–1970), have argued that the attribution to al-Masʿudi is reliable.[49] Al-Tihrani defended this position by noting that al-Masʿudi's Twelver Shiʿa inclinations are clear in *Meadows* and *Notification;* that there are other theological similarities between

Establishment and *Meadows*;[50] and that Shiʿa scholars have considered *Establishment* a work of al-Masʿudi from at least the mid-eleventh century onward.[51] The observations made by those on both sides are fair, and the question remains unresolved. But if *Establishment* was indeed a work of al-Masʿudi, the only way to make sense of Khalidi's observations is to argue that al-Masʿudi wrote secretly and that he purposely adopted a different writing style than he used in his major historical works. Such a scenario is unlikely, but not unthinkable, given the more controversial nature of the content in *Establishment*.[52]

Regardless of these uncertainties, the more central issue for this study is that the Shiʿa have frequently regarded *Establishment* as an important source on the lives of the imams. The book is of moderate length, numbering 232 pages in the 1983 edition. The first half focuses on accounts of the prophets from Adam to Muhammad; in this sense the work closely resembles the *qisas al-anbiya* genre. The second half of the book details key events and features of the life and leadership of each of the twelve imams. Though relatively brief in his treatment of each figure, the author was careful to include birth accounts, miracle stories, and death narratives for each imam. Furthermore, the author places great emphasis on the moment of transference of the spiritual inheritance (*wasiya*) from each imam to the next.[53] I return to the significance of these narratives in the coming chapters.

The authorial attribution of *Proofs of the Imamate* is on similarly shaky ground. This work has traditionally been ascribed to the Baghdadi Shiʿa scholar Muhammad b. Jarir al-Tabari (d. 310/923), henceforth Ibn Jarir (the elder).[54] Ibn Jarir shares a name, death date, and *kunya* (Abu Jaʿfar) with the famed historian and Qurʾanic commentator. As a result, the two have often been confused.[55] Ibn Nadim, for example, attributed a book on the imamate entitled *The Seeker of Guidance* (*al-Mustarshid*) to the more famous Muhammad b. Jarir al-Tabari, but nearly all subsequent Shiʿa scholars corrected him, noting that *The Seeker* was written by our lesser-known Shiʿa Ibn Jarir.[56] Unfortunately, for our purposes, references to Ibn Jarir are few, and most Sunni sources failed to mention him at all.[57]

In addition to knowing very little about Ibn Jarir, giving him authorial credit for *Proofs of the Imamate* is complicated by the fact that some portions of *Proofs* clearly postdate his life. Several of the authorities cited in *Proofs* are scholars who lived at the turn of the eleventh century, making it impossible for this Ibn Jarir (who died a century earlier) to have transmitted from them. Furthermore, in at least one case, the text of *Proofs* cites a report from the scholar al-Ghadaʾiri (d. 411/1020) and appends the phrase "may God have mercy on him" (*rahmahu Allah*) to his name, an indication that he had already died at the time of writing.[58] Assuming that these are not later additions to the text (an assumption I address below), this would mean that *Proofs* could not have been written prior to 1020, making its author a contemporary of al-Mufid. Agha Buzurg al-Tihrani has suggested that *Proofs* was written by a third, entirely different, Abu Jaʿfar Muhammad b. Jarir al-Tabari who died a century later—henceforth Ibn Jarir (the younger).[59]

Al-Tihrani's observations call into serious question the assumption by premodern Shiʿa scholars that *Proofs* was the work of the elder Ibn Jarir.[60] But al-Tihrani's solution is also problematic. No other sources, even Shiʿa ones, appear to contain any mention of the younger Ibn Jarir. Al-Tihrani's evidence is that the later (younger) Ibn Jarir must have existed because *Proofs* is said to have been written by a person of that name who couldn't, in light of the dating problems mentioned above, have been the known (elder) Ibn Jarir. Recent scholars like Kahhala and Etan Kohlberg have accepted al-Tihrani's thesis.[61] I am not entirely convinced, however, that *Proofs* is entirely an eleventh century compilation, or that it can be attributed to the younger Ibn Jarir, whose very existence I doubt. It seems more likely that an earlier draft of this book—perhaps simply a collection of notes—was written by the elder Ibn Jarir (whose existence is more certain) in the early tenth century and that a later scholar edited the draft, interpolating additional stories without attempting to take credit for the work. This is, admittedly, my own conjecture and cannot be proven. And in any case, enough changes/additions were made to the book in the early eleventh century that it cannot be considered a purely tenth century product. Although I am inclined to think that most of the material may be attributable to the elder Ibn Jarir, this claim remains tentative. Here too, however, uncertainty about authorship should not distract us from the significance of a given work. As is the case with *Establishment of the Inheritance,* most Shiʿa scholars believed *Proofs of the Imamate* to be the product of a known and reliable source, and it is cited by later biographers of the imams.[62]

Another issue to note in relation to Ibn Jarir's *Proofs of the Imamate* is that at some point after the thirteenth century, significant portions of the text were lost. By the time Majlisi wrote in the seventeenth century, the sections on Muhammad and ʿAli (the beginning of the book) were missing. We know that they existed in the original, however, based on extensive quotes in the writings of Ibn Tawus (d. 664/1266).[63]

The original version of *Proofs* is structured in a way that became conventional in the genre; namely, the life stories of the twelve imams are presented chronologically along with a section on the Prophet Muhammad and a sizeable account of the life of the Prophet's daughter, Fatima al-Zahra. This format anticipated the standardization of "the fourteen infallibles" (*al-maʿsumun al-arbaʿat ashar*) within the genre. Although al-Mufid's *Book of Guidance* did not have a biographical section devoted to Muhammad or Fatima, nearly all contributions to this genre in subsequent centuries would. When we talk about the collective biographies of the imams, therefore, we are typically referring to works that contain biographies of all fourteen infallibles.[64]

There are limitations to what can be said about the context of these works, given that we cannot be certain of the authorship of either. Nonetheless, they are the two earliest extant books devoted to the lives of all twelve imams, and they foreshadowed the genre that developed. The very fact that these two works survived into the modern period is a testament to their enduring relevance. Although both were eventually overshadowed by later biographies of the imams (particularly that of al-Mufid), the works were meaningful enough to warrant preservation. Prominent Shiʿa scholars throughout history have considered them a part of their tradition. For all their oddities, the vision of the imams they propagated was broadly in consonance with the form of Twelver Shiʿism that emerged as predominant.

Several features set *Establishment* and *Proofs* apart from the other collective biographies in this study. These qualities may give us some insight into the general tenor of Shiʿism in the early tenth century, the period when the semipermanent absence of the twelfth imam began to find widespread acceptance. Both *Establishment* and *Proofs* represent a prescholastic stage of explicitly Shiʿa literature. By prescholastic, I do not mean that the authors lacked education; far from it. Rather, they did not base their compositions on the norms or forms of other finalized texts. They did not cite other published books, relying instead on a wide variety of oral narratives.[65] Many of these oral traditions can also be found in the writings of their contemporaries, including in al-Kulayni's semicanonical hadith collection, *al-Kafi* (*The Sufficient*). But even when stories in *Establishment* and *Proofs* overlap with accounts contained in *al-Kafi*, there are significant enough differences that it does not appear that the authors of either *Establishment* or *Proofs* relied on al-Kulayni's work, or other extant works of the period.

Though both works appear to have relied on oral narratives, the structures of each suggest they were composed in writing (as opposed to having originated as oral lectures preserved in writing by students). *Establishment* is particularly clear in this regard, and it was almost certainly composed by its author as a single written work. The book's carefully crafted form, structure, and style are markedly different from dictated works from the same period. The precise balance between the treatment of pre-Islamic prophetic figures and that of the post-ʿAli imams is remarkable. The biographies of Muhammad and ʿAli form the crux of the book, and the unquestionable climax of the narrative is the body of elaborate accounts of the birth of ʿAli. The climactic role of this material is indicated both by its location at the exact midpoint of the book and by the notable incorporation of numerous poetic quotes (otherwise nearly absent from the book) that direct the reader's attention to the critical importance of that event. The author went to great lengths to highlight the crucial and seamless transition from the era of prophethood to the era of the imamate.

Another feature shared by *Establishment* and *Proofs* is the emphasis placed on the last four imams. Both devote more pages to each of the ninth, tenth, eleventh, and twelfth imams than to any of the other imams besides ʿAli.[66] The treatment of al-Husayn is particularly noteworthy; he is given no more attention than the other imams. This stands in stark contrast to the balance found in later collective biographies, which, beginning with al-Mufid, tend to devote far more space to al-Husayn than to any of his successors.

An emphasis on miracle stories is another unique feature shared by *Establishment* and *Proofs*. The vast majority of Shiʿa biographies of the imams, and all of the biographies considered in this study, contain miracle accounts—a subject to which I return in Chapter 4. But *Establishment* and *Proofs* have a particularly high number of such accounts relative to other works in the genre. In this respect, *Proofs* in particular straddles another genre boundary, resembling books written primarily to record the miracles of the imams. An early example of this genre is Ibn ʿAbd al-Wahhab's eleventh century book, *Springs of Miracles* (*ʿUyun al-muʿjizat*), which draws upon *Establishment* and perhaps on *Proofs* as well. The miracles of the imams are one of the important "proofs" (*dalaʾil*) that demonstrate the imams' legitimacy. But Ibn Jarir's *Proofs,* despite its emphasis on the supernatural, is much more than a collection of miracle accounts, and it better fits the genre outlined in this study.

One of the more divisive topics among scholars of Shiʿism today is the extent to which the early followers of the imams were inclined toward extreme esotericism (as argued by Mohammed Ali Amir-Moezzi)[67] or not (Hossein Modarressi).[68] The general tenor of *Establishment* and *Proofs* is largely in line with descriptions given by Amir-Moezzi of early Shiʿa esotericism. Though there are differences between these two collective biographies, each presents an array of cryptic and spectacular stories of the imams that emphasizes the connection of these holy men to the Prophet Muhammad and the prophets of pre-Islamic history. Some might make a case that these works are not representative of normative Twelver Shiʿism of the period and should instead be considered extremist writings (*ghulat*). More will be said about this important term in Chapter 3, but it should be emphasized here that the problem with placing these works in the category of *ghulat* (an inherently discrediting description) is that both *Establishment* and *Proofs* were read, used, quoted, and relied upon for preaching by mainstream Shiʿa teachers in subsequent centuries.[69] These works have been preserved by multiple generations of Shiʿa scholars and were considered part of the broad Shiʿa tradition up to the modern period. Dismissing them as *ghulat* flies in the face of their reception within the Shiʿa tradition.

On the other hand, it would be equally tenuous to suggest that the spectacular display of esotericism found in these early works was representative of an original form of Twelver Shiʿism. While many of the extant Imami Shiʿa writings up to the tenth century exhibit strong esotericism (after which a type of Baghdadi rationalism became common), this nonetheless may tell us more about subsequent centuries than it does early Shiʿism. Many of the earliest Shiʿa writings are no longer extant. The survival of early esoteric Shiʿa writings means that those ideas were somehow meaningful to transmitters of later generations. Praise for the imams, even taken to some extremes, would become a classic theme for broader Twelver Shiʿa piety. Early works enshrining such praise, therefore, were ultimately more useful for maintaining a social memory of the imams than more down-to-earth treatments. This later trend helped determine which books were copied and which fell into disrepair and were lost to history.

In short, as mentioned at the outset of this chapter, no normative mainstream Shiʿism existed prior to the tenth century, even among the followers of the twelve imams. Explicit forms of Shiʿism were often esoteric in nature, but they were also regularly perceived as politically rebellious. The social implications of Shiʿism radically shifted once the Twelver Shiʿa paradigm took root. This transition is exemplified in a shift in scholarly discussions of religious dissimulation (*taqiyya*). *Taqiyya* was a means to permit the imams' followers to keep their loyalties to the imams secret. Prominent ninth century Shiʿa scholar Ibn Babawayh advised all Shiʿa to practice *taqiyya* and to keep their Shiʿa loyalties private. But after the Buyids took control of Baghdad and permitted various public displays of ʿAlid loyalism, perspectives on *taqiyya* also changed. Ibn Babawayh's most influential student, al-Mufid, restricted the use of *taqiyya* and recommended it only when one's life was in clear danger.[70] Once the greater occultation was accepted, with the corollary that there would be no further imams, a different religious vision for society took shape. A new era was dawning that empowered the imams' followers to be more open about their convictions. It was no coincidence that rationalism, with its emphasis on rhetoric, began to prevail in public discourse among the Shiʿa at this time as well.

Legitimizing the Narrative: *The Book of Guidance* and *Informing Humanity*

Under the protection of the Buyids, leading Shiʿa scholars built a case for the legitimacy of Shiʿism as an orthodox school of thought while defending the legitimacy of the imams' authority and the inheritance of the *wasiya*. Control over how the story of the imams was told and remembered went hand in hand with debates on these issues. Not only did the way the stories were presented shift; their content was different. A genre of collective biographies of the imams began to take its enduring form and style.

Of all of the works considered in this study, the most famous is *The Book of Guidance* (*Kitab al-irshad*). The work was composed by the immensely influential Baghdadi scholar al-Shaykh al-Mufid (d. 413/1022),[71] and it is the book most commonly referenced by subsequent Shiʿa biographers of the imams, including those of the present era. *The Book of Guidance* is also the only work studied here that has been fully translated into English.[72] The influence of this work on the genre of collective biographies of the imams can hardly be overstated—it became the prototype. Even if it was not actually the first of its kind,[73] it set the bar. And yet, later Shiʿa authors did not simply repeat al-Mufid's perspective; nor did the ideas, symbols, and motifs of the genre cease developing after him. In fact, scholars in subsequent centuries contradicted al-Mufid in key ways, an important example of which will be explored in the next chapter.

Al-Shaykh al-Mufid (meaning the "useful" or "instructive")[74] was born around 950 in a town called ʿUkbara, situated on the west bank of the Tigris river, halfway between Baghdad and Mosul. His father moved the family to Baghdad when al-Mufid was still young, at a time when many Shiʿa enjoyed greater freedom to study, teach, and express their views.[75] With the Shiʿa-friendly Buyid rulers in Baghdad, Imami scholarship flourished. Al-Mufid played a central role in lasting changes that took place in the larger Shiʿa community over the course of the following century. By 987, when he was less than forty years old, the famous Baghdadi bibliographer Ibn al-Nadim considered him a leader of the Shiʿa.[76]

Al-Mufid was educated by a wide variety of well-known scholars, not all of whom were Shiʿa,[77] and he became an immensely prolific writer, authoring nearly two hundred books.[78] He was also a devoted teacher whose students carried on his legacy of scholarly engagement and community leadership. Two of his most prominent students, al-Sharif al-Radi (d. 406/1015) and al-Sharif al-Murtada (d. 436/1044),[79] were the sons of the ʿAlid *naqib* (registrar) of Baghdad.[80] Each of the two brothers eventually served as *naqib* and contributed to the canon of Shiʿa scholarship.[81] It appears al-Mufid had some contact with, and influence on, the Buyid rulers; ʿAdud al-Dawla (d. 372/983) is said to have attended al-Mufid's lectures.[82] He also participated in public debates on a range of topics. His activity in each of these areas put him in the spotlight whenever sectarian tensions flared and earned him a memorable legacy among later Sunni and Shiʿa communities.

Though he proved himself in the fields of history, law, and hadith, al-Mufid's most enduring scholarly contribution is generally considered to be his work in theology. In line with broad scholarly trends of the time, Shiʿa intellectuals were divided between those who were inclined toward a highly rationalized understanding of religious knowledge (*al-ʿilm al-ʿaqli*)—particularly as represented by the Muʿtazili school of thought—and those who preferred to organize religious thought around transmitted knowledge (*al-ʿilm al-naqli*). Among the latter were many Shiʿa hadith scholars whose center of intellectual activity had recently moved from Kufa to Qum.[83] Two of the great representatives of this persuasion were al-Kulayni (d. 329/941) and Ibn Babawayh (d. 381/991–2). Such scholars were often concerned about the spread of Muʿtazili thinking among the Shiʿa in Iraq, especially in Baghdad, where the influence of the Banu Nawbakht (a then-prominent Shiʿa family)[84] was facilitating the adoption of rationalist discourse. Al-Mufid studied under the preeminent scholars among both of these groups, including Ibn Babawayh and Abu al-Jaysh al-Balkhi (the latter was a student of Abu Sahl al-Nawbakht). Many have credited al-Mufid with guiding the Shiʿa community to a middle ground between the extreme positions of either side of this debate and charting a path that allowed Shiʿa scholarship and religious thought to flourish.[85] It does appear that al-Mufid had a significant influence on the widespread adoption of rationalist discourse among the Shiʿa of subsequent centuries; whether or not it was a middle position is debatable.[86]

Judging from the full range of al-Mufid's activities, intra-Shiʿa debates were not his primary concern. He appears to have been more deeply invested in articulating a Twelver Shiʿism that stood against ʿAbbasid claims to represent the family of the Prophet. He defended Twelver Shiʿism within the central Baghdadi institutions of education, and some of his most famous public exchanges were with the ʿAshari and Maliki scholar al-Baqillani (d. 403/1013) over issues of legal theory and the imamate.[87] Al-Mufid's philosophy was similar to that of the Muʿtazilites, and his public disputations gained him followers among the Shiʿa and respect among the elite. When considered alongside the scholarly developments of his time, his activities seem bent toward organizing a Twelver school of law and theology (a *madhhab*). An array of schools was already in existence, with the Shafiʿi and Hanafi *madhhab*s being the most fully formed and prominent. Other schools were still developing,[88] a number of which, including the Zahiris and Jariris, died out in later centuries. The idea of an orthodox Sunni Islam comprising four schools of law was not yet on the horizon. It was in this context that al-Mufid laid out the foundations for a Twelver school that his students would go on to complete. But times were quickly changing.

The submission of the ʿAbbasid caliphate to the foreign—and apparently Shiʿa—rule of the Buyids sparked a surge of anti-Shiʿa polemics. The public expression of previously banned forms of Shiʿa piety provoked particular outrage. In 963, the Buyid amir Muʿizz al-Dawla granted the Shiʿa official permission to publicly commemorate two events that increasingly functioned as representations of Shiʿism: ʿAshuraʾ (the martyrdom of al-Husayn) and Ghadir Khumm (an occasion when the Prophet is believed to have designated ʿAli as his successor). For some, these developments in Baghdad appeared connected to disturbing developments in the western portion of the empire. In 969, the Ismaʿili dynasty took control of Egypt and was quickly expanding its domain. Conflating the various Shiʿa-friendly groups in Baghdad with the political threat from outside was a strategic move to delegitimize the Buyids. The historiographical convention of referring to this period as the "Shiʿa century" arguably submits to the same logic.[89]

In response to the perceived encroachment of Shiʿism, opposing groups organized alternative and competing festivals. In 999, just eight days after ʿAshuraʾ, the death of ʿAli's opponent al-Zubayr (d. 36/656) was publicly commemorated. Similarly, eight days after Ghadir Khumm came a celebration of Yawm al-Ghar that commemorated Abu Bakr hiding with the Prophet in the cave.[90] These festivals, which were themselves a type of competition over public memory and social identity, appear to have prompted many of the street riots between 1002 and 1018 that were mentioned at the beginning of this chapter. Each riot saw Baghdad ravaged by rival sectarian groups, and in at least three cases in this period, the ʿAbbasid caliph banished al-Mufid from the city.[91] He was allowed to return each time, though he refused to abandon his public activities. *The Book of Guidance* was composed in this dynamic and tumultuous context.

Al-Mufid claimed to have written *Guidance* in direct response to a request for instruction.[92] He does not identify the person who made the request, but al-Mufid seems to have had an educated, but not strictly scholarly, audience in mind. Like *Establishment of the Inheritance* and *Proofs of the Imamate,* al-Mufid's *Guidance* is structured according to the conventions of the time, as a collection of short traditions/accounts (*akhbar*) placed in an order that creates a full narrative. This standard historiographical style had an air of authority and authenticity, and its credibility was buttressed by al-Mufid's use of chains of transmission (*asanid*) in many of the narratives.

Al-Mufid did not limit himself to explicitly Shiʿa sources. Whenever suitable, he availed himself of the broader historical corpus.[93] *Guidance* is a carefully crafted work, and al-Mufid refrained from protracted theological discussions and cumbersome expectations, arranging the accounts of the imams in a way that ensured a smooth narrative flow. *Guidance* is polemical in the sense that it engages a host of disputed issues, but it refrains from unnecessary provocations. Unlike the authors of *Establishment of the Inheritance* and *Proofs of the Imamate,* al-Mufid puts heavy emphasis on the life and martyrdom of al-Husayn, the third imam. This increased the book's usefulness for religious leaders, many of whom have read directly from this work at public gatherings and commemorations.[94] It came to be al-Mufid's most widely read work, and its success is part of the reason a genre of literature solidified in its image.

On November 29 (the third of Ramadan) in 413/1022, al-Mufid died. His funeral was a major event in Baghdad, and several accounts suggest that around 80,000 mourners were in attendance.[95] His opponents were relieved by his death. In his monumental history of Baghdad, Khatib al-Baghdadi (d. 463/1071) said of al-Mufid, "He was an imam of error. He intimidated many people until God granted the Muslims relief from him."[96] Al-Mufid was a key figure in the transformation of Twelver Shiʿism from a loosely affiliated group of ʿAlid sympathizers to a coherent religious community with defined boundaries, specific theological positions, and unique cultural patterns. *The Book of Guidance* was engaged with these developments.

The intellectual legacy of al-Shaykh al-Mufid is apparent in the twelfth century work by al-Fadl b. al-Hasan al-Tabrisi (d. 548/1154), titled *Informing Humanity of the Signs of Guidance* (*Iʿlam al-wara bi-aʿlam al-huda*).[97] Al-Tabrisi is remembered today primarily for his commentary on the Qurʾan, but he taught many subjects and played an important role in the development of Shiʿa thought during the Seljuq period. Dwight Donaldson went so far as to call him "the only Shi'ite theologian of importance in the twelfth century,"[98] an overstatement, but one that gives a sense of his significance.

The scholarly lineage from al-Shaykh al-Mufid to al-Tabrisi was direct: one of al-Tabrisi's main teachers was a scholar known as al-Mufid al-Thani ("the second al-Mufīd"), who was the son and student of al-Shaykh al-Tusi.[99] The latter was one of al-Mufid's most influential protégés, who played a major role in the formation of Twelver Shiʿism as a school of thought. *Guidance* had a marked impact on al-Tabrisi's *Informing Humanity,* which followed al-Mufid's book section by section. Al-Tabrisi often repeated large portions of *Guidance* verbatim, a common and accepted practice of the day.

Western scholarship has paid little attention to al-Tabrisi. Prior to Bruce Fudge's recent contribution,[100] only Musa Abdul—who referred to al-Tabrisi as "the unnoticed *mufassir*"—had written anything substantial on him in English. Al-Tabrisi was born around 1077 into a significantly different political context than the previously mentioned authors.[101] Most of his life was spent in Khurasan, specifically in Mashhad and Sabzevar. Much of the region from Baghdad to the Transoxiana had come under control of the Seljuq sultans by his time. This amorphous dynasty of Turkish rulers signaled the end of Shiʿa influence upon the ʿAbbasid caliphs. The Seljuqs committed themselves to extensive sponsorship of a select few schools of interpretation, none of which had any major Shiʿa connections. This period is often referred to as the "Sunni revival," though numerous scholars have noted the problems with this phrase.[102] A revival suggests there was already a Sunni identity or program that could be restored, a tenuous claim at best. The "emergence of Sunni Islam" may be a more apt description, for this was the critical period when the idea of Sunni Islam became operative as something that encompassed multiple schools of law and theology, but that excluded Shiʿism.

The political and educational policies instituted by the powerful vizier Nizam al-Mulk (d. 485/1092)[103] were fully in place by the time al-Tabrisi was beginning his academic career. Nizam al-Mulk's system of state-sponsored colleges (the *nizamiyya*) favored the Shafiʿi school of legal thought.[104] This exacerbated certain sectarian tensions, not between Sunnis and Shiʿa, but between adherents of the Hanafi and Shafiʿi schools of law. The former school was often connected with Muʿtazili theology, which was adopted by many tenth- and eleventh-century Shiʿa scholars as well. Shafiʿi law, in contrast, was associated with ʿAshari theology. A number of Shiʿa scholars were also trained in and affiliated with Shafiʿi law, and thus Shiʿa could be found on both sides of this conflict,[105] though they typically stayed out of the fray.

The Shiʿa were generally excluded from Seljuq centers of power, but some of the scholarly elite among the Sunni Seljuqs elite remained worried about a potential Shiʿa resurgence. The capture of Alamut by the Nizari Ismaʿilis in 1090 exacerbated these fears dramatically. The Ghaznavids to the east, located mostly in modern Afghanistan, justified many of their military campaigns on these grounds and were particularly active in battles against Ismaʿilis.

Al-Tabrisi lived and taught in Mashhad until 1129, when he retired to the nearby town of Sabzevar.[106] While in Mashhad, he navigated the precarious role of a Shiʿa public intellectual in a Sunni-majority environment. He studied with prominent Sunni and Shiʿa scholars and engaged himself with the defense of Shiʿism.[107] The move to Sabzevar, however, enabled him to teach his Shiʿa convictions more openly. The circumstances of his death in 1154 are uncertain, though some accounts claim that he was a martyr.[108] Biographers in subsequent centuries attributed semimiraculous stories and saintly qualities to him as well.[109]

Sabzevar, a growing town located west of Nishapur, was a hub of Shiʿa activities and came to be associated with Shiʿa movements.[110] Al-Tabrisi wrote three works of Qurʾanic commentary while in Sabzevar and probably lived there until his death. His service as a teacher eclipsed his role as a writer, and his students included the most highly regarded names of the next generation of Shiʿa scholars:[111] Qutb al-Din al-Rawandi (d. 573/1177–1178),[112] Muntajab al-Din (d. ca. 585/1189),[113] Ibn Shahrashub (d. 588/1192), and Shadhan b. Jibraʾil al-Qummi (d. ca. 659/1261).[114] Al-Tabrisi's teaching years coincided with the relatively stable decades of rule under Ahmad Sanjar (r. 1118–1157), the capable son of Malik Shah. According to Ibn Funduq, al-Tabrisi was the head of a college in Sabzevar called the Madrasa of the Gate of Iraq.[115] Each of his books was dedicated to a Shiʿa leader with some political power,[116] often a ruler of a nearby vassal state. This suggests he found sufficient patronage for his scholarship among the Shiʿa elite despite possible exclusion from schools in the capital Nishapur. The Seljuq policy of sponsoring specific Sunni schools of education, therefore, was not a consistently applied anti-Shiʿa program. It did, however, help solidify the perception of Shiʿism as heterodox and outside the bounds of Sunni Islam.

Al-Tabrisi penned more than twenty works over the course of his career,[117] and *Informing Humanity* was probably composed during his time in Sabzevar. The book is dedicated to the Bavandi king in Mazandaran,[118] ʿAla al-Dawla ʿAli b. Shahriyar (d. 534/1140).[119] The small Shiʿa kingdom was a vassal state of the Seljuqs at the time, and it served as a political sanctuary for Zaydi and Imami Shiʿa groups up to the fourteenth century. The particular relationship between Sanjar and ʿAla al-Dawla was rocky, and al-Tabrisi's praise of the latter may be an indication that his loyalty to Seljuq authority was superficial.

As mentioned above, *Informing Humanity* was shaped by *The Book of Guidance* in multiple ways. Beyond quoting extensive passages in nearly the exact same order as al-Mufid, al-Tabrisi shared the latter's preference for using broadly authoritative rather than strictly Twelver Shiʿa sources wherever possible. Like al-Mufid, al-Tabrisi cited historians like al-Waqidi, Ibn Ishaq, and al-Zuhri in the sections on Muhammad and ʿAli. *Informing Humanity* also emphasized ʿAli and al-Husayn rather than the later imams.

However, al-Tabrisi did make his own contributions to the genre. His preface provides an outline that divides the book into four main sections (*arkan*): I. On Muhammad (which includes a section on Fatima); II. On ʿAli b. Abi Talib; III. On the second through eleventh imams; and IV. On Twelver Shiʿism and the twelfth imam.[120] The first of these four sections is different from al-Mufid's work, which begins with ʿAli. Moreover, like Ibn Jarir's *Proofs,* al-Tabrisi's work includes a substantial section on Fatima, thus helping solidify the idea of the fourteen infallibles.

The tone and style of al-Tabrisi's work is scholarly and organized, much like al-Mufid's. But his narratives, as will be shown in subsequent chapters, reveal the increased alienation of the Shiʿa. The study of *Informing Humanity* was likely a key inspiration for the works of al-Rawandi and Ibn Shahrashub. The latter is the author of one of the greatest collective biographies of the imams: *Virtues of the Descendants of Abu Talib.*

Putting Stories to Work: *Virtues of the Descendants of Abu Talib*

The most important and influential biography of the twelve imams after al-Mufid's *Guidance* was composed by Ibn Shahrashub (d. 588/1192), the last great Shiʿa scholar of the twelfth century.[121] *Virtues of the Descendants of Abu Talib* (*Manaqib al Abi Talib*) remains among the most frequently quoted works of its type, and it exemplifies the uniqueness of the genre.[122] In keeping with the scholarly trend of his day, Ibn Shahrashub produced a large, encyclopedic work. At the time of completion, *Virtues* was the longest and most detailed work of its type, a literary achievement that reflected the sensibilities of a mature religious tradition. The author worked less to contest the boundary between Sunni and Shiʿa than to exploit it for rhetorical purposes, and *Virtues* is thus a fitting end to the formative stage of this literature. The logic, themes, and strategies of the collective biography were firmly in place, solidified into a genre that would serve Shiʿa communities well for centuries to come.

Although our information on the life of Ibn Shahrashub is limited, the little we know is intriguing.[123] He was born in Sari (in Mazandaran of modern Iran) around 1096 and was groomed for scholarship from an early age. He began studying with his grandfather, al-Shaykh Shahrashub b. Kiyaki (d. early sixth/eleventh cent.), who had been a student of al-Shaykh al-Tusi.[124] Like many of the great masters of his age, Ibn Shahrashub traveled extensively to study with the most prestigious scholars possible. He studied and taught for nearly forty years (ca. 1112–1150) in Sanjar's Nishapur, a bustling center of economic and intellectual activity. He spent a decade of that period studying with the great Sunni theologian and Qur'anic commentator al-Zamakhshari (d. 538/1144), and he also spent time with teachers in surrounding towns. Sometime after 1141 he studied with al-Tabrisi in Sabzavar.

Around 1151, Ibn Shahrashub began traveling westward. The Battle of Qatvan near Samarqand in 1141 was a sign of weakening Seljuq power, and just a couple of years after Ibn Shahrashub left Nishapur, the city was sacked by nomadic groups of the Turkish Ghuzz tribe. By that time, Ibn Shahrashub was far away, having studied and taught with scholars in Rayy, Kashan, Isfahan, and Hamadan before making his way to Baghdad. He remained in that city, teaching and preaching, for over a decade. His work caught the attention of the caliph's court, and he was invited to preach from the pulpit (*minbar*) on occasion during the reign of al-Muqtafi (r. 530–555/1136–1160).[125] Since al-Tusi had been forced to flee Baghdad a century before in 1055, very little Shiʿa preaching had been attempted in the city, and Ibn Shahrashub's foray into this arena was an intriguing, albeit short-lived, experiment. The flourishing of Hanbalism at the time inhibited Ibn Shahrashub's activities, and in 1170 he felt obliged to leave the city.[126] He lived in Hilla for a short time and then in Mosul before finally settling in Aleppo (Halab) around 573/1177. Despite his advanced age, he continued his work in Aleppo. He died there at nearly one hundred years of age.

As we have seen, Ibn Shahrashub studied with an extraordinary number of scholars throughout his career.[127] He interacted with the greatest Shiʿa teachers of his day and incorporated a wide range of source material into his own works.[128] He studied with several notable Sunni scholars of his time as well—with Ahmad al-Ghazali (d. 520/1126) in addition to al-Zamakhshari—and he incorporated many Sunni sources into his writings.

His professional activities were by no means limited to academics. Ibn Shahrashub was devoted to preaching, and he criticized Shiʿa who shrank from this public mission.[129] Despite his role in the defense of Shiʿism and the difficulties he encountered with Hanbalis in Baghdad, his vast erudition, humble demeanor, and rhetorical skills earned him widespread respect. Ibn Abi Tayyi (d. ca. 625–630/1228–1233),[130] who spent time with Ibn Shahrashub in Aleppo, wrote a substantial notice on him in his work of history which, although lost to us today, was quoted often among later Sunni scholars and contributed to a semifavorable legacy for Ibn Shahrashub among Sunnis.[131]

Virtues was likely written while Ibn Shahrashub was in Baghdad, and his lessons on the topic may have contributed to his conflict with Hanbalis there. His incorporation of major Sunni sources—a method already employed by al-Mufid and al-Tabrisi—was elaborate and strategic. The number of Sunni sources listed in the preface of *Virtues* is massive (far more than the number listed by his predecessors).[132] He included scholars like Ibn Hanbal (d. 241/855), the eponymous founder of the Hanbali school of law; Abu Hamid al-Ghazali (d. 505/1111), the famous Shafiʿi jurist and Sufi; and Ibn al-Jahiz (d. 255/868–869), a controversial Muʿtazili belle-lettrist. The reliance on such a wide variety of material was by no means haphazard or lacking in methodology. Ibn Shahrashub articulated his approach in the preface to *Virtues*, where he defended his decision to put Sunni (*ʿamma*) and Shiʿa (*khassa*) narratives side by side. By utilizing many sources seen as antithetical to the Shiʿa understanding of history, Ibn Shahrashub recontextualized certain narratives and put them in conversation with Shiʿa accounts. In his own words, this was an attempt "to bring forth what they [the Sunnis] have suppressed" and "to draw attention to what the chosen [the Shiʿa] have reported."[133] The nature of the reports themselves, he suggested, would resolve any differences between them. As I have argued elsewhere, this was an effective rhetorical strategy that Ibn Shahrashub helped popularize among Shiʿa scholars.[134] Ibn Shahrashub's approach to his sources distinguishes him from al-Mufid and al-Tabrisi. Whereas the latter two used sources that are often considered Sunni (though the sources predate the category and were used widely by various groups), they did so in order to strengthen the legitimacy of their understanding of history. Ibn Shahrashub, however, used Sunni sources (even quite late ones) specifically *because* they were considered Sunni. His purpose was not to uphold his own account, but to undermine and challenge what he perceived to be hegemonic Sunni views by putting their sources to use for Shiʿa purposes. He turned the tables on Sunni presumptions of authority by using their own works against them.

In addition to its innovative use of sources, *Virtues* is also unique for its incorporation of devotional poetry and elegies, some of which were Ibn Shahrashub's own compositions. As a preacher, Ibn Shahrashub had a keen eye for the devotional aspect of his work. He didn't simply stake out an intellectual position; he also cultivated a specific disposition toward the subject of his work: the imams. All of the biographers in this study were concerned with the devotional aspects of their material, but Ibn Shahrashub put it on full display. Subsequent centuries of Shiʿa scholars utilized his style to profound effect. Shiʿism had increasingly moved away from being simply a school of thought in competition (or potential inclusion) with the Sunni schools. The division between Sunni and Shiʿa Islam was increasingly about social memory, shared stories, and perceptions of those stories. The biographies of the imams helped erect a seemingly insurmountable wall between the Shiʿa and other Muslim communities.

Summary: A Sacred History for a Distinct Community

The precise historical audience that received each of the five works considered in this study is exceedingly difficult (perhaps impossible) to determine with any certainty, and few uniform statements will apply. The *Establishment of the Inheritance* and *Proofs of the Imamate* seem to have been compiled with devotional concerns at the foreground, whereas Mufid's *Guidance* and Tabrisi's *Informing Humanity* had more academic and text-oriented interests at play. Ibn Shahrashub brought all of that together in his masterful *Virtues.* But these tentative sketches tell us little. Furthermore, there is also good reason to resist the urge to cast these works as either "scholarly" (thus elite, and read by few) or "popular" (and therefore widespread among the masses).[135] Jonathan Berkey argues that during this general period in the Arabic-speaking world, the boundaries between scholarly and lay discourses were often blurred. The role of preaching and storytelling was particularly important in this regard.[136] And here, the biographies of the imams appear as a likely crossover genre for the Shiʿa. Not only do the stories have a strong narratological quality to them, which lent them well to preaching, but this literature appears to have been a resource for scholars throughout this period.[137] We also know that the biographies of the imams grew as a genre in subsequent centuries and were utilized by later Sufi/chivalry circles.[138] The infamous propagator of Twelver Shiʿism of the Safavid period, Muhammad Baqir Majlisi, worked on expanding the audience for the collective biographies of the imams by writing a version of his own in Persian, titled *A Lens on the Luminaries for the Cleansing of the Eyes* (*Jalaʾ al-uyun*).[139] By writing in Persian, rather than the standard scholarly medium of Arabic, Majlisi clearly intended to reach a broader audience.

The social historian Peter Burke has suggested that when reading texts we ask, "who wants whom to remember what, and why? Whose version of the past is recorded and preserved?"[140] This line of inquiry takes us beyond assessments of the historical accuracy of the narratives and helps illuminate the social context and experiences of those who recorded them. Why were certain narratives in Muslim historical writings remembered as they were? Who benefitted from such a memory? What were the social conditions under which one version of history prevailed over another?

These types of critical questions are just as important to ask of premodern biographies as any other genre. As Alan Shelston notes, "any biography is inextricably linked with the priorities and assumptions of the age which produced it."[141] This is an approach that Patricia Cox Miller has called the "author as prism" approach, noting the ways biographies reflect their authors' sociopolitical settings and cultural landscapes.[142] When applied to the texts at hand, this approach reveals some of the general concerns facing the Shiʿa communities that produced and transmitted biographies of the imams. Instead of reading the accounts of the imams with the desire to find out if the described events *really* happened, the goal is to learn something about why it was remembered in this way and what were the conditions that made it a meaningful story.[143]

When we release the biographies from "the tyranny of bland facticity,"[144] a rich spectrum of issues emerges. The following chapters explore some of these issues. Grief, hope, loyalty, gender, family, and the body are all concerns that permeate the texts. The stories enshrined in the biographies offer unique perspectives on these topics, illuminating the religious milieu that gave the texts meaning. Twelver Shiʿism coalesced around these shared stories, and the systems of meaning embedded have continued ramifications in Shiʿa communities today.

Claims about the social memory of the Twelver Shiʿa in the medieval period, however, must be held loosely, not least because the boundaries of the Shiʿa community were porous and ambiguous. Indeed, this ambiguity—the instability of the lines dividing Sunni and Shiʿa Muslims—is the dynamic against which the biographies can most fruitfully be read. The mere existence of "Sunni Twelvers,"[145] to recall but one example, is a testament to the range of interpretive possibilities that were open when this literature took shape. Part of what makes these biographies so fascinating is that they helped dismantle those possibilities. They buttressed an increasingly coherent discourse on the imams and helped solidify the division between Sunni and Shiʿa Muslims.

My analysis of these texts examines how particular ways of remembering the imams helped erect sectarian boundaries that have largely endured until today. This helps us appreciate the canonizing process of a particular sacred history centered around what Jan Assmann has called "figures of memory."[146] These memories, maintained through stories, poems, and rituals, have a durability that endures across time, but they are continually reinterpreted as the community to which they are meaningful undergoes change. Sunni and Shiʿa identities also developed gradually, with both continuity and ever-constant change. Forgetting this leaves us prone to the reductionist perspective of viewing Sunni–Shiʿa differences as inevitable. In tenth century Baghdad, the current lines of division were anything but inevitable.

CHAPTER TWO

Consolation for a Community

"Will anyone visit (our graves) after we are killed?" asked [al-Husayn]. "Yes, my little son," [the Prophet] told him, "a group (*ta'ifa*) of my community will gain my beneficence and favour through visiting [your graves]. On the Day of Resurrection, I will bring them to the place so that I may take them by the arms and save them from its terrors and sorrows."

—Book of Guidance[1]

THE STORIES OF THE IMAMS are inspiring and entertaining, but short on surprising plot twists. The tragic fates of the infallibles are foreshadowed and mourned long before their deaths are described in the texts. It's fitting, therefore, to begin our analysis with the ends of their lives, because their martyrdoms shape the emotional dispositions and the general mood set by the biographers. Their deaths help us make sense of the specific type of reasoning and emoting that persists throughout the biographies.

Like most literary genres, the collective biographies have their own internal logic and assumptions.[2] One of the most pervasive assumptions demonstrated by the authors was that the imams' personal qualities were in keeping with the office of the imamate. To state the obvious, the imams acted like imams. Practically speaking, this means that the biographers' visions of the imamate informed how they portrayed their subjects.

The salient themes and motifs of the biographies are informed by the authors' views of their own social order and the legitimacy of claims to religious authority. As Shiʿa communities' memories of their imams coalesced, so too did the genre. Each section in the remainder of this book examines those memories by focusing on a single important theme or motif as it appears in the life story of one of the fourteen infallibles. Narrowing the scope of each section to the story of a single figure allows for brevity without sacrificing specificity and detailed analysis. As I will demonstrate, the assumptions about the nature of the imamate throughout the biographies resulted in a high degree of thematic consistency across the lives of the imams, which means that observations about one of the infallibles is generally applicable to the others as well.

The present chapter deals with a cluster of themes surrounding the martyrdoms of the imams.[3] Martyrdom is not only a central component of these texts, but also of Shiʿa cultural memory of the imams. The omnipresent consciousness of martyrdom may all but eliminate the element of surprise from the biographies, but at the same time it gives the texts emotional complexity and depth. The suffering endured by the Prophet's family was meant to have an impact on the audience—an impact intensified by stories of the imams' own displays of emotions. The significance of certain events in the biographies is highlighted by the grief of the imams themselves, and this is especially the case when it comes to their deaths.

Although grief permeates the biographies, it is important to note that sorrow does not subsume all other emotions. The stories also provide reason for sustaining hope. Indeed, one of the primary themes throughout the biographies is consolation—a consolation that assumes and affirms grief, but points beyond it as well.

The Necessity of Martyrdom: The Poisoning of Imam al-Jawad

Most classical sources state that Muhammad b. ʿAli b. Musa b. Jaʿfar died in the year 835 of the Common Era. The man whom Twelver Shiʿa revere as the ninth imam was about twenty-five years old at the time of his death. Known for his extreme munificence, he was given the honorific al-Jawad ("the generous").

The sources may agree on these points, but they diverge when it comes to the matter of *how* Muhammad al-Jawad died. With surprising consistency, the best-known classical historians were silent on the issue.

Al-Tabari, Khatib al-Baghdadi, Ibn al-Jawzi, Ibn Athir, Ibn Khallikan, al-Dhahabi, and al-Safadi (in short, all major medieval scholars without Shiʿa commitments who mention al-Jawad's death) did not comment on the cause of the ninth imam's demise.[4] In contrast, nearly all Shiʿa scholars discussed the circumstances of his death, which they blamed on the ʿAbbasid Caliph al-Muʿtasim (d. 227/842). The eminent tenth century Shiʿa traditionist Ibn Babawayh, for example, asserted plainly in his *Shiʿite Creed* (*Risalat al-iʿtiqadat*) that Imam al-Jawad was poisoned by al-Muʿtasim.[5]

Martyrdom was a theme in ancient Near Eastern cultures and literatures long before the advent of Islam. It played a similar symbolic function across many different contexts, as Moses Hadas and Morton Smith have observed in their study of ancient Near Eastern biographies. "Martyrdom," they note, "implies a minority devoted to spiritual beliefs that the representatives of the dominant majority disapprove and seek to suppress."[6] This statement is made in reference to biographies that predate those of the imams by several centuries, but it holds true for the Shiʿa communities and texts at hand.

For centuries Shiʿa scholars have asserted that the ʿAbbasid government assassinated multiple Shiʿa imams. These assertions have often been accompanied by concerns that authorities antagonistic toward the Shiʿa enforced silence on the subject in an attempt to erase the event from public memory. A modern Shiʿa biographer of al-Jawad expresses this concern explicitly, saying, "All books of history and tradition written by Sunnite [*sic*] scholars are silent about this fact [the martyrdom of al-Jawad]. This is all due to the awesome influence of the Government and feeling of fear on the part of these writers and scholars and nothing else."[7] Many centuries earlier, our own Ibn Shahrashub said that he took the time to write *Virtues* in order "to bring forth what they [the Sunnis] have suppressed."[8]

Divergent memories of the deaths of the imams prompt us to ask the key question: "who wants whom to remember what, and why?"[9] Why is a particular death account embraced or rejected? The story of Imam al-Husayn's martyrdom at Karbala was often the focal point of the collective biographies, and that event is discussed further in the next chapter. But the less-studied stories of other imams' deaths give us important insight into Shiʿa notions of martyrdom and its cultural significance. The martyrdom accounts of some of the imams, like al-Jawad, tend to have less historical attestation than more famous stories like those of al-Husayn and ʿAli. But it is precisely this lack of consensus that makes these lesser-known martyrdoms important starting points for discussions of communal boundaries, social memory, and sacred history.[10]

One of the fascinating aspects of al-Jawad's death is that the different narratives were not always neatly split along Sunni-Shiʿa lines. Despite Ibn Babawayh's erudition and influence, not all Shiʿa scholars agreed with his account of the ninth imam's passing. Ibn Babawayh's most important and influential student, al-Shaykh al-Mufid, explicitly contradicted his teacher on this point. In his *Book of Guidance,* al-Mufid claimed that there were no reliable reports that al-Jawad was poisoned or murdered.[11] The two scholars differed in their accounts of other imams' deaths as well. Ibn Babawayh recorded martyrdom accounts for each imam (excluding the twelfth, of course), in each case citing the person responsible for the murder. In the *Book of Guidance,* however, al-Mufid argued that only five of the imams were killed: ʿAli (the first imam), al-Hasan (second), al-Husayn (third), Musa al-Kazim (seventh), and ʿAli al-Rida (eighth). Despite the tremendous influence of al-Mufid's *Guidance* on the genre of biographies of the imams, most medieval Shiʿa writers ignored al-Mufid's claims on this issue. By the Safavid and early modern periods, scarcely a reference can be found that acknowledges the possibility that any of the first eleven imams died of natural causes. The notion that all imams but the twelfth were killed came to be accepted as a given. Such assumptions about the imams' helped constitute the interdependent narratives around which Shiʿa constructions of sacred history were built. Treatments of the imams became typologies, and thus the stories told about one imam influenced what kinds of stories could be told about other imams. The accounts of al-Jawad's death illustrate this phenomenon, and stories of his martyrdom give us insight into the canonization of memory. To shed light on this process and show how this literature developed over time, I will trace the story of his death chronologically through the five key biographies.

In the *Establishment of the Inheritance*, the ʿAbbasid caliph al-Muʿtasim is said to have plotted with his nephew, Jaʿfar, to have the imam killed. At the caliph's behest, Jaʿfar approached his sister, Umm al-Fadl, who was married to the imam. Stoking his sister's jealousy over al-Jawad's preference for another wife, Jaʿfar induced her to poison her husband. The account reads:

> Al-Muʿtasim and Jaʿfar b. al-Maʾmun continued to plot and plan a trick to kill al-Jawad. So Jaʿfar said to his sister, Umm al-Fadl—she was his full sister—that he was aware of her disinclination toward al-Jawad and her jealousy over al-Jawad's preference for the mother of Abu al-Hasan, al-Jawad's son, and the mother's intense love for al-Jawad since she had been blessed with a son by him. Umm al-Fadl responded to her brother, Jaʿfar, and they made poison in something made from Raziqi grapes.[12]

This brief quote raises a host of overlapping issues related to gender, familial loyalties, and deception. These topics and their related motifs will be explored further in subsequent chapters, but it is worth noting the strong gendered assumptions about the innate trickery of women at play here and in other places in the biographies. The motif of a deceptive wife recurs frequently in these texts: at least three of the imams are said to have been killed by their wives.

The account in *Establishment* goes on to describe the enactment of divine justice upon Umm al-Fadl and her brother for their treachery and murder. Despite apparent regret over her involvement, Umm al-Fadl was cursed with an affliction called *nasura,* an archaic term for an ulcer or tumor. The author added that the tumor appeared on her genitalia:

> Al-Jawad was delighted by the Raziqi grapes, but when he ate from them Umm al-Fadl began to cry. He said to her, "Why are you crying? Truly God will strike you with an unyielding poverty and an affliction without protection." She was then afflicted with a condition in the most hidden parts of her body, which became a tumor. It constantly afflicted her such that she spent all her money and possessions on the illness until she became dependent on the support of people. It is said that the tumor was in her genitalia.[13]

For his part, Jaʿfar escaped the shame of tumor-inflicted genitals only to meet his end at the bottom of a well, which he fell into while staggering about in a drunken stupor.[14] The fact that the author of *Establishment* took the time to describe the fate of these two siblings is in keeping with a common theme throughout the biographies: the worst of the evildoers are justly punished. Sometimes those punishments occurred immediately,[15] and at other times future punishment was foretold.[16] Portrayals of the imams' betrayers coming to bad ends provided a glimmer of hope for the audience, which could take comfort in small displays of justice in the wake of greater injustice.

Turning to Ibn Jarir's *Proofs of the Imamate,* we find a martyrdom account similar to the one above. As in *Establishment,* Umm al-Fadl's jealousy is related to her childlessness, and the murder weapon is said to have been poisoned grapes.[17] The author of *Proofs* also included the story of the imam's curse, noting that Umm al-Fadl was stricken with an affliction "in her most hidden parts" from which she died. However, *Proofs* also contains an intriguing alternate account of the poisoning:

> [Others] have said that she poisoned him using a handkerchief (*mandil*)[18] by rubbing it on him during sexual intercourse. And when he sensed it, he said to her, "God will test you with a disease without cure." Then a gangrenous sore (*akila*) appeared in her genitalia. She was shown to doctors and they looked at her and prescribed medicines for her, but they were without any benefit. She died from her condition.[19]

This variant account of the murder has an added symmetry and a heightened sense of poetic justice. The imam's wife killed her husband in a sexual context (presumably by rubbing a poisoned cloth on his penis), and she in turn was visited by a similar fate. Neither *Establishment* nor *Proofs* cites a specific source for their accounts of al-Jawad's death, though both share in common the assertion that the imam's childless wife, daughter of the ʿAbbasid caliph al-Maʾmun, was the perpetrator. In addition to the motif of feminine trickery, the virtues of childbearing and the suspect nature of barrenness are assumed here (see Chapters 3 and 5 in this volume), and the vulnerability of the imam's body is significant as well (see Chapter 4).

In response to the circulation of accounts like the ones above,[20] al-Mufid made clear his opinion that the rumors about al-Jawad's poisoning were unsubstantiated and unreliable.[21] Al-Tabrisi, whose work closely follows that of al-Mufid, appears to have hedged his bets on the matter. Retreating into the passive voice, he stated merely, "it has been said (*qila*) that [al-Jawad] died by poisoning."[22] Later biographies, however, expressed no such ambiguity or hesitance to declare al-Jawad's death a martyrdom. As collective biographies proliferated in the twelfth and thirteenth centuries, the conventions of the genre solidified and narratives at odds with prevailing notions of how the imams lived and died fell by the wayside. A few later works contain the occasional reference to al-Mufid's position, but the impulse to view the imams as a type, alike in their lives and deaths, made his position increasingly unthinkable.[23]

Ibn Shahrashub's twelfth-century biography is the fruit of this homogenizing impulse, and its more uniform presentation of the different imams' lives is far more representative of the genre than al-Mufid's earlier, anomalous work. The former's *Virtues* was the lengthiest collective biography at the time of its writing, and, as noted already, Ibn Shahrashub culled reports on the lives of the imams from an array of Sunni and Shiʿa scholars' works. His method of using wide-ranging source material but organizing it according to Shiʿa sensibilities and devotional perspectives was the dominant model followed by biographers in subsequent centuries.

Despite his use of many different sources, Ibn Shahrashub included no reports that contradict the notion that al-Jawad was murdered. He clearly believed the imam was poisoned, though he did not commit himself to a specific account of how that occurred. Instead, he presented two versions of the story. In the first, the caliph himself poisoned the imam:

> Once al-Muʿtasim was recognized [as caliph] he began to evaluate his circumstances. So he wrote to ʿAbd al-Malak al-Zayyat to send al-Taqi [Imam al-Jawad] and Umm al-Fadl to him. So al-Zayyat's son, ʿAli b. Yaqtin, was sent to him. Al-Jawad prepared and left for Baghdad. Then al-Muʿtasim honored and praised al-Jawad and sent Ashnas with gifts for him and Umm al-Fadl. Then al-Muʿtasim sent him a citrus drink with his seal by way of Ashnas, and he said, "Have Amir al-Mu'minin [al-Jawad] taste it before Ahmad b. Abi Dawad and Saʿd b. al-Khasib and the rest of them." And he ordered him to mix it with ice water; and Ashnas prepared it in this way. But al-Jawad said, "I

> will drink it in the evening." He [al-Muʿtasim?] replied, "But it is good cold, and by then the ice will have melted." He persisted in this way. So al-Jawad drank it, with full knowledge of their actions.[24]

The second account in *Virtues* is very similar to the story in *Proofs:* Umm al-Fadl poisoned al-Jawad with a handkerchief (*mandil*) during sexual intercourse, after which she succumbed to a gangrenous sore on her genitalia.[25] Ibn Shahrashub's version, however, contains an additional component to the story that likewise appears in several other sources. In *Virtues,* Umm al-Fadl complains to her father, al-Maʾmun, about her husband taking a concubine. The caliph responds to her jealous tirade by saying, "I did not marry you to Abu Jaʿfar [al-Jawad] to prohibit for him what is permissible (*halal*)."[26] This is a curious addition, and like many highly gendered stories in the biographies, it helps us understand some of the social concerns and perspectives of the Shiʿa communities. Al-Maʾmun's response emphasizes al-Jawad's blamelessness, making it clear that he did nothing wrong by having a concubine. This detail may suggest that Shiʿa communities had defensiveness concerning the imams' number of concubines. Having al-Maʾmun—a mortal enemy—take al-Jawad's part in the marital dispute was a way of addressing the concern and buttressing Shiʿa claims about the imam's character. Al-Jawad must have been innocent, for if there were any fault in his actions, his enemy would surely have seized upon it.

Returning to the larger issue of how Ibn Shahrashub framed al-Jawad's martyrdom narratives, we see that the central question is *how* the imam was poisoned. This evades entirely the question of *whether* the imam was poisoned, making it all but irrelevant. Most subsequent biographers followed this model, which is nearly universal in contemporary literature of this genre. The reinforcement of assumptions about the imams through the repetition of certain types of narratives was a regular aspect of works composed in later centuries. In the Safavid period, the seventeenth-century Shiʿa preacher Muhammad Baqir Majlisi made an impressive contribution to the genre: *A Lens on the Luminaries for the Cleansing of the Eyes: History of the Fourteen Infallibles* (*Jalaʾ al-ʿuyun: tarikh-i chahardah maʿsum*). Majlisi's collective biography was one of the first major works in the genre to be written in Persian, and the author made no mention of the fact that al-Mufid or any other scholar ever doubted that Imam al-Jawad was martyred. Instead, like Ibn Shahrashub and many others, Majlisi simply presented different versions of the martyrdom. Though he accumulated more stories of the imam's death than previous scholars, his assumption that Umm al-Fadl was involved seems relatively clear.[27] As one of history's most avid compilers of Shiʿa narratives on the imams, there can be no doubt that Majlisi was aware that al-Mufid and others were unsure about al-Jawad's martyrdom. And yet Majlisi saw no reason to mention it.

Although this study does not focus on modern Shiʿa biographies of the imams, even a cursory look at them reveals the impact of the literary tradition shaped by scholars from Ibn Jarir to Majlisi. For example, Shaykh ʿAbbas Qummi, best known for an immensely popular devotional work entitled *The Keys of Heaven* (*Mafatih al-jinan*), also wrote a work on the lives of the imams titled *The Greatest of Hopes* (*Muntaha al-amal*). In it Qummi noted the debate concerning *how* Imam al-Jawad was poisoned, but he never questioned whether the imam was in fact poisoned or whether al-Muʿtasim had anything to do with it.[28] Similarly, in the popular book *Shiʿite Islam* (*Shiʿa dar Islam*), ʿAllamah Tabatabaʾi stated matter-of-factly that al-Muʿtasim used Umm al-Fadl to poison the imam, even providing commentary on the caliph's motives.[29] Consider also ʿAli Dukhayyil's *Our Imams* (*Aʾimmatuna*), which contains a similar confidence in the fact that al-Jawad was poisoned,[30] as does Muhammad Muhammadi Ishtihardi's *The Tragedies of Muhammad's Descendants* (*Masaʾib al Muhammad*).[31] Not only have I been unable to find any noteworthy modern Shiʿa biography of Imam al-Jawad that raises the question of whether or not he was poisoned, I have yet to find any that mention there ever existed any doubt on the matter.[32] The act of remembering is simultaneously an act of forgetting.

This is but one example of how the preservation and promotion of a certain memory in a body of literature can make alternative memories unthinkable. The canonization of a narrow range of death narratives in the collective biographies was not limited to the martyrdom of Imam al-Jawad. As mentioned above, al-Mufid considered only five of the eleven deceased imams to have been martyred. The circumstances of the deaths of the other six imams were originally considered ambiguous, engendering at least some debate among Shiʿa groups as to their cause. Yet the eventual consensus within the genre was that all of the deceased imams were martyred. By the time Majlisi wrote in the Safavid period, there was little—if any—room for the conception that an imam might not have been a martyr. It had ceased to be a meaningful consideration.

The homogenization of the infallibles' death accounts is part of a larger rhetorical process that happened as the collective biography genre took shape, one that is often overlooked. Increasingly over time, the imams functioned as a type. The typological impulse in this body of Shiʿa literature is similar to that in the premodern hagiographies of other traditions. For example, Michael Stuart Williams notes in his analysis of fourth- and fifth-century Christian biographies that "typology . . . concern[s] itself with 'historical recurrence'—with the repetition in history of previous historical events. The aim is to identify 'something real and historical' which corresponds to something else 'real and historical.'"[33] Recognition of this rhetorical feature should not obscure the "real and historical" significance of the stories in the minds of the biographers. Although the accounts of the imams are laden with symbolism, they were not intended as allegories, nor as *merely* symbolic. By telling the stories of individual imams in similar ways, the biographers projected their conceptions of a type—their convictions about the uniquely meaningful category of humanity into which the imams fit. The biographies had a purpose beyond chronicling the isolated circumstances of each imam's life. Rather, the biographies demonstrated how each of the lives of the "real and historical" imams were meaningful in light of the category of the imamate that bound them together.

Despite the homogenizing effect of the typology, the biographers and their audiences clearly were cognizant of the twelve imams as distinct people with individual lives in different time periods. The texts preserved some of the unique qualities of each imam: the fourth and fifth imams (al-Baqir and al-Sadiq) distinguished themselves with their scholarly achievements, and the superlative leadership qualities of ʿAli b. Abi Talib were often highlighted. But the placement of the imams' life stories together in one work meant that characteristics of each individual imam influenced how the others were understood. The biographers were not simply recording history for its own sake. Nearly all of them were skilled in the science of hadith, a discipline with its own methodology for discerning reliable accounts of history,[34] but the authorial decision-making process in the biographies went far beyond disputes over the integrity of transmitters.[35] Despite the unique speculative details sprinkled throughout each authors' accounts, the stories were increasingly presented in a way that served larger thematic truths about the nature of the imams and the imamate. The erudition of the fourth and fifth imams became a proof of the intellectual qualities of the imams, and the leadership skills displayed by ʿAli formed a lens through which to view the interactions of the subsequent imams with their followers.

Each element of this typological impulse is significant and deserves attention. In the case of the imams' death stories, what was accomplished by propagating the assumption that each of the first eleven imams was a martyr? Why were the martyrdom narratives canonized, and what function did they serve?

Theology played a significant role. By the time the early collective biographies were composed, some Shiʿa scholars like Ibn Babawayh considered the martyrdom of the first eleven imams an article of faith.[36] This claim was typically directed against other competing Shiʿa groups that were inclined to think that a previous imam such as Musa al-Kazim (seventh) or ʿAli al-Rida (eighth) had not died but was alive in a state of occultation.[37] Ibn Babawayh's insistence that the imams were martyred was rooted in this debate. Asserting the martyrdom of each of the first eleven imams emphasized the historicity of their deaths and bolstered the legitimacy of the Twelver line of imams.

An interesting facet of the martyrdom accounts is that the imams were murdered. In our present context this may seem like a statement of the obvious, but as David Cook has shown, the parameters of what counted as a martyr's death have traditionally been quite flexible.[38] Death by the plague or natural catastrophe was categorized as a martyr's death by some, as was dying in a state of purity.[39] Ultimately, our authors did more than claim martyrdom for al-Jawad and the other imams: they provided murder accounts. The issue at stake in these texts, then, was not only whether the imams were martyrs in a technical sense (which would suffice to defend Twelver theology). There is also significance in the fact that the imams were betrayed and murdered.

Recognizing the typological nature of the biographies gives us more tools to help us understand their significance. The individual imams were assumed to have interacted with the world in ways that were in keeping with the imamate. The biographers reinscribed their assumptions with each portrayal of the imams. Their conceptions of what constituted a plausible death for an imam could only be expressed within the framework of martyrdom. And thus the impulse to assume al-Jawad's martyrdom was less about his individual story and more about the nature of the imamate. His death communicated something about what kind of people the imams were: they were men who embodied a threat to illegitimate authorities and who were thus murdered for that reason.

The assimilating process at work in the imams' life stories was simultaneously at work in the portrayals of their enemies. That one imam's adversary would plot and kill him served as evidence that the same thing could—and would—happen again to another imam. A paradigmatic enemy existed across time, treating all the imams in a similar fashion. This assumption was usually implicit in classical sources, but it is made explicit in modern texts. Returning to the work of a contemporary Shiʿa biographer, we read these comments about al-Jawad's martyrdom:

> Whatever device out of these various methods was acted upon under instructions of Motassim should not cause any surprise. Those people who have read the life-accounts of these sacred personalities [the fourteen infallibles] fully know that various kinds of devices were used for killing or murdering these sublime personalities. The assassins adopted whatever method was considered by them to be suitable keeping in view the existing state of affairs at that time. The various means adopted by Haroon [al-Rashid] to kill the solitary personality of Imam Musa Kazim (A. S.) are well-known to the world. *If any intelligent and wise person carefully observes the variety of methods adopted by him he can easily understand that it is not very much surprising if Motassim also adopted both these means for the assassination and martyrdom of Imam Mohammad Taqi (A. S.) [al-Jawad].*[40] (emphasis mine)

This author asserts that it is reasonable to assume that Imam al-Jawad was poisoned because we know that previous imams suffered similar fates. The imams not only blend together as twelve men sharing the same office, but illegitimate rulers (a category I discuss more in Chapter 3) function as a monolithic enemy with singular intentions. The cultivation of this mentality in the collective biographies promoted a particular logic and an organization of narratives that reinforced certain viewpoints. In this way, the genre preserved and promoted a social memory that became a form of sacred history. Each martyrdom account was a way of contesting the official memory of the rulers, challenging their authority, and asserting a Shiʿa interpretation of God's plan for humanity.

Michael Cooperson hints at this logic in his discussion of the eighth imam's biography. "If the imams were not a threat," he says, "the caliphs would not have to murder them."[41] The flip side of this, of course, is that if the caliphs did not try to murder the imams, it would call into question whether they posed any threat and thus whether their status as imams was legitimate or meaningful. The only ending that could possibly surprise Shiʿa readers would be an imam living to a ripe old age and dying peacefully in his sleep. Such a conclusion to an imam's life could not happen, however; the symbolic system and narrative arc that held the literature together rendered a nonviolent death for an imam impossible. A sensibility was cultivated that not only rendered the natural death of an imam unthinkable, but made the killing of the imams inevitable.

Emotional Displays: The Tears of Imam al-Sajjad

Death engenders grief, and betrayal and murder add an element of injustice that heightens sadness and leaves survivors with the poignant sense that all is not as it should be. As we move on to examine grief over the imams' martyrdoms in the biographies, we turn to the story of ʿAli b. al-Husayn (the younger), who is most commonly known by the honorifics al-Sajjad and Zayn al-ʿAbidin ("ornament of the worshippers"). The fourth imam is the only son of Imam al-Husayn who survived the slaughter at Karbala in 680; he is said to have escaped only because he was too sick to go to battle on that fateful day and remained in the tents with the women. Most Shiʿa groups believe that the imamate passed on to him, though he had only a small following for the remainder of his life, most of which was spent quietly in Medina.[42] The fourth imam's grief over his father's death was a focal point in Shiʿa writings for centuries to come, and he was a catalyst for reflection upon the suffering of al-Husayn. Imam al-Sajjad is an excellent example of the emotions performed by the imams within the biographies, especially those related to grief and mourning.

There are numerous reasons why the tragedy at Karbala is the most famous narrative of suffering within the Shiʿa tradition. It was a devastating event that resulted not only in the death of the third imam, al-Husayn, but of many of his closest companions as well. The Prophet's lineage through his daughter Fatima was decimated, and stories of Imam al-Sajjad reflect the losses of the battle and the tragedy of his father's life and death. Ibn Shahrashub recorded a testimony that al-Sajjad wept for twenty years after Ashura.[43] This claim and many other accounts reveal how the memory of the fourth imam was entwined with images of his mourning. The fourth imam earned the honorific *al-sajjad,* a reference to his dedication to prayer, because he was said to have prayed so much that his body became marked and contorted from long hours of prostration.[44] His devotion to God went hand in hand with his connection to his family, the *ahl al-bayt.* This was a painful connection: al-Mufid, for example, recorded a tradition in which al-Sajjad's son, al-Baqir, described seeing his father's body as discolored, his face bruised and mashed, and his legs swollen from the length of his prayers. The mere sight of his father was said to have caused al-Baqir to weep uncontrollably.[45] This and many other similar stories linked the imams together in a chain of piety, suffering, and tears.

These accounts are examples of another feature of the collective biographies: the imams were often depicted thinking or talking about the other infallibles. They spent extensive time and emotion dwelling on the plight and circumstances of their predecessors and successors. This motif not only allowed the authors to eschew a strictly chronological presentation of content (the stories of imams past and future could be told in the contexts of a given imam's memories and foreknowledge), but it also emphasized the miraculous ability of the infallibles to know the future. A number of stories feature the Prophet, Fatima, and the early imams having insight into subsequent imams' lives and fates. These accounts not only highlighted the miraculous capabilities of the infallibles; they also provided opportunities to depict an imam displaying his love and emotion for another imam. Grief and mourning—particularly expressed in displays of weeping—stand out among the emotional performances attributed to the imams. Imam al-Sajjad's mourning over the death of his family at Karbala' took on monumental proportions. He wept for the rest of his life and was unable to eat a meal without crying,[46] and he referred to himself as "the son of the one for whom the angels of heaven weep."[47] Each of the biographers in this study depicted him in tears, and most of the prayers in a collection attributed to him have an undeniably somber tone.[48]

By frequently portraying the fourth imam weeping, the authors reflected and reinforced the complex and nuanced emotional system of the biographies. Al-Sajjad's tears made his concerns clear, but his grief was not focused solely on his father and the tragedy on 'Ashura'. The imam cried for other reasons as well,[49] including the fate of the entire family, the *ahl al-bayt*.[50] Contrary to common conceptions of Shi'ism, and despite the fame of the story, the martyrdom of al-Husayn at Karbala' was not the central cosmic event that defined the tradition,[51] as I explain further in Chapter 3. Karbala' was an event that pointed to a larger reality—an overarching system of injustice that inflicted suffering on the entire *ahl al-bayt*. The system of injustice was the ultimate cause of sorrow; 'Ashura' was simply one of its most powerful manifestations.

The fourth imam is but one example of a pervasive theme. Al-Sajjad is distinguished by his proximity to the tragedy at Karbala', but his displays of sorrow are not unique. All of the infallibles wept. Crying appears in these texts with compelling frequency. At nearly every turn the imams reacted in tears, and their emotional performances reinforced the logic of the biographies. The Prophet wept many times, particularly over the fate of Fatima and 'Ali.[52] Fatima, in turn, sobbed over her father's death and for other reasons.[53] 'Ali's tears were for events both past and future: he wept over Muhammad's death[54] and over his son's coming fate.[55] Al-Hasan and al-Husayn wept for their father[56] and for the deaths that they would suffer.[57] In short, all the imams from 'Ali to al-'Askari performed such emotional displays.[58] Their crying was often portrayed as loud and intense, with statements like "he wept violently" (*baka buka' shadid*).[59]

The imams were not the only ones who wept profusely. The many stories of people close to the imams crying suggest that the imams' weeping was invitational.[60] On occasion, the exhortation and recommendation to weep is explicit. Al-Husayn, for example, said, "I am dead in tears;

believers do not remember me except in tears."[61] More often, however, the invitation was merely implied by the examples of characters within the stories: the people around the prophet's deathbed are said to have lamented and wept loudly;[62] Zaynab wailed and tore her clothes;[63] and Muslim b. ʿAqil cried near the end of his life, saying "I would not weep for myself . . . but I am weeping for my family who are coming to me. I am weeping for al-Husayn and the family of al-Husayn."[64] Along with other instances, these displays of mourning and tears are testaments to the appropriateness of crying over the fate of the imams and the Prophet's family.[65] The biographies, Ibn Shahrashub's *Virtues* in particular, contain many poems that exhort people to tears.[66] There is little doubt that a mood of sadness was cultivated throughout the biographies. The high levels of grief and mourning on display invited the audience to empathize and to emote similarly. And as one Arab proverb indicates, the Shiʿa were widely associated with their weeping: "More subtle than the teardrop of the Shiʿa that weeps for ʿAli b. Abi Talib."[67]

In a study entitled *The Cultural Politics of Emotion,* Sara Ahmed provides helpful insight into the way words, texts, and discourses evoke specific emotions.[68] Emotion, Ahmed argues, is irrevocably connected to communication. Discourse is not only a vehicle for expressing emotions, but also a catalyst for the controlled reproduction of them. As Luisa Passerini writes, "if cultural history is, as I believe it to be, a history of forms of subjectivity, we cannot understand subjectivity unless we see emotions as constituents of it. Memory, which is a form of subjectivity, would not exist without its emotional undertones and components, and the same applies to identity, of course."[69] Central to this understanding is what Ahmed refers to as the "outside in" aspect of emotion.[70] Rather than understanding emotions as something generated within the individual and expressed outwardly in various manners, she describes emotion as a social and cultural practice that communities regulate through discursive norms. People internalize certain emotions through rituals and narratives that meaningfully affirm social identity. The sense that specific emotions are appropriate in a given context is affirmed through such social performances. Ahmed also points out that emotion and rationality are not opposed to one another. They are connected and interdependent, when distinguishable at all. Intelligence is, therefore, never devoid of emotion.

Ahmed's observations suggest that even the most rationalist (or traditionalist, for that matter) discourses in the medieval Islamic context functioned in part to shape "emotional intelligence."[71] The biographies of the imams may seem more emotional than other literatures, but this may not be the most accurate way of describing the unique emotive aspects of these works. The ostensible lack of emotion in non-Shiʿa literature that deals with the events described in the biographies is itself an emotional response, even if less obviously so. It is tempting to describe the biographies of the imams as "emotional," implicitly suggesting that other literatures (legal manuals, hadith collections, etc.) are unemotional. Other types of biography and historical writing may be less explicit about their affect on the reader, but emotion and rationality are nonetheless discursively entwined in these works. For example, the proto-Sunni pietists' insistence on reacting to death with patience and austerity was not a negation of emotion but a claim about what constitutes proper emotion. The collective biographies were simply making different claims about what displays of emotion were appropriate. The biographies had their own emotional norms, and through the repetition of those norms, new "worlds materialize," and communal boundaries stabilize.[72] Stories of weeping and mourning help us understand the moods and emotions evoked by the biographies.

It is not enough to say merely that the biographers of the imams cultivated a specific mood. The cultural dynamics of such acts, specifically the significance of public mourning in the ʿAbbasid period, must be considered. The ritual act of mourning and its representation in Arabic literature had specific connotations that come into play here. Proper rituals around funerary practices (*al-janaza*) in early Muslim communities were the subject of numerous debates among jurists and other religious leaders.[73] Public displays of mourning, such as crying (*buka*ʾ) and wailing (*niyaha*), were often topics of contention.[74] Proto-Sunni traditionalists collected many hadith narratives that denounced such activities. Lamenting loudly in public was associated with pre-Islamic (*jahili*) paganism, and loud crying and wailing were understood to be part of a pre-Islamic Arab belief in fate. By wailing, the mourner protested against an unwelcome fate that befell them. Within the developing theological horizons of Islam, in which God was seen to be in control of all things, some felt that excessive wailing and mourning were unsuitable, as they implied that something had happened that wasn't God's will. Numerous influential proto-Sunni pietists explicitly recommended austerity and patient restraint as the proper behavioral mood at funerals, though silent tears were permitted.[75] The type of mourning depicted in the collective biographies had a negative association for many Muslims, and some of the Shiʿa sources featuring the theme of grief contain accompanying descriptions of the imams responding to accusations of pagan-like behavior.[76]

The debate over proper mourning practices was highly gendered, particularly when it concerned crying and wailing. As Leor Halevi explains in his book *Muhammad's Grave,* mourning the dead was a social activity "dominated by women."[77] For added effect at a funeral, women could be hired to wail for the deceased, and a woman who offered her services in this capacity was known as a *naʾiha* (wailer). For some, the public presence of crying women, hired or otherwise, was an unacceptable disruption of public order and a manifestation of social discord (*fitna*). It was associated both with an improper view toward fate and an unsuitable public role for women, and the two infractions went hand in hand. Some Muslim leaders sought to create a distinctly Islamic social order by imposing greater restrictions on women's public activities, but despite frequent condemnations of wailing, the ritual remained common. In this context, the wailing of the *naʾiha* and the public weeping and crying by women at funerals were gender transgressions, instances where the normative rules of gender were not upheld.

In practice, observes Nadia Maria El Cheikh, "mourning was essentially women's work," but it had to be controlled by men.[78] Some traditionalists completely forbade wailing, collecting hadith in support of their stance.[79] In the eighth century Iraqi city of Kufa, where antiwailing campaigns were strongest, some men went so far as to lock women into buildings to keep them away from funerals.[80] Wailing was certainly not an activity considered suitable for men, at least according to many proto-Sunni traditionalists. These restrictive attitudes on wailing contrasted sharply with early and classical Shiʿa legal literature on the topic, which avoided taking a particular position on the issue.[81]

The gendered nature of mourning in early and classical Arabic-speaking settings is further evident in *marthiya* poetry, also known as *rithaʾ*. This genre of Arabic verse was used primarily for eulogizing a deceased beloved.[82] It was a vehicle for expressing lamentation of the deceased and inciting vengeance against those responsible for the death. Such mourning was a poetic ritual that was, according to Suzanne Stetkevych, "preeminently incumbent upon the female."[83] In fact, *ritha'* poetry was one of the only domains of classical Arabic literature dominated by female authors. Both of the earliest major figures associated with the development of *marthiya* were women: al-Khansa' (d. mid-first/seventh c.) and Layla al-Akhyaliya (d. early second/eighth c.).[84] Although numerous men wrote *marthiya* poetry as well, this type of verse remained associated with the disruptive role of women's mourning, which was as ubiquitous in the medieval Islamic context as it was contentious.

Against this backdrop, it is clear that the mourning scenes in the imams' biographies intersect with issues of gender as well as communal boundaries. The biographers depicted the imams in ways that resisted Sunni traditionalist sensibilities concerning masculinity and public order. Halevi notes that when disputes over mourning rituals took shape, funerary practices had distinct political relevance. Graveside mourning during the Umayyad period, for example, was often a politically provocative act, especially in southern Iraq where numerous anti-Umayyad rebellions had emerged. He posits that "the Kūfan attempt to ban women from funerals appears grounded in the proto-Sunni endeavor to prevent wailers from igniting rebellion. Perhaps, then, Kūfan traditions against the presence of women at funerals were on occasion directed polemically against proto-Shīʿites."[85] Halevi's observation is helpful for understanding the social implications of mourning in the biographies. The debate over weeping and wailing overlapped with general concerns about political authority and social stability. By denouncing the female mourners, proto-Sunni pietists effectively reinforced the gendered nature of mourning and asserted male control over female expression. Since those expressions were often politically charged with antigovernment sentiments, proto-Sunni condemnation of the mourners doubled as an anti-Shiʿa agenda.

The mourning practices of women, particularly in Shiʿa-friendly communities, were potential disruptions in the normative order of a male system of power that was generally anti-Shiʿa. The public sphere was primarily controlled by men who opposed Shiʿa claims and grievances. Disrupting that order with emotional laments over past deaths was a feminized form of protest against a masculinized political system. In some ways, therefore, the broader Shiʿa use of mourning as a form of protest, seen clearly within the biographies and exemplified by the imams, drew its power from the gendered dynamics of the discourse.

The significance of the stories of the imams' bitter laments and the eulogies of their followers now stands in sharper relief. As David Herman has noted, "Stories do not just emanate from cultural understandings of emotion but also constitute a primary instrument for adjusting those systems of emotion terms and concepts to lived experience."[86] The biographies did not merely represent a different emotional sensibility or an alternate concept of masculinity; they also protested the established social order through the appropriation of a feminized vocalization. By refusing to consent to an emotional logic that would strip power from the deaths of the imams, the biographers insisted upon the relevance of mourning as a marker of the enduring, unjust nature of their societies.

Another aspect of *marthiya* poetry is relevant to this discussion. Stetkevych points out that *marthiya* poetry structurally and ritually included an incitement to vengeance (*tahrid*) along with the lamentation. The two elements had an important reciprocal relationship—or as Stetkevych calls it, an "interreferentiality." In these poems, the execution of vengeance is situated as the fulfillment of the lament. The tearful mourning (prescribed to women) comes to an end once the vengeance (prescribed to men) has been achieved; and so, she writes, "women's lamentation/*rithāʾ* is in perception and expression the inverse parallel of men's blood vengeance/*rithāʾ*."[87] *Rithaʾ* implies lamentation and vengeance together.

The mourning performances in the biographies, like the performative aspects of *marthiya,* were intended not only to invite the audience to share in the grief of loss. They were also designed to evoke emotions of protest and desire for injustice to be rectified. Stetkevych writes, "women's mourning must thus be understood, above all, as an obligatory public lamentation that was ritually prescribed and served to express a typically liminal defiled and yet sacral state."[88] Likewise, the bodies of the imams were both sacred and defiled—sacred because of the infallibles' holy status and virtue, and defiled by those who denied them their rights, abused them, and murdered them. Mourning the imams functions as a constant reminder of that injustice and as a call for rectification. The lamentation cannot be fulfilled until vengeance comes to pass, and thus it must be reproduced across centuries and generations until justice comes.

Cathartic Hope: The Role of the Audience

Focusing on the imams and their stories runs the risk of making us lose sight of one of the most important aspects of this study: the audience. As noted in Chapter 1, we do not know the immediate audience of many of the collective biographies. And so I cast a broader net, considering not only those who read the texts when they were first composed, but also those who heard the stories in subsequent centuries through orations, preaching, and storytelling. My interest lies not exclusively with the readership the biographers had in mind, but rather with the community for whom these works proved meaningful. The latter are those who deemed these books worth remembering and thus ensured their survival. I have noted several ways in which audiences may have engaged with the texts in the communal process of constructing meaning, but I will make a few more comments before proceeding to the rest of this study.

Rather than attempting to determine the identity of the immediate audience of each work, it is worth considering what response the biographers appear to have expected or desired. Thinking about the broader community that received and passed on these stories brings the social functions of the texts to the fore. The response engendered in the audience by stories of the emotional outpourings of the imams is merely one example that shows that these texts were not only saying, but *doing* something. Discourse is a social performance that has certain effects,[89] and it is my intention to examine how the biographies emotionally affected their audiences. As Judith Perkins writes, "although discourses do not represent 'reality,' they do have very real effects."[90] How did the biographies guide their readers' thoughts and feelings about themselves, their community, and their world?

The emotional qualities of the biographies are readily visible. In a lecture to his students, al-Mufid recited a tradition in which Imam al-Sadiq said, "tests and trials begin with us and then with you, and the times of ease begin with us and then with you."[91] This direction of emotional transmission from the imams to their followers is assumed throughout the biographies. The trials that affected the imams affect their followers, and release from those trials would come to the community from the imams as well. Thus the emotions displayed by the imams are central to our reflection on the effects of the literature as a whole.

The suffering of the imams undoubtedly evoked sorrow, but their sadness on each other's behalf also served as an emotional prompt. Their tears were exemplary in that they embodied the appropriate emotional response to the stories. The imams modeled the way their life stories ought to be received. In another lecture, al-Mufid recited an elegy attributed to Fatima al-Zahraʾ. The final portion of it reads:

> Men have attacked us and humiliated us,
> after the Prophet, and all wealth has been usurped;
> The perpetrator of injustices to us will know his fate
> on the day of judgment, where he will finally land.
> We have come across things which no one before us,
> neither from Arabs nor from the Ajam [non-Arab] have suffered;
> So, we shall continue weeping over you as long as we live,
> and as long as we have eyes which well up with flowing tears.[92]

In this portion of the elegy Fatima was grieving Abu Bakr's denial of her right to Fadak. This was a sensitive topic for ʿAlids, who believed that Fatima was robbed of her rightful inheritance upon the Prophet's death. This poem, however, reveals how quickly grief over a specific instance of injustice morphed into mourning for the fate of the entire family. Fatima's injustice at the hand of Abu Bakr was one and the same with the injustice that befell all the infallibles, and the vengeance requested would come at the Day of Judgment. The call to mourning as a type of protest was clear, and many Shiʿa poets took up this call. In an excerpt quoted by Ibn Shahrashub, the poet al-Suruji said:

> Don't be surprised that I have followed
> your noble and strong voice
> With good intention and insight
> and patience for my victorious savior.
> Truly I want to stand
> before you as a funerary mourner (*naʾihat al-janaʾiz*)

Who, while striking wounds, keeps
 remembrance amidst the commotion.[93]

Another piece in *Virtues,* attributed to Ibn al-Rumi:

O, family of Muhammad's house! My sorrow is for you,
 it has weakened my patience and strength.
How the fangs of calamities have penetrated
 into you, dividing the oppressor from oppressed.
Every mourner is wailing for you
 lamenting you in an ever-renewing funeral commemoration (*maʾtam*).[94]

Such examples are numerous. But just as *marthiya* poetry combined backward-looking mourning with a forward-looking call for vengeance, the imams engaged in mourning while also inspiring hope for the future. The centrality of the theme of suffering in Shiʿa literature is undeniable, but alongside it come glimmerings of hope that are often overlooked. The biographies did not leave their audiences in despair: they provided something immensely meaningful and important—consolation. The idea of consolation carries with it a consciousness of grief, but it is also a testament to the possibility of surviving and processing suffering and loss. Consolation links sorrow and hope, encapsulating a central function of the biographies in the communities that found them meaningful.

In some cases in the biographies the imams encouraged their followers to cease weeping, even when they wept for good reasons.[95] Justice belonged to God, after all, and it could be enacted at any moment. Those who betrayed the imams often encountered divine retribution in their own lifetimes, as was the case with the murderers of Imam al-Jawad. Even those enemies who did not suffer bitter fates were clearly understood to be awaiting the judgment of God in the next life. In many stories, the hope of justice being meted out in a world to come served as consolation. When Zaynab, the daughter of ʿAli and Fatima, wept and mourned the tragedy occurring at Karbala, her brother, Imam al-Husayn, said to her, "Sister, fear God and take comfort in the consolation of God [*bi-ʿazaʾ Allah*]. Know that the people on the earth will die and the inhabitants will be destroyed except the face of God Who created creation by His power (*qudra*)."[96]

Those mourning the fate of the imams were consoled by confidence in divine power and by the expectation that God would restore direct contact between the people and the imamate with the return of the twelfth imam, the Mahdi. The return of the Mahdi and the establishment of just leadership is a vision of inspiration throughout the biographies. An account in *Proofs* includes a story in which one of the Prophet's companions (ʿAbd Allah b. Masʿud) asked Muhammad why he was crying. The Prophet responded:

> It's the *Ahl al-bayt.* God has chosen the world's last days for us. My *Ahl al-bayt* will endure being killed, chased, and banished from their land until God ordains the banner to come from the east. The one who waves [the banner] will do so, and the one who delights in it will do so. Then a man will emerge among them from my *Ahl al-bayt;* his name is like mine and his features are like mine. My people will return to him like birds return to their nests. For he will fill the land with justice like [it] is filled with oppression.[97]

Misfortune was thus embraced as part of God's plan for the select. But the community was reassured that every trial endured would be met with retribution. The world might be filled to the brim with cruelty, but al-Mahdi would return to fill it equally with justice. Various versions of the final line of this quote were widely cited by many proto-Shiʿa revolutionary and apocalyptic movements, including some that originally supported the ʿAbbasid revolution. The placement of this passage here, after countless tales of the imams' sufferings and at the end of the section on al-Mahdi, was a clear assurance to the readers that the Prophet's promise was still valid. Hope remained.

Many scholars have attempted to clarify what makes Shiʿa forms of Islam distinct from Sunni ones. As I will explain later, the differences between Sunni and Shiʿa Muslims cannot be reduced to a debate about historical events, even events the biographers themselves considered to be of great importance. These biographies do not simply present a particular narrative of history: they have influenced how people felt about that history. The biographies make indifference impossible. They have moved readers to sorrow and provided tangible hope. The narrative of consolation they supply has been immensely meaningful for a community that found itself on the losing side of history.

When writing about historical narratives, Peter Burke said, "what happens in the case of these myths is that differences between past and present are elided, and unintended consequences are turned into conscious aims, as if the main purpose of these past heroes had been to bring about the present—our present."[98] This approach to historical narratives proves fruitful when considered against the biographies. By placing the accounts of all of the infallibles side by side, the authors elided the differences between the imams. Chronology was constantly thwarted through visions, dreams, memories, and miraculous journeys, and no matter what injustices were suffered by the imams, the story always ended with the twelfth imam escaping into hiding and preparing to return with power and justice. This is part of what makes this genre so enduring: it was no great leap of reasoning for the Shiʿa to align their own grief with that of the imams and to find a parallel hope for a just redemption. The biographies, therefore, may tell us much more about how Shiʿa communities have understood their own social predicament than they do about the historical sufferings of the imams.

Conclusion

The biographies of the imams are good stories, not because they engage the reader through surprising plot twists, but because they accomplished something transformative. They helped solidify collective memories of the imams and forge a relationship between the imams and the community of memory. Judith Perkins, in her work on early Christian narratives of pain and suffering, writes:

> The power of discourse inheres precisely in this remarkable ability it has to set its agenda and mask the fact that its representation both has an agenda and that there could be other representations and other agendas. Every representation is by its very nature partial and incomplete. A representation of "reality" must leave something out, even as it puts something in. A culture's discourse represents not the "real" world, but rather a world mediated through social categories, relations, and institutions operating in the specific culture.[99]

The biographers of the imams were making claims about history. Their works contested one version of history and supplanted it with another.

But the power of this literature, in Perkins's words, was in its authors' ability to "set its agenda and mask the fact . . . that there could be other representations and other agendas." Communal memory was at stake, and the biographers focused on stories they felt were suppressed. They presented the imams as having died martyrs' deaths, and they intended those deaths to be perceived as sorrowful events.

The example of the martyrdom of the imams is instructive precisely because, as al-Mufid's work demonstrates, it was not universally agreed upon or considered necessary in early Shiʿa communities. As Twelver Shiʿism developed, however, the weight of the larger narrative of salvific history made any finale but martyrdom unthinkable for the imams. Despite al-Mufid's unparalleled influence on this genre, his comments on this matter were largely ignored and have essentially been forgotten in the metanarrative of Shiʿa social memory. The cultural negotiation of meaning restricted the possibilities of what could be said on this subject, even as it broadened them in other areas. The unnatural and unjust deaths of the imams helped stabilize the tone and homogenize the narrative of the biographies.

Memories have effects on a community, and the biographies of the imams impacted their audience as much as they informed them. The authors provoked an emotional response to the memory of the imams. The biographies are unique not because they cultivated emotion; rather, they are unique in the specific mood they engendered and in the emotional logic they constructed for the community. The biographers consistently represented the imams as men who mourned and cried over the tragedy of *ahl al-bayt,* and their tears reinforced the appropriateness of such a reaction. By embracing this feminized form of protest against the social order dominated by Sunnis, Shiʿa Muslims challenged the notion that any just social order could exist prior to the return of the Mahdi. Tethering religious identity to the necessity of justice for *ahl al-bayt* shaped the contours of Shiʿa social memory and provided the community with a lasting "boundary, fixity, and surface."[100]

CHAPTER THREE

Betrayal and the Boundaries of Faithfulness

They summoned us so that they might support us
and then they became hostile to us and killed us.

—*Imam al-Husayn*[1]

ALL THE INFALLIBLES WERE BETRAYED. Stories of treachery permeate the collective biographies, and the theme of betrayal had a valuable social function and reveals the cultural assumptions of Shiʿa audiences. Chapter 2 explored the themes of mourning and consolation in the biographies, making clear that the authors and their audiences were attempting to understand how the failure of the imams to acquire leadership over the greater community of Muslims fit into the broader arc of sacred history. The afflictions of the infallibles and the denial of their rights occupied a central place in the narrative that made Shiʿism intelligible. Finding religious meaning in narratives of suffering is not unique to Shiʿism; it is a common theme in human religiosity.[2] The biographies of the imams provide us with an excellent window into this phenomenon, helping us understand how and why it transforms memory.

The present chapter examines several different betrayals in the biographies, focusing not only on the literary motifs used and the cultural assumptions they enshrined, but also on the way these narratives served the social function of distinguishing community boundaries. Narratives of the imams' sufferings fortified porous and unstable boundaries of religious identification, and accounts of treachery were the places where the borders of the community were most clearly delineated. The betrayals made clear who was outside of the community and acted as warnings to those who were inside. The stories drew lines not only between Shiʿa and non-Shiʿa, but also between true Shiʿa and the imposters and their followers.

The best-known betrayal in Shiʿa sacred history is undoubtedly the massacre of al-Husayn and his family at Karbalaʾ. The retelling of this event has rightly been said to capture the essence of Shiʿa social memory,[3] and thus we begin this chapter with the third imam's story. It is important, however, not to overlook the betrayals of the other infallibles. This genre contains a pattern of treachery, and biographers and their audiences operated under the assumption that each imam would be denied his natural and divinely appointed rights.

The authors of the biographies dealt with betrayal in various ways. The death of al-Husayn was the focal point for explicit discussions of perfidy, but the effects of treacherous acts were felt at every turn. The dispossession of the imams' rightful authority and their persecution at the hands of their enemies was at the core of the metanarrative that bound the individual biographies together into a memorable and meaningful story. Certain assumptions regarding historical continuity undergirded this process. We have seen how the imams functioned as a type in the biographies, and we now see that their betrayers were also assumed to be one and the same.

Betrayal on Stage: The Murder of al-Husayn at Karbalaʾ

The martyrdom of al-Husayn and his companions on the plains of Karbalaʾ in 680 is the center of gravity for Shiʿa religious emotion. Kamran Aghaie has called the battle at Karbalaʾ "the most important symbolic event for Shiʿites, after the death of the Prophet,"[4] and Nakash argues that it has a "central role in shaping Shiʿi identity and communal sense."[5] Most general studies of Shiʿism devote substantial attention to this event and the rituals that commemorate it.[6]

The Shiʿa biographers of the imams were cognizant of the symbolic significance of al-Husayn's death. In some cases, these authors went so far as to link the events at Karbalaʾ to the eternal fate of each believer. Ibn

Shahrashub, for example, recorded Imam al-Rida saying, "he for whom ʿAshuraʾ is his disaster, his sadness, and his tears, God will make the Day of Resurrection his joy, his ḥappiness, his delight in heaven."[7] The salvific significance of al-Husayn's fate has been compared to Christian ideas of atonement and redemption.[8] Such comparisons, however, obscure the memory of al-Husayn more than they reveal it. There is no sense, at least not in the literature under consideration in this study, that the events at Karbalaʾ had any salvific power in and of themselves. Rather, their significance was in relationship to the family of the Prophet, the love members of the family had for each other, and the duty of the believer to participate in that love. This is a critical difference between Shiʿism and Christianity. For Christians, the life, work, and death of Jesus was entirely unique. Jesus was the center of creation in a fundamental and unrepeatable way. The biographies, however, regularly emphasized the ontological similarity between the imams and the prophets. Al-Husayn was unique only in how starkly his life displayed the realities and qualities that all imams faced and displayed. Devotion to al-Husayn was also a symbol of devotion to the entire family of the Prophet and to the Prophet himself.

The imams' biographers seem to have operated under two key assumptions. First, a person's feeling toward al-Husayn's death was a reliable indicator of whether or not that person truly loved the Prophet and his family.[9] ʿAshuraʾ was a litmus test of the heart. Second, a person who loved the Prophet's family would receive the favor of the Prophet and the other infallibles, who would intercede on his or her behalf on judgment day.[10] Al-Tabrisi, for example, in his section on al-Husayn, related the following saying by the Prophet: "al-Hasan and al-Husayn are my sons. Whoever loves them, loves me. And whoever loves me loves God. And whoever loves God will be taken to heaven. Whoever hates them, hates me. Whoever hates me, hates God. Whoever hates God will be put into the fire on his face."[11]

The massacre at Karbalaʾ was used by Shiʿa as a powerful symbol of injustice from an early date,[12] but it was some time before the collective biographies began to incorporate extensive reflections on the event. The *Establishment of the Inheritance* devotes only slightly more attention to al-Husayn's martyrdom than it does to that of the other imams. Similarly, Ibn Jarir's *Proofs of the Imamate* includes only brief narratives covering the affair.[13] This suggests that the conceptual link between al-Husayn's martyrdom and the significance of the imamate was still weak in the early tenth century. Al-Mufid was the first of the five biographers studied here to include a lengthy exposition of the Karbala' tragedy. He devoted around 15 percent of *Guidance* to the event—far more space than he allotted to any other single topic. The Karbala' story was the apex of his work, and his treatment of it was perhaps his most important contribution to the genre. His powerful narrative of the event drew mainly upon the writings of the Kufan traditionist Abu Mikhnaf,[14] with added portions from other sources. Abu Mikhnaf, like other early writers on the events of Karbala', wrote from an anti-Umayyad, pro-Kufan perspective, but one that was not necessarily "Shiʿa" in the later sectarian sense.[15] By incorporating such literature into his book, al-Mufid introduced a broader retelling of Shiʿa history into the biographies of the imams. Al-Tabrisi, Ibn Shahrashub, and all other later writers of this genre followed al-Mufid's lead in this regard. It was only from al-Mufid's writing forward that the martyrdom of al-Husayn became the emotional focal point of this literature. It is not clear that al-Mufid caused this shift in emphasis, but his book facilitated it. He was clearly at the forefront of a trend in which accounts of al-Husayn's death became increasingly aligned with a specifically Twelver Shiʿa social memory.

By al-Mufid's time, when the Buyids had control of Baghdad, ʿAshura' had begun to be commemorated through a set of public rituals.[16] Some of these rituals receive explicit attention in these biographies, including visits to the graves of imams. This suggests a connection between this literature and the production of religious practices.[17] It is perhaps not a coincidence that al-Mufid's narrative was the first to include theatrical components of the story of Karbala' that became standard fare in later works of this type. This is not to say that al-Mufid foresaw the development of public theatrical renditions of the battle at Karbala' (commonly referred to as *taʿziya*), which seem to have occurred in the Safavid period.[18] But his *Guidance*, al-Tabrisi's *Informing*, and Ibn Shahrahsub's *Virtues* all contain relatively long, continuous stories of the event that include dramatic monologues and theatrical physical gestures by the characters. Furthermore, these accounts feature some of the most jarring displays of blood and gore found anywhere in these works. The bodies of al-Husayn and his companions, whole and pure at the outset of the story, are stripped naked, broken, abused, and defiled. The imagery is startling and at times grotesque. For example, the biographers give a description of al-Husayn's baby son, ʿAbd Allah b. al-Husayn, being pierced through with an arrow as his father held him on his lap.[19] Later the arm of al-Husayn's nephew is severed, and his companions watch it dangle by a piece of skin.[20]

One character after another dies a gruesome death. The tormentors curse their victims, and the family members shed tears, which again modeled for the audience the proper reaction to such events. The immoral—indeed, barbaric—nature of the imam's oppressors is conveyed through depictions of the Umayyad army decapitating the imam and trampling his body under the feet of the cavalry.[21] It is further emphasized by the army's plundering of the imam's body, the stealing of his clothes, and the abandonment of his broken, naked corpse in the heat of the desert sun. In one particularly sobering scene, Ibn Ziyad, the Umayyad governor in charge, casually pokes a stick at the teeth in the imam's severed head. This degree of disrespect for an imam's body is too repulsive to have gone unrebuked. The biographers tell us that Zayd b. Arqam scolded the governors, saying, "Take your cane away from those lips. For, by God, other than whom there is no deity, I have seen the lips of the Apostle of God, may God bless him and his family, touch those lips countless times."[22]

The connection between the bodies of the Prophet and the imams, as well as the vulnerability of those bodies, opens up more questions than can be addressed here. We will return to the imams' bodies in the next chapter, but it is worth noting here that normative gender roles were exploited to efface the humanity of the enemies. The way in which the army treated the women at Karbalaʾ was a clear indictment of their lack of masculine chivalry, epitomized by their act of stripping the women of their clothing.[23] One Umayyad officer described the battle in this way:

> It was nothing but the slaughtering of animals. . . . There were their naked bodies, their blood-stained clothes, their faces thrown in the dust. The sun burst down on them; the wind scattered [dust] over them; their visitors were [scavenging] eagles and vultures.[24]

The single most pervasive image in these accounts, however, is blood. It is mentioned everywhere, and blood is even a major component of narratives of al-Husayn's life that take place prior to Karbalaʾ. Each of the biographers included an account in which Umm Salama (one of the Prophet's wives) recalls being given a clod of dried, red dirt by the Prophet, who explains to her that it was made of al-Husayn's blood at Karbalaʾ. Decades later, on the day of al-Husayn's death, the blood in that dirt flowed fresh, a sign to Umm Salama that the Prophet's grandson had died.[25]

Dreams, visions, and other miracles served to incorporate a larger cast of characters than would otherwise be possible into the story of al-Husayn's martyrdom. Blood was a symbolic link that tied together foreshadowing accounts and the stories of the tragedy. In the battle itself, blood imagery takes on apocalyptic proportions. Beyond references to blood in the death description of nearly every person killed at Karbalaʾ, we learn that the very heavens wept blood on that day. Al-Tabrisi's account says, "when al-Husayn b. ʿAli (peace be on them) was killed, the sky rained blood. It, along with everything around us, became full of blood."[26] In other accounts, people in distant cities claim to have found fresh blood under every stone.[27] The heavens and earth suffered under the grief of this tragedy.

Despite the dramatic ways al-Husayn's martyrdom gave expression to a profound sense of injustice and grief, the collective biographies of the imams are not, fundamentally, about al-Husayn or the events at Karbalaʾ. Such a view of Shiʿism obscures the relationship between al-Husayn/Karbalaʾ and the other imams. A broader consideration of Shiʿa ideas of the imamate compels us to look beyond al-Husayn.

In the biographies, the drama of al-Husayn's betrayal had a reciprocal relationship with the fate of the other imams. On the one hand, the brutal treatment of the Prophet's grandson set the emotional tone for the entire story: those who preceded the Karbalaʾ tragedy and those who came after participated in the suffering and mourning of this event. As such, the betrayal stakes out the parameters of a division within the larger Muslim community that spanned all of history. "Every day is ʿAshuraʾ, every land is Karbalaʾ,"[28] goes a saying popular in Shiʿa circles.[29] Those who betrayed al-Husayn are identified with those who later denied the other imams. And thus every imam was betrayed at Karbala'.[30]

On the other hand, al-Husayn's death derived meaning from its immediate literary context. Within the collective biographies of the imams, al-Husayn's pure character and pious intentions are affirmed by the qualities of the other infallibles, by the typological category in which he belongs. Thus, in the biographies, al-Husayn's story is freed from Abu Mikhnaf's anti-Umayyad concerns and given broader significance. ʿAshura' ceased to be a story about how a particular government or group of immoral people abused their power. Instead, it became a story about the enemies of the Prophet in all time periods and how "they" treat "us" (those who love the Prophet). Putting al-Husayn's biography alongside those of the other imams transformed his death into a statement about the universal significance of the imamate for all Muslims.[31] His martyrdom functioned as more than a call for all people to mourn him. It was an admonishment to all those who cared about the Prophet to love (and grieve the fate of) all twelve imams.

The Original Betrayal: Muhammad's Mantle

The denial of Muhammad's dying wishes—specifically his attempt to appoint ʿAli as his successor—stands alongside the battle of Karbala' as one of the defining scenes in the broader narrative arc of the biographies. Each of the authors studied here provided a detailed account of how the Prophet was betrayed.[32] Even al-Mufid, whose *Book of Guidance* does not include a delineated treatment of the Prophet's life, devoted significant attention to this event. According to each of the authors, the prophet gave clear instructions on multiple occasions that ʿAli should be his successor as leader of the community of believers (*amir al-mu'minin*). The most important instance of this, and the most widely attested in early Muslim sources, was a speech the Prophet gave on his way back from hajj in the final months of his life. At *Ghadir Khumm*,[33] the angel Gabriel told the Prophet that the time had come to reveal his successor to the people. The word of God came to Muhammad at that moment, saying, "Messenger, proclaim everything that has been sent down to you from your Lord."[34] Then, according to al-Tabrisi:

> [Muhammad] took hold of ʿAli's two arms and lifted them high until people could see his white underarms. He said: "Of whomever I am the master, ʿAli is his master. O Allah, befriend those who are loyal to him, and be an enemy to those who are hostile towards him. Grant support to those who support him, and abandon those who abandon him!"[35]

Those present, including ʿUmar b. al-Khattab, came forward and pledged their allegiance to ʿAli, congratulated him, and addressed him as *amir al-muʾminin*. The biographers' assumptions about Muhammad's intent and the perspicuity of his actions are apparent in the prominent placement of this narrative in the biographies. The *Ghadir Khumm* story is a defining, climactic event at the end of the Prophet's life that typically segues into a description of the circumstances of his death, which are also entwined with the issue of successorship.

Several biographers recalled that when the Prophet was on his deathbed, he feebly asked those present to send for his "brother" and "companion." ʿAʾisha maintained that he meant Abu Bakr, her father, and she had him come. But as Abu Bakr approached, the Prophet turned his head and repeated the original request. Hafsa, another wife of the Prophet, interjected that he must have intended for them to call her father, ʿUmar. But when ʿUmar was summoned, the Prophet turned his head away once again, saying again that he wanted his brother and companion. Finally Umm Salama spoke up, saying that the Prophet meant ʿAli. When ʿAli was summoned, the Prophet spoke privately to him for a long time. ʿAli remained with Muhammad, and the Prophet expressed a desire to die with his head in ʿAli's lap. As Muhammad's spirit departed from him, ʿAli caressed his own face with it.[36] This last point stands in stark contrast to mainstream Sunni narratives, which generally state that the Prophet died in ʿAʾisha's lap.[37]

The biographers' version of Muhammad's death story is an emotionally compelling protest against the ultimate betrayal of the Prophet of God. The motif of the deceptive wife appears here as it does in many other places: ʿAʾisha and Hafsa, beloved wives of Muhammad, shamelessly try to secure their own interests while the Prophet is at his most vulnerable. Moreover, two of Muhammad's closest friends, Abu Bakr and ʿUmar, are complicit in the treachery. Though their role in death narratives is a passive one, they are shown in other stories to have aggressively manipulated the situation and disobeyed the Prophet in order to snatch power for themselves.[38] In several accounts collected by the imams' biographers, Muhammad makes multiple attempts to clarify his wishes, at one point even asking for a pen so that he can write his will down,[39] but those closest to him repeatedly deny him. Ibn Shahrashub's account of this event cites Ibn ʿAbbas, who said that this was "the most disastrous thing to happen to the Prophet."[40]

Within the framework of these biographies, the betrayal of the Prophet is the betrayal of the entire imamate. It initiated the dispossession of the imams from their rightful authority and symbolizes the fate of the Shiʿa. In the metanarrative of sacred history constructed by the biographers, all problems in the Muslim community can be traced to this betrayal, which functions as an origin story for all that went wrong.[41] This is communicated implicitly in the early biographies, but became more explicit in subsequent centuries. A popular saying among Shiʿa preachers in the modern period—one that is found in Majlisi's *Ocean of Lights* (*Bihar al-anwar*)—is "al-Husayn was killed on the day of Saqifa."[42] Saqifa was the portico where Abu Bakr and ʿUmar vied for authority over the community while ʿAli was busy washing the Prophet's corpse.[43] By saying al-Husayn was killed on the day of Saqifa, Majlisi and countless preachers since have linked the Prophet's legacy with the fate of all the imams. Just as important, this saying conflates the enemies of the Prophet and the enemies of the imams.[44] Furthermore, the fact that ʿAli was attending to the deceased body of the Prophet while the events of Saqifa unfolded accentuates the intimacy between the two men and the bodily connection between them. As a whole, these accounts make clear the boundaries of the community: "we" are those who truly love Muhammad; "they" are the betrayers of the Prophet and his family.

A Tradition of Betrayal: The Appointment of Imam al-Rida

The biographers emphasized the ontological connectedness of the fates of all the infallibles. The disturbing events of Karbalaʾ and the grab for power at Saqifa functioned as symbolic examples of the kind of betrayal enemies have committed and will always commit against the imams and their followers. Treachery became logically necessary in the same way as martyrdom. The way this logic played itself out in the story of Imam al-Rida sheds further light on enduring patterns of how the category of enemy was conceived. The betrayal of al-Rida is particularly poignant, for it is his life that came closest to unsettling the boundary between Shiʿa and non-Shiʿa in the biographies.

Reviewing some of the details of the ʿAbbasid revolution[45] against the Umayyads in 750 helps set the stage for understanding al-Rida's untimely end. The movement seems to have originated in Merv (in northern Khurasan) and was able to unite (if only temporarily) a wide spectrum of people with anti-Umayyad sentiments. Persian converts to Islam and a range of proto-Shiʿa groups who favored the idea of tying leadership more closely to the Prophet's clan/family (both of whom had largely been excluded from Umayyad institutions of power) were among the most important supporters of the movement. The leadership of the movement expressed an ambiguous commitment to establishing the rule of "the chosen from the family" (*al-rida min ahl al-bayt*), which proved to be a solid enough foundation for a successful revolution. In many ways, the ʿAbbasid revolution was a Shiʿa revolution, and it occurred at a time when Shiʿism existed on a spectrum rather than as a category or identifiable community. At the outset, ʿAbbasid policies appeased and satisfied many constituents and charted a middle ground where the first three caliphs were respected, but ʿAli was not cursed, and the Prophet's family was honored. Followers of the Shiʿa imams were given significant freedom of expression, but the imams of the Twelver tradition did not emerge as political leaders under ʿAbbasid rule. That is, not until the year 817, when ʿAli b. Musa al-Rida was named heir to the caliphate.

Al-Maʾmun, the seventh ʿAbbasid caliph (r. 813–833),[46] had attempted to align the ʿAbbasid family with ʿAlid loyalists in various ways, and his appointment of al-Rida to the caliphate/imamate was apparently intended to complete the transition of power over to the descendants of the Prophet.[47] Before that transition could occur, however, al-Rida died. Shiʿa sources claim that he was betrayed by the caliph and poisoned at his directive less than a year after being named heir.[48]

From the perspective of the biographers, Imam al-Rida's life served as clear proof of the true nature of the ʿAbbasid caliphate. Al-Maʾmun's betrayal was all the more perfidious because of the sharp contrast between his public actions and reality: al-Maʾmun appeared to be supportive of the imams, but in reality he was a traitor. This gave al-Rida's story great instructive value, for it underlined the treacherous nature of a social order that may at times appear safe. The ʿAbbasid caliph raised the hopes of al-Rida's followers that the moment of justice had come, only to have the imam killed. Ibn Jarir covered this dramatic turnaround in *Proofs:*

> [Al-Maʾmun] minted coins with [Imam al-Rida's] name on them—these were known as "Rida coins" (*al-dirahim al-radiya*). [Al-Maʾmun] gathered the ʿAbbasid clan together and argued with them. He compelled them to accept his reasoning and espoused the merits of al-Rida and returned Fadak to the son of Fatima. But then later he betrayed him and thought about his murder (*thumma ghadara bihi wa-fakara fi qatlihi*). And then he killed him in Tus in Khurasan.[49]

Al-Maʾmun's culpability in the death of al-Rida is unquestioned in the Shiʿa biographies. This assumption conflicts with some non-Shiʿa sources, which claimed that al-Rida died by overeating grapes.[50] No similar accounts appear within the biographies. Similar to the case of Imam al-Jawad's martyrdom, al-Rida's death by martyrdom was not initially universally accepted among the Shiʿa. Al-Maʾmun's involvement was a rumor from the outset, but Cooperson notes that the early tenth-century Shiʿa scholars Yaʿqubi and al-Kulayni did not presume al-Maʾmun's involvement.[51] The biographers we are examining here, however, expressed unanimous confidence that al-Maʾmun had al-Rida murdered. Other aspects of the story, however, invite exploration.

In relation to al-Rida's death, the biographers attempted to provide an answer to two thorny questions. First, why would the ʿAbbasid caliph appoint al-Rida as his heir, only to betray him later?[52] Second, why would the imam accept the appointment? Each of the authors offered reports designed to address these matters. In regard to the caliph's motives, the more detailed biographies provided stories that portrayed the caliph transitioning from genuine respect for al-Rida to jealous anger at him.[53] In some cases, the imam's boldness in correcting al-Maʾmun's behavior was presented as the event that led al-Maʾmun to hate the imam.[54]

Al-Rida's motives in accepting the appointment, however, are more opaque. By the tenth century, when these accounts were being compiled into collective biographies, the end of the larger story had already been set. Key assumptions about the imams' fates on earth were already crystallizing. When our authors wrote, the story of an imam believing he might attain the position of leadership he deserved was even more problematic than a betrayal. The imams could be betrayed, but they were not naïve or foolish. To make sense of al-Rida's actions and to salvage his imam-like qualities, biographers were compelled to portray him as reluctant to accept the designation of heir to the caliphate.[55] Moreover, the larger story was cast around the presumption that al-Rida knew the event would not actually come to pass.[56] In the biographers' accounts, al-Rida essentially accepts the appointment as a way to call al-Maʾmun's bluff and make his hidden nature more visible to the world. Transforming messy history into a coherent narrative of this kind was a possibility reserved for generations removed from the confusing tangle of events. When al-Rida died, his followers were shocked, confused, and unprepared for the transition.[57] The biographers, however, had the temporal distance necessary to construct a narrative that fit the emerging vision of the history of the imams.

The story of al-Rida had an important function in the metanarrative being composed about the lives of the imams. It removed all doubt about the true nature of the ʿAbbasids and streamlined historical complexities. Notably, it put the ʿAbbasid caliphate into the same category as the Umayyad usurpers. Both were equally condemned, totally outside God's will. Al-Rida's father, Imam al-Kazim, said, "whoever wrongs the right of this son of mine and denies his imamate after me is like those who wronged ʿAli b. Abi Talib, peace be on him, and denied his right after the Apostle of God, may God bless him and his family."[58] There could be no doubt: all who opposed this family were the same. Differences in time and space were irrelevant; barriers easily surmounted through the conventions of this genre.

"A Woman Who Poisons Her Husbands": The Wife of Imam al-Hasan

When the second imam (al-Hasan) died, his brother and heir to the imamate, al-Husayn, assumed the burial responsibilities. In a story recounted in each of the main biographies, al-Husayn's attempt to fulfill the dying wish of his brother was thwarted by ʿA'isha, the daughter of Abu Bakr and the beloved and infamously young wife of the Prophet. Al-Hasan had desired to be buried next to his grandfather, the Prophet Muhammad, but the burial site was part of the property on which ʿA'isha still lived. As al-Husayn approached with the funeral party, ʿA'isha mounted a mule and bodily prevented the attempt to use that space for al-Hasan's burial. A verbal altercation between al-Husayn and ʿA'isha ensued. Eventually, due to al-Hasan's other dying request that blood not be shed, al-Husayn led the party to the burial site of Fatima al-Zahra', their mother.[59] There he buried his brother's body.

This brief story is told with varying levels of detail in the biographies, and it is another instance of an account made memorable due to its intersection with a host of highly contested symbols. Such stories are the fodder of sectarian discourse, and the narrative of al-Hasan's burial reflected a polarized debate over religious identity and served to entrench those identities. The level of culpability ascribed to ʿA'isha in these accounts varies. In some versions, she is the only person who stands in the way of the deceased imam's wish.[60] In other versions, she is encouraged by the Umayyad governor of Medina (and future caliph), Marwan I (d. 65/685),[61] to block the path of al-Husayn.[62] But in all cases, her presence is central. It set up the most memorable line of this story—found in every account—when Ibn ʿAbbas criticizes ʿA'isha by saying, "What mischief you bring about, one day on a mule and one day on a camel!"[63] This allusion to ʿA'isha's role in the Battle of the Camel (named for the steed on which she sat and watched) is both humorous and tragic, and it serves to remind the audience that ʿA'isha had already betrayed one imam when she led the community of believers into civil war against ʿAli.[64]

For the biographers, ʿA'isha was a symbol of one of the types of people who harbored ill intent toward the imams. She is the archetype of the treacherous wife, and she represents a particular kind of threat. Her proximity to the Prophet only heightens the sense of betrayal and heaps further condemnation on her and those who would follow in her path. In al-Mufid's account, Ibn ʿAbbas goes on to say to ʿA'isha, "Do you want to extinguish the light of God and fight the friends (*awliyāʾ*) of God? . . . By God, victory will come to this house, even if it is after some time."[65]

Distrust of and even disdain for some of the Prophet's wives (particularly ʿA'isha) is a common feature of early and classical Shiʿa writings.[66] Sunni and Shiʿa narratives suggest a significant amount of bad blood between ʿA'isha and ʿAli even during the Prophet's lifetime.[67] One of the best-known examples is when ʿAli was said to have counseled the Prophet to divorce ʿA'isha after some called into question her sexual fidelity to Muhammad.[68] The question of whether such disputes reflected a genuine rift between the historical ʿA'isha and ʿAli, or whether later generations contrived such tales to reinforce their own version of events (perhaps in the wake of the better-attested Battle of the Camel), cannot be settled with any certainty. In either case, however, the effect on ʿA'isha's legacy was the same.[69] Shiʿa sources regularly cast her as a suspect character with sinister motives, and the biographers of the imams rarely passed up an opportunity to criticize and deride her. Even in portions of the texts unrelated to ʿA'isha's lifetime, one finds examples of this. In a frequently recounted story, Imam Musa al-Kazim displayed a supernatural ability to speak while still an infant (see Chapter 5 of this volume), using this gift to instruct a visitor to change the name of his newborn daughter. The daughter had been named al-Humayraʾ, another name for ʿA'isha, and the infant imam explained that God hated that name.[70] ʿA'isha's role as wife of the Prophet did not protect her from the antipathy of the Shiʿa community; on the contrary, it added fuel to the fire. Furthermore, ʿA'isha's hypersexual legacy was a shaping force in the gendered rhetoric undergirding this type of Shiʿa literature.[71]

The biographies of the imams often portray the female body as a site of mistrust and fear. The biographers praised many women, but only those who fulfilled one of a limited number of sanctified roles allowed to them. A woman's merit was tied primarily to her status as mother or daughter of an imam; ʿA'isha was neither, and, moreover, she bore no children at all. The biographies, therefore, reflect and enforce gendered values in their judgment of her. In basing the praise of women almost exclusively on their connection to the imams, the stories reinforced the theological underpinnings of an androcentric paradigm of human destiny. As we will see in Chapter 4, the woman whom the biographers elevated most highly (Fatima) was regendered in a way that completely obscured her connection to her sexual organs. Assumptions about gender played a particularly acute role in the representations of wives of the imams.

The wives of the imams had physical, emotional, and legal ties to the imams. But marital bonds, unlike the blood ties between the imams and their mothers/daughters/sisters, were not enough to secure the wives a favorable legacy within the biographies. The marriage relationship functioned differently, and not simply in regard to legal issues such as rights and inheritance. At a typological level, wives did not participate in the divine plan and were not included in the chosen family, the *ahl al-bayt*. A wife remained an outsider until she attained the elevated role of mother to an imam's child. She was redeemed through childbirth, at least insofar as her portrayal in this literature is concerned. The recording of the wives' names illustrates this matter all too clearly: only the wives (or concubines) of the imams who bore them children are named within the biographies. The names of the rest have been forgotten. The only exceptions to this rule are those wives who murdered their husbands. They are named and condemned. And with striking consistency, those murderous wives did not bear children for the imams.

The implicit assumptions about the weakness of the marital bond gave space for criticisms of some of the Prophet's wives (most notably ʿAʾisha), which established a pattern that allowed some of the imams' wives to be blamed for treacherous and murderous acts. Such blame often intersected with the sexual bond between wife and husband. As we'll see in the Chapters 4 and 5, Fatima and other holy women were separated from their sexual performances, but the sexuality of deceptive wives was amplified.

Time and again we see that the biographers of the imams inherited and built upon an array of literary motifs found in late-antique and early medieval storytelling. Stories of the deceptive wife, the jealous wife, and the "killer wife" were ubiquitous in Near Eastern literatures of the period.[72] In the case of the biographies of the imams, the deceptive wife motif was connected to another common motif: poisoning. As mentioned above, the idea that an imam might die a natural death, or die of unknown causes, became increasingly inconceivable. Poisoning was a reasonable and memorable explanation for the deaths of the imams, and most Shiʿa accounts claim that nine of the twelve imams (plus the Prophet) were poisoned. In at least two of those cases—though sometimes more—the fatal deed is attributed to a deceptive wife. Agreement that Imam al-Hasan and Imam al-Jawad were poisoned by their wives was nearly universal among the Shiʿa. The story of al-Jawad's death was covered in the Chapter 2, and so we turn now to the matter of al-Hasan's death. His poisoning at the hands of his wife, and his burial, which was disturbed by ʿAʾisha, gives us a sense of the types of concerns addressed and unaddressed in the betrayal accounts.

Not surprisingly, al-Mufid's narrative of al-Hasan's death did much to set the standard for later Shiʿa retellings.[73] Al-Mufid based his account extensively on Abu al-Faraj al-Isfahani's (d. 356/967) narrative in *Killings of the Talibids* (*Maqatil al-talibiyin*),[74] making it clear that al-Muʿawiya, the Umayyad caliph with whom al-Hasan made a treaty following Imam ʿAli's death, chose to openly betray that agreement. Muʿawiya's malice toward *ahl al-bayt* is legendary; among other things he is said to have instituted the public cursing of ʿAli. The story of al-Hasan's death begins with a plan by Muʿawiya to have the imam killed. The caliph had decided to pass the reign of the empire over to his son, Yazid, rather than handing power back to a descendent of ʿAli, as the treaty with al-Hasan is said to have specified. To carry out his plan, Muʿawiya contacted one of al-Hasan's wives, Jaʿda bt. al-Ashʿath b. Qays. By promising her 100,000 dirhams and the chance to marry his son Yazid, Muʿawiya persuaded Jaʿda to give al-Hasan a poisonous drink that killed him after a forty-day period of lingering sickness. Al-Mufid also included an account of the event that states that Muʿawiya paid Jaʿda the money but did not fulfill his promise to marry her to Yazid. Instead, he married her to "a man from the family of Ṭalḥa as a substitute."[75] This story has the dual function of providing further evidence of Muʿawiya's deceptive character and emphasizing once again that betraying the imams may even carry negative results in this lifetime.

In each of the Shiʿa biographers' accounts, the real blame for al-Hasan's death is placed on the caliph. Jaʿda was merely a tool, a relatively inconsequential character who warranted no more than a passing gloss. The author of the *Establishment of the Inheritance* did not mention her at all, though he referred to Muʿawiya as Ibn Akila al-Akbad ("son of the liver-eater")[76]—a reference to Muʿawiya's infamous mother, Hind bt. ʿUtba, who is widely remembered in Sunni and Shiʿa sources for having eaten the liver of Hamza b. ʿAbd al-Muttalib on the battlefield of Uhud. As for Jaʿda, the portrayal of her as a tool of the caliph removes her agency and further dehumanizes her. It implies that Jaʿda was not simply immoral, but also irrelevant. Like Umm al-Fadl, who poisoned Imam al-Jawad, Jaʿda was not considered to have had her own serious motivations. The characters of genuine importance are the men. The story of al-Hasan's poisoning is told in connection to the dispute over leadership of the community, and the significance of his death lies in its relation to the question of the imamate. Al-Hasan's true killer—Muʿawiya—was motivated solely by his desire to prevent the imams from acquiring their rightful position of authority. The possibilities that someone else might have wanted to kill al-Hasan, or that Jaʿda had her own motivations unconnected to the rewards offered by the caliph are completely absent from the account. This is particularly interesting when considering accusations by later Sunni writers that al-Hasan was a "habitual divorcer" (*mitlaq*).[77] Some accounts claim that he married and divorced as many as ninety women, though sixteen appears to be the highest number of names produced for the women he supposedly married.[78] The biographers in this study made no attempt to address this issue. Like the childless (and thus nameless) wives, al-Hasan's marital proclivities simply do not figure into the account in any meaningful way. In a system constructed around assumptions about male leadership and the denial of the imams' rightful place of authority, Muʿawiya's political motivations provide the most sensible explanation for al-Hasan's murder.

The story of Jaʿda's murder of al-Hasan and the way in which it typically leads directly into the burial account and al-Husayn's confrontation with ʿAʾisha gives us excellent fodder for reflecting on cultural assumptions about gender, family, community, and sexuality that influenced the way the biographers' stories were told. One salient point is that the portrayals of the wives of the imams differed very little from portrayals of their concubines. In both cases, the women remain nameless and absent unless they bore the imams children. Marriage, in the context of these stories, does not necessarily entail a bond of trust, companionship, or even inclusion into the religious community.[79] Those bonds *are* consistently assumed, however, in the cases of the mothers and daughters of the imams, as I explain in the Chapters 4 and 5.

Accounts of wives poisoning their husbands show us the extent to which public discourse, slanderous discourse in particular, was highly gendered. The Jaʿda narrative is peripheral to the murder of al-Hasan; the biographers' primary intent was to attack Muʿawiya and other male enemies of *ahl al-bayt*. The women in the stories, even ʿAʾisha, were not real threats. They were merely tools of the men around them. In a world where trickery and deception were seen as weaknesses of women, Muʿawiya's decision to use secretive and conniving tricks implicitly feminized the caliph.

Muʿawiya's bribery of Jaʿda paralleled Marwan I's manipulation of ʿAʾisha, further strengthening the caliphate's connections to wily femininity. This short narrative connects enemies to women at multiple junctions, and these connections are a way of discrediting the usurpers. This is evident even in the sources that do not mention ʿAʾisha's involvement, like *Establishment of the Inheritance*. In that case, the author's derisive reference to Muʿawiya as Ibn Akila al-Akbad serves as another layer of association with evil women. Muʿawiya was not the only man subjected to highly gendered slander in this story. Generations of men who descended from Jaʿda and her second husband are collectively ridiculed as the "sons of a woman who poisons her husbands."[80] Authentic leadership over the community was assumed to be the right of the best man. To attack the masculinity of the unjust rulers was to attack their legitimacy.

Betraying the Masters: Imam al-Sadiq and the *Ghulat*

Those who tried to murder and/or usurp the power of the imams were not the only enemies mentioned in the biographies. The authors also placed another group, the ʿAlid loyalists known as the exaggerators (*ghulat*), outside the boundaries of the Twelver Shiʿa community. In a section devoted to denouncing this group, Ibn Shahrashub quoted Imam al-Sadiq: "The *ghulat* are an evil among God's creation. They reduce the greatness of God and ascribe lordship to God's servants. Truly the *ghulat* are given to the evil of the Jews, Christians, Magians, and those who ascribe partners with God." Ibn Shahrashub followed this account with this anonymous Shiʿa couplet:

> Do not go beyond what is attributed to the prophets
> for in ignorance they exaggerate about the inheritors (*al-awsiya*ʾ)
> And do not forget what He said
> "I have created someone hostile to every prophet."[81]

Who exactly were these exaggerators, and what earned them such strident criticism? Scholars have grappled with these questions, but few reliable answers have been provided.[82] The term *ghuluw* was universally applied as a term of derision, echoing a famous Qurʾanic passage from Surat al-Nisaʾ that reads, "People of the Book, do not exaggerate in your religion."[83] Not surprisingly, no group of people appears to have accepted this label for themselves. Attempting, then, to identify the religious sect to whom the term *ghulat* applied is a fraught endeavor. In many ways, it was a catch-all pejorative for groups with whom one disagreed. Indeed, many traditionalist figures accused the entire Shiʿa community of such exaggeration. For their part, however, the biographers of the imams also adamantly condemned the *ghulat*. For our Shiʿa authors, *ghuluw* was associated with the elevation of someone to a religious position beyond his rank, whether this meant elevating an imam to the level of divinity or elevating a normal person to the level of imam. The legendary story of Ibn Sabaʾ,[84] the archetypal heretic of early Islam, served as one proof that the imams condemned such beliefs. Ibn Shahrashub's account, like many Twelver Shiʿa works, told of ʿAli ordering Ibn Sabaʾ to be burned to death for his heresy (assumed to be worshipping ʿAli as a god). One finds such sayings, which served to distance the imams from the *ghulat*, throughout the biographies.[85]

Although this topic appears throughout the biographies, the accounts of Imam al-Sadiq have a particularly high number of anti-*ghuluw* statements. This accords with the frequent portrayal of al-Sadiq as a teacher whose guidance and advice were packaged and transmitted by his students for the benefit of subsequent generations.[86] An example of al-Sadiq's opposition to the *ghulat* is found in an account in which he converts a famed Shiʿa poet, al-Sayyid al-Himyari, to the Shiʿism of the twelve imams.[87] Al-Himyari had been a follower of the Kaysaniya, a group labeled as *ghulat* by the Twelver Shiʿa because they elevated Muhammad b. al-Hanafiya (d. 81/700), a half-brother to al-Hasan and al-Husayn, to the level of imam. At al-Hanafiya's death, the group claimed he had in fact gone into occultation (*ghayba*) and would return one day as the Mahdi. Al-Himyari's affiliation with this group, however, did not prevent his poetry from resonating with the broader Shiʿa community. His verse was a powerful vehicle for Shiʿa social memory and was widely transmitted. Ibn Shahrashub, for example, used al-Himyari's poetry extensively in composing *Virtues,* and the story of al-Sadiq's conversion of al-Himyari served the useful purpose of bringing a treasured poet into the community of salvation.

Ghuluw was also a form of betrayal in the biographies—another way in which the parameters of the community were defined. It was a different form of betrayal than those we have examined so far in that it did not end in an imam's death, but it nonetheless represented a dangerous rejection of the imams' teachings. All acts of betrayal—whether they involved a failure to recognize the imams' authority or an exaggeration of their ontological nature—belonged in the same category of the aberrant "other." Al-Sadiq's uncle, ʿUmar b. ʿAli b. al-Husayn, was recorded as saying, "The one who is excessive (*al-mufrit*) in his love for us is like the one who is excessive in his hatred for us."[88] All of those who betrayed the imams lacked proper guidance. Whether they strayed to one side or the other made little difference. The equivocation of excessive love and excessive hate for the Prophet's family was a valuable rhetorical strategy, however: it allowed the Shiʿa to position their own vision as the middle way. The category of *ghuluw* was useful for the Shiʿa because it provided an alternate extreme from which they differentiated themselves.

The boundaries between the Twelver Shiʿa and the *ghulat,* even if we limit the term to those at whom our Shiʿa authors directed it, remain obscure and porous. Just as the lines dividing Shiʿa and Sunni were often blurred by the complex beliefs and devotional practices of real people, so too were the distinctions between faithful Shiʿa and *ghulat.* The attempt of the biographers to distance themselves and the imams from the *ghulat* is yet another example of how this literature helped to clarify and reify identities. By creating a normative account for the other group's nature and intent, the authors marked them as aberrant and different.

The demarcation between the faithful and the *ghulat* did not mean the latter were incorrect on every point or that their sources weren't useful. In fact, the biographers' conscious incorporation of *ghulat* sources gives us special insight into their intellectual process. As the narrative became increasingly codified, the authors of the biographies (beginning especially with al-Mufid) incorporated accounts and stories that fit snugly into their own overall vision, whether those stories originated in non-Shiʿa communities (including those that would later be considered Sunni) or in *ghulat* circles. This was particularly the case with Ibn Shahrashub, who drew ambitiously from a wide variety of sources. Considering certain groups *ghulat* did not prevent him from including their stories if they aligned with his sensibilities. At times, he did this in the very sections of *Virtues* where he criticized the exaggerators. While writing about some miracles performed by Imam ʿAli, for example, Ibn Shahrashub reported several stories in which ʿAli is said to have flown through the air—in one case, while riding atop a shield.[89] He explicitly stated that these accounts came from the *ghulat,* but his desire to convey the stories despite their suspicious origins demonstrated the compatibility of the accounts with the metanarrative of Ibn Shahrashub's biographies.

Thus we see that whether or not a given story conveyed a truth about the imams often proved a more salient issue than historical facticity. The latter simply was not the primary guiding impulse for what accounts the biographers decided to include in their works. The willingness to transmit narratives from unreliable or suspicious origins was not, of course, unique to Shiʿa writers and scholars, as Jonathan Brown has shown in relationship to Sunni hadith collections.[90] But, it gives us a glimpse into what the particular authors of these accounts found plausible and meaningful. Shared assumptions about what constituted a believable story provided a filter for the types of narratives included in the biographies, and thus stories were accumulated along culturally contingent contours of expectation. Narratives that portrayed the imams acting in ways that fit how their nature was understood could be included, no matter the source. Occasionally, the authors even acknowledged the possibility that a story might not be factual. For example, Ibn Shahrashub followed the story of ʿAli flying by saying, "If [these stories] are true, then it is like the flying and descending of the angels or the flight (*isra*ʾ) of the Prophet."[91] Here he admitted that the account might be not be true (due to its connection to a *ghulat* source), but he followed up that admission by drawing parallels between ʿAli's flight and more widely accepted stories like that of the Prophet's night journey from Mecca to Jerusalem. The implication is that the story of ʿAli's flight was plausible because, after all, God had enabled other beings to perform similar feats. This process of reasoning helped solidify and stabilize Twelver Shiʿa expectations of the imams, and it contributed to the canonization of a collective memory.

Warning against Heresy: The Brother of Imam al-ʿAskari

Betrayal narratives filled another role not mentioned above: they served as a warning against other Shiʿa groups who had diverged from the Twelver lineage of imams. Each retelling of deception or disloyalty reminded the audience of treacherous mistakes that should be avoided. Accounts of betrayal were symbolic exhortations to remain faithful and served a similar function to the practice of hanging the corpses of criminals in public spaces as a visual warning. There had been times, readers were reminded, that the imams were betrayed by those closest to them, even by immediate family members. A particularly memorable example of an intrafamily betrayal was canonized in the accounts of Jaʿfar b. ʿAli, the brother of Imam al-ʿAskari who is known in Shiʿa sources as Jaʿfar al-Kadhdhab ("the liar").[92]

In most of the collective biographies, Jaʿfar al-Kadhdhab is first mentioned in the biography of the sixth imam, Jaʿfar al-Sadiq. Not only do the two men share first names; they also have parallel honorifics: al-Sadiq means "the truthful," and al-Kadhdhab translates as "the liar." The biographies contain a story that foretells the betrayal and contrasts the sixth imam with the traitor who would eventually share his name. In some versions the account contains a statement attributed to the Prophet that reads, "When Jaʿfar b. Muhammad b. ʿAli b. al-Husayn—my son—is born, call him al-Sadiq. As for his descendent, call him Jaʿfar al-Kadhdhab. Woe unto him who has insolence before God and hostility toward his brother, the possessor of the right of imam of his time."[93]

The despised brother of al-ʿAskari (the eleventh imam) is remembered for his rejection of God's appointed heir (al-ʿAskari's son, al-Mahdi) and his attempt to claim the imamate for himself. Modarressi suggests, however, that there may have been a rift in the family that preceded the death of al-ʿAskari, and that the brothers may have had competing claims to the imamate from an early age.[94] These ambiguities are clarified in the biographies; the brothers' father (al-Hadi) and al-ʿAskari warn their followers explicitly about Jaʿfar.[95] His character was condemned on numerous fronts: among other things, he was accused of wine bibbing.[96] The ultimate display of Jaʿfar's betrayal came in the form of a story of him going to the ʿAbbasid authorities and attempting to bribe them into recognizing his claim to the Shiʿa imamate.[97] This narrative has been widely repeated, and it is difficult to imagine a more singularly discrediting act.

Jaʿfar al-Kadhdhab is not an entirely unique figure within the biographies. Each of the major splits within Shiʿism had to do with some type of intrafamily—often brotherly—dispute. Similarities can be found, for example, in the accounts about Muhammad b. al-Hanafiyya (the half-brother of al-Hasan and al-Husayn),[98] and ʿAli b. Ismaʿil b. Jaʿfar (the nephew of Imam al-Kazim and grandson of al-Sadiq).[99] Interestingly, however, the biographers at times went to great lengths to exonerate certain characters, as was the case with al-Mufid, who sought to redeem the memory of Zayd b. ʿAli (son to the fourth imam and the eponymous founder of Zaydi Shiʿism).[100] This may reflect al-Mufid's desire to not offend the Buyid sensibilities of his day. While the exact religious commitments of the Buyid princes are unclear, they hailed from a region of Iran where Zaydi Shiʿism was quite popular.

The followers of Jaʿfar, Modarressi notes, constituted "a large number, possibly even the majority," of the Imamis in the period immediately after the death of al-ʿAskari.[101] It took time for the narrative of a hidden twelfth imam to become widely accepted. By the time our biographers were writing, however, the followers of Jaʿfar al-Kadhdhab had ceased to exist, and decrying him bore none of the potential risk of slandering Zayd b. ʿAli. This is apparent in the strident tone in which these writers condemned Jaʿfar. For the biographers and their contemporaries in the tenth century and beyond, serious consideration of Jaʿfar's claims was no longer thinkable. The *Establishment* gave Jaʿfar's claims little attention, and the subsequent biographers preferred to specify Jaʿfar's vices rather than refuting his claims.[102] His legacy remained relevant not as a contending claim to the imamate that needed to be taken seriously, but as a symbol of betrayal. As such he was even more useful to the biographers than a figure with plausible claims to the imamate might have been.

As the genre developed, the texts' condemnations of Jaʿfar become increasingly elaborate and poignant. In some cases, his betrayal is even cited as the event that forced the twelfth imam into hiding.[103] Jaʿfar's treachery, then, was the catalyst that set in motion the epoch of occultation that continues to the present day. Since allegiance to Jaʿfar was a moot point when the collective biographies began to be written, the authors' condemnations of him cannot be read as warnings against accepting his claims. Instead, Jaʿfar serves a different cautionary end. His example was a warning against all types of betrayal of the imams—a warning that even the followers of the imams needed to hear. Familial betrayal had fractured the Muslim community at its inception, and familial betrayal had sent the last imam into hiding. The stories of the imams sandwiched in-between do not stand alone; they form a composite narrative that resists partial acceptance. This way of organizing and remembering history made allegiance to the imamate an all-or-nothing affair. Those who might honor some of the imams but not others were outside of the imagined community. Ambivalence was dangerous and unwelcome.

Conclusion

Those not invested in the Shiʿa tradition may wonder why the retelling of the stories of the imams is so important. Wouldn't forgiving and forgetting be less divisive? This line of reasoning, however, misses the implications of the larger narrative. The biographers' utilization of the socially feminized performance of mourning was not simply to protest the imams' deaths (however unjust they may have been), but it also creates a rupture in the story that draws attention to the dysfunctional social order imposed upon them by others. The biographies give expression to an understanding of history that differentiated between the faithful (victims) and the treacherous (oppressors). The stories make clear who belongs to the community and who does not, making visible boundaries that are otherwise often obscure. The betrayal narratives are not necessarily the longest or most emphasized aspect of the imams' biographies, but the accounts play a critical role in heightening the memorability of their lives. The pains and losses experienced by the imams are the central features that bind the individual biographies into a collective whole and transform them into a meaningful genre of Shiʿa storytelling and literature.

This chapter and Chapter 2 reveal how the infallibles shared in each other's sufferings. Differences between the historical imams were effaced as the stories began to follow consistent patterns. Symbols in these biographies were increasingly self-referential, and the suffering of one imam often mirrored, represented, or even fulfilled the story of another imam. This phenomenon gives us a better understanding of the significance of ʿAshuraʾ. The importance and power attached to the memory of al-Husayn was dependent upon and derived from the assumption that his martyrdom was *not* a unique event. Instead, it was the natural, even expected, outcome of the betrayals that befell all of the imams.

Further, betrayal accounts were key tools through which the authors asserted and regulated normative conceptions of communal boundaries. Those who perpetrated crimes against the imams became symbols of all outsiders. This enabled the authors to connect the Umayyad and ʿAbbasid caliphs (who betrayed the imams) with those who betrayed the Prophet (and even those who betrayed pre-Islamic prophets). This framing of the imams' lives tied their memories to the life of the Prophet and encouraged the audience to equate the error of the *ghulat* with the error of Sunnis: both groups were disloyal to the imams and their divinely appointed roles. The faithful, therefore, were not extremists of either type, but were on the narrow middle path.

As the collective biography genre solidified, implicit criteria for truth coalesced. The veracity of an account was judged, at least partly, on the extent to which it conformed to what was already understood to be the case. Namely, once the nature of the imams and their enemies was reified, it became the standard by which future accounts were judged. Historical nuance and psychological complexities were less meaningful to the larger narrative and less useful for the broader functions of the literature. The continuity facilitated by a stable image of the imams (along with a consistent use of certain tropes and motifs) was more useable to the authors than ambiguities of historical process.

Finally, in developing a narrative that helped shape communal identity, the authors drew upon their understandings of the body, sexuality, and family relationships. In this literature, the imams' wives are often portrayed as a threat to the imams. Their access to the vulnerable and intimate parts of the imams' bodies made their disloyalty both memorable and especially pernicious. As we will see more clearly in Chapters 4 and 5, the treacherous wives stand in sharp contrast to the daughters and mothers of the imams. The threat posed by wives was not ameliorated by the bond of marriage, and familial bonds of all types were threatened by rivalries. This was particularly the case with brothers, whose betrayals of the imams were arguably the most nefarious, since they shared a blood relationship with the imams. As such, we begin to see how the boundaries of the community were often conceptually linked to the bodies of the imams. In Chapter 4 we turn our attention more directly to those bodies.

CHAPTER FOUR

Vulnerable Bodies and Masculine Ideals

There is no sword but Dhu al-Faqar;
there is no man but ʿAli.

—a popular saying attributed to the Prophet

In the eyes of the biographers, the imams were infallible men. The significance of infallibility has been discussed by scholars,[1] but very little attention has been paid to the significance of the imams' masculinity. Like any gender category, masculinity is a fluid concept constantly negotiated by societies. Within the biographies, the imams' bodies were platforms for displaying the biographers' visions of virtue, manliness, and group loyalty (*ʿasabiya*).[2] The interweaving of these three traits in the imams' lives stood in stark opposition to the abuses of the ruling authorities portrayed in these works—authorities who perverted justice and censored public memory. An analysis of the biographies of the imams would not be complete without an exploration of their masculinity, especially given the dearth of academic study on the topic. A decade ago, Nadia Maria El Cheikh expressed an apt criticism:

> The conceptualization of men is not a developed area of study. While women and their construction in historical and literary texts is now considered a valid object of study seen in a proliferation of works on the subject and in a large entry in the *Encyclopedia of Islam* entitled "al-mar'a," no equivalent scholarship can be found on men. We read

> about men as caliphs, judges, bureaucrats and military officers but not "men" as a defined gender category. By not making men or masculinity an object of study the secondary literature sustains a political construction into our sources.[3]

It is my hope that this chapter, which focuses on how the imams were idealized through their masculine bodies, represents a small measure of progress in this field. But we should not leave behind our knowledge that the stories of the imams' lives stood in the shadow of their impending death. In the biographies, the betrayals and deaths endured by the imams are foreshadowed throughout their lives, sometimes with specific predictions. Their bodily performances must be read with that foreknowledge as well.

Modern norms of polite conversation make discussions of the body and gender challenging, especially when dealing with the works of medieval storytellers who were constrained by different social niceties and cultural assumptions. Understanding the interaction between portrayals of the imams' revered bodies and the biographers' assumptions about masculinity requires a willingness to put aside our discomfort and transgress into irreverence. This chapter begins by highlighting explicit descriptions of the imams' physical appearances and masculine performances using the example of Imam al-Baqir. Next, I turn to the story of Imam al-Kazim as I focus upon the miraculous achievements of the imams. Finally, I look at the example of Fatima al-Zahra᾽ to round out my discussion of the interplay between gender and conceptions of the human ideal. The presence of Muhammad and Fatima in the collective biographies ultimately serves to communicate ideas about the imams. Descriptions of Fatima's bodily performances are necessary points of comparison and contrast that tell us as much (perhaps more) about the biographers' ideas of men as they do about their understandings of women. Ultimately, the biographers' portrayals of both male and female bodies helped negotiate social memory and convey hope for the community and aspirations for a more ideal social order.

Bodily Inheritance: The Masculinity of Imam al-Baqir

A number of patterns and motifs recur in the bodily portrayals of the imams, who are presented as beautiful, capable, and ideal physical specimens. Their bodily actions convey strength and dexterity as well as love and piety. These patterns are not accidental or inconsequential, and thus they give us valuable information about the assumptions, concerns, and hopes of the authors. The imams' bodies reflect a set of shared perspectives that were meaningful for particular communities.

Descriptions of the imams' bodies are integral to understanding the social memories of those bodies. The physical descriptions affirm the imams' spiritual significance; they function as concrete representations of divine light, guidance, and blessing.[4] Unsurprisingly, the imams were beautiful, and their bodies were both objects of devotion and models of physical perfection.

Most forms of classical Arabic biography give little, if any, information about the physical appearance of their subjects. Such comments, when they exist at all, are typically made in passing and reserved for people with a disability or deformity. Prophets and saints tend to be exceptions to this rule, however, and their biographies often contain references to their physical presence and appearance. Sunni and Shiʿa communities have a rich legacy of remembering the physical characteristics of the Prophet Muhammad, perhaps best captured in a comparatively late genre of literary works called *hilya,* which contain physical descriptions of Muhammad often recorded in elaborate calligraphy.[5] The biographies in this study predate the *hilya* by several centuries, but like the later works, they describe for their readers the physical beauty of the prophets and imams. Al-Tabrisi, for instance, included an account in *Informing Humanity* that explicitly states that God protected Muhammad in battle from being disfigured.[6] With rare exceptions, holy men and women are consistently portrayed as physically beautiful—the archetype being Joseph, whose attractiveness is memorialized in the Qurʾan.[7] In keeping with the expectation that the holiness of saintly men is reflected in their physiques, the biographies of the imams often contain references to their physical beauty, particularly that of their faces, which are special loci of the light that shone from their bodies.[8] Some of the descriptions contain unusual detail. Ibn Shahrashub said of Imam al-Baqir: "He was of medium height, with delicate skin and slightly curly hair. There was a brown birthmark on his cheek and a red one on his body. He had a slender waist, a beautiful voice, and a bowed head."[9] It's a pleasant image.

As seen already, the physical descriptions of the imams go beyond clarifying that they had no deformities or disabilities (which would have detracted from their presumed manliness and raised questions about their qualifications for leadership). The biographers assumed that an ideal body was the most attractive body, and thus the physical descriptions of the imams enshrine idealized conceptions of male beauty and physical constitution. As social standards changed, so did the descriptions. Gender categories are never static, and the tenth to twelfth centuries were likely a time of transition in the way Muslims valorized masculinity.[10] Unfortunately, little research has been done on this topic,[11] and I can make only passing note of it here. But the contrast between Ibn Shahrashub's twelfth-century description of al-Baqir quoted above and al-Mufid's tenth-century description of him as "big-bodied"[12] is clear. Ibn Shahrashub's image of al-Baqir is decidedly more delicate and refined than that of al-Mufid. Nonetheless, both biographers make the connection between the imams' physical beauty and their exemplary lives. Simply put, their bodies were virtuous in both form and function. At times, physical attributes act as proofs of their imamate,[13] and thus their bodies reflect the perfection that characterizes their spirits.[14] The connection between a pure spirit and a perfect body is an ancient one, and it is reflected in this literature in many ways.

The beautiful bodies of the imams were sites of devotion, affection, and blessing. This is particularly clear in their birth stories. Those narratives will be explored further in Chapter 5, but it is worth noting here that the fathers' tender and loving treatments of their child-imams reaffirmed for the community the significance of the imams' bodies. Interactions between the imams and their devotees recorded in the biographies are further indications to the community of how to properly orient oneself toward the imams. In a widespread account of Imam al-Baqir's boyhood, the young imam is taken to Jabir al-Ansari by his father.[15] The highly revered, elderly companion of the Prophet demonstrates his love and affection for al-Baqir (and vicariously, for the Prophet) by kissing the boy's head, hands, and, in some accounts, his feet.[16] Jabir conveys the Prophet's greetings to al-Baqir, emphasizing the legitimacy of his imamate in connection to the authority of the Prophet. In the process, the audience witnesses the outpouring of the devotee's love toward an imam in the form of Jabir's physical affection toward al-Baqir.

Stories like this one can be plausibly linked to the increasing popularity of grave visitation (*ziyara*) rituals. The same authors who wrote these biographies often compiled instructions for visiting an imam's grave as well as prayers to recite while there. It seems relevant to note that the biographies contain many instances of imams magnanimously granting the requests of those who came to them. Al-Mufid, for example, recorded this statement about al-Baqir, "he never tired of bestowing generosity on the brethren, and on those who came to visit him, and on those who place their hopes and trust in him."[17] Statements like this reaffirmed the expectation that physical visitation went hand in hand with the bestowal of blessing.

Love for the imams and their bodies is portrayed in many ways and encouraged throughout the biographies. It is exemplified by the love of the imams' family members and of the imams toward one another, it is emulated by their followers, and it is explicitly enjoined by the imams in their teachings. Believers ensure their own salvation by cultivating love for the imams, and those who do not love the imams condemn themselves to the fire. Examples of this abound, but the central example of this type of love is that displayed by the holy family comprising the first five infallibles: Muhammad, Fatima, ʿAli, al-Hasan, and al-Husayn.[18] For the Shiʿa, these five individuals make up the core of the *ahl al-bayt,* also known as *ahl al-kisaʾ*.[19] The biographers prominently described the love these five had for each other. Muhammad's love for these members of his family was particularly intense, and it served as a testament to the legitimacy of the imams' claims to authority.[20] The love and affection demonstrated were not at odds with masculinity; in fact, they were an integral part of these men's performance of gender. The imams' love for their family was a model for what every man's love for his family should look like.

The love displayed by members of the holy family for one another did more than provide a proof for Shiʿa doctrinal claims about succession.

It set a devotional example for people to follow. Imam al-Sajjad said, "Love us, for it is love for Islam. May your love for us never cease even if it becomes a public disgrace."[21] Loving the imams was consistently positioned as a core facet of religious practice.[22] Those who fulfilled this duty could expect rewards, and not just heavenly ones. Loving the imams gave one the right to call upon them in times of need. This reciprocal relationship of love and protection is emphasized repeatedly through the way the imams responded to their followers. Al-Mufid recorded many stories of Imam al-Baqir giving money to those of his community who were in need. He went on to say, "[al-Baqir] never tired of bestowing generosity on the brethren, and on those who came to visit him, and on those who placed their hopes and trust in him."[23] These stories about the imams reinforced the hopes of audiences who heard them long after the final imam went into hiding and physical contact was lost. Even if love for the imams was "a public disgrace" (perhaps especially in that case), devotees could visit the imams' entombed bodies and have faith that their devotion would be rewarded.

Other aspects of the bodily portrayals of the imams deserve attention. Like the other imams, Muhammad al-Baqir was much more than an object of admiration and devotional affection. The biographies also remember him as a man who did manly things—a person who enacted social performances presumed to be uniquely suited to men. The gendered performances of the imams were not natural or haphazard.[24] The way the literature displays their masculinity carries with it certain assertions. These depictions of the imams enshrined cultural expectations of what it meant to be a man while concomitantly defending the legitimacy of their claims to be the best of all men and the rightful leaders of the community.

References to various masculine qualities are sprinkled throughout the biographies. The texts make many passing mentions of the imams' courage, strength, and fearlessness in the face of death.[25] Such characteristics have little relevance to questions of law or doctrine; their clearest purpose is to display the imams' excellence at being men. Descriptions that contribute to their masculine images abound. For example, the imams are frequently associated with, and interact with, lions. Numerous ancient Near Eastern cultures used the lion as a symbol of ideal masculinity.[26] This symbolic use is evidenced in the biographies by the appearance of lions in conjunction with the miraculous powers of the imams,[27] masculine performances of power that will be discussed further below.

Another central way in which the manliness of the imams was confirmed was through the fathering of children, particularly their male heirs. The assumption that the ability to father a male heir was a requirement for an imam is occasionally made explicit. In an encounter between Imam al-Rida and Ibn Qiyama, the latter accuses al-Rida of not being the real imam since he had not proven himself able to father an heir. Tellingly, the imam does not disagree with the reasoning presented, but simply promises that he will fulfill this requirement in the future.[28] Each of the imams fulfilled this task (apart from the twelfth imam, who went into hiding as young child). Bodily perfection and virility are conceptually linked, and the imams' fulfillment of their reproductive tasks helps confirm God's favor upon them. The imams' sexual vitality is further demonstrated by the number of wives and concubines they had. Imam al-Baqir is said to have fathered children with at least two wives and two slaves, and other imams had at least as many sexual partners.[29]

That all the imams fathered male children who inherited their roles and legacies is an interesting contrast with the Prophet's lack of a male heir. Each of Muhammad's natural-born sons (perhaps as many as five in all) died as a young child.[30] Not all of the sources attempt to smooth out this dissonance or account for Muhammad's failure to produce an heir, but *Establishment of the Inheritance* offers an explanation: Muhammad allowed his son to die in order to save his community. This unusual account relates that, after Muhammad's last son, Ibrahim, dies, the angel Gabriel appears to offer the Prophet a choice. He can have his son revived to inherit his spiritual leadership, but his son will be betrayed by the entire community and killed. As a result, all of Muhammad's followers will be condemned to hell. The alternative is to allow his son to rest in peace and have his spiritual leadership pass to al-Husayn, who will be betrayed and killed by only half of the community. That half will wind up in hell, but the other half will be saved. Muhammad chooses al-Husayn, saying, "I do not want all of my community to enter hell."[31]

This narrative removes any doubt about the Prophet's ability to father an heir, while at the same time making explicit his alignment with the Shiʿa.

Other narratives ascribe additional masculine accomplishments to the imams. In accordance with conceptions of male leadership found across many cultures and times, the imams are portrayed has having knowledge of and facility with weaponry. Demonstrations of their military prowess helped create full, robust presentations of them as ideal men. In the longest single narration about al-Baqir in *Proof of the Imamate,* the imam goes to Damascus with his son, Jaʿfar al-Sadiq, at the request of the Umayyad caliph, Hisham b. ʿAbd al-Malik (d. 125/743).[32] The occasion provides the setting for a poignant story in which Imam al-Baqir embarrasses the caliph with his extraordinary archery skills.[33] In the account, al-Sadiq describes how the Caliph Hisham was "sitting on the throne with his army and chiefs at his feet." An archer's target is set up, and the caliph, who is watching his men practice shooting, orders al-Baqir to join them. This, recalls al-Sadiq, was because the caliph "wanted to laugh at my father, thinking that he would come up short and thus miss the target on account of his old age and by this [the caliph could] take out his anger on him." With a proper show of humility and social etiquette, al-Baqir at first declines, saying "I have grown old and think it better if you excuse me"; but the caliph foolishly misses the chance to save face and insists on putting the imam on the spot.

After reluctantly accepting a bow and quiver from of the soldiers, Imam al-Baqir takes out an arrow and shoots it directly into the middle of the target. The story continues: "Then he shot another [arrow] which split apart the first one down to its arrowhead. He continued until he had split nine arrows—they ended up one inside the other." The caliph is unable to contain his frustration, saying, "you are the best archer of all the Arabs and non-Arabs, but you claimed you were old!" Hisham immediately regrets praising the imam, and he tarries for some time before eventually getting up to embrace al-Baqir and al-Sadiq, praising the father again for his unparalleled skill with the bow. The caliph then asks al-Baqir where he learned to shoot with such precision. The imam casually responds that he had practiced for a short time with the people in Medina. The crux of this story, however, is contained in the imam's answer to the caliph's subsequent query as to whether Jaʿfar al-Sadiq is equally skilled. Al-Baqir responds, "We inherit perfection, completeness, and religion."[34] With this one line, al-Baqir takes the conversation beyond him and his son to make a broader comment about the imamate. This bold statement in the face of the Umayyad caliph links the imams' physical superiority over the caliph to their spiritual superiority.

The political relevance of fulfilling standards of masculinity is clear in this narrative. The caliph displayed all the markings of an emasculated leader:[35] laziness, arrogance, trickery, short-sightedness, lack of hospitality, and, presumably, lack of skill with the bow,[36] while the imam displayed the opposite of these shortcomings, putting on an admirable performance of manly ideals.[37] Al-Baqir's masculine prowess with the bow suggests greater ability to function as leader of men. The imams were designated by God to lead the community, and they are clearly the more capable leaders. Michael Cooperson makes some relevant observations in his discussion of the biographies of Imam al-Rida. Regarding the literary role of the caliph in these stories, he writes:

> Structurally, the *ṭāʾifa* [faction] of caliphs in Twelver biography serves as the demonic double of the *ṭāʾifa* of Imams. The caliphal claim to heirship represents a perversion of the true Alid one, just as oppressive caliphal rule represents a perversion of the imamate. As counterpoints to the Imams, the caliphs serve an important purpose in Twelver biography. Most notably, their persecution of the Imams confirms the rightness of Imami claims.[38]

Like most antagonists in these stories, the caliph is a character whose comments serve to set up a teaching moment. As the story from *Proof* continues, the caliph is infuriated by al-Baqir's claim to a special inheritance. He objects to the imam's claim, saying, "Are we not both children of ʿAbd Manaf? Our descendants and your descendants are the same." The imam replies, "God has specified us [the imams] for his innermost secrets and his pure knowledge. He has not singled out anyone else except for us." The caliph and the imam, in a scene packed with symbolic significance, continue their debate on the nature of God's revelation, Muhammad's mission, and ʿAli's relationship to them both. Throughout the dialogue, the physical as well as spiritual nature of ʿAli's (and implicitly the imams') inheritance is emphasized. The imam explains to the caliph that Muhammad had commanded that ʿAli should

> collect the Qurʾan after him and to take care of the [ritual] washing of his deceased body, the embalming, and the wrapping of it—not anyone else from among his people.[39] For [the Prophet] said to his people and his followers, "It is forbidden for any of you to look upon my genitals (*ʿawrati*) except my brother ʿAli, for he is from me and I am from him. Whatever is mine is his; and whatever is his is mine. He is the judge of my religion, the fulfiller of my promises." And [the Prophet] said, "ʿAli fights according to the true meaning of the Qur'an (*ta'wil al-Qur'an*) just as I fought on the basis of its revelation (*tanzilihi*).[40]

Eventually, the caliph falls silent, unable to counter the imam's superior arguments. In his embarrassment, he bids the imam to return home. Throughout this story, the imams are presented as physical—not just spiritual—heirs of the Prophet, and the legitimacy of their claim to authority is displayed through their masculine qualities. Alongside his humility, generosity, and profound wisdom, al-Baqir is able to prove himself with weaponry, an ability rife with masculine associations that he construes as an inheritance. The mandate passed to ʿAli, as described in the debate with the caliph, is framed both in terms of spiritual knowledge (taking care of and interpreting the Qurʾan) and in bodily intimacy (the sole right to look upon and touch the naked corpse of Muhammad).[41] The bodies of the two men are discursively linked together. The imams inherited the physical capabilities of the perfect man, Muhammad, just as they inherited his authority. Disregard for the authority of the imams, therefore, was parallel to dishonoring the body of the Prophet of Islam. Just as the imams carried on the physical bloodline of the Prophet, they carried on his divinely blessed ability to rightly interpret the tradition for their followers.

The imams embodied the most basic masculine ideals, but the biographers' conceptions of masculinity were nuanced. Their desire to present the imams as the right kind of men included the downplaying of some overtly aggressive forms of masculinity and an emphasis on more refined performances.[42] The refined, even urbane, masculinity of the imams was tempered by asceticism, scholarship, and suffering.[43] The teachings of Imam al-Baqir emphasized the reigning in of physical desires. He is recorded saying that "the best worship is chastity of the womb and genitals."[44] Chastity, in this context, does not refer to the renunciation of sexual activity, but its strict limitation to legally/morally licit encounters. This overlay of moralism onto the imams' bodies gives us an image of men in full control of their bodily urges, enjoining others to exercise similar restraint.[45]

Cultivating the intellect was an even greater charge than controlling bodily impulses. The relationship between imam and believer was often construed as that of teacher and student. Al-Baqir proclaimed, "A scholar is better than seventy-thousand worshippers."[46] The image of the imams as moral teachers was a critical compliment to their virility and facility with weapons. Imam al-Sadiq said, "People are of three types: possessor of knowledge, student, and rubbish (*ghutha'*). We are the knowledgeable (*al-ʿulama*). Our Shiʿa are the students. The rest of the people are scum."[47] Not only were the imams positioned as the true holders of knowledge (*ʿulama*), but their followers were the only real students. All those who fell outside this relationship were dehumanized and categorically positioned as the other.[48]

Bodily portrayals were also influenced, however, by the tragedy of the greater Muslim community's failure to recognize the imams as teachers. The imams endured persecution, ridicule, and rejection, and they went to their graves as martyrs.[49] The imams' bodies were vulnerable. Shiʿism is a story of loss, and the imams' bodies were a testament to that story. "The people cause us great trouble," says Al-Baqir in *Guidance.* "We summon them but they do not answer us. If we abandoned them, they would be guided by no one."[50]

Rightful leadership was displayed through physical skill, intellectual acumen, and moral integrity. It was a beautiful thing to behold. The imams' suffering did not distract from this display; it enhanced it. It provided an opportunity to contrast the sincerity of the imams with the hypocrisy of ordinary men. Some men pretended to be ascetics, but the imams gave everything they had to those who loved them. Some posed as scholars, but the imams had true knowledge to share. Some feigned grief, but the imams endured unimaginable trials at the hands of their enemies. Some called themselves men, but their masculinity paled in comparison to that of the imams. These contrasts not only revealed the perfection of the imams, they revealed their isolation and alienation.

This sense of imams as outsiders says much about the concerns of the biographers and their communities.[51] The authors appear to have reacted to persecution by embracing a distinctive identity and drawing a rigid line around themselves, lumping all outsiders together as enemies. They may have spoken of the imams' abilities as leaders and warriors, but the mood of the texts is far from triumphant. There is none of the optimism one finds in early biographies of the Prophet aimed at a community that had conquered far-reaching lands (or was expected to do so sometime soon). Instead, the collective biographies are colored by a disappointment expressed through the unfulfilled potentiality of the imams' bodies. It seems fair to say that the depictions of the imams reflect the circumstances and identities of the men who wrote about them: they are portrayed as capable, urbane men of letters who know life-giving secrets but were prevented from taking full leadership by their adversaries.

Power over the Body: The Miracles of Imam al-Kazim

The array of miracles attributed to the imams is one of the few aspects of the biographies that has garnered attention in contemporary scholarship.[52] The collective biographies place varying degrees of emphasis on the miraculous events of the imams' lives. Some have sections of text explicitly devoted to miracles, and others do not, but all fully embrace the notion that every imam performed miracles. The biographies are saturated with the miraculous; those texts that have portions demarcated for miracles feature supernatural events in many other portions as well. It should be noted that Shiʿa scholars rarely made the distinction between prophetic miracles (*muʿjiza*) and nonprophetic miracles (*karama*). This categorization was common among Sunni scholars, who made the distinction to contrast the purposes of each miracle type. Such categories were less useful for the Shiʿa. For the Shiʿa, the imams' miracles functioned similarly to prophetic miracles in that they verified and authenticated the imams' divinely appointed role.[53] The nature, meaning, and functions of miracle accounts of the imams warrant attention, though I do not argue that miracle stories all serve a universal function. Arie Schippers has demonstrated the limited utility of Claude Bremond's theories, which Bremond believed would apply to all miracle stories.[54] In this section, then, I identify pervasive patterns rather than outlining a comprehensive paradigm by which all miracle accounts of the imams can be read. Narratives of the seventh imam, Musa b. Jaʿfar al-Kazim, show how miracles allowed the imams to transcend their bodily limitations and revealed their true nature to the community of believers. Imam al-Kazim is not exceptional among the imams; his biography merely demonstrates the pervasiveness of miracle accounts in these texts.[55]

The miracles attributed to the imams in the biographies are astonishingly varied and thus difficult to neatly categorize.[56] However, a few identifiable types of miracles reappear continually across the biographies of all twelve imams. Among the most frequently recurring are miracles related to speech and vision. These two types encompass a large number—if not the majority—of the miracles of the imams. In most cases, they bridge the gap between the imams' physical vulnerability and their role as leaders. The imams were hampered by the difficulty of their circumstances: some of them had scarcely any followers,[57] and the biographies regularly mention the intimidation those followers faced at the hands of ruling authorities. This atmosphere of fear and uncertainty is precisely the context in which many of the miracles are performed. The miracles were a clear message that eased fears while condemning unjust leaders. In a famous account, Hisham b. Salim[58] tells of his despair after the death of al-Kazim's father (Imam al-Sadiq), a despair caused by not knowing the identity of the next imam. Hisham weeps in the streets and contemplates joining other Muslim groups like the Muʿtazilis or the Zaydis. But at a critical moment, a man appears to him and motions for him to follow. Despite his fears that the man is a spy for the caliph, Hisham follows him. The man takes Hisham to the house of Musa al-Kazim, who is supernaturally already aware of the latter's doubts and concerns. Al-Kazim then answers all Hisham's questions in a way that proves he is the imam. He then cautions Hisham not to tell people about him, lest they all be killed. In spite of this warning, Hisham cannot contain his joy and quickly spreads the word.[59]

Earlier in this chapter, we saw how the vulnerability of the imams is mitigated through the idealization of their manliness. Here we find that the cultivation of mystery, miracles, and knowledge of the unseen was another way that the pain and suffering of the imams was shaped into an intelligible and memorable narrative by their biographers. The miracle accounts also deepen the connection between the imams and the prophets, something that will resurface in the birth accounts described in Chapter 5.

Miracles of speech are attributed to all the imams. Each biographer commented on the imams' supernatural knowledge of all human languages. In some instances the texts specify the number of languages known by an imam. Al-Tabrisi, for example, asserted that Imam al-Hadi knew seventy-three languages.[60] The number seventy-three likely refers to a popular hadith in which the Prophet is said to have predicted that his community would be split into seventy-three groups.[61] More often, the biographers included stories that showcased the linguistic prowess of the imams. Ibn Shahrashub recorded Abu Basir's account of asking Imam al-Kazim how one could recognize the real imam. Al-Kazim responds by listing some of the criteria for an imam, including designation from the father, an ability to answer any question, knowledge of coming events, and speaking to people in all languages. Abu Basir's account continues:

> Then [the imam] said, "Abu Muhammad [Abu Basir], I will provide a sign for you before you get up [to leave]." And shortly thereafter a man from Khurasan approached [the imam]. The man spoke to [the imam] in Arabic but Abu al-Hasan [al-Kazim] answered him in Persian. Then the Khurasani said, "The only thing that kept me from speaking to you in Persian was that I thought you did not know it well." [The imam] replied, "Praise God. If I did not speak well enough to answer you then I would not have any superiority over you which is a requirement of the imamate." Then [the imam] said, "Abu Muhammad [Abu Basir], the speech of no one is hidden from the imam, nor the speech of birds (*mantiq al-tayr*),[62] nor the speech of anything which has a spirit (*ruh*).[63]

As seen here, the omnilingual capability of the imam acts as an explicit proof of his uniquely superior status—and as such, implicit proof of his right to the authority of the imamate. As an intellectual power, his knowledge of languages highlights his superiority over those who claim elite religious knowledge: jurists, theologians, philosophers, and so on. The function of these narratives, however, is not limited to apologetics. The imams' fluency in all languages facilitated their intercessory role in Shiʿa religious life, giving confidence to Muslims across the centuries that they could pray directly to the imams in their own language.[64] This emphasis on multilingual capability reflected—and perhaps influenced—the popularization of Shiʿism outside of ʿArab circles in the tenth to twelfth centuries.

The quote above also shows that the imams' linguistic abilities were not limited to human languages. The imams are repeatedly shown communicating with animals, jinn,[65] and (occasionally) inanimate objects.[66] None of this would have been shocking to the Shiʿa community; conversing with animals was a common motif in stories about pre-Islamic prophets and some later Sufi saints.[67] The account contained in the twenty-seventh sura of the Qurʾan (Surat al-naml), in which the Prophet Solomon speaks with birds and ants, is but the most famous of many such stories.[68] Other prophets are also said to have communicated with animals, and the assumption by the Shiʿa that the imams would do the same is not surprising. Several scholars have recently commented upon the link between the imams' miracles and those of previous prophets. As an example, Judith Loebenstein makes this helpful observation in her study of miracles attributed to Imam al-Sadiq:

> One of the striking patterns in these traditions is the link between al-Ṣādiq and characters mentioned in the Qurʾān. This link is created in several ways, one of which is the comparison of a miracle performed by al-Ṣādiq with a miracle mentioned in the Qurʾān. Thus al-Ṣādiq's deeds are compared to the *sunna* of Maryam, Mūsá and Sulaymān. The use of the word *sunna* raises the association of *sunnat al-nabi,* thus implying that the Imams, like the Prophet, also have a defined *sunna* which is characterized, among other things, by the routine performance of miracles. This subtle and associative comparison treads the thin line which differentiates between the concepts of prophecy and Imamate in Imamī thought. The tension between these two concepts, which stems from the Imamiyya's wish to elevate the Imams' status without undermining that of the Prophet, comes to

light in such allusions which recur throughout the traditions dealing with the Imams' miracles.[69]

My own reading of the imams' miracles supports Loebenstein's assessment and lends support to Khalid Sindawi's general observation that "The Ŝīʿites miss no opportunity to compare the prophets and the imams in this respect."[70]

Each of the imams' biographers included accounts of the holy men speaking with animals. Al-Kazim spoke with cows,[71] lions,[72] and birds,[73] for example. The exchanges between imam and animal were often quite personal in content, as when a lion came to al-Kazim requesting prayer for his partner, who was experiencing great difficulty during childbirth (a request the imam obliged).[74] Such stories reinforce the full authority of the imams, which may be hidden from many humans, but is apparent to the animal kingdom. The range of animals we find across the biographies is fascinating and suggests a desire on the part of the biographers to amaze and entertain while meeting their other goals.[75] In addition to the above-mentioned animals, the biographies of other imams include conversations with wolves,[76] sheep,[77] geese,[78] donkeys,[79] fish,[80] and geckos,[81] to name but a few. A comprehensive study of the interactions of the imams with animals would be a worthwhile endeavor. In addition to increasing our understanding of animal imagery used in medieval Islamicate literature, it would likely provide insight into the social contexts of the authors. The imam-animal dialogues often revolve around personal or familial problems that prompted the animal to seek advice from the imam and have obvious parallels to issues faced by the imams' human followers. These interchanges have the potential to increase our knowledge of family relations, gender, and general social life in the biographers' era.

These conversations with animals also alert the audience to the imams' place in the cosmic order, and they invite the community to align themselves with that order by recognizing the absolute authority of the imams. We see this in the animals' cognizance of the imams' powers and authority, an understanding that leads them to approach the holy men. Only in a small number of cases is an animal an enemy of the imam.[82] The imams' interactions with animals display their potential as effective leaders, and they illustrate what constitutes proper deference to an imam.

These encounters provide glimpses of an alternate storyworld that remains largely outside the audience's view. The animal kingdom isn't treated in a systematic way, but it is presumed to have its own narrative, in which the imams have an authoritative role. In this sense, the animal stories give us glimpses of a reality that the human world ought to resemble, but does not. Ibn Shahrashub, for example, recorded a story that portrays all the animals on land and sea mourning the death of Imam al-Husayn.[83] Another commonly reported account has Imam ʿAli pointing out a group of geese who were grieving in the knowledge that his death would occur.[84] Khalid Sindawi, in his analysis of the role of birds in classical Shiʿa literature, reveals an array of similar activities ascribed to these animals, including general mourning for the Shiʿa, expressing love for the Shiʿa, showing sympathy for the imams, and doing charitable acts for the sake of *ahl al-bayt*.[85] Each of these activities is an important ritual that has helped sustain the Shiʿa community.[86] The idealized animal storyworld evoked by the biographers stands in stark contrast to their own realities and serves as an indictment of the unnatural and ungodly corruption of the corporeal world, where the imams' authority was widely rejected.

Another dominant motif of the miracle stories is the imams' preternatural ability to see the unseen and to give sight to others.[87] The imams could see through walls and in the dark;[88] they could view far-off lands,[89] discern people's thoughts,[90] perceive the future,[91] see deceased ancestors, view heaven and hell,[92] and behold other unseen events that symbolized or took place in the spiritual world. My grouping together of physical sight, spiritual sight, mystical visions, and the power of foresight is intentional. These frequently overlap in meaning within the stories themselves, where physical sight is often used as a metaphor for spiritual and miraculous knowledge.[93] The imams also had the power to make people see things that were hidden. They healed the blind[94] and provided spiritual visions to those who needed or requested guidance.[95] Obstructing the vision of others—namely the enemies of the Shiʿa—was also within the imams' thaumaturgic capabilities. In a similar vein, al-Kazim once made himself invisible to the ill-intentioned Caliph Harun al-Rashid.[96]

The imams also enabled select people to have mystical visions that emphasized the role of the imams as guides and impressed upon the faithful the importance of remaining near to the imams. *Establishment* records a story from Dawud al-Riqqi, who asks Imam al-Sadiq about the day of resurrection. The imam asks Dawud whether he prefers to hear a hadith on the matter or to have a visual experience of the last day. When Dawud requests the latter, al-Sadiq instructs his son, Imam al-Kazim, to fetch "the rod" (*al-qadib*). This is presumably the rod of Moses, which is often said to have been among the physical items passed down through the prophets and imams.[97] Al-Kazim returns with the rod and, at his father's command,

> struck the ground with it [causing] such a blow that a black sea burst forth. Then he struck the sea with the rod and [the water] was divided by a black rock. Then he struck the rock and a door opened up into it. And there was a group of people crammed together. Their faces were rough and their eyes were blue (*mazraqa*). And each one of them was tightly tied to the rock. And there was an angel in charge of each one of them. They [the people] would cry out, "Oh, Muhammad!" But the angels of hell (*al-zabaniya*) would strike their faces and say to them, "You have lied! Muhammad is not with you and you are not with him!" Then I said to [Imam al-Kazim]: "May I be your servant. Who are they?" He said to me, "They are al-Jibt and al-Taghut.[98] They are filth. They are the cursed son of the devil (*al-laʿin ibn al-laʿin*). They will always be known by their names, from their first to their last, including the people of Saqifa,[99] the sons of al-Azraq,[100] and the groups of people from the descendants of Abu Sufyan and Marwan.[101] God renews the punishment upon them each day."
>
> Then [the imam] said to the rock, "Be closed upon them until the known time."[102]

This story reflects the deep anger and vindictiveness that seems to have resonated in the Shiʿa community toward its opponents. It is telling that the consolation offered in this story is a vow to remember the perpetrators' names, not erase them from history. Victors attempt to erase the memory of others; the persecuted vow to remember. The imam assures Dawud that the identity of these gross offenders of God's plan will not be forgotten. Their sins against God, God's Prophet, and the Prophet's family will be met with justice. The entire genre of biographies of the imams is a testament to this determination to remember.

Through miracles, the imams demonstrated their care for their followers. This is another important motif in many of these accounts, particularly in miracle stories related to the imams' ability to foresee the future. The imams cared for the Shiʿa and protected them against those who sought to bring them harm. Once again, the imams are assumed to be honorable, just, manly leaders who have the ability to protect their followers when called upon. One example of this is the rescue of ʿAli b. Yaqtin by Imam al-Kazim, a story recorded in several sources. In one account, ʿAli b. Yaqtin is given a beautiful robe by the Caliph Harun al-Rashid. As a follower of the imam, ʿAli decides to donate the expensive item to his leader. But al-Kazim, prompted by his powers of premonition, warns ʿAli that he will need the item and that he should keep it for the time being. Later, one of the caliph's informants who knew of ʿAli's intention to donate the item to the imam attempts to betray ʿAli and have him punished. He tells the caliph that ʿAli gave the gift to Imam al-Kazim, and the ruler furiously questions ʿAli about the robe. ʿAli is able to prove that he did not give it to the imam by bringing it forward to show the caliph. The latter's anger subsides, and ʿAli is safe. The informant, however, is given a hundred lashes and dies.[103] Many such stories are among the miracle accounts, and they facilitated the faith of those who relied on the imams for guidance and protection, reminding them that the Shiʿa will ultimately prevail.

The miracles related to speech and vision presented to the audience an understanding of the imams as loci of true knowledge (*ʿilm*).[104] Clear demonstrations of the imams' superior embodiment of *ʿilm* helped offset their lack of temporal authority. Knowledge was the most regularly referenced proof of the authority of each imam, and the biographies contain many stories that pit the imams against known scholars of their day. Key representatives of each of the classical Sunni schools appear in these texts, and the historical personas of esteemed proto-Sunni jurists are exploited for the greater glory of the imams.[105]

The overarching narrative of the biographies is one in which the imams cannot achieve physical victory. They lose out in this world. In light of this reality, many of the imams exhibited a somewhat passive, almost fatalistic, attitude toward the political rulers' abuses of power and the lack of just governance. Pessimism about the historical trajectory dominated Shiʿa literature for several centuries, and the prevailing sense in many Shiʿa communities was that the world was drowning. The Shiʿa were destined to be rescued from this ill-fated world through right guidance, but the possibility of achieving political leadership seemed out of reach and was not entertained seriously in this literature and many others like it. This may be part of the reason Shiʿa discourse has been such a powerful means of protest, but so at odds with the assumption of power.[106]

But hope triumphs over despair. The miracle accounts opened the eyes of the audience to the imams' connection with the spiritual world, to a metanarrative where they did not lose out. In the cosmic scheme of things, the imams were in complete control of their fate, and their physical impediments in this world only highlighted their spiritual transcendence. Such ideas are not unique to Shiʿism. Hujwiri, for example, argued that human saints are better than angels because the saints overcome human frailty in their spirituality, whereas the angels do not have to transcend corporeal limitations.[107] Greatness through weakness was modeled by the imams, who were subjected to ridicule and persecution only to ascend to even greater spiritual heights than the saints. Miracles played a key role in helping the biographers move the locus of the imams' power from their bodies to their spirits, effectively redefining the nature of their struggle against their enemies and placing that struggle in a framework where victory was assured.

The metanarrative of the imams began long before their births, and their essence was composed of pure light passed on from time immemorial. They knew the languages of all humankind and were able to lead everyone willing to follow. Even the animal kingdom was aware of their spiritual powers, and the animals were regularly portrayed as servants and helpers to the imams, just as they had been to the prophets before them. The greatest figure in the animal kingdom, the lion, was particularly prominent in this regard. This strong and majestic animal, full of masculine connotations, showed himself to be a servant of the imam.[108] The vision of the imams extended beyond their temporal and geographical confines and even penetrated the immaterial world.

Perhaps the most straightforward example of spiritual power compensating for physical limitations is the imams' ability to move their bodies to other locations on earth in a flash.[109] In numerous instances, the imams transport themselves from one city to another instantly, or temporarily remove themselves from captivity in order to fulfill a task.[110] The author of *Proofs,* for instance, recorded a fascinating story attributed to Ahmad al-Tabban, who recalls being awakened by Imam al-Kazim and taken on a journey. The uniqueness of this trip is apparent from the start. Al-Tabban relates, "he [the imam] took me from my house, but the door was locked and I do not know how he got me out." The imam places Ahmad behind him on his camel, and the two journey together. When they stop, the imam prays, performing twenty-four prostrations, and then asks Ahmad if he knows where they are. When Ahmed says he does not, the imam informs him that they have come to the grave of Imam al-Husayn, and then they set out on another journey. At the next stop, the imam again prays twenty-four prostrations and informs Ahmad of his whereabouts; they are now at the Mosque of Kufa, where Imam ʿAli was killed.[111] Following the same pattern, they visit the tomb of Abraham, the holy sites of Mecca, and Muhammad's mosque and grave in Medina. After the imam performs a few additional miracles,[112] their travels end at the top of a great mountain range where Ahmad admits that he is exhausted from the journey. The imam, notably, suffers no such physical exhaustion. Bringing the story full circle, the imam offers to take the tired man back to his home so that he can go back to sleep.[113]

The story makes clear that this journey to far-off places occurred over the course of a single night.[114] The imam easily overcame physical obstacles that would stymie the average person, passing through locked doors and travelling impossible distances. This ability to transcend natural corporeal confines not only served as proof of the imamate, it emphasized the voluntary nature of his suffering/confinement, salvaging his masculinity in the process. The author of *Proofs* used this account and others like it to assure the audience of the imam's identity and to display his spiritual power over the frail material world.

Gendered Ambiguity: Imam-like Daughters and the Infallible Fatima

Despite the undeniable centrality of men in the biographies, this literature contains no shortage of important women. The mothers and daughters of the imams appear most frequently, often playing critical roles in the narratives. In fact, nearly every woman portrayed positively by the biographers is either a mother or a daughter of one of the imams. As a daughter of the Prophet and mother to two imams, Fatima al-Zahraʾ is the crowning example of the elevation of both roles.[115] But other daughters of imams figure prominently as well.

After Fatima, no woman stands out quite as powerfully in the literature as Zaynab (d. 62/682), the daughter of ʿAli and Fatima.[116] And no moment of her life is remembered more than her role following the massacre at Karbalaʾ.[117] In the midst of that central tragedy of Shiʿism, Zaynab boldly shamed the murderers of her brother. Al-Mufid included a powerful portrayal of Zaynab's resistance to ʿUbayd Allah b. Ziyad (d. 67/686), the Umayyad governor to whom the freshly decapitated head of al-Husayn is brought after the battle. The governor summons Zaynab, who has likewise been brought to his palace. She puts on "her dirtiest clothes" in protest of her lavish surroundings and refuses to acknowledge his summons.[118] When she finally engages him, she calls judgment down upon him, saying, "God will gather you and us together. You will plead your excuses to Him, and we will be your adversaries before Him." In the days after Imam al-Husayn's death, Zaynab is the most prominent voice of resistance, and she becomes the spokesperson for the remnants of the holy family. Just moments after her altercation with Ibn Ziyad, the governor threatens to kill the new imam, ʿAli b. al-Husayn al-Sajjad. Zaynab functions as the imam's protector, quickly stepping in to intercede on his behalf and declaring that they will have to kill her to get to him.[119] Zaynab again performs the roles of spokesperson, intercessor, and protector when the family is taken before the Umayyad caliph Yazid in Damascus. There, one of Yazid's guards points to Fatima, the younger daughter of al-Husayn, and demands that she be given to him. The young girl clings to the skirt of her aunt, Zaynab, who assures Fatima that this will not happen. Zaynab then lambasts the man for his presumption that he has comparable social rank. Yazid is enraged by Zaynab's confidence and declares that he is the only one who can decide such matters. But Zaynab does not consent to his authority in any form. Instead, she assumes a position of power, declaring herself to be "led by the religion of God." She rebukes the caliph for his treachery and oppression, and the caliph grudgingly backs down from the confrontation.[120]

Although Zaynab and Fatima al-Zahraʾ are the most famous daughters of the infallibles, other daughters also appear as spokespersons for the family or defenders of the family's rights. For example, on numerous occasions the biographies put Hakima, the daughter of Imam al-Jawad, in a prominent role. Hakima's life spanned the imamates of the last four imams, and she acts as their messenger to the public and is involved in their education and protection.[121] Other daughters who play roles include Fatima bt. al-Hasan,[122] Fatima bt. al-Husayn (whom Zaynab saved from Yazid's guards),[123] and Hakima bt. Musa.[124] The legacies of these women have endured through the passing centuries, and they have been revered to various extents by Shiʿa communities in different eras. One need only visit the city of Qum, Iran, to see the devotion exhibited toward some of these relatively lesser-known daughters of imams. The shrine to Fatima bt. Musa (d. 201/816), the daughter of the seventh imam, dominates the city and is visited by millions of pilgrims each year.

The honored position of the daughters as children of the imams, but their simultaneous exclusion from the imamate on account of their bodies illuminates the gendered nature of the imamate itself. It helps foreground what was at stake with the portrayals of the imams as ideal men. As Derek Neal has argued, "the history of masculinity will be strong when it takes more account of women."[125] The daughters of the imams participate in many of the distinguishing characteristics of their fathers, but their bodily differences justify a parallel but unequal purpose for their constructed legacies.

There is no doubt that Fatima al-Zahraʾ is the most elevated female relative of the imams in the biographies. As the only woman to be counted among the fourteen infallibles, she shares in the primordial origins of these figures, which play a significant role in the overarching cosmology of these works and will be discussed in Chapter 5. Fatima is tied to the divinely ordained lineage of male inheritors (*awsiyaʾ*) in three distinct ways: as daughter of the Prophet, wife of Imam ʿAli, and mother of Imams al-Hasan and al-Husayn. The role of daughter is arguably the most important of the three—as Ibn Shahrashub remarked, "Women's honor is through their fathers" (*sharaf al-nisaʾ bi-abaʾihim*).[126] Ibn Shahrashub used this statement to demonstrate Fatima's superiority over Mary. In his turn, Ibn Jarir noted that "daughters of prophets do not menstruate," thus suggesting another way in which those daughters are inherently superior to other women.[127]

Fatima's feminine intrusion into the otherwise all-male club of infallibles is a matter worthy of scrutiny. Among the most striking portrayals of Fatima are those in which she functions like—or even stands in for—the imams at key moments. Fatima is clearly not like other women:[128] she is part of the preexistent light (*nur*) from which the other imams were formed;[129] she speaks from the womb;[130] she is infallible (*maʿsuma*);[131] angels communicate with her;[132] she possesses a divinely revealed message (usually referred to as her *mushaf*);[133] she is made aware of future events;[134] she performs extreme displays of piety;[135] she partakes in the Prophet's inheritance;[136] she publicly confronts Abu Bakr and ʿUmar about their claims to the caliphate;[137] and she dies a martyr's death at the hands of enemies of the Shiʿa.[138] In each of these extraordinary ways, Fatima is like the imams. In some cases, Fatima is even assigned a role in the judgment of humanity at the end of the world.[139] Majlisi wrote in his seventeenth-century contribution to the biographies of the imams that "Fatima is not like the women of the children of Adam: she is not defective as they are defective."[140]

Nevertheless, despite the many ways in which Fatima is equated with the imams (functionally and as an object of devotion), she is never considered to be a full imam. Despite her many qualifications for the position, she is disqualified by one critical feature: her body. Fatima's anatomy separates her from the imams. It should come as no surprise, then, that an exceptionally large number of the narratives about Fatima focus on her body and her bodily performances. Her physical form is portrayed in uniquely idealized ways that rival the portrayals of any of her fellow infallibles.

The birth and death of Fatima provide obvious opportunities for examining portrayals of Fatima's body in the text. All of the infallibles are said to have been created from a single spermatic light substance often referred to as the Muhammadan light (*nur muhammad*), which is said to have been passed down through history via a pure race of inheritors (*awsiyaʾ*) or directly given to each mother in some other manner. This will be discussed more fully in Chapter 5, but narratives about the conception of Fatima deserve attention here. These narratives make up part of a larger body of stories about Muhammad's famous journey into the heavens (known as the *miʿraj*).[141] A common form of the conception story is told in the Prophet's voice as he explains to ʿA'isha what happened while he was in heaven. "Gabriel brought me to the Tuba tree and gave me an apple from it," relates Muhammad. "I consumed it and sperm formed in my loins. When I came down to earth, I had intercourse with Khadija and she became pregnant with Fatima."[142] The story functions as an assertion that Fatima's essence was heavenly and pure, and most biographers place it alongside the story of ʿA'isha's disconcerted (perhaps jealous)[143] reaction to seeing the Prophet put his tongue into Fatima's mouth. Here again we can see the way in which ʿA'isha is cast in a contemptuous role that excoriated her legacy and those whom she represented, namely those who similarly prevented proper love and devotion to be paid to the Prophet's family. This type of kissing (which I discuss further in Chapter 5) is described frequently in the biographies and is generally presented as a means of transmitting spiritual knowledge from father to son. Fatima's case is somewhat unusual, however. The Prophet's assertion about Fatima's heavenly origin is a response to a puzzled remark by ʿA'isha. "I see you kissing Fatima's mouth excessively and putting your tongue into her mouth," she says.[144] After describing the heavenly origin of Fatima, Muhammad goes on to add, "Whenever I long for heaven, I kiss her and put my tongue into her mouth; for through her I encounter the breeze of heaven, and through her I encounter the scent of the Tuba tree. For she is a heavenly human (*insiya samawiya*)."[145]

Numerous other accounts speak to the Prophet's physical affection for Fatima. Imam al-Sadiq is recorded saying, "[the Prophet] would not go to sleep until he kissed the side of Fatima's face and put his face between Fatima's breasts (*bayn thadiyay Fatima*) and prayed for her."[146] These stories not only highlight Fatima's heavenly nature, but also her profound connection with the Prophet. There's no indication that the biographers perceived these stories to be sexual in any way, despite how they may sound to modern readers. The bond between the Prophet and his daughter was emphatically physical, but it reflected their closeness, love, and similar natures. This type of connection is made even more explicit in other narratives, as when the Prophet states that Fatima is a part of him,[147] or when Fatima is called the "mother of her father" (*umm abiha*).[148]

Fatima's body is also a focal point of stories about her death. Her unique status raised questions about who would be worthy to wash her corpse, and some early sources suggest that she actually performed her own ritual washings before her death and thus there was no need for anyone else to wash her dead body.[149] The story that came to dominate Shiʿa sources, however, was that ʿAli washed Fatima's body after her death and—in accordance with her wishes—buried her secretly at night in an undisclosed location.[150] It was not uncommon for scholars to jump immediately from this account to their concerns about the impact of this story on visitation to her grave. Al-Tabrisi, for example, listed several possible sites and recommended visiting each of them.[151]

Another way the texts focus on the body of Fatima is by describing her appearance. She is invariably portrayed as beautiful and radiant. She is likened to "the full moon or the sun hidden by the clouds,"[152] and is said to have been "fair and tender-skinned."[153] The latter description, as Soufi notes, matches that of the virgin maidens of paradise (*huriya*).[154] In some cases, Fatima is explicitly associated with the *huriya*.[155] Her beauty is tied to her heavenly origins, and light imagery pervades descriptions of her. Her most common honorific, al-Zahraʾ, is usually understood to be a reference to her radiance.[156] So magnificent was the light that appeared at her birth that the angels had never seen anything like it.[157]

These characteristics highlight the similarities between Fatima and the male imams. The difference between them lay in their different sexualities. Fatima's female genitalia categorically disqualified her for the imamate. And the biographers were not averse to commenting on her private parts (though sometimes in roundabout ways). References to genitalia are common in literature from this period when describing women. The vagina, projected as the most uniquely feminine part of the body, comes to implicitly define women—or at least to represent them.[158] As in many other premodern contexts, women's social status was heavily shaped by what went into their vaginas (sexual activity tended to be understood solely in terms of penetration)[159] and what came out of them (be it offspring or menstrual blood). The vagina was both a source of condemnation and the locus of redemption. Even the light attributed to Fatima was sometimes associated with her vagina. Majlisi, for example, interpreted the description of her being like a "sun hidden by the clouds" as a reference to her chastity and veiling.[160] Another example of a woman's genitals being associated with a radiant light is found in the stories of Abu Muslim, whose mother was described as having a light shining from underneath her skirt.[161] Kathryn Babayan offers insightful commentary on several narratives from this time period, demonstrating that writers who included women in their stories had to continually affirm their chastity.[162] Her observations substantiate the notion that women are regularly reduced to their genitals in the literature of this period. Within those norms, praising the mother or daughter of an imam necessitated a discussion of her sexual purity. Her sexuality was the most significant aspect of her person.

The most well-known and regularly remarked-upon aspect of Fatima's body is that she did not menstruate.[163] The "affliction" that plagues women did not afflict Fatima. Her vagina was completely untainted by the impurity of blood. Even at childbirth, she expelled no blood.[164] In some cases, she is said to have given birth through her thigh.[165] The biological mechanics of such a birth are difficult to imagine, but similar claims are made about Mary in some Christian sources.[166] The ways in which Fatima's biographers put her in competition with Mary also explains the somewhat confusing description of Fatima as "the virgin" (*al-batul*). Interestingly, this description was, at least in part, understood on account of the fact that she did not menstruate. In one story, the Prophet was asked how it was that Fatima was a *batul,* and the Prophet responded, "*al-Batul* is someone who never sees red [blood], that is, she does not menstruate. For menstruation is unsuitable (*makruh*) for the daughters of the prophets."[167] This aspect of Fatima was seen to have had a purifying effect on all of her progeny and—by extension—their followers. With this in mind (rarely missing an opportunity to deride their detractors), Shiʿa sources sometimes referred to their adversaries as "the defective cursed children of menstruation" (*bani al-tamth al-malaʿin al-ʿayb*).[168]

The significance of Fatima's body was made most explicit, however, in an oft-repeated phrase in the biographies: "Fatima kept her vagina chaste, so God has protected her progeny from the fire" (*inna Fatima ahsanat farjaha fa-harrama Allah dhuriyataha ʿala al-nar*).[169] Fatima exerted control and protection over her children through her sexuality; that is, through the safeguarding of her genitals and protecting them from any illicit activity. By this uniquely feminine accomplishment, Fatima secured the sanctification of herself, her children, and (implicitly) all of the Shiʿa. Her power resided in the proper use of her body, not in transcending it. One might reasonably argue that not bleeding in menstruation or at childbirth *is* a transcendence of the body, but within the cultural framework of the biographers, these were not natural bodily actions. They were deficiencies and evidences of the flawed qualities of most women's bodies.

What becomes clear to us is that Fatima represents an entirely distinct ontological category, separate from woman, man, or imam. She embodies a feminine ideal completely unattainable to women who are not part of the *nur muhammad*—women who menstruate, who bleed at childbirth, and to whom angels do not speak. Fatima is not alone in standing above normal (flawed) women. Other daughters of the imams are similarly described, as are women like Khadija and Mary. These superwomen stand in a category of their own, with Fatima at their head.[170] Their gender prevents them from being grouped with the prophets or imams, but they are not normal women, either. This conceptual category of the ideal female has been noted by other scholars and is found in other (Sunni and Shiʿa) literature.[171] The typological logic that supports this distinction—and which is a defining feature of these biographies in general—is nicely summarized by Denise Soufi: "how could a woman who was not of extraordinary caliber be born of the Prophet, be married to the venerated hero ʿAli, and be the mother of Hasan and the martyred Husayn, the Prophet's beloved grandchildren?"[172] The logic of the biographies makes it inconceivable that any normal woman could hold these honors. The uniquely fulfilled masculinity of the men in her life (the imams) necessitated that Fatima live up to a higher standard than other women. Her canonical inclusion among the fourteen infallibles solidified the distinctiveness of the "feminine ideal" category in mainstream Shiʿa literature.

How does this alternative category of "feminine ideal" impact the devotional purposes of the biographies of the imams? What function does it serve? There is a tendency to assume that these (primarily male) reflections on the feminine ideal were directed toward women and offered as a model for women to emulate. And indeed, this may to some extent be the case. Fatima, Zaynab, and other daughters of the imams are presented as ideal feminine forms toward which women might strive. In recent times, the legacy of Fatima and Zaynab has been increasingly utilized in elaborations of proper female behavior.[173]

It would be a mistake, however, to assume that the memory of Fatima and other prominent women was constructed solely for the devotional needs of women. In fact, it appears that Fatima's devotional relevance for women was a secondary concern. Fatima, and to a lesser extent the other ideal women, were important and powerful symbols that helped orient male Shiʿa devotion to the imams. Several aspects of Fatima's image in the biographies stand out in this regard. First of all, Fatima was in a special position that allowed her to express love to the original holy family in uniquely intimate ways. Her love and devotion for her father, her husband, and her children were models for all the Shiʿa as they sought to cultivate their love for the Prophet and imams.[174] Her devotion motivated her to speak out against those who usurped her family's rights,[175] and she was so unyielding in her position that the biographers often depicted her as the person who will judge her family's oppressors on the Day of Reckoning.[176] Fatima's exemplary qualities manifested themselves in and through her devotion to her perfect male counterparts. This way of positioning ideal women can be seen in other literatures of the period as well. According to Sulami, ʿAisha of Marv, an exemplary figure in early Sufism, credited her own spiritual light to her male counterparts.[177] Similarly, Fatima's light—although more ontologically complex—is inseparable from her relationship with men.

A second essential way Fatima served as an example to all Shiʿa was through her role as mourner of the tragedies that befell the family. Fatima frequently appears in the biographies as a eulogist for her family. Ibn Shahrashub included these verses, which Fatima is said to have spoken after her father's death:

> We have suffered from the loss of he who was of sincere disposition
> And of pure character, origin, and lineage.
>
> You were a full moon and a light which brought enlightenment.
> Books from the Powerful One used to descend upon you.
>
> And Jibril, the holy spirit, was our visitor.
> Then he disappeared and [now] all good is hidden.

If only death had found us before you
When you departed and veils obstructed you!

We suffered from a loss which was not suffered
By those who grieve, both Arab and non-Arab.

The countries have become narrow for me after they had [once] been spacious.
Your two cubs have been disgraced along with me.

By God, you are the best of all creation
And the most honest person with regard to truth and falsehood.

So we will cry for you for as long as we live and as long as our eyes
Remain bathed in tears which pour forth.[178]

The significance of elegies like this can hardly be overstated. As I argued in Chapter 2, they express the prevailing emotional mood of the biographies.[179] In the piece quoted above, Fatima models the appropriate response to the tragedy that befell the holy family. She praises the Prophet, indicts those who betrayed him, experiences immense grief over the affair, and vows never to cease remembering. Her example beckons those who hear her to join her in her unending mourning.[180] Having a woman enact this emotional role seems to heighten the intended reaction by the male audience.[181] The physical closeness between Muhammad and Fatima provides a sensible platform on which to stage the deep intimacy with the Prophet that the male audience hoped to spiritually and emotionally emulate.[182]

There is a complex network of relationships found in these biographies that have devotional utility. The way in which these stories are utilized for devotional purposes is fluid and partly determined by the gendered ontological categories through which the stories are read. The biographers themselves appear to assume a dual-gendered ontology that is symmetrical, parallel, and hierarchical. As men of the community look to the prophets/imams as ideal models of manhood, they also direct their gaze of devotion toward the feminine ideal represented in these stories. For men, the feminine ideal also serves a model for devotion in that the ideal women help facilitate the desired emotional disposition in relation to the imams. This feminized devotion, therefore, is another means for men to approach the imams. In parallel fashion, women can look to the feminine ideal as a model of femininity. But the biographies already frame the feminine ideal through the concerns and perspectives of men, thus proscribing a kind of feminine devotion that entails striving to be more like men while remaining in the service of men.

For the Shiʿa, Fatima is a uniquely suitable representative of the feminine ideal. Her physical and emotional connections to the Prophet and the imams were utilized by the biographers as an example of how to praise, love, and mourn the imams. Removing any faults or defects from the character and body of Fatima constructed a useful legacy toward which men could gaze. Most of the miracles attributed to Fatima have to do with removing bodily defects. In the biographies, Fatima is primarily a passive receptor of miracles, for example, her spiritual origins, lack of menstruation, marriage being appointed in heaven,[183] bloodless/painless childbirth, and so on. In each case, Fatima's miracles relate to her body and her lack of deficiency, but she does not transcend her body entirely. Her power is in her perfected body (by removing the feminine deficiencies), not beyond it. She does not, for instance, perform the kind of miracles described earlier in this chapter in relation to the imams.[184] Her miracles functionally separate her from the category of "woman," making her more useable for men (and simultaneously unattainable for women).[185] She has countless similarities to the imams, but her body ensures that difference always remains.

Conclusion

Attention to the representations of the imams' bodies and their bodily performances exposes the extent to which the authors of their biographies framed their stories around ideals that were important to them and their (androcentric) community. Calling attention to the androcentric nature of the biographies should not be misunderstood as a criticism. One could certainly critique the biographies on those grounds, but that is not my concern here. Instead, I am simply attempting to take seriously the gendered context of the communal production and receptions of these stories. Scott Kugle, in his *Sufis and Saints' Bodies,* argues that "the saint's body acts as a mirror for the religious virtues around which society can adhere."[186] In our case, the hopes of the imams' biographers and the community that remembered these accounts are manifest in the presentations of the imams' lives. The ideal physical bodies of the imams are projections of some of the authors' own desires for a masculine fulfillment of power and leadership, even as the imams exhibited those qualities in ways that went beyond what normal men could hope to achieve. The imams function simultaneously as role models for behavior and as unattainable, utopian imaginations of the human form. By presenting an unachievable ideal, the authors offered ways of coping with personal and communal constraints, whether through intervention by an imam or with the confidence that injustices will eventually be rectified. These narratives not only serve as spaces of contested masculinity in specific historical contexts, but the ideals embodied by the imams also point to the authors' hopes for an ideal order, ideal community, and ideal leadership.

Idealized women within this literature, particularly Fatima, reinforce the masculinized construction of the ideal human form by functioning like imams but remaining outside of that category. At the same time, the idealized women were often more "manly" than the men around them and were utilized as potent shaming tools in the authors' critiques of other men. These women also helped model an intimate and loving relationship with the imams that men and women alike could use to cultivate a proper spiritual and emotional disposition.

Although the imams had perfect male bodies, their true potential was unfulfilled in this world. Their miracles reveal that the locus of the imams' powers was ultimately grounded in the spiritual realm, reflecting uneasiness about the vulnerability of the community of believers and their lot in history. Fatima, in contrast, rooted the feminine ideal in her female body.[187] Her fulfillment of a perfect body was a source of praise and inspiration for the Shiʿa—for men and women, though in different ways. In general, we can say that the body is not portrayed as inherently evil or bad in this literature, though it may be dangerous (especially the female body). Instead, the body has the potential to be fruitfully put to use, as long as it is properly pure. The texts do not enforce a strict spirit-body dualism (something found in numerous religious contexts of the ancient Near East), but there exists a gendered hierarchy rooted in conceptions of the body. That hierarchy prioritizes the spiritual over the physical while more closely aligning spiritual power with the male (via the imams) and the physical with the female.[188]

This gendered hierarchy—overlaid with a spirit-body hierarchy—is mitigated by the mutually reinforcing utility of the existing conceptions of masculinity and femininity. Women who achieved heights of spirituality were understood to be more like men, and men made use of the example of ideal women to cultivate a more profound connection to the imams. Throughout the biographies of the imams, the binary categories of man and woman are cast in ways that alter the meaning of both in relationship to the anxieties of a religious community determined to resist outside pressures to forget their past. Against the backdrop of the betrayal of the imams, the nature and significance of their bodies achieves its tragic fulfillment.

Caroline Bynum suggests in her article "Why All the Fuss about the Body?" that she is not alone in noticing "the complex link between body, death, and the past."[189] That link is clearly apparent in this literature. By focusing on the bodies of the imams, we see how important it was to the authors that the imams not only fulfilled their physical potential but also overcome the obstacles laid before them. The limitations placed on the imams' bodies, therefore, are critical and necessary to the narrative structure of the genre and for the explication of the true power of the imams. But nowhere is the inherent nature of the imams more clear than in the stories of their births, to which we now turn.

CHAPTER FIVE

Entering the Cosmos

Then you descended to earth, not as a human being,
Nor as a morsel or congealed blood,
But as a drop of sperm [in Adam's loins]. You sailed the ark
While the flood had reached the mouth of Nasr and his followers.
You were transmitted from loins to wombs;
. . . When you were born, the earth shone
And the horizons beamed with your light;
We proceed fast in this brightness
And light, and in the right paths.

—*attributed to al-ʿAbbas b. ʿAbd al-Muttalib (quoted in* Virtues*)* [1]

ALL THE KEY WORKS examined in this study describe the imams' nativities, and these birth stories are some of the biographies' most spectacular narratives.[2] The tone and level of detail differ from account to account, but the biographers consistently treated the time, place, and manner of the imams' births as matters of significance. This simple observation is worth emphasizing, because most Arabic biographies and Muslim hagiographies from the same era contain few, if any, details about the births and childhood experiences of their subjects. Consider, for example, Farid al-Din ʿAttar's (d. 618/1221) *Remembrance of the Saints (Tazkirat al-awliya')*,[3] a hagiographical collection that opens with a biography Jaʿfar al-Sadiq. This account of the imam's life begins with what may be a nod to the collective biography genre:

> We have said that if we were to memorialize the prophets, Mohammad's companions, and his family, it would require a separate book.

> This book [*Remembrance of the Saints*] will consist of the biographies of the masters of this clan, who lived after them. But as a blessing, let us begin with Sādeq (may God be pleased with him) for he too lived after them. Since he among the Prophet's descendants said the most about the path and many traditions have come down from him, I shall say a few words about this esteemed man, for they are all as one.[4]

This short introduction leads directly to descriptions of the adult imam's virtues and attributes. In addition to bypassing Jaʿfar al-Sadiq's birth and childhood entirely, ʿAttar paid little to no attention to the historical context of the stories he transmitted. His primary concern was with the spiritual lessons that could be extracted from tales about al-Sadiq's life.

By contrast, the collective biographies contain detailed information on the births of the imams. The time and place of their nativities are always given, and narratives about their early childhoods frequently appear. Interestingly, early Shiʿa reflections on the births of the imams, particularly Imam ʿAli, further contributed to the development of popular stories concerning the birth of the Prophet Muhammad in broader Muslim circles beyond Shiʿism.[5]

The birth accounts in the biographies display many of the same concerns, themes, and strategies already discussed in this study. Once again we see tension between the biographers' impulse to depict the imams as strong, capable leaders and their desire to emphasize the Muslim community's tragic failure to recognize the imams' right to lead. But the birth narratives also reveal the concrete devotional purposes of the biographies. The stories do not simply teach theology or doctrine, they also accomplish things for the community.[6] Take, for example, the relative abundance of dates in the collective biographies. The biographers not only provided birth and death dates for the imams, but also the dates of various life events. In addition, they tended to note what king or caliph was in power at the time of these events.[7] But this is not just history for history's sake. Providing dates and a historical context accomplished important objectives: it grounded the imams as corporeal beings in a temporal world and emphasized that they were historically—not just spiritually—significant. The biographers' concern with indicating the time and place of each birth also met the devotional needs of a community that viewed the imams as embodiments of spiritual blessing and divine favor.

In her discussion of Muslim narratives of the Prophet's birth, Marion Katz observes that "the idea that time is inherently patterned, with some days or months intrinsically privileged over others, is deeply rooted in the Islamic tradition and is addressed by the earliest *mawlid* authors."[8] The dates in the collective biographies helped determine which time periods the Shiʿa would privilege. Specifying when an imam's birth occurred enabled believers to commemorate the nativity each year, providing them with a consistent opportunity to seek God's blessing and favor as they remembered the imam. Indicating a birthplace also had a concrete devotional effect: it provided a physical locus of God's merciful encounter with humanity, a place to be visited by those in search of divine blessing. In addition, the birth stories of the imams were a practical resource for Shiʿa leaders. The accounts have immense popular appeal, and they have been used in Shiʿa preaching across the centuries.[9]

This chapter explores portrayals of three different aspects of the imams' early lives: their primordial existence, the significance of the maternal connection, and their behaviors in infancy and young childhood. These themes can be found in accounts about all the imams, but this chapter uses the stories of the first, tenth, and twelfth imams as entry points for discussion. Narratives about Imam ʿAli lend themselves particularly well to explorations of the first topic, because his position as the first imam is marked by a proliferation of narratives about primordial existence.

Spiritual Origins: Preexistence and the Conception of Imam ʿAli

"Light is one of the most prevalent representations of Muhammad's prophetic mission," says Uri Rubin in his insightful analysis of *nur Muhammad,* the Islamic concept of divine prophetic light.[10] The notion that this preexistent light was passed down through generations of prophets from Adam to Muhammad is not a distinctly Shiʿa concept. Accounts of Muhammad's reception of the divine light are found in the works of Ibn Saʿd (d. 230/845) and al-Tabari (d. 310/923), as well as in the writings of later Sunni scholars like al-Suyuti (d. 911/1505).[11]

The exact nature of this light is not easily defined. Early descriptions of *nur Muhammad* in both proto-Sunni and proto-Shiʿa works offer little by way of doctrinal explanation, which itself confirms that dogma was not the primary concern. Ibn Hisham's (d. 213/828 or 218/833) biography of the Prophet contains the idea that Muhammad's essence predates the creation of the world, and that it passed through Muhammad's ancestors until it reached him.[12] The idea is often associated with the primordial covenant (*al-mithaq*) between God and his prophets.[13] Rubin observes that the notion of a "spermatic substance" reflects conceptions of heredity and nobility found in pre-Islamic poetry and that, over time, Muslim sources increasingly used light imagery to describe this substance and its transmission.[14] Most descriptions portray God as having created this light prior to the rest of creation. Then, as part of his covenant with his creation, God placed the light into the loins of Adam. The luminous substance was then passed from prophet to prophet (or alternately, through an unbroken line of infallible progenitors) until it reached Muhammad.[15]

This idea was not limited to the Shiʿa, but it had special significance for them. Unlike narratives from other traditions, Shiʿa accounts hold that ʿAli and the imams received and passed on the divine light, the luminous substance that marked and empowered true prophets across time. According to most Shiʿa descriptions, the light was divided between Muhammad and ʿAli. For example, the section on Imam ʿAli in *Establishment of the Inheritance* begins with these words attributed to the Prophet Muhammad:

> ʿAli and I were a light on the forehead of Adam. We were passed along from the pure loins to the chaste pure wombs until we reached the loins of ʿAbd al-Muttalib. The light was then separated into two parts. One part came to ʿAbd Allah and the other part to Abu Talib. I came forth from ʿAbd Allah and ʿAli came forth from Abu Talib.[16]

Light is a recurring image throughout the biographies. It permeates the memories of God's messengers, marking events from their births to their deaths.[17] It is one of many symbolic and literary motifs that link these narratives to the larger hagiographical tradition. In his broad study of Islamic hagiography, John Renard notes several recurring motifs in birth narratives, including dreams in expectation of the awaited birth (Abraham, Moses), emissions of light (Kanuh, Moses), painless childbirth (Muhammad), and speaking infants (Jesus).[18] These themes and many others like them appear frequently in the birth accounts considered in this study, linking the imams to pre-Islamic prophets and placing them firmly within sacred history.

Light imagery is particularly prominent in birth accounts of Imam ʿAli. It undergirds claims about ʿAli's preexistence, his relationship to the Prophet, and his foreordained role as *wasi* ("trustee/inheritor") of the Prophet's divinely appointed authority. In passages like the one above, *Establishment* conceptualizes the entire sacred history of the *wasiya* ("inheritance") as the transference of light. The central understanding of the book is that God created the primordial light of Muhammad and ʿAli before all else and secured its transference from Adam through an unbroken succession of "trustees" (*awsiya'*) to al-Mahdi.[19] Nearly half the work is devoted to listing and describing the trustees of the holy substance and the pure women (the mothers) through whom the substance passed.[20]

The other collective biographies also use light imagery to validate and embellish the stories of the imams. Ibn Shahrashub relied on such imagery throughout his work, and, like the author of *Establishment,* he explicitly stated Muhammad and ʿAli existed as light prior to the creation of the world. Beginning with Muhammad's birth, Ibn Shahrashub recounted narratives from various perspectives in which light is a central feature.[21] The connection between Muhammad and ʿAli is explicit. "ʿAli and I were created from one light," says the Prophet in one account.[22] Other narratives extend the conception of primordial light beyond Muhammad and ʿAli to include Fatima, al-Hasan, al-Husayn,[23] or, in some cases, all fourteen of the infallibles.[24]

Narratives related to ʿAli's conception are particularly fascinating. His similarity to the Prophet is affirmed in nearly every story. When his mother told her husband about the visions seen by Muhammad's mother at the Prophet's birth, Abu Talib replies, "Are you surprised by this? Truly you will conceive and give birth to his trustee and his advisor. . . . Have patience with me for a valiant child, for it will come upon you in the same way, except for the prophethood."[25] Other stories describe ʿAli's transition from primordial light/seed to physical presence in the womb of his mother, Fatima bt. Asad. One story that appears in numerous biographies describes the spermatic substance being transferred directly from a heavenly fruit to the loins of Abu Talib, who then passes the light on to Fatima bt. Asad. In a version found in Ibn Shahrashub's

Virtues, Jabir al-Ansari[26] tells the story of Abu Talib going to see a monk (*rahib*) named al-Mithram b. Daʿib, one of the oldest surviving followers of the true God. Al-Mithram kisses Abu Talib and expresses deep gratitude to God for the encounter.[27] Then al-Mithram informs Abu Talib that he will become the father of the next saint (*wali Allah*), who will be named ʿAli. The story continues:

> Then [Abu Talib] said, "What proof is there of this?" [Al-Mithram] responded, "What would you like?" [Abu Talib] said, "food from heaven, at this moment." So the monk prayed for this and he had not finished his words before a tray arrived with fruits from heaven—fresh dates, grapes, and pomegranates. [Abu Talib] ate some pomegranate and it transformed into liquid in his loins. Then he had intercourse with Fatima and she became pregnant with ʿAli and the earth trembled for days and quaked.[28]

In this narrative, the generative act that created ʿAli occurs prior to sexual intercourse. The essence of ʿAli is transmitted through the fruit to Abu Talib, and the sex act is but a transference of the spermatic seed from one vessel (the father) to another (the mother).

As the story continues, the violent shaking of the earth caused by ʿAli's conception frightens Abu Talib's tribe and topples their idols. Abu Talib takes the opportunity to stand before his people and preach to them about the reason for the quake. He calls them to obedience, saying, "O people, truly God has brought forth the event of this night. He has created in it a man whom if you do not obey him and consent to his rule (*wilaya*) and testify to his imamate, God will not cease [this calamity] that is upon you." The people consent, and the story goes on to describe the moment of ʿAli's birth:

> Fatima went to the house of God [ie., the Kaʿba] and said, "Lord, I am a believer in you and in what has come from you among prophets and scriptures, [and I am] a testament to the words of my grandfather Abraham and thus to the right of the family of this house and to right of the child in my belly whose birth has become easy on me." Then the house opened and she entered it. And then she was with Eve, Mary, Asiya [wife of Pharaoh], the mother of Moses, and others who attended to her as they had at the birth of the Prophet of God.

> When [ʿAli] was born he prostrated on the ground and said, "I testify that there is no god but God; and I testify that Muhammad is the prophet of God; and I testify that ʿAli is the *wasi* of Muhammad the prophet of God; by Muhammad God has sealed the prophethood and by me God has sealed the *wasiya.* I am the commander of the faithful (*amir al-mu'minin*)." Then he greeted the women and asked about their well-being. And the heavens radiated with his light.[29]

The immense importance of ʿAli's birth is clear. It takes place in the most sacred site on earth and is attended by the most virtuous women of history. At birth, ʿAli displays complete knowledge of his mission and its relationship to the Prophet's mission. He greets Eve, Mary, Asiya, and the mother of Moses in a way that suggests a familiarity developed prior to his birth.

Later in the account, ʿAli instructs his father to return to al-Mithram and inform him of his birth, bringing the periscope full circle. When Abu Talib goes to the mountain described by ʿAli to seek out al-Mithram, the monk is dead. He is revived to life long enough to be given the news and responds with tears and gratitude before returning to his burial shroud.[30]

Many of the motifs and thematic elements mentioned in previous chapters are contained in this single narrative. But this account of the fruit tray coming down from heaven to Abu Talib (or, in other versions, Fatima bt. Asad directly)[31] contrasts with birth stories that indicate that the spermatic substance was physically passed from generation to generation beginning with Adam and ending with the imams. *Establishment* contains only the latter story, but all major Shiʿa biographers from about the twelfth century on appear to have been comfortable with the tension, retaining stories that represented both perspectives.[32] The varying theological implications of the two stories do not appear to have troubled the authors. Their scholastic prowess notwithstanding, the biographers were concerned less with theological consistency in these works than with cultivating piety and facilitating its expression.

Different accounts of ʿAli's conception may have circulated among the Shiʿa, but agreement was unanimous that he was born inside the Kaʿba. In his *Book of Guidance,* Al-Mufid commented on ʿAli's birth, remarking,

> He was born in the Sacred House [i.e., the Kaʿba] in Mecca on Friday, the thirteenth day of the month of Rajab, thirty years after the Year of

> the Elephant [c. 570]. Nobody before or after him has ever been born in the House of God, the Most High. [It was a mark] of him being honoured by God, the Most High, may His name be exalted, and of his position being dignified in its greatness.[33]

This passage highlights the concern with identifying dates and locations that serve as reference points for communal devotion. This simple act—the impulse to demarcate times and places where human beings may encounter divine favor—has long been the focus of traditionalist Sunni opprobrium. Ibn Taymiya is particularly famous for his condemnation of popular Shiʿa practices like pilgrimages to the imams' graves.[34] Standard Shiʿa rebuttals of such objections rely on comparisons to the Hajj—comparisons invoked by theologians like al-Mufid, who explicitly defended Shiʿa pilgrimages.[35]

The birth of ʿAli in the Kaʿba also strengthened the first imam's ties to the prophetic traditions of Abraham and Ismaʿil (who are often considered the original founders of the site of worship) and to Muhammad (through whom God restored the Kaʿba to its proper purpose after it had become a place of idol worship).[36] The "house of God," as it was often called in medieval sources, was the central locus of God's engagement with humanity and a symbol of pure, authentic Islam. When Fatima bt. Asad was inside the Kaʿba awaiting the birth of her son, God cared for her. In addition to sending her attendants from among the holy women of history, he also, according to other accounts, sustained her with heavenly fruits.[37] The idols in the Kaʿba are said to have fallen on their faces before her (or alternatively, at the sound of ʿAli's voice from within her womb).[38] For the biographers, ʿAli's birth within the walls of the Kaʿba is a profound and powerful testament that God selected him and his descendants. The image of his birth within the sacred precincts affirms the conviction that the imams have a place at the heart of the prophetic tradition, not on the fringes of it.

Physical Beginning: Mothers of the Imams and the Birth of Imam al-Mahdi

Another unique aspect of the biographies is the care taken to identify the mother of each imam, something rarely found in other medieval Muslim biographies and hagiographies. The birth stories are frequently accompanied by a description of the mother's virtues and background, and at times they include her first-person account of childbirth. The veneration of the imams' mothers as a class displays again the typological logic of the biographies and confirms the importance placed on the maternal figures in these stories.

Not all the mothers are alike, however. One area in which they differ from one another is socioeconomic status and religious pedigree. The mothers of the first six imams were women of high status, but the mothers of the last six imams were not. ʿAli's mother, Fatima bt. Asad, was a Hashimite and one of the first converts to Islam. Fatima al-Zahra, mother to al-Hasan and al-Husayn, was of course the daughter of the Prophet. The mother of the fourth imam, the wife of al-Husayn, is said to have been the daughter of the last king of Persia, Yazdigird b. Shahriyar.[39] The *Establishment* claims that this princess (who is called Jahanshah) and her sister (called Shahrbanu) were captured during the conquests of ʿUmar, who intended to have them sold in the marketplace.[40] ʿAli stopped this from happening, insisting that the daughter of a king could not be sold. He then sought someone to marry them. Al-Hasan and al-Husayn volunteered, and the sisters readily agreed. The story concludes with ʿAli telling al-Husayn to take care of Jahanshah and to treat her well, for she would bear him the "best people of the earth."[41] The mother of the fifth imam, Fatima (known as Umm ʿAbd Allah), was the daughter of Imam al-Hasan. This meant that the subsequent imams were both Husaynid and Hasanid in genealogy or, as Majlisi said, "doubly honored" (*naqib al-tarafayn*).[42] The mother of the sixth imam was a scholar of hadith known as Umm Farwah. She was the daughter of al-Qasim b. Muhammad, a jurisprudent and companion of Imam al-Sajjad, and al-Mufid suggested her mother was also a Persian princess.[43]

The high status accorded these six women is noticeably absent from the lives of the remaining mothers, but the latter are no less praised in the biographies. The mother of the seventh imam (al-Kazim) was a foreign slave (*jariya*) purchased by his grandfather for his father,[44] and the mothers of each subsequent imam, down to al-Mahdi, were also slaves. Rather than ignoring this reality, the authors of the biographies tackle it head-on, seizing the opportunity to emphasize the purity of the women and the unique, divinely ordained nature of the imams' lives. This is particularly the case with the mother of the seventh imam, since she was the first of the mothers to be an *umm walad* (lit. "mother of a son," a term used for a slave who gives birth to her owner's child).[45] In the account found in al-Tabrisi's *Informing Humanity,* Hisham b. Ahmar recalls a story of Imam al-Sadiq sending him out on a very hot day to see an African slave trader. Al-Sadiq describes a slave girl Hisham will find there, but Hisham does not see a slave matching the description. When he returns to al-Sadiq, the imam tells him to go back and look again. Hisham obeys, but when he returns to the slave trader, he once again fails to find the girl. Hisham insists that the man must be hiding someone, and the man says reluctantly, "I have a sick servant girl with a shaved head whom I have not shown." He brings her out, and Hisham recognizes her based on the imam's description. The man tells him to take her, explaining,

> I wanted her [sexually] since I took possession of her, but I wasn't strong enough to prevail upon her. And the man from whom I purchased her also said that he did not have relations with her.[46]

When Hisham relays to the imam what the trader has said, the imam sends him back with a hundred *dinars,* but the trader refuses the money and instead gives her away for free (*li-wajh Allah*). The story concludes with a proclamation from the imam that the girl "will give birth to a child for whom there is no barrier between him and God."[47] It makes it clear that al-Kazim's mother was chosen by God for the purpose of giving birth to the imam, and that her virginity was protected for this purpose. She was a pure vessel, counted among the great mothers of the trustees (*awsiya'*). Similar accounts can be found that validate and defend the purity of the other *umm walad* mothers of the imams.[48]

The story of al-Mahdi's mother, another *umm walad,* is particularly interesting. Usually called Narjis, the twelfth imam's mother was a slave, but she was not purchased from a slave trader. She was born to a slave who served in the house of Hakima, the daughter of Imam al-Jawad. The *Establishment* tells her story as follows:

> The trustworthy from among our teachers have reported that one of the sisters of Abu al-Hasan ʿAli b. Muhammad [Imam al-Hadi] owned a slave girl who was born in her house and over whom she had authority named Narjis. When she matured and filled out Abu Muhammad [al-ʿAskari] came upon her and looked at her and she was pleasing to him. Then his aunt [Hakima] said to him, "I see you are looking at her." And he said, "I have not looked at her except with delight." And the noble birth from God—the great and most high—is through her.[49]

In these stories, the honor and integrity of Hakima provides an aura of purity around Narjis, and the al-Mahdi's birth story is preserved primarily in Hakima's voice.[50] Most versions, like the one below from al-Tabrisi's *Informing Humanity,* relate that Narjis's pregnancy was unmarked by any physical sign. The infant's father, Imam al-ʿAskari, is nonetheless aware of the pregnancy:

> [Hakima bt. Muhammad b. al-Rida (i.e., daughter of Imam al-Jawad) reported to me and she said]: Abu Muhammad al-Ḥasan b. ʿAli [al-ʿAskari] called on me and said, "Aunt, break your fast with us tonight for in this night, in the middle of Shaʿban, God will reveal the proof (*al-hujja*) and he is the proof of his world." I said to him, "Who is his mother?" He said, "Narjis." So I said to him, "May God make me your sacrifice; there is no sign [of pregnancy] in her." He said, "It is as I said to you."
>
> [Hakima said]: So I came and when I greeted [her] and sat down she began to remove my shoe. She said to me, "O my lady, how are you this evening?" I said, "No, you are my lady and the lady of my people."
>
> [Then Hakima said]: She did not acknowledge my words and she said, "What?" So I said to her, "Daughter, God most high is going to grant you tonight a boy, head of the world and the thereafter."
>
> [Hakima said]: She felt embarrassed and shy.[51]

Imam al-ʿAskari lived under house arrest for much of his adult life, and he was allowed few visitors. Shiʿa sources maintain that government authorities actively attempted to prevent the conception/birth of the next imam.[52] An invisible pregnancy is an effective counterargument against widespread accusations that al-ʿAskari never fathered a child, and it simultaneously emphasizes God's providence over the imams' offspring.

The story in *Informing Humanity* goes on to say that Hakima wakes up several times that same night to check on Narjis. As daybreak draws near, Hakima feels creeping doubts about the pregnancy, and so she sits and begins to recite the Qurʾan. Her story continues:

> Then [Narjis] woke up in fear and I rushed to her and said, "God's name be upon you." Then I said to her, "Do you feel anything?" She said, "Yes." I said to her, "Collect yourself and your heart, for this is what I said to you."
>
> [Hakima said]: A weakness took hold of me and took hold of her.[53] Then I woke up from the feeling of my lord, then I pulled back the dress from her and there he was prostrated, receiving the earth with his prostrations, so I drew him to me and he was completely clean. Then Abu Muhammad [al-ʿAskari] called out to me, "Bring me my son, Aunt." So I brought [the child] to him and he put his hands under his bottom and his back and put [the child's] feet on his chest. Then he placed his tongue into [the child's] mouth and passed his hand over [the child's] eyes, ears, and joints. Then he said, "Speak, my son." And [the child] said, "I witness that there is no god but God; and I witness that Muhammad is the prophet of God." Then [the child] blessed *Amir al-Muʾminin* [i.e., Imam ʿAli] and [each of] the imams until he came to his father, then he stopped.[54]

Soon thereafter, Hakima leaves. She returns the next day to find the child gone, and Imam al-ʿAskari explains his absence by saying, "we have entrusted him with the one whom Moses's mother entrusted Moses." On the seventh day, Hakima returns again, and al-ʿAskari holds the child as before, putting his tongue into the child's mouth "as if he were feeding him milk or honey." The child repeats the words he spoke before, and concludes by reciting two verses of the Qurʾan (28:5–6).[55]

The case of Narjis is an example of how, in many respects, the mothers of the imams functioned as "holy incubators," saintly vessels with minimal agency in the process of childbirth.[56] Not only does Narjis seem to have had no knowledge of her own pregnancy, her role in the birth is completely overshadowed by al-ʿAskari, who guides his wife and aunt through the mysterious and miraculous event and bonds closely with his infant son.[57]

All of the mothers are relatively passive in their roles as carriers of the holy seed, and their significant physical sacrifices are not recorded. The natural process of childbirth—characterized by impure fluids and significant pain—is replaced in the narratives by blood-free, painless births. This is a common motif in ancient literatures,[58] and Shiʿa biographers adopted and further developed it. In the sixteenth century, Majlisi drew upon the authority of al-Kulayni to record this description of the imams' births:

> Whenever a mother of an imam became pregnant, that day she would feel tired and weak and fall into a faint state where she would be given glad tidings by a man and when she awoke, she would hear the voice of a person beside her that she could not see who would tell her that she had become pregnant with one of the best people of the earth and that she was doing a great deed. Afterwards, the weight of her pregnancy would be gone until the ninth month. Then she would hear the sound of many angels and she would see a great light, which only she and the father could see, and when the child came out he would be facing *qibla* and then sneeze three times and then praise God. Each imam was born circumcised, with a cut umbilical cord, and without any blood. The imam also has all of his teeth and all of that day and night the child would shine with a yellow light from his hands.[59]

In addition to erasing the mothers' childbirth experiences, the narratives downplay their roles in nourishing and comforting the infant imams. Instead, the bond between father and child is emphasized. The fathers are often portrayed as the ones who feed the infants, carry them, sleep by their sides, and instruct them.[60] As in the previous account, the father-imams sometimes put their tongues into the infants' mouths, indicating a transmission of spiritual knowledge.[61] The transmission of mystical truth through saliva is a concept seen in other hagiographies as well.[62] In the biographies of the imams, it is often compared to breastfeeding the child, and at times it explicitly takes the place of breastfeeding—thereby erasing another conventional role of the mother.[63] Of course, nursing was not always a role assigned to mothers; wet nurses were quite common. But in any case, the effort to highlight the role of the father-imam in the physical and spiritual nourishment of the child-imam obscured the role of women who participated in that process.[64]

The priority of the father is emphasized in other, more explicit ways as well. According to al-Mufid, the Prophet told ʿAli, "On the Day of Resurrection (all) the people will be summoned by the names of their mothers except our Shīʿa. They will be summoned by the names of their fathers because of their good birth."[65] The presumption behind this statement is that if the identity of the father were known, then the person would be called by that name. By quoting this tradition of the Prophet, al-Mufid echoed a common Shiʿa polemic that all non-Shiʿa were bastards. Al-Baqir is said to have remarked, "All people are offspring of fornicatrices (*awlad baghaya*), with the exception of our Shiʿa."[66] As Etan Kohlberg has pointed out, this accusation was sometimes accepted as literal truth and buttressed with claims rooted in Shiʿa legal thought.[67]

However, to say that the mothers' roles are often obscured does not give justice to the complexity of their portrayals in the biographies. The mothers are frequently shown to have been engaged, honored participants in the pregnancies and births. The narratives are often told at least partly in their voices.[68] They commonly have visions or dreams before their pregnancies in which the significance of their roles is announced. Mothers' accounts are presented as legitimate and trustworthy throughout the biographies, which reveals positive assumptions about their integrity, intelligence, and reliability. The biographers went out of their way to praise the mothers' virtues,[69] and stories like that of ʿAli's birth demonstrate that these women played a notable role in constructing and defending the nature of the imamate.[70] Many of the mothers are said to have received knowledge about the divine mission of their child prior to the birth, and their testament reinforces that mission.[71]

Even biographies like al-Mufid's *Guidance,* which does not contain detailed discussions of the mothers, make clear the identity of the women and incorporate them into the overall presentation of the nature of the imams. Attention to the character of a person's mother or maternal ancestor had cultural significance and rhetorical weight. The integrity of an imam depended on the integrity of his mothers' sexuality, as we saw in Chapter 4. Al-Suyuti recorded an instance in which the Prophet clarifies his own maternal heritage, saying, "a whore (*baghiy*) has never given birth to me since I came out of Adam's loins."[72] A common perspective underlying these stories was summed up in the twelfth-century by

Muhammad b. Mahmud al-Tusi, who said, "There are also good women: they are few, but the existence of the world depends upon them: they give birth to great men."[73] This is the flip side of praising the imams' mothers: deriding those of opponents. An example cited in Chapter 3 is apropos: after al-Mufid related that the wife responsible for poisoning Imam al-Hasan later married a man from the family of Talha, he noted, "Whenever any argument occurred between them and the clans of Quraysh, they would revile them saying: 'Sons of a woman who poisons her husbands.' "[74]

In summary, stories of the imams' mothers bolster the leaders' credentials and affirm the latter's right to authority while simultaneously reinforcing cultural assumptions about the sanctity of motherhood and the relationship between a mother's honor and that of her child. The mothers of the imams are highly revered in this literature, which presumes them to be, or explicitly defends them as, virtuous, pure, and blameless. Their virtue is determined by their sexual purity, and guarding that purity is their most valued achievement. Class and race do not determine their worth; despite vast differences in circumstances and backgrounds, each is honored as the mother of an imam, a blessing bestowed upon only the most deserving of women.[75]

Out of the Mouths of Babes: The Child-Imam, al-Hadi

The final aspect of the imams' early lives considered here is their preternaturally precocious development. As seen in the birth narratives quoted above, the infant imams are regularly described as having powers of speech and knowledge of religion at the moment of birth.[76] At times, as in the birth account of ʿAli at the beginning of this chapter, the imams exhibited fully developed language skills, knowledge, and reason. In other cases, like the narrative of al-Mahdi, the infant imams display more limited faculties and linguistic ability, often connected to the exchange of saliva with the father and the declaration of the *shahada*. In *Establishment of the Inheritance*, following the story al-Mahdi's birth, Hakima describes returning to al-ʿAskari's house after forty days to find that the young imam was walking on his own. He is described as having a most beautiful face and speaking in the most eloquent language.[77] Upon seeing him, Hakima proclaims, "My lord! Do you see what I see of his power yet he is only forty days old!?" Imam al-ʿAskari smiles and responds, "My aunt, I told you that we are the company of the trustees (*maʿashir al-awsiyaʾ*). We grow in a day as others grow in a week; and we grow in a week as others grow in a month; and we grow in a month as others grow in a year."[78]

Similarly, the story of the tenth imam, al-Hadi, is another excellent reference point for exploring the imams' childhood development. *Establishment* affirms that his birth was "like that of his fathers," and that he was born from a pure mother, a slave named Sumana[79] about whom Imam al-Hadi later says, "My mother knows of my rights; she is from among the people of heaven."[80] Immediately after the birth narrative, *Establishment* proceeds to a story about the young child and his father, Imam al-Jawad, as the latter prepares to go on a trip. The father asks his two sons what they would like him to bring them. Al-Hadi replies, "a sword like fire;" while his brother, Musa, asks for house cushions. The father responds, saying, "Abu al-Hasan [al-Hadi] is like me, and he [Musa] is like his mother."[81] Once again, the presumption of idealized masculinity is entwined with the claims to the imamate. Not long after the events of this story, Imam al-Jawad is killed, and al-Hadi becomes imam of the community at approximately seven years of age.

The stories of the imams' childhoods, like the stories of their adult lives, are informed by many social and religious debates, including the nature of the imamate, legitimacy and authority in the Muslim community, and the content of public memory.[82] One recurring anecdote that appears in relation to many of the imams pertains to their supernatural awareness of the imamate entering them at the moment of their fathers' deaths. In the case of al-Hadi, this occurred when he was still a child. *Proofs of the Imamate* describes a gathering of women in the family during which the young al-Hadi suddenly becomes frightened and climbs into his grandmother's lap. When asked what is wrong, he replies, "I swear by God that my father has died at this hour." Witnesses record the date, and when they later receive news of al-Jawad's death, they are able to confirm the veracity of al-Hadi's claim.[83] This story reinforces the ontological reality of the imamate and functions as further proof to the community that al-Hadi was indeed the chosen successor of his father; the child and those nearest him were certain of this fact.

Other narratives from al-Hadi's youth reveal the overlap of religion and politics in this literature more clearly. *Establishment* paints a picture of ruling authorities who constantly seek to undermine the family of the Prophet. Muhammad b. Saʿid relates that after al-Hadi's father dies, a government official (ʿUmar b. al-Faraj al-Murakhaji) is sent to Medina on a mission to eliminate the Shiʿa community. His plan is to place the education of the child-imam in the hands of someone extremely erudite but antagonistic toward the Shiʿa, and after consulting people in Medina, he chooses a stern man named Abu ʿAbd Allah (known as al-Junaydi). The teacher is given a slave girl as compensation and entrusted with the task of educating al-Hadi in a way that will put an end to the imams' community.

The plan backfires, however, when al-Junaydi finds the child-imam more knowledgeable than himself. The teacher tells Muhammad b. Saʿid, "By God, I teach him a portion of literature in which I think I have excelled, then he dictates to me the section which follows it! The people think that I am teaching him, but by God, I am learning from him!" Several days later, the teacher says once again:

> By God, he is the best of all people and the most virtuous of God's creation. Often upon entering I say to him, "Look and read your tenth." Then he says to me, "Which *suras* do you want me to read?" I tell him: "from the long *suras* in which you have not excelled." He takes them, reading more perfectly than I've ever heard from anyone.

Muhammad b. Saʿid then adds that al-Hadi "was certain [of the meaning] of the best Psalms of the Prophet David, applying the proverbs from his reading." Finally, driving the point home, al-Junaydi exclaims, "His father died in Iraq, and he was a small boy in Medina who grew up among black slaves. So where did he learn this?!" The story ends by saying that al-Junaydi became a follower of the imam.[84]

The political and religious commentary in these tales stands out in sharp relief. The passage about Imam al-Hadi's education speaks to the nature of the imamate while critiquing those who plot against the will of

God. In the process, the connection between the imams and the divine guides of pre-Islamic history is strengthened. The works considered in this study portray all of the imams as having high levels of innate knowledge even as children.[85] Even al-Mufid—whose work is considered by most Shiʿa to epitomize reliable, unexaggerated accounts of the imams—claimed that ʿAli embodied "perfection of his intellect, dignity and knowledge of God and His Apostle, despite his youth and his being in outward form still only a child."[86] The biographies explicitly tie claims like this to religious ideas in the Qurʾan that can be traced back to preexisting traditions. The Hebrew Psalms, for example, contain a well-known prayer: "Out of the mouth of babes and nursing infants, You have ordained strength, Because of Your enemies, That You may silence the enemy and the avenger."[87] In the Christian gospels, Jesus recites this passage in response to his accusers.[88] The Qurʾan in turn famously attributes powers of speech to the infant Jesus, saying, "He will speak to people in the cradle."[89] This passage is regularly cited in the biographies whenever an infant imam speaks, and al-Mufid's claim about ʿAli's youthful abilities is introduced by a reflection on Jesus's speech from the cradle.[90]

Once again we see the biographies assigning religious significance to narratives aimed at a community seeking to defend itself and its legitimacy. The fact that multiple imams are said to have inherited the imamate at a young age raised questions about their fitness for leadership, and stories of their preternaturally precocious development helped answer those questions and validate Twelver Shiʿa claims. In fact, the preservation of the imamate in the face of the tender ages, losses, and trials of the imams is cast as evidence of God's clear designation of them. Al-Hadi foiled his enemies' attempts to put an end to his leadership despite his youthfulness, proving in the process that his claims to leadership were authentic. Even as a child, he was more of a man than his contenders. By connecting this account to the preexisting prophetic tradition, the biographers met the broader community's need for legitimacy, confidence, and inspiration.

Conclusion

The birth accounts of the imams are meant to inspire awe and to demonstrate that the imams were ordained by God to be followed. The stories give meaning to their followers' devotion, and they make that devotion comprehensible. The legitimacy of these twelve men is tethered to an accepted discourse about the prophetic light created by God and passed down through countless generations of pure mothers and fathers.[91] Images of light appear in the birth stories of all the imams, representing a light created by God prior to the creation of the world.

The birth of each imam is depicted as a momentous event of universal relevance that reveals the ontological reality of the imamate as a timeless institution. The cosmic significance is emphasized not only with light imagery, but through other signs and wonders that occur when the imams are conceived or born. Many of these signs connect the imams to popularly known stories of Muhammad and the pre-Islamic prophets, further buttressing the biographers' claims. Muhammad was preceded by divinely appointed prophets who guided humanity, and the imams were ordained to fill a similar role after him. The similarities between their births and the births of the messengers who came before them make this clear. These narratives make loyalty to the imams sensible, even those imams who were only children when the mantle of the imamate passed to them.

Several specific functions of the birth narratives are worth highlighting. First, the biographers were clearly concerned with the lingering question of succession. Ultimately, each imam's claim to the imamate was contested, not just that of ʿAli. Even as the collective biographies were written, the existence of non-Twelver Shiʿa groups meant that the right to leadership of all twelve imams had to be defended. The birth accounts suited this purpose by providing signs that each imam was the designated heir of the *wasiya*. Reinforcing the legitimacy of this group of imams was also a way of reinforcing the legitimacy of their followers. The biographers, then, were engaged in the demarcation of communal boundaries: those who did not assent to the rightful claims of these imams were outside the community. The borders of the community were porous (al-Hadi's teacher converted, after all), but they were distinct, and those on the inside had a common identity and a secured eternal destiny.

Yet we must also avoid reading the biographies as nothing more than assertions of their authors' theological or doctrinal positions. Those positions helped trace the dividing lines between communities, but those lines were reinforced by rituals and by the very act of storytelling. By recording the time and place of the imams' births, deaths, and other significant events in their lives, the biographers encouraged communal expressions of piety at those special times and places. Moreover, the stories of loyalty and love that fill the biographies are intimately connected to the piety of a community staking its hopes on the imams' guidance. Such stories lend themselves far better to inspiring devotion than a theological treatise.

Lastly, preoccupation with purity in the birth accounts cannot be overstated. The blemish-free nature of the imams' bodies and the honor of their lineage are emphasized time and again. The sacred spermatic substance and the light of their preexistent nature were transmitted to the imams through an undefiled lineage of fathers and mothers who served as perfect *awsiya'* (trustees). Even stories that disrupt this narrative and speak of more direct transference of the light/seed from heaven to the fathers or mothers of the imams are primarily concerned with the purity of the imamate. The blameless mothers and their bloodless births are the means by which the imams emerged in splendorous light to live and lead in a treacherous world.

Epilogue

> Communities, in the sense in which we are using the term, have a history—in an important sense are constituted by their past—and for this reason we can speak of a real community as a "community of memory," one that does not forget its past. In order not to forget that past, a community is involved in retelling its story, its constitutive narrative, and in so doing, it offers examples of the men and women who have embodied and exemplified the meaning of community.
>
> —*Robert Bellah et al.*[1]

AT A RECENT national conference on religion, I attended a discussion devoted to the topic of sectarian conflict in the Middle East. In a lighthearted moment, a panelist joked that American foreign policy experts don't even understand the difference between Sunni and Shiʿa. We all laughed, but I was also somewhat uneasy, because years of studying Shiʿism have made me increasingly aware of the challenges inherent in making a simple distinction between Sunni and Shiʿa Islam. Policymakers may indeed be ignorant on the matter (something that may be an indictment of those of us who are educators), but how would the panelist and audience have described the difference between Sunni and Shiʿa Islam? Is the matter really so simple?

Most Western scholarship on Islam has focused on Sunni Islam, projecting it as the normative version of the religion.[2] Shiʿism has largely been regarded as the "other" version—the less-authentic, sectarian branch of Islam. This conceptualization is rooted in the accidents of history and dictates of geography: early modern Europeans encountered Muslim communities primarily, or at least most directly, through engagements with the Ottomans, who presided over an officially Sunni empire. European access to Shiʿa texts was limited until well into the twentieth century. Much of what was known about Shiʿism, therefore, was apprehended through the lens of Sunni interpretation.[3] Demographic realities have also buttressed the treatment of Sunni Islam as the standard: roughly 85 percent of the global Muslim population identifies as Sunni.[4]

Contemporary scholarly discussions of Shiʿism tend to prioritize one of three aspects of the tradition. The aspect most commonly highlighted is the issue of succession, which frequently serves as a starting point for general surveys of Shiʿism.[5] The issue of who was the rightful heir to the Prophet's leadership over the Muslim community is paramount in Sunni-Shiʿa polemical writings of the classical period. Immeasurable ink was spilled in arguments over the comparative merits of Abu Bakr and ʿAli and other similar debates.[6] Emphasizing the original dispute over succession aligns nicely with a straightforward reading of classical Muslim sources, which often linger on that controversy. It also provides a manageable account of Shiʿa origins: a succinct explanation that frames the Sunni-Shiʿa split as a succession dispute that led to the evolution of separate religious communities.[7] Whether it is possible to trace key Shiʿa or Sunni concepts back to that crisis of leadership is debatable, but the dispute continues to be invoked to explain the division.[8] Explaining Shiʿism in this way, however, sheds little light on the dynamics of Sunni-Shiʿa relationships through most of history, and even less so today.

Other scholars take a slightly different approach to explaining the nature of Shiʿism, one that privileges the propositional and normative discourses within the tradition, especially theology and law. Marshall Hodgson traced Shiʿism's origins to the teachings of the sixth imam, Jaʿfar al-Sadiq.[9] Etan Kohlberg, who has produced some of the most formative work in the field of Shiʿa studies, emphasizes theological developments in the ninth and tenth centuries, highlighting the doctrine of the occultation (*ghayba*), which maintains that the twelfth and final imam is in a state of semipermanent hiding.[10] Despite differences in emphases, both scholars effectively define Shiʿism as a set of beliefs, and their approach remains prominent among those who study early and classical Shiʿism.[11]

A third approach to Shiʿism may be discerned in the work of a few scholars whose methods are influenced by the overlapping insights afforded by the disciplinary theories of sociology and anthropology. These studies generally emphasize distinctive Shiʿa practices and rituals. The most prominent and frequently discussed rituals are those that commemorate the death of the third imam, al-Husayn. The public rituals performed on ʿAshuraʾ have come to symbolize Shiʿa difference, and they have often served as the flashpoint of many Sunni-Shiʿa conflicts.[12] Some scholars have invoked the importance of these rituals in support of the conception that the martyrdom of al-Husayn at Karbalaʾ was the seminal event from which Shiʿism emerged.[13]

There is no universal agreement on how best to understand the difference between Sunni and Shiʿa forms of Islam. Each of the above three ways of describing the nature of Shiʿism has its own merits and shortcomings,[14] and there remain other ways the issue can be approached.[15] Much of the question turns on how we define religion, and how we assess the role it plays in communal identity. Scholars of religion define religion differently for different purposes, and in this study, I have emphasized the conception of religion as a community of memory. Eric Hobsbawm once noted that, "To be a member of any human community is to situate oneself with regard to one's (its) past, if only by rejecting it."[16] Twelver Shiʿa conceptions of the past are profoundly shaped by stories of the imams. In many real ways, the biographies attempt to define what it means to be Shiʿa. This is not to say that the biographies are situated at the historical origin (if such can be identified) of Shiʿism. Rather, they shed light on a different question: how did Shiʿism come to be *understood* (by Shiʿa and non-Shiʿa) as something distinct? Or, perhaps more broadly: how and why did the two fundamental categories of "Sunni" and "Shiʿa" come to be seen as oppositional analogues?

The terms Sunni and Shiʿa exist today in reciprocal relationship, and any attempt to understand one is simultaneously a journey into the other.[17] Unfortunately, the tendency to see Sunni as the normative (natural) form of Islam means that there have been comparatively fewer efforts to delineate the origins of Sunnism as a sectarian category.[18] But leaving that aside, the biographies of the imams may give us insight into the development of a distinct religious group. Social boundaries are not created in a vacuum; they are closely connected to historical narratives and to the stories of individuals who play a role in those narratives. If we consider Twelver Shiʿism to be a community of believers who share a common relationship to the twelve imams, then stories of those imams serve as reliquaries of social memory that mark the boundaries between communities, namely between Sunni and Shiʿa communities. These stories help make certain practices and beliefs sensible, and make them feel appropriate. The very rituals and doctrines that are evoked to explain the distinctness of Shiʿism are made thinkable and compelling by the stories of the imams. And yet, religious differences are never simple or static: like all social boundaries, the line of division between Sunni and Shiʿa is constantly in flux. Thus, with each biography of the imams, we have a window into how religious boundaries were negotiated by prominent Shiʿa thinkers at a certain point in history.

The complete development of Shiʿa stories of the imams still deserves further research. The collective biographies in particular have not been sufficiently studied as a literary genre distinct from the closely related genres of hadith, history, prosopography, and hagiography. The biographies clearly exhibit unique structural and thematic patterns, and they produce and conform to their own norms and expectations. Grouping these texts into a genre allows us to better discern the moods and motivations of this literature and the way it crafts a comprehensive vision of the holy lives and purpose of these men. If we take seriously the understanding that, in the tenth to twelfth centuries, Shiʿism was still in the process of becoming a distinct community of memory, then these texts reflect formative socioreligious concerns of that gradually solidifying Twelver Shiʿa identity.

Reflecting back on the themes and motifs of the biographies, we can see some of the ways in which a distinct Shiʿa orientation to the past was developing. The imams' exceptional births, the miracles they performed, and the betrayals they suffered are critical components of that vision. Moreover, the narratives evoke communal responses, a phenomenon seen most clearly in the stories of weeping and mourning. By recording lamentation in so many forms and circumstances, the biographers went directly against the grain of their times, when excessive weeping and mourning were deemed inappropriate activities in which only irrational women would engage. The imams and their followers, however, wept at every turn—a contrast that helped demarcate Shiʿa identity. Weeping, wailing, and mourning were presented as appropriate communal performances, and such performances made the differences between communities public and visible. The biographers played a role in broadcasting difference by asserting the appropriateness of specific responses to the imams and their stories. They staked the religious claims of the Shiʿa community on the cosmic meaning and eternal relevance of the imams' lives. This gave critical importance to the act of remembering their stories.

The recurring theme of betrayal sheds unique light on the relationship between the community and the stories. The Shiʿa biographers wrote for people who felt threatened, and the betrayals experienced by the imams reflect a sense of the alienation those communities experienced and feared. Underlying the imams' biographies is a pervasive sense of social anxiety. The dramatic martyrdom of al-Husayn at Karbalaʾ may be the most famous injustice suffered by a descendant of the Prophet, but all the imams suffered at the hands of traitors, as Muhammad had before them. The Prophet, the imams, and the Shiʿa community itself were irrevocably connected by their collective experience with treachery. The *ahl al-bayt* had been deprived of their rights by an unjust order, and the rights of the community continued to be trampled. The biographers sought to stake out the boundaries of their own community and to warn members about treachery lurking without and within. They did this by emphasizing the fateful cycle of the imams' lives, which functioned as a reminder to the faithful of the dangers posed by others.

But the imams were not merely portrayed as victims who were subject to the unjust actions of others. The biographers portrayed the imams as strong, beautiful, learned, and pious. They were the best and most capable of all men. This inherent tension is reflected in the imams' physical bodies, which were sites of both intense devotion and great anxiety. The tension impacted how the imams' masculinity was constructed and how it functioned in the broader discourse of these works. The inherent contradiction between being God's chosen men for the imamate and yet lacking temporal authority functioned as another analogue of the Shiʿa community. The biographers offset the emasculating position of victimhood by showcasing the imams' masculine capabilities and miraculous talents. The thaumaturgic powers of the imams enabled them to transcend the restrictions placed on their bodies, thus providing readers with a demonstration of the imams' true power and authority.

History, faith, and community are combined to highest effect in the imams' birth stories, which are replete with symbolism and imaginative flourishes but still highlight concrete, practical concerns. God chose the imams before the beginning of time for their integral role as preservers and leaders of humanity and the material world. Narratives of the imams' entrances into the world emphasize their physical and spiritual ties to the entire prophetic tradition of divine guidance from Adam to Muhammad. The earth trembled at their presence, and miraculous events validated their roles as heirs to the Prophet's authority. Such validation was critical to the legitimacy of this particular lineage of men, as it distinguished the Twelver community from other, erroneous groups (Shiʿa or otherwise) that might claim authority. The divine light of the imamate was transferred from father to mother to infant imam in ways that dazzle, inspire, and demand loyalty.

Communal constructions of history through storytelling and the systems of meaning that emerge from this process regulate what is asserted about the past. The biographies of the imams, with all their idiosyncrasies and unique features, are examples of this social memory. The fantastical nature of many of the stories discussed in this study could lead some to presume that Shiʿa writers were especially prone to altering historical accounts to suit their purposes and bolster their belief systems. But this phenomenon is not unique to Shiʿism. By cross-referencing similar stories in other traditions (Islamic and otherwise), I have attempted to be mindful that all communities manipulate the past. There is no unbiased telling of history. The alternative historical perspectives enshrined within the biographies were meaningful precisely because of the relative marginalization of the Shiʿa community from broader circles of influence. The flourishing of stories of the imams suggests they were an effective form of self-defense against a perceived attack on the community's "constitutive narrative"[19] and treasured ideals. Although there are examples of Sunni-Shiʿa cooperation throughout the medieval and modern periods—not to mention contexts in which Shiʿa scholars have had privileged access to rulers or became political leaders themselves—these biographies enshrine a deep suspicion of, and alienation from, reigning institutions of power. The endurance of these biographies suggests the concerns of the authors have continued to resonate with, and shape the views of, generations of followers of the imams.

APPENDIX 1

The Fourteen Infallibles: A Quick Guide

For those unfamiliar with Shiʿa stories of the imams, keeping track of the names and identities of the infallibles can be arduous. As we have seen, this group includes the Prophet and his daughter Fatima along with the imams. It seems prudent, therefore, to provide a brief introduction to each of these individuals here for reference purposes. I am providing below the extended form of each person's name, along with his or her most famous honorifics, generally agreed-upon death dates, and a brief note about historical context. Throughout the book, I have consistently used one name for each individual, and I indicate that name in bold here for easy reference. Some of the useful secondary literature on each person is provided in the endnotes.

Traditional Arabic names contain several components. In addition to one's proper name (*ism*), such as Muḥammad, Fāṭima, or al-Ḥasan, most individuals were given a *kunya* (patronymic, beginning with Abū ["father of"] or Umm ["mother of"]), a *nasab* (indicating lineage, each generation being connected with *ibn* ["son of"] or *bint* ["daughter of"]), and a *nisba* (adjectival indicator typically specifying one's place of origin, such as "Egyptian," or vocation, such as "bookseller"—rarely used for the imams and therefore excluded from the present list with the notable exception of the eleventh imam). Further, some individuals, particularly those of social prestige, were provided with a *laqab* (honorific nickname)—sometimes several of them. I have provided the *kunya* of each of the infallibles in parentheses. Many of the classical Shiʿa sources use an imam's *kunya* as the preferred name of reference. Later medieval and modern sources tend to prefer the imams' *laqab,* the most famous of which I've provided after each *nasab.* My own choice for which name to adopt for consistent reference in this study (those indicated in bold) relates to the names I felt were most commonly used in contemporary Shiʿa discourse or, in some cases, the name which I felt would best limit confusion for readers.

Prophet (Abū al-Qāsim) **Muḥammad** b. ʿAbd Allāh b. ʿAbd al-Muṭṭalib, al-Amīn (d. 11/632): the Prophet of Islam. He is said to have begun his mission in Mecca and established the first Muslim community in Medina in 622.[1]

Daughter of the Prophet (Umm Abīha) **Fāṭima** bt. Muḥammad, al-Zahrāʾ (d. 11/633): the daughter of Muḥammad. Fāṭima is unique in her position at the nexus of the Prophet's family; in addition to being his daughter she is the husband of Imam ʿAlī and mother of Imams al-Ḥasan and al-Ḥusayn. She lived most of her life in Medina and died just a few months after her father.[2]

First imam (Abū al-Ḥasan) **ʿAlī** b. Abī Ṭālib, Amīr al-Muʾminīn (d. 40/661): nephew and son-in-law of the Prophet. The Shiʿa generally adhere to a belief in his rightful inheritance of the Prophet's authority. Mainstream Sunni positions hold him to be the fourth of the "rightly guided" caliphs, ruling from 656–661. He spent most of his final years trying to secure his unified leadership over the emerging empire but was assassinated without having achieved complete success.[3]

Second imam (Abū Muḥammad) **al-Ḥasan** b. ʿAlī b. Abī Ṭālib, al-Ṣibt (d. 49/669–670): grandson of the Prophet and son of ʿAlī and Fāṭima. After his father's death, al-Ḥasan made a treaty with the main rival leader, the Umayyad caliph Muʿāwīya (d. 60/680). Al-Ḥasan spent the rest of his years in relative quiet in Medina.[4]

Third imam (Abū ʿAbd Allāh) **al-Ḥusayn** b. ʿAlī b. Abī Ṭālib, al-Shahīd (d. 61/680): brother of the second imam and famed martyr at Karbalāʾ. After his brother's death and the death of Muʿāwīya, al-Ḥusayn and seventy-one of his companions were killed by Umayyad forces on their way to meet supporters in Kūfa.[5]

Fourth imam (Abū Muḥammad)[6] ʿAlī b. al-Ḥusayn b. ʿAlī b. Abī Ṭalib, **al-Sajjād,** Zayn al-ʿĀbidīn (d. 94–95/712–714): son of the third imam. After the events at Karbalāʾ, he lived quietly, mostly in Medina, for his remaining years. Toward the end of his life he witnessed the Umayyad transition from Sufyānid to Marwānid lines of leadership as well as an array of unsuccessful anti-Umayyad rebellions.[7]

Fifth imam (Abū Jaʿfar) Muḥammad b. ʿAlī b. al-Ḥusayn, **al-Bāqir** (d. 117/735):[8] son of the fourth imam. He also lived a fairly quiet life in Medina, following his father's example of refusing to support any anti-Umayyad uprisings. Apparently taking an interest in the emerging discipline of hadith transmission, he gained a reputation as an important teacher.[9]

Sixth imam (Abū ʿAbd Allāh) Jaʿfar b. Muḥammad b. ʿAlī, **al-Ṣādiq** (d. 148/765): son of the fifth imam. From his home in Medina, al-Ṣādiq followed the tradition of his father as a teacher. Although he is not known to have made any attempts at political power, he is often seen as a key figure for bringing attention to this particular lineage of descendants of the Prophet. He lived through the fall of the Umayyad Empire and the establishment of rule of the ʿAbbāsid caliphs.[10] Twelver Shiʿa legal traditions are often referred to as "Jaʿfarī" law, on account of al-Ṣādiq's influence.

Seventh imam (Abū al-Ḥasan)[11] Mūsá b. Jaʿfar b. Muḥammad, **al-Kāẓim** (d. 183/799): son of the sixth imam. Al-Kāẓim inherited leadership over an increasingly fractured group of followers and spent his energies trying to secure his authority through his teachings. ʿAbbāsid rulers were often suspicious of him and arrested him on occasion. Eventually, the Caliph Hārūn al-Rashīd kept him permanently under arrest, mostly in Baṣra and Baghdad until his death.[12]

Eighth imam (Abū al-Ḥasan) ʿAlī b. Mūsá b. Jaʿfar, **al-Riḍá** (d. 203/818): son of the seventh imam. The eighth imam spent most of his life in Medina but eventually attracted the interest of ʿAbbāsid caliph al-Maʾmūn

(d. 218/833), who appears to have planned to appoint al-Riḍá as successor of the empire. The imam was killed before this came to fruition.[13]

Ninth imam (Abū Jaʿfar) Muḥammad b. ʿAlī b. Mūsá, **al-Jawād,** al-Taqī (d. 220/835): son of the eighth imam. He appears to have been a mere seven years old when he inherited the imamate. He too spent most of his life in Medina, though he was obliged to stay in Baghdad for brief periods several times.[14]

Tenth imam (Abū al-Ḥasan) ʿAlī b. Muḥammad b. ʿAlī, **al-Hādī,** al-Naqī (d. 254/868): son of the ninth imam. Like his father, al-Hādī inherited the imamate while still a child himself, probably around the age of eight. He was later forced by the Caliph al-Mutawakkil (d. 247/861) to take up permanent residence in Sāmarrāʾ where he could remain under watch.[15]

Eleventh imam (Abū Muḥammad) al-Ḥasan b. ʿAlī b. Muḥammad, **al-ʿAskarī,** al-Naqī (d. 260/873–874): son of the tenth imam. He grew up with his father in Sāmarrāʾ, living nearly his entire life under house arrest or general surveillance. Immense uncertainty about the imamate ensued following his death.[16]

Twelfth imam (Abū al-Qāsim)[17] Muḥammad b. al-Ḥasan b. ʿAlī, **al-Mahdī,** al-Qāʾim, Ṣāḥib al-Zamān: son of the eleventh imam, whose birth was kept a secret and therefore disputed by many. He is believed to have gone into a temporary *ghayba* (occultation) in 260/873–874 and into a long-term *ghayba* in 329/941. He is generally believed to be continually sustained supernaturally by God in his *ghayba* until the right time for his return at the dawn of the final apocalypse.[18]

APPENDIX 2

Collective Biographies of the Imams: A Genre Survey

In addition to the five works analyzed in this study, I want to draw attention to other early and late contributions to the genre of collective biographies of the imams.[1] I briefly mention here some of the works that fit the genre outlined in this study but upon which I did not focus. In three groupings, there are: (1) the smaller and lesser-known works up to the thirteenth century; (2) works from the thirteenth century through the Safavid period, especially those of al-Bahrānī and Majlisī; and (3) modern works.

Lesser-Known Early Works

There are several works from the first few centuries of this genre that were considered for comparison's sake. Some of them are simply too brief to have been particularly useful to this study, occasionally consisting of no more than a few pages. This includes Ibn Abī al-Thalj's (d. 325/936) *Tārīkh al-aʾimma*,[2] Ibn Khashāb al-Baghdādī's (d. 567/1172) *Tārīkh mawālīd al-aʾimma wa wafīyātihim*,[3] and Faḍl b. al-Ḥasan al-Ṭabrisī's *Tāj al-mawālīd*.[4] Several other important early works focus only on one particular theme throughout the lives of the imams. Such is the case with Ibn ʿAbd al-Wahhāb's (eleventh c.) *ʿUyūn al-muʿjizāt*[5] and Quṭb al-Dīn al-Rāwandī's (d. 573/1178) *Kharāʾij wa-al-jarāyih*,[6] which both center on the miracles attributed to the imams. I also consider al-Ḥasan b. ʿAlī al-Ḥarrānī's (tenth c.) *Tuḥaf al-ʿuqūl ʿan āl al-Rasūl* in this group due to the heavy emphasis on the teachings of the imams,[7] creating a work more closely akin to conventional hadith collections than the genre I am outlining. A few other works overlap significantly in content with the biographies but are structured in alternate fashions. Here I would mention the early work by Naṣr b. ʿAlī Jahḍamī (d. 250/854–855), *Tārīkh ahl al-bayt: naql^an ʿan al-aʾimma al-Bāqir wa-al-Ṣādiq wa-al-Riḍā wa-al-ʿAskarī ʿan ābāʾihim.*[8] Also of note is Abū Manṣūr al-Ṭabrisī's (d. ca. 620/1223) *al-Iḥtijāj,*[9] which preserves many disputations of the imams with their opponents, and Muḥammad b. al-Ḥasan al-Fattāl's (d. 508/1114–1115) *Rawḍat al-wāʿiẓīn,*[10] which addresses many theological and ethical questions of Shiʿism.[11]

Thirteenth Century through the Safavid Period

The genre of collective biographies of the imams continued to flourish after Ibn Shahrāshūb and was masterfully utilized during the Safavid period. These works stand outside the formative stage of the genre, but it is only through these later works that the full impact of the earlier works is perceived. Among the well-known works from this period are: *Maṭālib al-suʿūl fī manāqib āl al-rasūl* by Ibn Ṭalḥa (d. 652/1254);[12] *Kashf al-ghumma fī maʿrifat al-aʾimma* by al-Irbilī (d. 692/1293);[13] *Rāḥat al-arvāḥ* by Shīʿī Sabzavārī (fourteenth c.);[14] *Mashāriq anwār al-yaqīn fī asrār Amīr al-Muʾminīn* by al-Bursī (fl. late-fourteenth c.);[15] *al-Ṣirāṭ al-mustaqīm ilá mustaḥiqq al-taqdīm* by ʿAlī b. Yūnus al-Bayāḍī (d. 877/1472);[16] *Rawẓat al-shuhadāʾ* by Kāshifī (d. 910/1504–1505);[17] and *Tawḍīḥ al-maqāṣid* by Bahāʾ al-Dīn al-ʿĀmilī (d. 1031/1622).[18]

There are two scholars from the Safavid period, however, that deserve particular mention: Hāshim b. Sulaymān al-Baḥrānī (d. 1107/1696)[19] and ʿAllāma Majlisī (d. 1110/1698–1699).[20] The two of them are giants of Shiʿa scholarship from the seventh century whose contributions stand apart for a couple of reasons. First, the sheer magnitude of their contributions was unprecedented. Al-Baḥrānī penned three separate collections on the lives of the imams, each of which was several volumes in length: (1) *Ghāyat al-marām wa-ḥujjat al-khiṣām fī taʿyīn al-imām min ṭarīq al-khāṣṣ wa-al-*

ʿāmm;[21] (2) *Ḥilyat al-abrār fī aḥwāl Muḥammad wa-Ālihi al-aṭhār;*[22] and (3) *Madīnat maʿājiz: al-aʾimma al-ithna ʿashar wa-dalāʾil al-ḥujaj ʿalá al-bashar.*[23] Majlisī also made significant contributions to this genre of literature. His unparalleled collection of Shiʿa hadith, *Biḥār al-anwār,*[24] includes within it several volumes devoted to the lives of the imams. Furthermore, he also composed a more accessible version of the biographies in Persian, entitled *Jalāʾ al-ʿuyūn: tārīkh-i chahārdah maʿṣūm.*[25] Second, though al-Baḥrānī and Majlisī were contemporaries, they represented two distinct geographical settings of the Shiʿa intellectual tradition. The former lived in Bahrain, was heavily influenced by the thought of al-Astarābādī, and is counted among the great Akhbārī Shiʿa of his time. The latter worked closely with the Safavid court in Isfahan and is noted for his role in the persecution of Sunnis and Sufis. Together, they demonstrate the extent to which the genre considered here was a useful and popular literature across the major Twelver Shiʿa subgroups.

Modern Works

The genre of collective biographies of the imams is vibrant and growing to this day. Shiʿa scholars over the last two centuries have continued to reformulate and retell the lives of the imams in this literary form, demonstrating the ongoing utility and relevance of the literature to their religious lives. I have made occasional notes in this book of which formative features of the genre have been retained or changed across time, particularly in contemporary expressions. I give special attention to the works of two scholars due to the weight of their perceived authority among many contemporary Shiʿa. ʿAbbās Qummī (d. 1941), who was the compiler of the hugely popular collection of Shiʿa prayers *Mafātiḥ al-jinān,* also penned an acclaimed two-volume work on the lives of the imams entitled *Muntahá al-āmāl.* It is carefully written in a user-friendly manner and is read among many contemporary Shiʿa. Another work that deserves special mention, though much shorter, is ʿAllāma Ṭabāṭabāʾī's *Shīʿeh dar Islām.* Although this work does not fit the genre exactly and is written as a general introduction to Shiʿism, the author devotes a significant portion of the book to retelling the lives of each of the imams—itself indicative of the central significance of these stories to Shiʿa identity. Furthermore, the work has been translated into English and has been a critical resource for the growing number of English-speaking Shiʿa across the world today.[26]

A few other notable modern works relevant to this study include Sharīf al-Jawāhir's (d. 1897) *Muthīr al-aḥzān fī aḥwāl al-aʾimmah al-ithnā ʿashar;*[27] Hāshim Maʿrūf Ḥasanī's two-volume *Ṣīrāṭ al-aʾimma al-ithnā ʿashar;*[28] ʿAlī Muḥammad ʿAlī Dukhayyil's two-volume *Aʾimmatunā;* Muḥammad Muḥammadī Ishtihārdī's three-volume *Sīrat al-maʿṣūmīn al-arbaʿat ʿashar;* and Mahdī Pīshvāʾī's recent *Sīrah-yi pīshvāyān.* A few scholars have recently expanded further on this genre and produced some truly massive scholarly contributions. In 2009, Mahdī Khalīl Jaʿfar published a sixteen-volume work on the lives of the imams entitled *al-Mawsūʿa al-kubrá li- Ahl al-Bayt.* And Bāqir Sharīf al-Qurashī has recently finished having his biographies of each of the imams collected and translated into English in a fourteen-volume set entitled *The Fourteen Infallibles in the History of Islam.* In a unique modern twist on the genre, Mahmood Davari has put together *Taṣvīr-i khānavādeh-i Payāmbar dar Dāʾirat al-maʿārif-i Islām: tarjumeh va naqd.* In it, Davari has collected and translated into Persian the articles on each of the imams found in EI^2 and added his own commentary and critique at the end of each.[29]

Abbreviations

Primary Sources

Dalā'il	Ibn Jarīr b. Rustam al-Ṭabarī, Muḥammad (attributed). *Dalā'il al-imāma.* Beirut: Mu'assasat al-Aʿlamī lil-Maṭbūʿāt, 1408/1988. Other editions, where indicated: *Dalā'il al-imāma,* (Qum: Mu'assasat al-Baʿtha, 1413 [1992–1993]); *Dalā'il al-imāma,* (Najaf: Manshūrāt al-Maṭbaʿah al-Ḥaydarīyah, 1963).
Iʿlām	al-Ṭabrisī, Abū ʿAlī al-Faḍl b. al-Ḥasan. *Iʿlām al-wará b-aʿlām al-hudá.* Edited by ʿAlī Akhbār al-Ghaffārī. Beirut: Mu'assasat al-Aʿlamī lil-Maṭbūʿāt, 1464/2004. The biographies of Muḥammad and Fāṭima are translated: *Beacons of Light: Muhammad: The Prophet and Fatimah: The Radiant.* Translated by Mahmoud Ayoub and Lynda Clarke. Tehran: World Organization for Islamic Sciences, 1986/1406.
Al-Irshād	al-Mufīd, Muḥammad b. Muḥammad b. al-Nuʿmanī. *Kitāb al-irshād: fī maʿrifat ḥujaj Allāh ʿalá al-ʿibād.* 2 volumes. Beirut: Mu'assasat Āl al-Bayt li-Iḥyā' al-Turāth, 1429/2008. English translation: *Kitāb al-Irshād: The Book of Guidance into the Lives of the Twelve Imams.* Translated by I. K. A. Howard. London: Muhammadi Trust, 1981.
Ithbāt	al-Masʿūdī, ʿAlī b. al-Ḥusayn (attributed). *Ithbāt al-waṣīyah lil-Imām ʿAlī ibn Abī Ṭālib.* Qum: Ansarian, 1384/2005.
Manāqib	Ibn Shahrashūb, Abū Jaʿfar Muḥammad b. ʿAlī. *Manāqib āl Abī Ṭālib.* 5 volumes. Edited by Yūsuf al-Biqā'ī. [Qum:] Dhawī al-Qurbá, 1421 [2000].

Secondary Sources

ALC	*Arabic Literary Culture, 500–925.* Edited by Michael Cooperson and Shawkat Toorawa. Detroit: Thomson Gale, 2005.

BSOAS	*Bulletin of the School of Oriental and African Studies.*
CHALAP	*Cambridge History of Arabic Literature: Religion, Learning and Science in the ʿAbbasid Period.* Edited by M. J. L Young, J. D. Latham, and R. B. Serjeant. Cambridge: Cambridge University Press, 1990.
CHALUP	*Cambridge History of Arabic Literature to the End of the Umayyad Period.* Edited by A. F. L. Beeston, T. M. Johnstone, R. B. Serjeant, and G. R. Smith. Cambridge: Cambridge University Press, 1983.
CHIr	*Cambridge History of Iran.* 7 volumes. Cambridge: Cambridge University Press, 1968–1990.
DMBI	*Dāʾirat al-maʿārif-i buzurg-i Islāmī.* Edited by Kāẓim Mūsavī Bujnūrdī. Tehran: Markaz-i Dāʾirat al-Maʿārif-i Buzurg-i Islāmī, 1368– [1989–]. Some entries have been translated: *Encyclopaedia Islamica.* Edited by Wilferd Madelung, Farhad Daftary. London: Brill, with The Institute of Ismaili Studies, 2008–.
EAL	*Encyclopedia of Arabic Literature.* 2 volumes. Edited by Julie Scott Meisami and Paul Starkey. London: Routledge, 1998.
EI^1	*The Encyclopedia of Islam,* 1st ed. Edited by M. Th. Houtsma, T. W. Arnold, R. Basset and R. Hartmann. Leiden: Brill, 1913–1936.
EI^2	*The Encyclopedia of Islam,* 2nd ed. Edited by P. J. Bearman, Th. Bianquis, C. E. Bosworth, E. van Donzel, and W. P. Heinrichs. Leiden: Brill, 1960–.
EI^3	*The Encyclopedia of Islam,* 3rd ed. Edited by Kate Fleet, Gudrun Krämer, Denis Matringe, John Nawas, Everett Rowson. Leiden: Brill, 2007–.
EIr	*Encyclopædia Iranica.* Edited by Ehsan Yarshater. London: Routledge, 1983–.
ER2	*Encyclopedia of Religion,* 2nd ed. Edited by Lindsay Jones. Detroit: MacMillan Reference USA, 2005.
GAL	Brocklemann, Carl. *Geschichte der arabischen Litteratur, Zweite den Supplementbänden angepasste Auflage.* Leiden: Brill, 1943–1949.
GAS	Sezgin, Fuat. *Geschichte des arabischen Schrifttums.* Leiden: Brill, 1967–2007.
IJMES	*International Journal of Middle Eastern Studies.*
IQ	*Islamic Quarterly.*
JAOS	*Journal of the American Oriental Society.*
JSAI	*Jerusalem Studies in Arabic and Islam.*

Notes

Prologue

1. Except where otherwise noted, all mentions of Shiʿism in this study are shorthand references to Twelver Shiʿism. For an excellent survey of Shiʿism more broadly, see Najam Haider, *Shīʿī Islam: An Introduction* (New York: Cambridge University Press, 2014).
2. Elizabeth Castelli, *Martyrdom and Memory: Early Christian Culture Making* (New York: Columbia University Press, 2004).
3. Cameron is drawing on Foucault's use of the phrase "totalizing discourse" here: Averil Cameron, *Christianity and the Rhetoric of Empire: The Development of Christian Discourse* (Berkeley: University of California Press, 1991), 2.
4. See especially Mahmoud Ayoub, *Redemptive Suffering in Islam: A Study of the Devotional Aspects of ʿĀshūrāʾ in Twelver Shiʿism* (The Hague: Mouton Publishers, 1978).
5. Khalid Sindawi has done extensive work on many of the individual themes and motifs of classical Shiʿa stories of the imams. Sindawi's work is scattered across an array of academic articles; see the bibliography for a partial list. His work has been very helpful in locating some extra references and identifying some of the concepts present in this literature.
6. For a list of some of the important works of this genre from the formative period and beyond, see Appendix 2. Unless otherwise stated, all references to "biographies of the imams" are meant to refer to the collective biographies of the twelve imams and/or fourteen infallibles.
7. See Chapter 1 for more details on each of these authors, including full citations to my research on them.
8. The importance of this literature is mentioned by Kamran Aghaei, "Gendered Aspects of the Emergence and Historical Development of Shiʿi Symbols and

Rituals," in *The Women of Karbala: Ritual Performance and Symbolic Discourses in Modern Shiʿi Islam,* ed. K. Aghaei (Austin: University of Texas Press, 2005), 10; Kathryn Babayan, *Mystics, Monarchs, and Messiahs: Cultural Landscapes of Early Modern Iran* (Cambridge, MA: Harvard University Press, 2002) [see Part II, especially 161–196, where she discusses stories about the imams in general]; Lloyd Ridgeon, *Morals and Mysticism in Persian Sufism: A History of Sufi-futuwwat in Iran* (London: Routledge, 2010), 1; John Renard, *Friends of God: Islamic Images of Piety, Commitment and Servanthood* (Berkeley: University of California Press, 2008); and Mahmoud Ayoub, *Redemptive Suffering,* 19–22.

9. Etan Kohlberg, for example, mentions al-Mufīd's *Kitāb al-irshād* in his survey of Shiʿa hadith, though he does distinguish it from other types of hadith collections: "Shīʿī Ḥadīth," *CHALUP,* 305. Within Ayoub's *Redemptive Suffering* alone we can see how differently these works have been categorized. He notes four genres of literature that he uses in his work: hadith material (where he lists *al-Irshād* among the works he uses), general historical works (listing *Ithbāt*), martyrdom/*maqātil* works (where none of our key works are listed), and works "relating to *taʾziyah* and *ziyarah*" (where he lists *Manāqib* and *Dalāʾil*) (20–21). So while Ayoub has these works spread out across three different literary genres and does not place any of them in the *maqātil* category, others have placed all of these works solely into the *maqātil* category. Although I argue that the collective biographies of the imams represent their own genre, the works do significantly overlap with all of the genres listed here.

10. The erudite works of M. A. Amir-Moezzi, Etan Kohlberg, and many others cited throughout this study all make excellent use of the biographies of the imams for this purpose.

11. The scholarship of Husayn Modarressi, Maria Massi Dakake, and S. H. M. Jafri is notable in this regard.

12. Renard mentions them to some extent in his *Friends of God,* 148–149.

13. For a survey of this topic, see Anna Taylor, "Hagiography and Early Medieval History," *Religion Compass* 7, no. 1 (2013): 1–14. Compare Felice Lifshitz, "Beyond Positivism and Genre: 'Hagiographical' Texts as Historical Narrative," *Viator* 25 (1994): 95–113.

14. See, for example, Martin Hinterberger, "Byzantine Hagiography and its Literary Genres: Some Critical Observations," in *The Ashgate Research Companion to Byzantine Hagiography.* Vol. 2, *Genres and Contexts,* ed. Stephanos Efthymiadis (Surrey: Ashgate, 2014), 25–48. Compare Taylor, "Hagiography and Early Medieval History," 5–7.

15. Lifshitz, "Beyond Positivism and Genre," 97.

16. Peter Brown, "The Rise and Function of the Holy Man in Late Antiquity," *The Journal of Roman Studies* 61 (1971): 81

17. I place my work within what has been called the "cultural turn" in religious studies, which entails the utilization of a "wide diversity of theories and methods borrowed from poststructuralism: various literary theories, discourse analysis, ideology critique, theories of the construction of the body and the self, feminist and gender studies, ritual studies" (Dale Martin, "Introduction," in *The Cultural Turn in Late*

Ancient Studies: Gender, Asceticism, and Historiography, eds. Dale Martin and Patricia Cox Miller [Durham, NC: Duke University Press, 2005], 9).

18. Collective/social memory studies is a field often traced to the writings of Maurice Halbwachs, especially his *Les cadres sociaux de la mémoire* (Paris: Librairie Félix Alcan, 1925) [new ed., Paris: Presses Universitaires de France, 1952; repr., Paris: Mouton, 1975], and his *La mémoire collective* (Paris: Presses Universitaires de France, 1950) [2nd rev., aug. ed., Paris: Presses Universitaires de France, 1968]. Other scholars, such as Marc Bloch, were also influential in the early development of this perspective. See his "Memoire collective, tradition et coutume," *Revue de Synthese Historique* 40 (1925): 73–83. More recent studies that have built on their ideas include Marie Noelle Bourguet, Lucette Valensi, and Nathan Wachtel, eds., "Between Memory and History," special issue of *History and Anthropology* 2, no. 2 (October 1986): 207–400; Jan Assmann, "Collective Memory and Cultural Identity," trans. John Czaplicka, *New German Critique* 65 (Spring-Summer 1995): 125–133, originally published as "Kollectives Gedachtnis und kulturelle Identitat," in *Kultur und Gedachtnis,* ed. Jan Assman and Tonio Holscher (Frankfurt am Main, 1988), 9–19; Peter Burke, *Varieties of Cultural History* (Ithaca, NY: Cornell University Press, 1997); Alon Confino, "Collective Memory and Cultural History: Problems of Method," *American Historical Review* 102 (1997): 1386–1403; Jan Assmann, *Religion and Cultural Memory: Ten Studies,* trans. Rodney Livingstone (Stanford, CA: Stanford University Press, 2006).

19. This concept is commonly referred to as "collective memory," but some scholars have steered away from this term in favor of "historical memory," "cultural memory," "public memory," or "social memory." In each case, the intended meaning is nearly the same, though occasionally slight differences are sketched: Jacob Climo and Maria Cattell, eds., *Social Memory and History: Anthropological Perspectives* (Walnut Creek, CA: AltaMira Press, 2002), 4, 5. I prefer to use "social memory" for reasons discussed by James Fentress and Chris Wickham, *Social Memory* (Cambridge: Blackwell, 1992), ix–x. See also Jeffrey K. Olick and Joyce Robbins, "Social Memory Studies: From 'Collective Memory' to the Historical Sociology of Mnemonic Practices," *Annual Review of Sociology* 24 (1998): 105–140, esp. 112.

20. The vantage point afforded by such a perspective has recently been helpful to scholars in a wide variety of fields, including history, religion, sociology, anthropology, and philosophy. For a discussion of the general contours of this field of research, see James V. Wertch, "Collective Memory," in *Memory in Mind and Culture,* eds. Pascal Boyer and James V. Wertsch (New York: Cambridge University Press, 2009), 117–137. For other definitions, see Climo and Cattell, *Social Memory and History,* 3–5; Fentress and Wickham, *Social Memory,* ix–xii; Burke, *Varieties,* 45.

21. I have found Burton Mack helpful for thinking beyond how individuals respond to the sacred due to their own personal needs and pressing larger questions about communities and collectives. See his "A Radically Social Theory of Religion," in *Secular Theories of Religion: Current Perspectives,* eds. Tim Jensen and Mikael Rothstein (Copenhagen: Museum Tusculanum Press, 2000), 123–136. Mack also

poses a question that lingers behind this study without being directly addressed: "Why does a group in the process of social formation produce the practices we call religion?" (129).

22. Castelli, *Martyrdom and Memory,* 22–32.
23. Thomas J. Heffernan, *Sacred Biography: Saints and Their Biographers in the Middle Ages* (Oxford: Oxford University Press, 1988), 15–18.
24. On the problem with drawing a clear line between fiction and nonfiction, see Marilyn Robinson Waldman, *Toward a Theory of Historical Narrative: A Test Case Study in Perso-Islamicate Historiography* (Columbus: Ohio State University Press, 1980), 3–19. Compare Cameron's discussion of the problem in relation to Christian hagiographical literatures in *Christianity and the Rhetoric of Empire,* 118–119. On the relationship between rationality and emotion in discourse, see Sara Ahmed, *The Cultural Politics of Emotion* (New York: Routledge, 2004).
25. See, for example, the exploration of this topic in relationship to modern Americans: Dan McAdams, *The Redemptive Self: The Stories Americans Live By* (New York: Oxford University Press, 2006).
26. See Ch. Pellat, "Ḳāṣṣ," EI[2].
27. There is, however, a similarity and even historical overlap that should not go entirely unnoticed. See Mohammad-Djaʿfar Mahdjoub, "The Evolution of Popular Eulogy of the Imams Among the Shiʿa," in *Authority and Political Culture in Shiʿism,* ed. S. Arjomand, trans. and adapt. John R. Perry (Albany: State University of New York Press, 1988), 54–79; Babayan, *Mystics, Monarchs, and Messiahs,* 175–182.

Chapter 1: Setting the Stage

1. Michael Cooperson, *Classical Arabic Biography* (Cambridge: Cambridge University Press, 2000), xi.
2. For example, Ibn Miskawayh (d. 421/1030), a contemporary of al-Mufīd, did exactly this. See, for example, Aḥmad b. Muḥammad b. Miskawayh, *Tajārib al-umam,* ed. D. S. Margoliouth and H. F. Amedroz (Baghdad: Maktabat al-Muthanná, 1914–1919) 2:328. See also the discussion by John Donohue, *The Buwayhid Dynasty in Iraq, 334H./945 to 403H./1012: Shaping Institutions for the Future* (Leiden: Brill, 2003), 171–183, 277–287, 329–334.
3. For a defense of the legitimacy of using the term "orthodoxy" in the Islamic context, see Devin Stewart, *Islamic Legal Orthodoxy: Twelver Shiite Responses to the Sunni Legal System* (Salt Lake City: University of Utah Press, 1998), 45–48.
4. George Makdisi, "The Sunnī Revival," in *Islamic Civilization: 950–1150,* ed. D. S. Richards (Oxford: Cassirer, 1973), 155–168. Marshall Hodgson also noted the problems with using the term "Sunni" in this period. See his *Venture of Islam* (Chicago: University of Chicago, 1974), 1:278–279. Compare Donohue, *The Buwayhid Dynasty,* 277–287, 315–356.
5. See Teresa Bernheimer, *The ʿAlids: The First Family of Islam, 750–1200* (Edinburgh: Edinburgh University Press, 2013).

6. See Donohue, *The Buwayhid Dynasty,* 315–346, where there are numerous examples of various Shiʿa or Shiʿa-friendly individuals found in various social groupings. But the trend toward a Sunni-Shiʿa dichotomy, as Donohue points out, was becoming the norm in Baghdad specifically (347–356).
7. Arent Jan Wensinck, "al-Nasāʾī," EI[2].
8. Mohammad-Djaʿfar Mahdjoub, "The Evolution of Popular Eulogy of the Imams Among the Shiʿa," in *Authority and Political Culture in Shiʿism,* ed. S. Arjomand, trans. and adapt. John R. Perry (Albany: State University of New York Press, 1988), 54–79. Among some non-Shiʿa groups, especially in certain Sufi traditions, ʿĀshūrāʾ continues to be celebrated into the modern period; see Kamran Aghaie, "ʿĀshūrāʾ (Shīʿism)," EI[3].
9. Some scholars use the terms "proto-Sunni" and "proto-Shiʿa" to describe figures who may have predated the solidification of the categories "Sunni" and "Shiʿa," or who may not have self-identified as such. Adding "proto" is a helpful nuance, though it can easily become a simple substitute for the category of Sunni and Shiʿa. I think we would generally do well to avoid using "Sunni" and "Shiʿa" as an identity markers for at least the first four centuries of Islamic history. Instead we can use more descriptive and specific categories, such as pro-Umayyad, *murjiʾa,* ʿAlid-supporter, or Imāmī. I reserve the use of "proto-Sunni" and "proto-Shiʿa" to indicate someone from the first four centuries of Islam that was specifically and nearly unanimously regarded by later Sunni or Shiʿa communities as a representative of their tradition. In this case, for example, "proto-Sunni" would not be used to indicate the "Sunni" nature of the person's views or historical identity, but rather to indicate how that person was viewed and appropriated by later generations.
10. See Rainer Brunner, "SHIʿITE DOCTRINE iii. Imamite-Sunnite Relations since the Late 19th Century," EIr.
11. Donohue, *The Buwayhid Dynasty,* 347–356.
12. Ronald Buckley has provided a useful description of some of the benefits of identifying the themes and motifs of Shiʿa accounts of the imams: Ron P. Buckley, "The Morphology and Significance of Some Imāmī Shīʿite Traditions," *Journal of Semitic Studies* 52, no. 2 (Autumn 2007): 301–334. He also suggests a useful adaption of Vladimir Propp's typology of folktale components. Buckley relies upon three categories: theme (the main abstract plot elements that carry the story), motif (specific ways a theme is manifest in a narrative), and narrative vocabulary (the actual terms and phrases used in a narrative). This typology has been useful for the present study as well.
13. See I. Goldziher, C. van Arendonk, and A. S. Tritton, "Ahl al-Bayt," EI[2]; C. van Arendonk and W. A. Graham, "Sharīf," EI[2]; Kazuo Morimoto, ed., *Sayyids and Sharifs in Muslim Societies: The Living Links to the Prophet* (London: Routledge, 2012).
14. On the different ways this slogan may have been understood, see Patrica Crone, "On the Meaning of the ʿAbbāsid call to al-Riḍā," in *The Islamic World: From Classical to Modern Times (Essays in Honor of Bernard Lewis),* eds. Clifford

Edmund Bosworth, et al. (Princeton, NJ: Princeton University Press, 1989), 95–111.

15. Dimitri Gutas, *Greek Thought, Arabic Culture: The Graeco-Arabic Translation Movement in Baghdad and Early ʿAbbāsid Society (2nd–4th / 8th–10th centuries).* (New York: Routledge, 1998), 5.
16. Gutas, *Greek Thought,* 5.
17. For an overview of *sīra* and *maghāzī,* see Josef Horovitz, *The Earliest Biographies of the Prophet and Their Authors* (Princeton, NJ: Darwin Press, 2002); ʿAbd al-Azīz Dūrī, *The Rise of Historical Writing,* ed. and trans. Lawrence Conrad (Princeton, NJ: Princeton University Press, 1983), 23–41; J. M. B. Jones, "The *Maghāzī* Literature," *CHALUP*; M. J. Kister, "The *Sīrah* Literature," *CHALUP;* M. J. L. Young, "Arabic Biographical Writing," *CHALAP;* Martin Hinds, "al-Maghāzī," EI[2]; W. Raven, "*Sīra,*" EI[2]; Martin Hinds, *Studies in Early Islamic History* (Princeton, NJ: Darwin Press, 1996), 188–198.
18. They overlap to a significant degree and at times appear to be interchangeable, but slight distinctions can be made. Maher Jarrar argues that *maghāzī* is simply a part of *sīra*: *Die Prophetenbiographie im Islamischen Spanien: Ein Beitrag zur Überlieferungs- und Redaktionsgeschichte* (Frankfurt: Peter Lang, 1989), 42–43. Jones is also of this opinion, calling *maghāzī* a "sub-category" of *sīra* ("The *Maghāzī* Literature," *CHALUP,* 344). See also Sean Anthony's comments in the introduction to his translation of the oldest existing work of *maghāzī*: Maʿmar ibn Rāshid, *The Expeditions: An Early Biography of Muḥammad,* ed. and trans. Sean W. Anthony (New York: New York University Press, 2014), xv–xxix.
19. Hinds, *Studies,* 188–198.
20. The most important examples of this genre are al-Zuhri's (d. 124/742) *Sira* and Ibn Hisham's (d. 218/833) redaction of Ibn Ishaq's (d. 150/767) *Sira.*
21. On the relatively short life of *maghāzī* literature, see Jones, "The *Maghāzī* Literature," *CHALUP,* 346. The *sīra* works on figures other than the Prophet tended to be connected with epic narratives, and their authors were even less concerned with historiographical method. See P. Heath, "Sīra Shabiyya," EI[2]; G. Canova, "Sīra Literature" EAL.
22. Asma Afsaruddin, "In Praise of the Caliphs: Re-Creating History from the *Manāqib* Literature," *IJMES* 31, no. 3 (1999): 329–350.
23. Asma Afsaruddin, *Excellence and Precedence: Medieval Islamic Discourse on Legitimate Leadership* (Leiden: Brill, 2002), 1–35.
24. For the degree of overlap between *manāqib* and *faḍā'il,* see R. Sellheim, "Faḍīla," EI[2]; Charles Pellat, "Manāḳib," EI[2]. For other general treatments of *manāqib* and *faḍāʾil* literatures, see Ernst August Gruber, *Verdienst und Rang: Die Faḍā'il als literarisches und gesellschaftliches Problem im Islam* (Freiburg im Breisgau: K. Schwarz, 1975); C. E. Bosworth, "Manāqib Literature," EAL; Afsaruddin, "In Praise of the Caliphs"; Afsaruddin, *Excellence and Precedence.*
25. Reynolds has noted that *manāqib* writings were often the continuation of the *sīra* form of biography under a new name. See Dwight Reynolds, ed., *Interpreting the Self: Autobiography in the Arabic Literary Tradition* (Berkeley: University of California Press, 2001), 39.

26. D. F. Eickelman, "Tardjama: In Literature," EI[2].
27. The earliest extant examples of this are Ibn Sa'd's (d. 230/845) *Ṭabaqāt al-kubrā* and Ibn Sallām al-Jumaḥī's (d. 231/845 or 232/846) *Ṭabaqāt al-shuʿarāʾ*.
28. On collective biographies, see Tarif Khalidi, "Islamic Biographical Dictionaries: A Preliminary Assessment," *Muslim World* 63 (1973): 53–65; Ibrahim Hafsi, "Recherches sur le genre "*ṭabaqāt*" dans la literature arabe," *Arabica* 23, no. 3 (1976): 227–265; and 24, no. 1 (1977): 1–41; and 24, no. 2 (1977): 150–186; Fedwa Malti-Douglas, "Controversy and Its Effects in the Biographical Tradition of al-Khaṭīb al-Baghdādī," *Studia Islamica* 46 (1977): 115–131; Malak Abiad, "Origine et développement des dictionnaires biographiques arabes," *Bulletin d'Etudes Orientales* 31 (1979 [1980]): 7–15; Fedwa Malti-Douglas, "Dreams, the Blind, and the Semiotics of the Biographical Notice," *Studia Islamica* 51 (1980): 137–162; Young, "Arabic Biographical Writing," *CHALAP*, 168–187; Paul Auchterlonie, *Arabic Biographical Dictionaries: A Summary Guide and Bibliography* (Durham, NC: Middle East Libraries Committee, 1987); Ruth Roded, *Women in Islamic Biographical Collections* (Boulder, CO: Lynne Reinner Publishers, 1994); Wadād al-Qāḍī, "Biographical Dictionaries: Inner Structure and Cultural Significance," in *The Book in the Islamic World*, ed. George N. Atiyeh (Albany: State University of New York Press, 1995), 93–122; Wadād al-Qāḍī, "Biographical Dictionaries as the Scholars' Alternative History of the Muslim Community," in *Organizing Knowledge: Encyclopædic Activities in the Pre-Eighteenth Century Islamic World*, ed. Gerhard Endress (Leiden: Brill, 2006), 23–75.
29. The distinction between biographical dictionaries (or *muʿjam* writings) and *ṭabaqāt* was not always made, but here I agree with Chase Robinson on the matter. See his *Islamic Historiography* (Cambridge: Cambridge University Press, 2003), 66–74.
30. Such as Ibn Sa'd's *Ṭabaqāt al-kubrā*.
31. Young appears to have been the first to categorize this literature as prosopography ("Arabic Biographical Writing," *CHALAP*, 170), and Robinson structures his literary categories in this way as well (*Islamic Historiography*, 55–79). R. Kevin Jaques further cemented conceptions of this literature as prosopography rather than biography in his article "Arabic Islamic Prosopography: The Tabaqat Genre," in *Prosopography Approaches and Applications: A Handbook*, ed. K. S. B. Keats-Rohan (Oxford: University of Oxford, 2007), 387–414.
32. See Charles Pellat, "Ḳiṣṣa: 1. The Semantic Range of *ḳiṣṣa* in Arabic," EI[2]; A. Abdel-Meguid, "A Survey of the Terms Used in Arabic for 'Narrative' and 'Story,'" *Islamic Quarterly* 1, no. 4 (1954): 195–204; H. T. Norris, "*Qiṣaṣ* Elements in the Qurʾān," *CHALUP*, 246–259.
33. See Raven, "Sīra," EI[2].
34. See William M. Brinner's introduction to al-Thaʿlabī, *ʿArāʾis al-majālis fī qiṣaṣ al-anbiyā*, trans. and anno. William M. Brinner (Leiden: Brill, 2002), xviii-xix. For an overview of this literature, see Dūrī, *Rise of Historical Writing*, 122–135; William M. Brinner, "Legends of the Prophets (*Qiṣāṣ al-anbiyāʾ*)," *EAL*.
35. T. Nagel, "Ḳiṣaṣ al- Anbiyāʾ," EI[2]. The most important contributions to this genre were by Wahb b. Munabbih (d. ca. 110/728), Ishaq b. Bishr (d. 206/821), al-Thaʿlabi (d. 427/1035–6), and al-Kisaʾi (d. tenth cent.)

36. See Ignaz Goldziher, *Muslim Studies,* ed. S. M. Stern, trans. C. R. Barber and S. M. Stern (London: Allen & Unwin, 1967–71), vol. 2, chap. 5. On the complex perspectives on the use of *qiṣaṣ,* see Merlin Swartz, *Ibn al-Jawzī's* Kitāb al-Quṣṣāṣ wa'l-Mudhakkirīn (Beirut: Dar el-Machreq Éditeurs, 1971), esp. Swartz's comments on 46–60.
37. Robinson, *Islamic Historiography,* 24–30.
38. Afsaruddin, "In Praise," 343–345.
39. Kister, "The Sīrah Literature," *CHALUP,* 362–367; Afsaruddin, "In Praise," 340–342; Afsaruddin, *Excellence and Precedence,* 1–35; Young, "Arabic Biographical Writing," *CHALAP,* 169–176.
40. T. Nagel, "Ḳiṣaṣ al- Anbiyāʾ," EI[2]; Brinner, introduction to al-Thaʿlabī, *ʿArāʾis al-majālis,* xi–xviii.
41. Some notable modern examples of the genre include Sharīf al-Jawāhir's (d. 1897) *Muthīr al-aḥzān fī aḥwāl al-aʾimmah al-ithnā ʿashar* (Najaf: al-Maṭbaʿah al-Ḥaydarīyah, 1966); Hāshim Maʿrūf Ḥasanī's two-volume *Ṣīrāṭ al-aʾimma al-ithnā ʿashar* (Beirut: Dār al-Taʿāruf, 1977); ʿAlī Muḥammad ʿAlī Dukhayyil's two-volume *Aʾimmatunā* (Beirut: Dār al-Murtaḍá, 1982); Muḥammad Muḥammadī Ishtihārdī's three-volume *Sīrat al-maʿṣūmīn al-arbaʿat ʿashar: al-musammá bi-Muntaqá al-durar: dirāsah mūjazah wa-muyassarah wa-hādifah ʿan ḥayat al-maʿṣūmīn al-arbaʿah ʿashar* (Beirut: Muʾassasat al-Balāgh, 2008); and Mahdī Pīshvāʾī's recent *Sīrah-yi pīshvāyān: nigarishī bar zindagānī-i ijtimāʿī, siyāsī va farhangī-i imāmān-i maʿṣūm ʿalayhum al-salām* (Qum: Muʾassasah-i Imām Ṣādiq, 1388 [2009]).
42. ʿAbd al-Jabbār al-Rifāʿī lists over 2,000 works that appear to fit the genre: *Muʿjam mā kutiba ʿan al-Rasūl wa-ahl al-bayt, ṣalawāt ʿalayhim Allāh* (Tehran: Sāzmān-i Chāp va Intishārāt-i Vizārat-i Farhang va Irshād-i Islāmī, 1371– [1992–]), see vols. 9–10. My gratitude goes to Hossein Modarressi for pointing me to this work.
43. See Appendix 2 for a description of other tenth to twelfth century works, as well as a description of later works of this genre.
44. Etan Kohlberg, "From Imāmiyya to Ithnā-ʿAshariyya," *BSOAS* 39, no. 3 (1976): 521.
45. Abū al-Ḥasan ʿAlī b. al-Ḥusayn al-Masʿūdī (d. Jumādá II 345/ September 956). The two monographs on al-Masʿūdī are Tarif Khalidi, *Islamic Historiography: The Histories of Masʿūdī* (Albany: State University of New York Press, 1975); and Ahmad M. H. Shboul, *Al-Masʿūdī and His World: A Muslim Humanist and His Interest in Non-Muslims* (London: Ithaca Press, 1979). Other relevant scholarship on al-Masʿūdī includes *GAL* I, 150–152, S I, 220–221; S. Maqbul Ahmad, "Al-Masʿūdī's contribution to Medieval Arab Geography," *Islamic Culture* 27 (1953): 61–77, and 28 (1954): 275–286; S. Maqbul Ahmad, "Travels of Abū al-Ḥasan ʿAlī ibn al-Ḥusayn al-Masʿudı," *Islamic Culture* 28 (1954): 509–524; S. Maqbul Ahmad and A. Rahman, eds., *Al-Masʿūdī Millenary Commemoration Volume* (Aligarh: Indian Society for the History of Science, 1960); *GAS,* 1: 332–336; Charles Pellat, "Masʿūdī et l'Imāmisme," in *Le Shîʿisme imâmite: Colloque de Strasbourg (6–9 mai*

1968) (Paris: Presses Universitaires de France, 1970), 69–90; Tarif Khalidi, "Masʿūdī's Lost Works: A Reconstruction of Their Content," *JAOS* 94, no. 1 (1974): 35–41; Julie Scott Meisami, "Masʿūdī on Love and the Fall of the Barmakids," *Journal of the Royal Asiatic Society of Great Britain and Ireland* 2 (1989): 252–277; Maria Kowalska, "Al-Masʿūdī's Stellung in Geschichte der arabischen Literatur," *Folia Orientalia* 32 (1996): 115–121; Julie Scott Meisami, "Masʿūdī and the Reign of al-Amīn: Narrative and Meaning in Medieval Muslim Historiography," in *On Fiction and* Adab *in Medieval Arabic Literature,* ed. Philip F. Kennedy (Wiesbaden: Harrassowitz, 2005), 149–176; Maysam J. Faruqi, "Is There a Shīʿa Philosophy of History? The Case of Masʿūdī," *Journal of Religion* 86, no. 1 (2006): 23–54; A. Azfar Moin, "Partisan Dreams and Prophetic Visions: Shīʿī Critique in al-Masʿūdī's History of the Abbasids," *JAOS* 127, no. 4 (2007): 415–427.

46. Ibn Khaldun (d. 808/1406) held this work in high esteem, and it captured the fascination of many modern scholars of Islam. See Ibn Khaldūn, *Tārīkh Ibn Khaldūn: al-Muqaddima,* (Beirut: Dār al-Kitāb al-Lubnānī, 1961), 1:52. See also Muhsin Mahdi, *Ibn Khaldun's Philosophy of History: A Study in the Philosophic Foundation of the Science of Culture* (London: G. Allen and Unwin, 1957), 152–153, 164, 255; W. J. Fischel, "Ibn Khaldūn and al-Masʿūdī", in *al-Masʿūdī Millenary commemoration volume,* ed. Ahmad and Rahman, 51–59.
47. For a list and description of his works, see Khalidi, "Masʿūdī's Lost Works."
48. Khalidi, "Masʿūdī's Lost Works," 40; Pellat, "Al-Masʿūdī, Abū ʿl-Ḥasan ʿAlī b. al-Ḥusayn," EI^2.
49. Muḥammad Muḥsin Āghā Buzurg al-Ṭihrānī, *al-Dharīʿah ilá taṣānif al-Shīʿah*(Najaf: Maṭbaʿat al-Qaḍā, 1936-), 1:110.
50. On this point, Pellat would likely concur. See "Masʿūdī et l'Imāmisme," 69–90.
51. The earliest account ascribing *Ithbāt* to al-Masʿūdī is in al-Najashi's (d. 450/1058) *Rijāl al-Najāshī,* ed. Muḥammad Jawād al-Nāʾinī (Beirut: Dār al-Adwāʾ, 1988), 2:76–77.
52. Despite uncertainty of authorship, the long tradition of attributing *Establishment* to al-Masʿūdī justifies a brief note on his life. *Meadows* and *Notification* contain many autobiographical references that give us insight into their author's life. He was born in Baghdad in the last decade of the ninth century. Al-Masʿūdī's references to various scholars lead us to believe that he studied with some of the most famous intellectuals of the early tenth century, including the historian Wakīʿ (d. 306/918) (al-Masʿūdī, *Tanbīh wa'l-ishrāf,* ed. Michael Jan de Goeje [Beirut: Maktabat Khayyāṭ, 1965], 293); the Imāmī theologian al-Ḥasan b. Mūsá al-Nawbakhtī (d. early fourth/tenth c.) (al-Masʿūdī, *Murūj al-dhahab wa-maʿādin al-jawhar),* ed. Charles Pellat [Beirut: Publications de l'Universite Libanaise, 1965–1979], 1, § 159 and 4 :77, § 2282 [in French: *Les prairies d'or,* trans. Charles Pellat (Paris: Société asiatique, 1962–1997), 1, § 159 and 4, 924, § 2282]; and the Muʿtazilī scholar al-Jubbāʾī (d. 303/915) (al-Masʿūdī, *Tanbīh,* 396). Pellat believes that al-Masʿūdī may also have been acquainted with the famed historian and Qurʾan commentator al-Ṭabarī (d. 310/923), the great Arabic grammarian al-Zajjāj

(d. 311/924), the influential theologian al-Ashʿarī (d. 324/935), and other notable scholars of the period: see Pellat, "Al-Masʿūdī, Abū 'l-Ḥasan ʿAlī b. al-Ḥusayn," EI². In keeping with the scholarly custom of the day, al-Masʿūdī traveled widely: see Maqbul Ahmad, "Travels," 509–521; Shboul, *Al-Masʿūdī and His World,* 1–28. He went to Persia (al-Masʿūdī, *Tanbīh,* 106) and India (al-Masʿūdī, *Tanbīh,* 224) in 915 and later to Syria and Arabia: al-Masʿūdī, *Murūj,* § 3326 [*Les prairies d'or,* 5:1333–1334, § 3326]. In 932 he traveled to Armenia and the Caspian Sea region (al-Masʿūdī, *Murūj,* 1 § 494 [*Les prairies d'or,* 1 § 494]), and from around 941 onward, he made his home in Egypt, where he wrote *Meadows* in 943 (*Establishment* dates to the same year): al-Masʿūdī, *Murūj,* 2:126, § 874 [*Les prairies d'or,* 2:330, § 874]; *Ithbāt,* 231–232). *Notification* was completed some years later in Fustat in 956, the year of his death: al-Masʿūdī, *Tanbīh,* 401.

53. On the importance of the concept of *wasīya* to the early Shiʿa, see Maria Dakake's *The Charismatic Community: Shiʿite Identity in Early Islam* (Albany: State University of New York Press, 2007).

54. His full name is Abū Jaʿfar Muḥammad b. Jarīr b. Rustam al-Ṭabarī al-Āmulī. I am following Etan Kohlberg's example here by referring to him as Ibn Jarīr in order to minimize confusion. See his *Medieval Muslim Scholar at Work: Ibn Ṭāwūs and His Library* (Leiden: Brill, 1992), 141.

55. As Franz Rosenthal has suggested, the confusion of these two individuals may have contributed to misunderstandings regarding the Shiʿa inclinations of al-Ṭabarī. See F. Rosenthal's introduction to his annotated translation of al-Ṭabarī's *The History of al-Ṭabarī,* ed. Ehsan Yar-Shater (Albany: State University of New York Press, c. 1985–2007), 39:13.

56. Notes from Muḥammad b. al-Ḥasan al-Ṭūsī, *Fihrist kutub al-Shīʿa wa uṣūlahum wa-asmā al-muṣannifīn wa-aṣḥāb al-uṣūl,* ed. ʿAbd al-Azīz Ṭabāṭabāʾī (Qum: Maktabat al-Muḥaqiq al-Ṭabāṭabāʾī, 1420 [1999–2000]), 447; al-Najāshī, *Rijāl,* 2:289; and Ibn Shahrāshūb, *Kitāb maʿālim al-ʿulamāʾ fī fihrist kutub al-muṣannifīn minhum qadīman wa-ḥadīthan,* ed. ʿAbbās Iqbal (Tehran: Maṭba Faradīn, 1353 [1934]), 106 (#716); Muḥsin al-Ḥusaynī al-ʿĀmilī, *Aʿyān al-Shīʿa* (Damascus: Maṭbaʿat Ibn Zaydūn, 1353–1379 [1935–1959]), 44:139–40.

57. Ibn Ḥajar al-ʿAsqalānī is one of the few Sunni scholars to mention him, but here too very little is given beyond his name and his Shiʿa affiliation: *Lisān al-Mīzān* (Ḥaydarābād al-Dakkan, Maṭbaʿat Majlis Dāʾirat al-Maʿārif al-Niẓāmīyah, 1331–1339 [1911–1913]), 5:103.

58. *Dalāʾil,* 545. If this were an interpolation added by a later scribe, one would have to wonder why the scribe didn't add similar interpolations to other people in the text.

59. Al-Ṭihrānī, *Dharīʿa,* 8:241–247 and 21:9–10. See also the editorial introduction to *Dalāʾil*'s 1992 edition: Ibn Jarīr al-Ṭabarī, *Dalāʾil al-imāma,* (Qum: Muʾassasat al-Baʿtha, 1413 [1992–1993]), 1–46.

60. Examples: Ibn Shahrāshūb, *Maʿālim al-ʿulamāʾ,* 106 (#716); Mirzā ʿAbd Allāh Afandī al-Iṣbahānī, *Rīyāḍ al-ʿulamāʾ wa-ḥiyāḍ al-fuḍalāʾ,* (Qum: Maṭbaʿat al-khayyām, 1401 [1980]), 5:103; introduction to the 1963 edition of *Dalāʾil* (Najaf: Manshūrāt al-Maṭbaʿah al-Ḥaydarīyah); *GAS* 1:540.

61. ʿUmar Riḍā Kaḥḥāla, *Muʿjam al-muʾallifīn: tarājim muṣannifī al-kutub al-ʿArabīyah* (Beirut: Muʾassasat al-Risālah, 1993), 3:190 (#12593); Kohlberg, *Medieval Muslim Scholar,* 140–141.
62. Examples include Ibn ʿAbd al-Wahhāb (d. fourth/tenth cent.) in his *ʿUyūn al-muʿjizāt* (Beirut: Muʾassasat al-Aʿlamī lil-Maṭbūʿāt, 2004); Abū al-Ḥasan, ʿAlī b. ʿĪsá b. Abī al-Fatḥ al-Irbilī, *Kashf al-ghumma fī maʿrifat al-aʾimma,* ed. ʿAlī al-Fāḍilī ([Iran]: Markaz al-Ṭibāʿa wa-al-Nashr lil-Majmaʿ al-ʿĀlamī li-Ahl al-Bayt, 1426 [2005–2006]), 4:22.
63. On Ibn Ṭāwūs, see Kohlberg, *Medieval Muslim Scholar,* 3–24.
64. On this category, see Hamid Algar, "Čahārdah Maʿṣūm," EIr.
65. Here I am relying upon Gregor Schoeler's terminology and observations about the spectrum of Arabic literature in early Islam. See his *The Genesis of Literature in Islam: From the Aural to the Read,* rev. ed., trans. Shawkat M. Toorawa (Edinburgh: Edinburgh University Press, 2002), 1–15.
66. Even here, however, the portion on ʿAli is lost from our manuscripts of *Proofs,* so we can only assume its section was substantive.
67. See Amir-Moezzi's *The Divine Guide in Early Shiʿism: The Sources of Esotericism in Islam,* trans. David Streight (Albany: State University of New York Press, 1994); or his collection of essays in *The Spirituality of Shiʿi Islam: Beliefs and Practices* (London: I. B. Tauris, 2011).
68. See Hossein Modarressi's *Crisis and Consolidation in the Formative Period of Shiʿite Islam: Abū Jaʿfar ibn Qiba al-Rāzī and His Contribution to Imāmite Shīʿite Thought* (Princeton, NJ: The Darwin Press, 1993).
69. Both al-Bahrānī and Majlisī quote directly from *Dalāʾil* and use some of the content of *Ithbāt* via Ibn ʿAbd al-Wahhāb's *ʿUyūn.*
70. Etan Kohlberg, "Some Imāmī-shīʿī Views on *Taqiyya,*" *JAOS* 95, no. 3 (Jul.–Sep. 1975): 400.
71. Two monographs have been written on al-Mufīd in English: Martin J. McDermott, *The Theology of al-Shaikh al-Mufīd* (Beirut: Dar el-Machreq, 1978); and Tamima Bayhom-Daou's introductory work, *Shaykh Mufīd* (Oxford: Oneworld, 2005). Other helpful scholarship includes *GAS,* 1:549–551; Wilferd Madelung, "Imāmism and Muʿtazilite Theology," in *Le Shiʿisme imamate,* ed. T. Fahd (Paris: Presses Universitaires, 1970), 13–29; S. Waheed Akhtar, *The Early Imāmiyyah Shīʿite Thinkers* (New Delhi: Ashish Publishing House, 1988), 79–122; Wilferd Madelung, "al-Mufīd," EI[2]; Niʿmat Āllāh Ṣafarī Furūshānī, "Shaykh Mufīd va-tārīkh nigārī-yi ou dar *Kitāb al-irshād,*" *A Quarterly for Shiʿite Studies* 5, no. 2 (2007): 7–36; Furūshānī, "*al-Irshād* wa-tārīkh nigārī zindagānī-yi aʾimmah," *A Quarterly for Shiʿite Studies* 6, no. 2 (2008): 37–76; Qāsim Khānjānī, "Mudawwanāt al-Shaykh al-Mufīd wa-qarāʾituhu al-kalāmīya lil-tārīkh" *Turāthunā* 25, no. 97/98 (1430 [2009]): 87–198.
72. *Al-Irshād*: Al-Mufīd, *Book of Guidance,* trans. I. K. A. Howard, pref. S. H. Nasr (London: Muhammadi Trust, 1981).
73. Per Akhtar, *The Early Imāmiyyah,* 96.
74. His full name was Abū ʿAbd Allāh Muḥammad b. Muḥammad b. al-Nuʿman al-Ḥārithī, though he was also sometimes known as Ibn al-Muʿallim ("the teacher's

son"). On the origin of his two honorifics, see McDermott, *The Theology of al-Shaikh al-Mufīd,* 10–12; Akhtar, *The Early Imāmiyyah,* 80.

75. Akhtar, *The Early Imāmiyyah,* 80–81.

76. Ibn Nadīm, *al-Fihrist,* ed. Yūsuf ʿAlī Ṭawīl (Beirut: Dār al-Kutub al-ʿIlmīyah, 2002), 178, 197; English: *The Fihrist of Ibn al-Nadīm: A Tenth-Century Survey of Muslim Culture,* trans. Bayard Dodge (New York: Columbia University Press, 1970), 1:443, 491. On al-Mufid's leadership of the Bagdadi Shiʿa, see also Donohue, *The Buwayhid Dynasty,* 331–333.

77. He studied *fiqh* with Jaʿfar b. Qulūya (d. 369/979–980) and Ibn al-Junayd al-Iskāfī (d. 381/991); theology with Abū al-Jaysh al-Balkhī (d. 367/977–978) and, perhaps, Abū Ṣahl b. Nawbakht; and hadith with Ibn Bābawayh, among others.

78. For a list and description of his known books, see McDermott, *The Theology of Shaikh al-Mufid,* 25–45; Akhtar, *The Early Imāmiyyah,* 88–101.

79. On these two brothers, see Akhtar, *The Early Imāmiyyah,* 123–204.

80. On the institution of *naqīb* among the ʿAlids, see L. Massignon, "Cadis et naqibs baghdadiens," in *Opera minora: Textes recueillis, classés et présentés avec une bibliographie,* ed. Youakim Moubarac (Paris: Presses Universitaires de France, 1969), 1:258–265; L. Massignon, "Naḳīb al-Ashrāf," EI²; Bernheimer, *The ʿAlids,* 51–70.

81. Al-Mufīd had many other prominent students as well. Madelung says, "Virtually all the leading Imami scholars of the following generation were his students" ("Mufīd," EI²). In addition to those listed above, were, notably, al-Shaykh al-Ṭūsī (d. 459–460/1066–1067), al-Najāshī (d. 450/1058), and Muḥammad al-Karājakī (d. 449/1057).

82. Muḥammad ibn Aḥmad al-Dhahabī, *al-ʿIbar fī khabar man ghabar* (Kuwait: Dār al-Maṭbuʿat wa-al-nash, 1960), 3:114. See also McDermott, *The Theology of Shaikh al-Mufid,* 14.

83. Andrew Newman helpfully illuminates this critical intra-Shiʿa debate in *The Formative Period of Twelver Shīʿism: Ḥadīth as Discourse between Qum and Baghdad* (Richmond, UK: Curzon, 2000).

84. On the Nawbakhtī family, see J. L. Kraemer, "al-Nawbakhtī, al-Ḥasan b. Mūsá," EI². On al-Mufīd's connection to them, see McDermott, *The Theology of Shaikh al-Mufid,* 22–25.

85. McDermott comes to this conclusion (*The Theology of Shaikh al-Mufid,* 395–397); and Bayhom-Daou agrees (*Shaykh Mufid,* 83). I am not convinced that al-Mufīd was taking a middle position as much as he was legitimizing rationalist discourse through slight, but emphatic, differentiation with the Muʿtazilīya. In any case, the end result was a dramatic shift among the most influential Imāmī scholars toward thoroughly rationalist—and often, as in the case of al-Murṭaḍá, fully Muʿtazilī—thought.

86. On the relationship between Imāmī theology and Muʿtazilī theology, see Madelung, "Imamism and Mu'tazilite Theology." Although al-Mufīd and his students were relatively successful in utilizing rationalist discourse while remaining distinct from Muʿtazilism, the debate between traditionalists and

rationalists reemerged in later centuries, particularly in the form of legal debates between the *Usūlī* and *Akhbārī* scholars. See Robert Gleave, *Scripturalist Islam* (Leiden: Brill, 2007).

87. McDermott, *The Theology of Shaikh al-Mufid,* 15.

88. On the development of the Sunni schools of law, see Christopher Melchert, *The Formation of the Sunni Schools of Law: 9th–10th Centuries* C.E. (Leiden: Brill, 1997).

89. Hodgson, *Venture of Islam,* 2: 36–39.

90. McDermott, *The Theology of Shaikh al-Mufid,* 17. The story of Abū Bakr in the cave was often cited in debates over his legitimacy as the first caliph (rather than ʿAlī).

91. On these riots, see H. Laoust, "Les Agitations Religieuses à Baghdād aux IVe et Ve siècles de l'Hégire," in *Islamic Civilization, 950–1150: Papers on Islamic History III,* ed. D. S. Richards (London: William Clowes & Sons Limited, 1973), 169–186; Makdisi, "The Sunni Revival," 155–168. For al-Mufīd's role in them, see McDermott, *The Theology of Shaikh al-Mufid,* 16–22.

92. *Al-Irshād,* 1:3–4 (English: xxxvii).

93. Among the non-Imāmī sources that he frequently uses are Ibn Ishāq, al-Wāqidī, Abū al-Farāj al-Isfahānī, and al-Ṭabarī.

94. See S. H. Nasr, in his preface to Howard's translation (*Book of Guidance,* xix); Muḥammad Riḍá al-Jaʿfarī, *Introduction to* Kitāb al-Irshād (Tehran: World Organizations for Islamic Sciences, 2004), 2–5.

95. Al-Dhahabī, *al-ʿIbar,* 3:114–115.

96. Khaṭīb al-Baghdādī, *Tārīkh Madīnat al-Salām wa-akhbār muḥaddithīhā wa-dhikr quṭṭānihā al-ʿulamāʾ min ghayr ahlihā wa-wāridīhā,* ed. Bashshār ʿAwwād Maʿrūf (Beirut: Dār al-Gharb al-Islāmī, 2001), 4:375.

97. For contemporary scholarship on al-Ṭabrisī, see *GAL* 1:513–514, S 1:708–709; Ḥusayn Karīmān, *Ṭabrisī va Majmaʿ al-bayān* (Tehran: Dānishgāh-i Tihrān, 1340–1341 [1961–1962]); Musa O. A. Abdul, "The Unnoticed *Mufassir* ShaykhṬabarsī," *IQ* 15 (1971): 96–105; Abdul, "The *Majmaʿ al-Bayān* of Ṭabarsī," *IQ* 15 (1971): 106–120; Abdul, *The Qurʾan: Shaykh Tabarsi's Commentary* (Lahore: Hafeez Press, 1977); al-Ṭihrānī, *al-Dharīʿa,* 2:240–242, (#957) and 3:213, (#789); Kaḥḥāla, 2:622 (#10821); Kohlberg, "al-Ṭabrisī (Ṭabarsī), Amīnal-Dīn," EI^2; Bruce Fudge, *Qurʾānic Hermeneutics: al-Ṭabrisī and the Craft of Commentary* (New York: Routledge, 2011). His name is sometimes mistakenly vocalized as al-Ṭabarsī. Karīmān gives an extensive and helpful discussion of this problem (1:167–205, 313–333), which Abdul unfortunately misunderstood, confusing "Arāk" with "ʿIrāq" (*The Qur'an: Shaykh Tabarsi's Commentary,* 6–7).

98. Dwight Donaldson, *The Shiʿite Religion: A History of Islam in Persia and Irak* (London: Luzac & Company, 1933), 292.

99. This was not al-Ṭabrisī's only connection to al-Mufīd. He studied under at least one other pupil of Shaykh al-Ṭūsī as well. See Kohlberg, "al-Ṭabrisī (Ṭabarsī), Amīn al-Dīn," EI^2.

100. First in an article, then incorporated into his book, see Fudge, *Qurʾānic Hermeneutics.*

101. For alternate birth dates, see Karīmān, *Ṭabriṣī,* 1:205–208.
102. See Makdisi, "Sunnī Revival," 159–168; Richard Bulliet, *Islam: The View from the Edge* (New York: Columbia University Press, 1994), esp. 146–148; Jonathan Berkey, *The Formation of Islam: Religion and Society in the Near East, 600–1800* (Cambridge: Cambridge University Press, 2003), 189–202.
103. On Niẓām al-Mulk, see S. R. A. Rizvi, *Nizam al-Mulk Tusi: His Contribution to Statecraft, Political Theory and the Art of Government* (Lahore: Muhammad Ashraf, 1978); Bowen and Bosworth, "Niẓām al-Mulk," EI²; Neguin Yavari, "Niẓām al-Mulk and the Restoration of Sunnism in Iran in the Eleventh Century," *Taḥqīqat-i Islāmī* 10, no. i-ii (1996): 570–551.
104. On the Niẓāmīya, see Muhammad al-Faruque, "The Development of the Institution of Madrasah and the Niẓāmīyah of Baghdad," *Islamic Studies* 26, no. 3 (Autumn 1987): 253–263.
105. On Shiʿa participation in Shafiʿi law, see Stewart, *Islamic Legal Orthodoxy.*
106. Karīmān, *Ṭabrisī,* 1:209.
107. Abdul, *The Qurʾan: Shaykh Tabarsi's Commentary,* 11–12. For a list of his teachers, see Karīmān, *Ṭabrisī,* 1:290–300.
108. Kohlberg says that some later scholars elaborated on this and supposed him to have been poisoned: "al-Ṭabrisī (Ṭabarsī), Amīnal-Dīn," EI². See also Fudge, *Qurʾānic Hermeneutics,* 33.
109. Fudge, *Qurʾānic Hermeneutics,* 33–34.
110. Wilhelm Barthold, *An Historical Geography of Iran,* trans. Svat Soucek, ed. with intro. C. E. Bosworth (Princeton, NJ: Princeton University Press, 1984), 110.
111. Kohlberg, "al-Ṭabrisī (Ṭabarsī), Amīnal-Dīn," EI². For a full list, see Karīmān, *Ṭabrisī,* 1:300–313.
112. Quṭb al-Dīn Saʿīd b. Hibat Allāh al-Rāwandī (d. 573/1177–1178); Kohlberg, "Rāvandi, Qoṭb-al-Din Saʿid," EIr; name of books: *al-Kharāʾij wa-al-jarāʾiḥ; Fiqh al-Qurʾān; Lubb al-lubāb; Makārim akhlāq* al-*Nabī wa-al-aʾimmah; Minhāj al-barāʿah fī sharḥ Nahj al-balāghah;* and *Qiṣaṣ al-anbiyāʾ.*
113. Author of an important Shiʿa *fihrist: Fihrist asmāʾ ʿulamāʾ al-Shīʿah wa-muṣannifīhim.*
114. Author of a work on Imam ʿAlī: *Risālah fī al-rasāʾil jāmiʿah li-daqāyiq al-Manāqib wa-al-Faḍāyil.*
115. Fudge, *Qurʾānic Hermeneutics,* 31, 32.
116. Ibid., 29.
117. For a list of these works, see, Karīmān, *Ṭabrisī,* 1:260–290.
118. On the Bāwandis, see Frye, "Bāwand," EI²; C. E. Bosworth, "The Political and Dynastic History of the Iranian World (A.D. 1000–1217)," in CHIr (1968), 5:27–29; W. Madelung, "Āl-e Bāvand," EIr.
119. *Iʿlām,* 14. On this king, see C. E. Bosworth, "'Alāʾ-al-Dawla ʿAlī," EIr.
120. *Iʿlām,* 16.
121. His full name was Abū Jaʿfar Muḥammad b. ʿAlī b. Shahrāshūb, known sometimes as ʿIzz al-Dīn or Rashīd al-Dīn. For contemporary scholarship on Ibn Shahrāshūb, see ʿĀmilī, *Aʿyān al-Shīʿa,* 46:136–137, #2556; al-Ṭihrānī, *al-Dharīʿa,*

22:318–319, #7264; *GAL* S I:710; Kaḥḥāla, 3:515–516, #14748; B. Scarcia Amoretti, "Ibn Shahrāshūb," EI[2]; Aḥmad Pākatchī, "Ibn Shahrāshūb," DMBI 4:90–92; Mohammad Ali Amir-Moezzi, "Ebn Ŝahrāŝub," EIr; Muḥammad Raḥīm Bayg Muḥammadī, *Ibn Shahrāshūb: dar ḥarīm-i vilāyat* (n.p.: Markaz-i Chāp va Nashr-i Sāzmān-i Ṭablīghāt-i Islāmī, 1374 (Shamsī) [1996]); Matthew Pierce, "Ibn Shahrashub and Shiʿa Rhetorical Strategies in the 6th/12th Century," *Journal of Shiʿa Islamic Studies* 5, no. 4 (Autumn 2012): 441–454.

122. Muḥammadī, *Ibn Shahrāshūb,* 71–72.

123. The dating for the events of Ibn Shahrāshūb's life is taken primarily from Pākatchī, "Ibn Shahrāshūb," DMBI, 4: 90–92.

124. Muḥammadī, *Ibn Shahrāshūb,* 30.

125. Pākatchī, "Ibn Shahrāshūb," DMBI, 4:90. Also referred to in al-Dhahabī, *Tārīkh al-Islām wa-wafayāt al-mashāhīr wa-al-aʿlām,* ed. ʿUmar ʿAbd al-Salām Tadmurī (Beirut: Dār al-Kitāb al-ʿArabī, 1989–), 309–310, #315.

126. For a description of the turn of events in Baghdad at this time, particularly Ibn al-Jawzi's enforcement of Sunni orthodoxy, see Swartz, *Ibn al-Jawzī's* Kitāb al-Quṣṣāṣ, 27–34.

127. For a full list of these, see ʿAbd al-Mahdī al-Ithnāʿasharī, "Mashyakha Ibn Shahrāshūb (1)," *Turāthunā* 24, 93/94 (1429 [2008]): 11–95; "Mashyakha Ibn Shahrāshūb (2)," *Turāthūna* 24, 95/97 (1429 [2008]): 7–95. See also Muḥammadī, *Ibn Shahrāshūb,* 31–44.

128. Particularly notable, in this regard, were his studies under al-Fattāl (d. 508/1114–1115, author of *Rawda al-waʿizin,* see Appendix 2), Abu ʿAli al-Tabrisi, Qutb al-Din al-Rawandi (d. 573/1177–1178, author of *al-Kharaʾij wa-al-jaraʾhḥ,* and Abu Mansur al-Tabrisi (d. ca. 620/1223, author of *al-Ihtijāj* and *Taʾrikh al-aʾimma* (lost). For more on these works, see Appendix 2.

129. *Manāqib,* 1:18–19. See also Muḥammadī, *Ibn Shahrāshūb,* 54–58.

130. On Ibn Abī Ṭayy, see Muḥammad Āṣif Fakrat, "Ibn Abī Ṭayy," DMBI; Cl. Cahen, "Ibn Abī Ṭayyiʾ," EI[2].

131. On this, see Pierce, "Ibn Shahrashub," 444–451. For an example of a favorable Sunni legacy, see Ibn Ḥajar, *Lisān al-Mīzān,* 5:310, #1034; Dhahabī, *Taʾrīkh,* 309–310, #315.

132. *Manāqib,* 1:19–32.

133. Ibid., 1:18–19, 34–35.

134. Pierce, "Ibn Shahrashub," 446–451.

135. See Alon Confino, "Collective Memory and Cultural History: Problems of Method," *American Historical Review* 102 (1997): 1402; Peter Burke, "History as Social Memory," in *Memory: History, Culture and the Mind,* ed. Thomas Butler (Oxford: Basil Blackwell, 1989), 109; Jeffrey K. Olick and Joyce Robbins, "Social Memory Studies: From 'Collective Memory' to the Historical Sociology of Mnemonic Practices," *Annual Review of Sociology* 24 (1998): 127; Marion Holmes Katz, *The Birth of the Prophet Muḥammad: Devotional Piety in Sunni Islam* (London: Routledge, 2007), 47–50.

136. Jonathan P. Berkey, *Popular Preaching & Religious Authority in the Medieval Islamic Near East* (Seattle: University of Washington Press, 2001), 88–96.

137. Al-Mufīd uses many of the same pieces in his lectures collected in *al-Amālī* as he does in his *Kitab al-Irshad*. Or consider the twelfth-century scholar al-Fattāl al-Nīshābūrī, whose book of sermons (*Rawḍat al-wāʿiẓīn*) draws upon this literature significantly.
138. For other examples of this genre in this period and later, see Appendix 2. Kāshifī's sixteenth-century *Futūvat-nāmah-i Sultānī* is an excellent example of how the material was used in Sufi circles. The undeniable popularity of another Kāshifī work that drew upon the biographies, *Rawḍat al-shuhadāʾ*, further suggests a broad appeal for this literature. See also Kathryn Babayan, *Mystics, Monarchs, and Messiahs: Cultural Landscapes of Early Modern Iran* (Cambridge, MA: Harvard University Press, 2002), 175–177.
139. Thanks to Franklin Lewis for this suggested rendering of the title of this book.
140. Peter Burke, *Varieties of Cultural History* (Ithaca, NY: Cornell University Press, 1997), 56.
141. Alan Shelston, *Biography,* in *The Critical Idiom* 34, ed. John D. Jump (London: Methuen & Co, 1977), 15. Quoted in Young, "Arabic Biographical Writing," *CHALAP,* 178, n. 28.
142. Patricia Cox Miller, *Biography in Late Antiquity: A Quest for the Holy Man* (Berkeley: University of California Press, 1983), 135, 145–148. This does not mean the stories themselves are fictitious, nor is this unique to Shiʿa literature—Calamawy, for instance, has described the artistic and creative literary elements within Sunni hadith collections as well. See Sahair EL Calamawy, "Narrative Elements in the *Ḥadīth* Literature," *CHALUP,* 308–316, esp. 311.
143. Consider also the observations by Jonathan Brockopp in his discussion of the shortcomings of focusing on the historicity of reports within the biographies of exemplary figures—stating that the meaning of reported events "overwhelms any sense of historicity": "Contradictory Evidence and the Exemplary Scholar: The Lives of Sahnun b. Saʿid (d. 854)," *IJMES* 43, no. 1 (2011): 124.
144. John Renard, *Friends of God: Islamic Images of Piety, Commitment and Servanthood* (Berkeley: University of California Press, 2008), 257.
145. See Mahdjoub, "The Evolution of Popular Eulogy," 54–79.
146. Jan Assmann, "Collective Memory and Identity," trans. John Czaplicka, *New German Critique* 65 (Spring-Summer 1995): 129.

Chapter 2: Consolation for a Community

1. *Al-Irshād,* 2:131 (English, 377).
2. David Herman, *Basic Elements of Narrative* (West Sussex, UK: Wiley-Blackwell, 2009), 139–143.
3. Much of the material in the following section was presented in a conference paper at the American Academy of Religion: Matthew Pierce, "Killing the Imams: Classical Shiʿi Narratives of the Twelve Imams and the Necessity of Martyrdom" (American Academy of Religion, Atlanta, GA, October 30, 2010).

4. See Muḥammad b. Jarīr b. Yazīd al-Ṭabarī, *The History of al-Ṭabarī,* 32:184–185; Khaṭīb al-Baghdādī, *Tārīkh Madīnat,* 4:88–90, #1261; ʿAbd al-Raḥmān b. ʿAlī b. al-Jawzī, *al-Muntaẓam fī tārīkh al-mulūk wa-al-umam,* ed. Muḥammad ʿAbd al-Qādir ʿAṭā, Muṣṭafá ʿAbd al-Qādir ʿAṭā, and Naʿīm Zarzūrmuntazam (Beirut: Dār al-Kutub al-ʿIlmīya, 1992), 11:62–3, #1257; ʿIzz al-Dīn ʿAlī b. Muḥammad Ibn al-Athīr, *al-Kāmil fī al-taʾrīkh,* ed. ʿUmar ʿAbd al-Salām Tadmurī (Beirut: Dār al-Kitāb al-ʿArabī, 1997), 6:18; Ibn Khallikān, *Wafayāt al-aʿyān,* ed. Iḥsān ʿAbbās (Beirut: Dar Assakafa, [1968?-1972?]), 4:175, #561; al-Dhahabī, *Tārīkh al-Islām,* 15:385–386, #372; Khalīl ibn Aybak Ṣafadī, *Kitāb al-Wāfī bi-al-Wafayāt,* ed. Muḥammad Ḥujayrī, Otfried Weintritt, Māhir Zuhayr Jarrār, and Benjamin Jokisch (Leipzig: Deutsche Morgenländische Gesellschaft, in Kommission bei F.A. Brockhaus, 1931), 4:105–106, #1587.

5. Muḥammad b. ʿAlī b. Bābawayh, *Iʿtiqādat al-imāmiyah,* in *Muṣannafāt li-Shaykh al-Mufīd* (Qum: al-Mu'tamir al-ʿĀlimī li-Alafīyah al-Shaykh al-Mufīd, 1413 [1992]), 5:98. English translation: *Shiʿite Creed,* 3rd ed., trans. Asaf A. A. Fyzee (Tehran: World Organization for Islamic Services, 1999), 89.

6. Moses Hadas and Morton Smith, *Heroes and Gods: Spiritual Biographies in Antiquity* (Freeport, NY: Books for Library Press, 1965), 94.

7. [Peer Mohamed Ebrahim Trust], *Biography of Imam Taqi (A. S.)* (Karachi: Peer Mohamed Ebrahim Trust, 1975), 70. Henceforth, Peer.

8. *Manāqib,* 1:18–19, 34–35.

9. Peter Burke, *Varieties of Cultural History* (Ithaca, NY: Cornell University Press, 1997), 56. See also my discussion of this in Chapter 1; Alon Confino, "Collective Memory and Cultural History: Problems of Method," *American Historical Review* 102 (1997): 1389–1393.

10. Daniel Boyarin's *Dying for God* makes an excellent case for how martyrdom accounts can be a useful place to explore religious boundaries: *Dying for God: Martyrdom and the Making of Christianity and Judaism* (Stanford, CA: Stanford University Press, 1999).

11. *Al-Irshād,* 2:295 (Eng: 495).

12. *Ithbāt,* 227. I added many of the names in this quote to my translation in order to reduce pronoun confusion.

13. Ibid.

14. Ibid.

15. Besides the fate of Jaʿfar and Umm al-Faḍl, other examples include: al-Ṭabrisī clarified that a few people who injured the Prophet did not die naturally, one of them being impaled by a ram in his sleep (Dalāʾil, 99; Eng: 129;see Chapter 4 in this volume for the role of animals); an informant for the caliph was killed during Imam al-Kāẓim's life (*al-Irshād,* 2:225–227; Eng: 444–445); al-Kāẓim's nephew who betrayed him to the caliph died unceremoniously while defecating (*al-Irshād,* 2:238–239; Eng: 452–453); al-Hādī's brother, who was tricked by the caliph, was made into a mockery during his life (*al-Irshād,* 2:307–308; Eng: 502–503).

16. Examples of future punishment being explicitly promised include: when al-Ḥusayn asked al-Ḥasan (after the latter was poisoned) if he wanted al-Ḥusayn to avenge his death, al-Ḥasan said he will oppose his murderer before God instead (*al-Irshād,* 2:16–18; Eng: 287–288); al-Mufīd said that all of those who murdered al-Ḥusayn were killed or punished by God in some way (*al-Irshād,* 2:125; Eng: 372); Imam al-Hādī assured one of his followers that his murderer will soon die (al-Irbilī, *Kashf,* 4:36–37 [taken from al-Rāwandī's *Kharā'ij*]). See Carlin A. Barton, "Savage Miracles: The Redemption of Lost Honor in Roman Society and the Sacrament of the Gladiator and the Martyr," *Representations* 45 (Winter 1994): esp. 51–52.
17. *Dalā'il,* 204.
18. Franz Rosenthal made some insightful notes about the use of this term in classical Arabic literature: *Four Essays on Art and Literature in Islam* (Leiden: Brill, 1971), 63–99. Particularly noteworthy is the attested use of a *mandīl* for cleaning oneself after sexual intercourse. Further, the secret application of poison to a person's genitals using a *mandīl* was a motif found elsewhere as well (84).
19. This quote is translated from the 1992 edition of *Dalā'il* (395). The 1988 edition (normally cited in this study) says that after the imam felt the infection, "he prayed a certain prayer and it worked. She showed it to doctors but they had no medicine for it, until she died" (*Dalā'il,* 204).
20. We can add to these the accounts recorded by Ḥusayn b. ʿAbd al-Wahhāb. He wrote just a few decades after al-Mufīd and included a detailed account pertaining to the ninth imam in his short book *ʿUyūn al-muʿjizāt,* which focused on the miracles of the imams. In his account, Umm al-Faḍl was said to have become enraged when she found a new wife of the imam in the house. She complained to her father, Caliph al-Maʾmūn, who went to al-Jawād's house in a drunken stupor and slayed him with his sword. When the caliph sobered, he was horrified to hear of his own actions. Dismayed and regretful, the caliph sent someone to find out about the status of the young man, only to learn that al-Jawād was uninjured (323–329). Though this story differed from the other accounts in that God miraculously preserves al-Jawād's life, it buttressed the general understanding of Umm al-Faḍl's deep jealousy toward al-Jawād and the deadly peril in which it put the imam. Ibn ʿAbd al-Wahhāb also confirmed that al-Muʿtaṣim had plotted to kill the imam. The account was almost identical to that in the *Establishment* (even the phrasing is much the same), with the exception that it contained no mention of Jaʿfar b. al-Maʾmūn. As in the other stories, the caliph manipulated Umm al-Faḍl's jealousy to induce her to poison al-Jawād, and once again she was cursed with a tumor *(nāsūr)* in her sexual organs (though it does not specify whether she died from the affliction) (331–332). The martyrdom of the ninth imam was further substantiated in this work by another miracle account that had the eighth imam, ʿAlī al-Riḍá, predicting the martyrdom of the ninth imam at his son's birth, saying, "He will be killed in rage and the company of heaven will weep for him" (309–310).
21. *Al-Irshād,* 1:295 (Eng: 495).
22. *Iʿlām,* 351.

23. As mentioned in the beginning, medieval Sunni writers, including Sibṭ b. al-Jawzī, were completely silent on the issue, though Umm al-Faḍl was typically mentioned as being with al-Jawād in Baghdad when he died: *Tadhkirat al-khawāṣ* (Qum: Manshūrāt Dhuwī al-Qurbī, [1427]), 446–447. See also al-Ṭabarī, *History,* 32:184–5; Khatīb al-Baghdādī, *Tārīkh,* 4:88–90, #1261; Ibn al-Jawzī, *al-Muntaẓam,* 11:62–3, #1257; Ibn Athīr, *Kāmil,* 6:18; Ibn Khallikān, *Wafāyat,* 4:175, #561; al-Dhahabī, *Tārīkh,* 15:385–6, #372; al-Ṣafadī, *al-Wāfī,* 4:105–106, #1587. In the thirteenth century, the Shiʿa scholar al-Irbilī, in his *Kashf al-ghummah,* prefaced his section with al-Mufīd's comments on the matter—one of the very few times al-Mufīd is mentioned regarding this topic by the Shiʿa—and al-Irbilī left out most of the other death accounts (3:520–530). This more skeptical approach to the question, however, was clearly in the minority when it came to the literature on the lives of the imams. Muḥammad b. al-Ḥasan Al-Fattāl in *Rawḍat al-wāʿizīn* refrains from giving any details, but he does unequivocally state that the imam was poisoned while in Baghdād: *Rawḍat al-wāʿizīn* (Beirut: Muʾassasat al-Aʿlamī lil-Maṭbūʿāt, 1986), 267. Even the fifteenth century Māliki scholar, Ibn al-Ṣabbāgh, in his *Fusūl al-muhimmah,* concedes that it is a possibility that he was poisoned—this is the only medieval Sunnī writer I've found to make such a concession: *al-Fuṣūl al-muhimmah fī maʿrifat al-aʾimma,* (Qum: Dār al-Ḥadīth, 1422 [2001 or 2002]), 2:1057–1058.
24. *Manāqib,* 4:416. This account may have been understood as a miracle account—that the imam was not killed, even though he was poisoned.
25. *Manāqib,* 4:423. Like most previous authors, Ibn Shahrāshūb also specified that Umm al-Faḍl did not bear any children for the imam (4:411).
26. *Manāqib,* 4:414.
27. Muḥammad Bāqir Majlisī, *Jalāʾ al-ʿuyūn: tārīkh-i chahārdah maʿṣūm,* ed. Sayyid ʿAlī Imāmiyān (Qum: Surūr, 1387 [2008–2009]), 959–972.
28. ʿAbbās b. Muḥammad Riḍā Qummī, *Muntahá al-āmāl* (Qum: Intishārāt-i Nigāh-i Āshnā, 1388 [2009 or 2010]), 2:403–406.
29. Muḥammad Ḥusayn Ṭabāṭabāʾī, *Shīʿeh dar Islām* (Qum: Daftar-i Tablīghāt-i Islāmī, 1348 [1969]), 144–145. English translation: *Shiʿite Islam,* trans. Seyyed Hossein Nasr (Albany: State University of New York Press, 1975), 207.
30. ʿAlī Muḥammad ʿAlī Dukhayyil, *Aʾimmatunā* (Beirut: Dār al-Murtaḍá, 1982), 2:162.
31. Muḥammad Muḥammadī Ishtihārdī, *Maṣāʾib Āl Muḥammad: fī bayān ḥayāt wa-al-maṣāʾib al-muʾlimah lil-maʿṣūmīn al-arbaʿat ʿashar wa-shuhadāʾ wa-sabāyā Karbalāʾ maʿa marāthīhim* (Beirut: Dār al-Kātib al-ʿArabī, 2002), 137–145.
32. For further examples, see Mahdī Pīshvāʾī, *Sīrah-ʾi pīshvāyān: nigarishī bar zindagānī-i ijtimāʿī, siyāsī va farhangī-i imāmān-i maʿṣūm ʿalayhum al-salām* (Qum: Muʾassasah-i Imām Ṣādiq, 1388 [2009]), 563–564; [World Organization for Islamic Sciences], *A Brief History of the Fourteen Infallibles* (Tehran: World Organization for Islamic Sciences, 1984), 158; Mahdī Khalīl Jaʿfar, *al-Mawsūʿah al-kubrá li- Ahl al-Bayt* (Beirut: Markaz al-Sharq al-Awsaṭ al-Thaqāfī, 2009), 11:154–160.

33. Michael Stuart Williams, *Authorized Lives in Early Christian Biography: Between Eusebius and Augustine* (Cambridge: Cambridge University Press, 2008), 12.
34. For a general overview of traditional hadith criticism, see Muḥammad Abdul Rauf, "*Ḥadīth* Literature—I," *CHALUP,* 271–288; Nabia Abbott, "*Ḥadīth* Literature—II," *CHALUP,* 289–298.
35. Even early traditionalists were influenced by a wider range of concerns when determining the "effective truth" of hadith reports: Jonathan A. C. Brown, "Did the Prophet Say It or Not? The Literal, Historical, and Effective Truth of *Hadiths* in Early Sunnism," *JAOS* 129, no. 2 (2009): 280.
36. Ibn Bābawayh, *Iʿtiqādat al-imāmiyah,* 5:98 (Eng: *Shiʿite Creed,* 89).
37. See M. Ali Buyukkara, "The Schism in the Party of Mūsā al-Kāẓim and the Emergence of the Wāqifa," *Arabica* 47, no. 1 (2000): 78–99. See also Hossein Modarressi, *Crisis and Consolidation in the Formative Period of Shiʿite Islam: Abū Jaʿfar ibn Qiba al-Rāzī and His Contribution to Imāmite Shīʿite Thought* (Princeton, NJ: The Darwin Press, 1993), 60–64.
38. David Cook, *Martyrdom in Islam* (Cambridge: Cambridge University Press, 2007), 31–36.
39. Muḥammad b. Muḥammad b. al-Nuʿmanī al-Mufīd, *al-Amālī* (Najaf: al-Maṭbaʿat al-Haydariyah, 1962), 46; Eng: *Al Amaali,* trans. Asgharali Jaffer (Middlesex: World Federation, 1988), 78.
40. Peer, *Biography of Imam Taqi,* 69–70.
41. Michael Cooperson, *Classical Arabic Biography* (Cambridge: Cambridge University Press, 2000), 99.
42. S. H. M. Jafri, *Origins and Early Development of Shiʿa Islam* (London: Longman, 1979), 235–244.
43. *Manāqib,* 4:179–180.
44. *Al-Irshād,* 2:140–143 (Eng: 382–384).
45. *Al-Irshād,* 2:142 (Eng: 383).
46. *Manāqib,* 4:179–180. See also al-Fattāl, *Rawḍat al-wāʿiẓīn,* 494.
47. *Manāqib,* 4:182.
48. See *Psalms of Islam,* trans. W. Chittick (Qum: Ansariyan, 2000). See also al-Fattāl, *Rawḍat al-wāʿiẓīn,* 492–496; and Mahmoud Ayoub's descriptions of al-Sajjād's mournings in other Shiʿa literatures: *Redemptive Suffering in Islam: A Study of the Devotional Aspects of ʿĀshūrāʾ in Twelver Shīʿism* (The Hague: Mouton Publishers, 1978).
49. See, for example, his tears while recovering the Kaʿba, presumably related to its sacredness: *Manāqib,* 4: 152.
50. Various examples: *Ithbāt,* 175; *al-Irshād,* 2:142–143 (Eng: 383); *Iʿlām,* 398–399; *Manāqib,* 4:158, 163–164.
51. This is where I feel Ayoub's otherwise excellent work, *Redemptive Suffering,* misleads. He directs the mourning of Imam al-Sajjād, and nearly the entire theme on sorrow, toward the tragedy of al-Ḥusayn.
52. See *Dalāʾl,* 27, 231–232; *al-Irshād,* 2:129–131 (Eng: 375–376); *Iʿlām,* 24 (Eng: 14), 100–101 (Eng: 131–132), 125 (Eng: 175), 199, 225; *Manāqib,* 1:89, 151, 279, 290; 2: 87, 91, 139; 3:311, 390; 4:67, 78, 88–89, 91–92.

53. See *Dalāʾil,* 27; *Iʿlām,* 97 (Eng: 128), 150 (Eng: 214); *Manāqib,* 3:365, 385, 411; 4:71. See also references in Denise Soufi, "The Image of Fāṭimah in Classical Muslim Thought" (PhD diss., Princeton University, 1997), 81–151.

54. See *al-Irshād,* 1:116 (Eng: 78), 1:165 (Eng: 115); *Iʿlām,* 115, 204; *Manāqib,* 2:139; 3:167, 356.

55. See *al-Irshād,* 1:332 (Eng: 251); *Manāqib,* 2:305.

56. See *al-Irshād,* 2:8 (Eng: 281); *Iʿlām,* 216; *Manāqib,* 4:76–77.

57. See *Iʿlām,* 236; *Manāqib,* 4:18, 93, 95, 117. See also Khalid Sindawi, "The Image of Husayn ibn ʿAlī in *Maqātil* Literature," *Quaderni di Studi Arabi* 20–21 (2002–2003):92–93.

58. For al-Sajjād, see *Ithbāt,* 175; *al-Irshād,* 2:142 (Eng: 383–384); *Iʿlām,* 398–399, *Manāqib,* 4:152, 158, 163–164, 179–180, 182. For al-Bāqir, *al-Irshād,* 2:142 (383); *Manāqib,* 211. For al-Ṣādiq, *Dalāʾil,* 102, 133; *Manāqib,* 4:94, 257, 261. For al-Kāẓim, *al-Irshād,* 2:231 (Eng: 448); *Iʿlām,* 307; *Manāqib,* 4:343, 348–349. For al-Riḍá, *Iʿlām,* 328, 330, 342–343; *Manāqib,* 4:366–367. For al-Jawād, *al-Irshād,* 2:298 (497); *Iʿlām,* 352; *Manāqib,* 4:366–367. For al-Hādī, *Ithbāt,* 229; *Dalāʾil,* 215; *Manāqib,* 4:440. For al-ʿAskarī, *al-Irshād,* 2:318 (510); *Iʿlām,* 364; *Manāqib,* 4:456. There are also instances of pre-Islamic figures crying: *Manāqib,* 1:229, 279, 4:67, 275, 384. See also Khalid Sindawi, "Noah and Noah's Ark as the Primordial Model of Shiʿism in Shiʿite Literature," *Quaderni di Studi Arabi nuova serie* 1 (2006): 33.

59. Some examples of this phrase can be found in *Manāqib,* 1:290 (speaking of the Prophet); *Manāqib* 4:158 and 399 (of Imam al-Sajjād); *Iʿlām,* 330 (of Imam al-Rida); *I'lām,* 423 (of Imam al-Jawād); *Dalāʾil,* 215 and *Ithbāt,* 229 (of Imam al-Hādī). See also Fāṭima screaming and throwing dirt (*Iʿlām,* 150; Eng: 214); al-Bāqir crying uncontrollably (*al-Irshād,* 2:142; Eng: 383); al-Ṣādiq's eyes being flooded with tears (*Manāqib* 4:94); al-Kāẓim soaking his beard with tears (*Iʿlām,* 307; *al-Irshād,* 448; *Manāqib,* 4:343, 348–349); and al-Hādī wailing while crying (*Dalāʾil,* 215; *Ithbāt,* 229).

60. For instances where this process was enacted (i.e., the weeping of an imam caused people around them to cry as well), see *al-Irshād,* 2:8 (281); *Iʿlām,* 216; *Manāqib* 4:67, 163–164, 257.

61. *Manāqib,* 4:95.

62. *Al-Irshād,* 1:184 (Eng: 130); *Iʿlām,* 147 (Eng: 210).

63. *Al-Irshād,* 2:93 (Eng: 348); *Iʿlām,* 244.

64. *Al-Irshād,* 2:59 (Eng: 321).

65. Some examples include *Dalāʾil,* 84, 139–140, 176–177, 200–201, 231, 260; *al-Irshād,* 1:17 (Eng: 10), 1:184 (Eng: 130), 1:319–320 (Eng: 241–242), 2:113–116 (Eng: 364–365), 2:129–131 (Eng: 376); *Iʿlām,* 147 (Eng: 210), 169, 411; *Manāqib,* 1:292, 2:93, 3:356, 4:23, 71, 73, 147, 163–164, 180, 211, 213, 335, 472–473.

66. Some interesting examples include *Manāqib,* 1:299–300, 2:245–246, 3:161, 359–360, 4:71, 126, 129, 133, 300. These are usually snippets taken from *rithāʾ* poems, see below.

67. Araqqu min damʿati shīʿa // tabkī ʿAlī b. Abī Ṭālib: this proverb comes from an anonymous *bayt* found in Aḥmad b. Muḥammad Maydānī, *Majmaʿ al-amthāl*, ed. Muḥammad Muḥyi al-Dīn ʿAbd al-Ḥamīd (Cairo: al-Maktabah al-Tujārīyah

al-Kubrá, 1959), 2:316, #1712. Ignaz Goldziher makes reference to this proverb in *Introduction to Islamic Theology,* trans. Andras and Ruth Hamori (Princeton, NJ: Princeton University Press, 1981), 179.

68. Sara Ahmed, *The Cultural Politics of Emotion* (New York: Routledge, 2004).

69. Luisa Passerini, "Connecting Emotions: Contributions from Cultural History," *Historein* 8 (2008): 121.

70. Ahmed, *Cultural Politics of Emotion,* 9. The "outside in" approach is what David Herman calls the "constructionist approach" to emotion; the alternate view, what Ahmed calls the "inside out," is referred to as the "naturalist" approach by Herman: "Cognition, Emotion, and Consciousness," in *Cambridge Companion to Narrative,* ed. David Herman (Cambridge: Cambridge University Press, 2007), 254–255.

71. Ahmed, *Cultural Politics of Emotion,* 3–4.

72. Ibid., 12.

73. The best survey of this topic is in Leor Halevi's *Muhammad's Grave: Death Rites and the Making of Islamic Society* (New York: Columbia University Press, 2007).

74. See Nadia Maria El Cheikh, "Mourning and the Role of the *Nāʾiḥa,*" *Estudios onomástico-biográficos de Al-Andalus* 13 (2003): 397–401.

75. Halevi, *Muhammad's Grave,* 114–142.

76. In a report recorded by al-Fattāl, one of Imam al-Sajjād's followers was so concerned by the imam's mourning that even he felt compelled to ask for clarity (*Rawḍat al-wāʿiẓīn,* 494).

77. Halevi, *Muhammad's Grave,* 115. See also El Cheikh, "Mourning and the Role," 395–412.

78. Nadia Maria El Cheikh, "The Gendering of 'Death' in *Kitāb al-ʿIqd al-Farīd,*" *Al-Qantara* 31, no. 2 (2010): 435.

79. Halevi, *Muhammad's Grave,* 123 n. 39, 128.

80. Ibid., 126–128.

81. Ibid., 133–135.

82. On *marthīya,* see Ch. Pellat, "Mar<u>th</u>iya: Arabic Literature," EI²; Suzanne Stetkevych, "The Generous Eye / I and the Poetics of Redemption: An Elegy by al-Fāriʿah b. Shaddād al-Murriyah," in *Literary Heritage of Classical Islam: Arabic and Islamic Studies in Honor of James Bellamy,* ed. M. Mir (Princeton, NJ: The Darwin Press, 1993), 85–105; Pieter Smoor, "'Death, the Elusive Thief': The Classic Arabic Elegy," in *Hidden Futures: Death and Immortality in Ancient Egypt, Anatolia, the Classical, Biblical and Arabico-Islamic World,* ed. J. M. Bremmer, Th. P. J. van den Hout, and R. Peters (Amsterdam: Amsterdam University Press, 1994), 151–176; Marlè Hammond, ed., *Transforming Loss into Beauty: Essays on Arabic Literature and Culture in Honor of Magda Al-Nowaihi* (Cairo: American University Press, 2008); El Cheikh, "The Gendering of 'Death,'" 411–436; Marlè Hammond, *Beyond Elegy: Classical Arabic Women's Poetry in Context* (Oxford: Oxford University Press, 2010).

83. Suzanne Stetkevych, "Obligations and Poetics of Gender: Women's Elegy and Blood Vengeance," in *The Immortals Speak: Pre-Islamic Poetry and the Poetics of Ritual* (Ithaca, NY: Cornell University Press, 1993), 164–165.

84. On al-Khansāʾ, see K. A. Fariq, "al-Khansāʾ and Her Poetry," *Islamic Culture* 37 (1957): 209–219; F. Gabrieli, "al-Khansāʾ," EI[2]; Clarissa Burt, "al-Khansaʾ," *ALC*. On Laylā al-Akhyalīya, see "Laylā al-Akhyaliyya," EI[2].
85. Halevi, *Muhammad's Grave,* 133.
86. Herman, "Cognition, Emotion, and Consciousness," 255–256.
87. Stetkevych, "Obligations and Poetics of Gender," 167.
88. Ibid., 165.
89. See Athena Athanasiou, Pothiti Hantzaroula, and Kostas Yannakopoulous, "Towards a New Epistemology: The 'Affective Turn,'" *Historein* 8 (2008): 5–16.
90. Judith Perkins, *The Suffering Self: Pain and Narrative Representation in the Early Christian Era* (New York: Routledge, 1995), 3.
91. Al-Mufīd, *Al Amaali,* 285.
92. Ibid., 61–62.
93. *Manāqib,* 3:161.
94. *Manāqib,* 4:245–246.
95. For example, the Prophet visited ʿAlī and his family in visions, consoling them at the time when ʿAlī was to die: *al-Irshād,* 1:14–17 (Eng: 8–10).
96. *Al-Irshād,* 2:94 (Eng: 348–349).
97. *Dalāʾil,* 232.
98. Burke, "History as Social Memory," 110.
99. Perkins, *The Suffering Self,* 2–3.
100. See Ahmed, *Cultural Politics of Emotion,* 12, quoting Judith Butler.

Chapter 3: Betrayal and the Boundaries of Faithfulness

1. *Al-Irshād,* 2:110–111 (Eng: 362).
2. For examples in other religious traditions, see Elizabeth Castelli, *Martydom and Memory: Early Christian Culture Making* (New York: Columbia University Press, 2004); Carlin Barton, "Savage Miracles: The Redemption of Lost Honor in Roman Society and the Sacrament of the Gladiator and the Martyr," *Representations* 45 (Winter 1994): 41–71; Judith Perkins, *The Suffering Self: Pain and Narrative Representation in the Early Christian Era* (New York: Routledge, 1995); Nouri Gana, *Signifying Loss: Toward a Poetics of Narrative Mourning* (Lewisburg, PA: Bucknell University Press, 2011).
3. The way in which Hamid Dabashi filters most of his discussions of Shiʿism through the "Karbala Complex" is indicative of this tendency: see *Shi'ism: A Religion of Protest* (Cambridge, MA: Belknap Press, 2011), esp. 73–100.
4. Kamran Aghaie, "The Origins of the Sunnite-Shiʿite Divide and the Emergence of the Taʿziyeh Tradition," *The Drama Review* 49, no. 4 (2005): 43.
5. Nakash, "An Attempt to Trace the Origin," 161.
6. Fred Donner has recently described the battle as Shiʿism's "defining event": *Muhammad and the Believers: At the Origins of Islam* (Cambridge: Harvard University Press, 2010), 190. More detailed examples of this can be found in the works of D. Pinault, H. Halm, M. Ayoub, and H. Dabashi.

7. *Manāqib* 4:94. See also *al-Irshād,* 2:124–125 (Eng: 371–372); *Manāqib* 4:91–95, 138–139. Discussions of this can be found in Mahmoud Ayoub, *Redemptive Suffering in Islam: A Study of the Devotional Aspects of ʿĀshūrāʾ in Twelver Shīʿism* (The Hague: Mouton Publishers, 1978), 120–139.
8. Henri Corbin, "De la philosophie prophétique en Islam Shî'ite," *Eranos Jahrbuch* 31 (1962): 49–116, esp. 101–105; Khalid Sindawi, "Jesus and Ḥusayn Ibn ʿAlī Ibn ʾAbū Ṭālib: A Comparative Study," *Ancient Near Eastern Studies* 44 (2007): 50–65. Ayoub, however, also notes that the imams might be collectively compared to Christ—a suggestion that has yet to receive sufficient consideration: *Redemptive Suffering,* 216–217.
9. For example, see *Manāqib* 4:91–92; *al-Irshād,* 2:27–28 (Eng: 296); *Iʿlām,* 227–228.
10. See *al-Irshād,* 2:131 (376–377); *Iʿlām,* 227; *Manāqib* 4:67.
11. *Iʿlām,* 227–228; *al-Irshād,* 2:27–28 (Eng: 296). The *isnād* here went through Salmān al-Farsī. See also Maria Massi Dakake, *The Charismatic Community: Shiʿite Identity in Early Islam* (Albany: State University of New York Press, 2007), 121–123. Many other narratives make a connection between love of the Prophet and love of the other infallibles. See *Ithbāt,* 134; *Dalāʾil,* 27; Bursi, *Mashāriq,* 99–102.
12. Ayoub, *Redemptive Suffering,* 148–196; Nakash, "An Attempt to Trace the Origin," 163.
13. For some of the early Shiʿa controversies regarding how the death of al-Ḥusayn would be understood, see Douglas Karim Crow, "The Death of al-Ḥusayn b. ʿAli and Early Shi'i Views of the Imamate," *al-Serat* 12 (1986): 71–116.
14. On Abū Mikhnāf, see Ali Bahramian, "Abu Mikhnaf," *DMBI* [trans. Azar Rabbani and Farzin Negahban, *Encyclopedia Islamica*]; Khalil Athamina, "Abu Mikhnaf," EI³.
15. Marshall Hodgson, "How did the Early Shi'a become Sectarian?," *JAOS* 75, no. 1 (1955): 1–13; reprinted in *Shīʿism,* ed. Etan Kohlberg, 3–16 (Burlington, VT: Ashgate, 2003); Etan Kohlberg, "From Imāmiyya to Ithnā-ʿashariyya," *BSOAS* 39, no. 3 (1976): 521–534; S. H. M. Jafri, *Origins and Early Development of Shiʿa Islam* (London: Longman, 1979), 211–216. Compare with P. Crone, "Uthmāniyya," EI².
16. Nakash, "An Attempt to Trace the Origin," 161–171. See also Ali J. Hussain, "The Mourning of History and the History of Mourning: The Evolution of Ritual Commemoration of the Battle of Karbala," *Comparative Studies of South Asia, Africa and the Middle East* 25, no. 1 (2005): 78–88.
17. *Dalāʾil,* 73; *Manāqib* 4:138–139. See also Khalid Sindawi, "Visit to the Tomb of al-Ḥusayn b. ʿAlī in Shiite Poetry: First to Fifth Centuries AH (8th–11th Centuries CE)," *Journal of Arabic Literature* 37, no. 2 (2006): 230–258. Al-Mufīd recorded a narrative that inferred powers of speech on the body of al-Ḥusayn long after his death: *Al-Irshād,* 2:117 (Eng: 367).
18. Hussain, "The Mourning of History," 85.
19. *Al-Irshād,* 2:108 (Eng: 360); *Iʿlām,* 252.
20. *Al-Irshād,* 2:110 (Eng: 361–362); *Iʿlām,* 253.
21. *Al-Irshād,* 2:113 (Eng: 364); *Iʿlām,* 255.
22. *Al-Irshād,* 2:114 (Eng: 364–365); *Iʿlām,* 255. See also Jafri, *Origins,* 193.

23. *Al-Irshād,* 2:112 (Eng: 363). Imam al-Ḥusayn, in contrast, and despite his ultimate demise, is remembered in these texts for his courageous and unparalleled fighting. *Ithbāt* says the imam killed 1,800 Umayyad soldiers before succumbing to death himself (168).
24. *Al-Irshād,* 2:118 (Eng: 367–368). Ayoub discusses other versions of this narration: *Redemptive Suffering,* 137.
25. *Ithbāt,* 165–166; *Dalāʾil,* 73; *al-Irshād,* 2:129–130 (Eng: 375–376); *Iʿlām,* 225–226; *Manāqib* 4:62–63. In some accounts, Muḥammad went on a night journey to Karbālāʾ, where he got the dirt. In other accounts, the angel Gabriel brought the dirt clod to the Prophet. Compare Ayoub, *Redemptive Suffering,* 74. As we will see in Chapter 4, the bodies of the imams and the Prophet were often presented as one substance.
26. *Iʿlām,* 227. *Dalāʾil* contains a similar narrative (72), though the other previous biographers simply reported that the sky was red: *Ithbat,* 167–168; *al-Irshād,* 2:132 (377). But Ibn Shahrāshūb follow's al-Ṭabrisī's lead and has even more reports of the sky raining blood, including descriptions of the valleys becoming flooded with the blood (*Manāqib,* 4:61–69, 94). The imagery evokes the Qurʾānic passage in Sūrat al-Dukhān (44):29.
27. *Iʿlām,* 226. Compare *Dalāʾil,* 72.
28. Or, as Douglas Crow has summarized, "For the Shi'a, all of history is stained by the blood spilt at Karbala": "The Death of al-Ḥusayn," 71.
29. *Kull yawm ʿāshūrāʾ, kull ʿarḍ karbalāʾ.* The origins of this famous saying are unclear, but Yitzak Nakash has some references: "An Attempt to Trace the Origin of the Rituals of ʿĀshūrāʾ," *Die Welt des Islams,* n.s. 33, no. 2 (1993): 164–165, n. 10.
30. This is seen played out in certain historical performances of the *taʾzīya.* Shireen Mahdavi mentions that *taʾzīya* was performed in memory of all the imams, not just al-Ḥusayn: "Amusement in Qajar Iran," *Iranian Studies* 40, no. 4 (2007): 485–486.
31. See also Crow, "The Death of al-Ḥusayn," 73.
32. *Ithbāt,* 123–126; *al-Irshād,* 1:7–9, 175–195 (3–5, 123–137); *Iʿlām,* 44–151; *Manāqib,* 1:290–302. The *Dalāʾil* was unlikely an exception, but the early portion of the work is not extant, so there are no means by which this can be verified.
33. On *Ghadīr Khumm* and the sources on the Prophet's speech, see Dwight M. Donaldson, *The Shi'ite Religion: A History of Islam in Persia and Irak* (London: Luzac & Company, 1933), 1–13; L. Veccia Valieri, "G͟hadīr K͟humm," EI[2]; Wilferd Madelung, *Succession to Muḥammad: A Study of the Early Caliphate* (Cambridge: Cambridge University Press, 1997), 253; Dakake, *Charismatic Community,* 33–48.
34. Sūrat al-Māʾida (5):67, trans. M. A. S. Abdel Haleem, *The Qur'an: A New Translation* (Oxford: Oxford University Press, 2004).
35. *Iʿlām,* 145 (trans. Ayoub and Clarke, 206). Compare *al-Irshād,* 1:175–176 (124).
36. *Al-Irshād,* 1:186 (132–133); *Iʿlām,* 148–149 (212–213); *Manāqib,* 1:293–294.
37. Example: Ibn Isḥaq, *The Life of Muhammad: A Translation of Isḥāq's* Sīrat Rasūl Allāh, intro. and trans. A. Guillaume (Oxford: Oxford University Press, 1955), 682.
38. *Al-Irshād,* 1:183–184 (130); *Iʿlām,* 147 (210).
39. *Al-Irshād,* 1:184 (130–131); *Iʿlām,* 147–148 (210–211).

40. *Manāqib,* 1:292–293.
41. In one tradition attributed to Fāṭima al-Zahrā᾿, once Abū Bakr seized the caliphate, there "was an earthquake that only ʿAlī could stop": *Dalā᾿il,* 5–6. Compare Denise Soufi, "The Image of Fāṭimah in Classical Muslim Thought" (PhD diss., Princeton University, 1997), 71.
42. Muḥammad b. Ibrāhīm Ṣadr al-Dīn Shīrāzī, *Risālah-᾿i Sih Aṣl: Bi-inẕimām-i Muntakhab-i Masnavī Va Rubāyīyāt-i ū,* ed. Seyyed Hossein Nasr (Tehran: Dānishkadah-᾿i ʿUlūm-i Maʿqūl va Manqūl, 1340), 122. Thanks to Ata Anzali for helping me locate this reference. Crow also discusses this topic, providing a quote from Ayatollah Khomeini as well: "The Death of al-Ḥusayn," 71–72.
43. On Saqīfa, see Jafri, *Origins,* 27–57; G. Lacomte, "al-Saḳīfa," EI^2; Madelung, *Succession,* 28–56, 356–363.
44. Compare al-Baḥrānī, *Ḥilyat al-abrār fī aḥwāl Muḥammad wa-Ālihi al-aṭhār, ʿalayhim al-salām,* ed. Ghulām Riḍā Mawlānā al-Burūjirdī (Qum: Mu᾿assasat al-Maʿārif al-Islāmīyah, 1411- [1990 or 1991-]), 111–117.
45. On the ʿAbbāsid revolution, see Patricia Crone, "On the Meaning of the ʿAbbāsid Call to al-Riḍā," in *The Islamic World: From Classical to Modern Times (Essays in Honor of Bernard Lewis),* ed. Clifford Edmund Bosworth, et al. (Princeton, NJ: Princeton University Press, 1989), 95–111; M. A. Shaban, *The Abbasid Revolution* (Cambridge: Cambridge University Press, 1970); Moshe Sharon, *Black Banners from the East: The Establishment of the ʿAbbāsid State: Incubation of a Revolt* (Leiden: Brill, 1983); Jacob Lassner, *Islamic Revolution and Historical Memory: An Inquiry into the Art of ʿAbbāsid Apologetics* (New Haven, CT: American Oriental Society, 1986); Ṣāliḥ Saʿīd Āghā, *The Revolution that Toppled the Umayyads: Neither Arab nor ʿAbbāsid* (Leiden: Brill, 2003); Daniel Elton, "ʿAbbāsid Revolution," EI^3.
46. On al-Ma᾿mūn, see Michael Cooperson, *Classical Arabic Biography* (Cambridge: Cambridge University Press, 2000), 24–69; Cooperson, *al-Ma'mun* (Oxford: Oneworld, 2005).
47. For a recent historical analysis of this fascinating moment, see Deborah G. Tor, "An Historiographical Re-examination of the Appointment and Death of ʿAlī al-Riḍā," *Der Islam* 78 (2001): 103–128.
48. See *Ithbāt,* 214–216; *al-Irshād,* 2:269–270 (Eng: 477–478); *Dalā᾿il,* 174–180; *Iʿlām,* 337–341; *Manāqib,* 4:394–407.
49. *Dalā᾿il,* 174.
50. Cooperson, *Classical Arabic Biography,* 74.
51. Ibid., 90.
52. I am, of course, looking at how this question is answered by the biographers at hand. For a contemporary historian's approach to this question, see Tor, "An Historiographical Re-examination," 103–128.
53. *Al-Irshād,* 2:259–271 (Eng: 469–478); *Iʿlām,* 332–341; *Manāqib,* 4:394–407.
54. *Al-Irshād,* 2:269–271 (Eng: 477–478); *Iʿlām,* 337. Core portions of al-Mufid's narrative here, and thus those of the subsequent authors, draw from Isfahānī, *Maqātil,* 566.
55. *Al-Irshād,* 2:259–260 (Eng: 469–470); *Iʿlām,* 332; *Manāqib,* 4:398–399. See also Cooperson, *Classical Arabic Biography,* 73–74.

56. Knowledge of their fates is characteristic of all the imams. In this case, see *Ithbāt,* 209–211; *al-Irshād,* 2:191–192 (417–419); Cooperson, *Classical Arabic Biography,* 84.
57. See Hossein Modarressi, *Crisis and Consolidation in the Formative Period of Shīʿite Islam: Abū Jaʿfar ibn Qiba al-Rāzī and His Contribution to Imāmite Shīʿite Thought* (Princeton, NJ: The Darwin Press, 1993), 62–64.
58. *Al-Irshād,* 2:253 (Eng: 465).
59. See *Ithbāt,* 163; *al-Irshād,* 2:18–19 (Eng: 288–289); *Dala'il,* 68–70; *Iʿlām,* 219–220; *Manāqib,* 4:50. Various versions of this story are also found in numerous early and classical sources: Abū al-Faraj al-Isfahānī, *Maqātil al-ṭālibyīn,* ed. Aḥmad Ṣaqr (Cairo: Dār Iḥyāʾ al-Kutub al-ʿArabīya, 1368 [1949]), 72.
60. See *Ithbāt,* 163.
61. On Marwan I, see C. E. Bosworth, "Marwān I b. al-Ḥakam," EI[2].
62. See *al-Irshād,* 2:18–19 (Eng: 288–289); *Dalāʾil,* 68–70; *Iʿlām,* 219–220; *Manāqib,* 4:50.
63. A variation of this line is also found in slightly different contexts: see Denise Spellberg, *Politics, Gender, and the Islamic Past: The Legacy of ʿAʾisha bint Abi Bakr* (New York: Columbia University Press, 1994), 114–119.
64. On the Battle of the Camel, see Madelung, *Succession,* 141–183; L. Veccia Vaglieri, "al-Djamal," EI[2]; Spellberg, *Politics, Gender, and the Islamic Past,* 101–132.
65. *Al-Irshād,* 2:18–19 (Eng: 289).
66. Wadad al-Qadi, for instance, mentions this in relationship to al-Himyari, an early Shiʿa poet: "al-Sayyid al-Ḥimyārī," EI[2].
67. See Denise Spellberg's excellent discussion in *Politics, Gender, and the Islamic Past.*
68. Spellberg, *Politics, Gender, and the Islamic Past,* 69–70. ʿA'isha is understood by most Sunni Muslims to have been vindicated from the charge of infidelity by Sūrat al-nūr (24):11.
69. As for contrasting legacies, Spellberg's work here again succeeds in explaining the significance of the evolution of these stories, particularly in her contrast of ʿĀʾisha and Fāṭima's legacies: *Politics, Gender, and the Islamic Past,* 151–190.
70. *Ithbāt,* 191; *al-Irshād,* 2:219 (Eng: 438–439); *Manāqib,* 4:312. In another particularly interesting (though entirely unique, as far as I am aware) account, the writer of *Ithbāt* claims that while al-Ḥusayn argued with ʿĀʾisha about the burial of al-Ḥasan, al-Ḥusayn "divorced" ʿĀʾisha. The text claims that Muḥammad had passed on the right to divorce his wives to his heirs. This right—presumably a symbolic gesture rather than having any legal ramifications—was passed on all the way to al-Ḥusayn, who then divorced ʿĀʾisha on this occasion. The text goes on to claim that the Prophet had said that one of his wives would be divorced by his descendants and that this woman would not see him in paradise (163).
71. On the sexualized nature of ʿĀʾisha's legacy, see again Spellberg, *Politics, Gender, and the Islamic Past,* 161–165.
72. See, for example, Mordechai A. Friedman, "Tamar, A Symbol of Life: The 'Killer Wife' Superstition in the Bible and Jewish Tradition," *AJS Review* 15, no. 1 (Spring 1990): 23–61; Afsaneh Najmabadi, "Reading 'Wiles of Women' Stories as

Fictions of Masculinity," in *Imagined Masculinities: Male Identity and Culture in the Modern Middle East,* ed. Mai Ghoussoub and Emma Sinclair-Webb (London: Saqi Books, 2000), 147–168; Margaret A. Mills, "Whose Best Tricks? Makr-i zan as a Topos in Persian Oral Literature," *Iranian Studies* 32, no. 2 (Spring 1999): 261–270; Afsaneh Najmabadi, "Reading: And Enjoying: 'Wiles of Women' Stories as a Feminist," *Iranian Studies* 32, no. 2 (Spring 1999): 203–222; Margaret A. Mills, "The Gender of the Trick: Female Tricksters and Male Narrators," *Asian Folklore Studies* 60, no. 2 (2001): 237–258; E. A. W. Budge, trans., *The Book of the Cave of Treasures: A History of the Patriarchs and the Kings, Their Successors from the Creation to the Crucifixion of Christ* (London: Religious Tract Society, 1927, rep. Kessinger Publishing), 175.

73. See *al-Irshād,* 2:13–17 (Eng: 285–288). See also *Ithbāt,* 162; *Dalāʾil,* 68–70; *Iʿlām,* 214; *Manāqib,* 4:34, 47–48.
74. See al-Isfahāni, *Maqātil,* 72–77.
75. *Al-Irshād,* 2:16 (Eng: 287).
76. *Ithbāt,* 162.
77. Madelung discusses these accusations in some detail in *Succession to Muhammad,* 380–387.
78. Ibid., 385–387.
79. Mohammad-Djaʿfar Mahdjoub talks about the Shiʿa tendency to scapegoat the wives of good men: "The Evolution of Popular Eulogy of the Imams Among the Shiʿa," in *Authority and Political Culture in Shiʿism,* ed. S. Arjomand, trans. and adapt. John R. Perry (Albany: State University of New York Press, 1988), 59.
80. *Al-Irshād,* 2:16 (Eng: 287); *Manāqib,* 4:48.
81. *Manāqib,* 1:324. The last line is a partial quote of Sūrat al-Anʿān (6):112.
82. See M. Hodgson, "Ghulāt," EI[2]; Wadād al-Qāḍī, "The Development of the Term *ghulāt* in Muslim Literature with Special Reference to the Kaysāniyya," in *Akten des VII Kongresses für Arabistik und Islamwissenschaft,* ed. Albert Dietrich, 86–99 (Göttingen: Vandenhoeck & Ruprecht, 1976) (reprinted in *Shīʿism,* ed. E. Kohlberg, 169–194 [Burlington, VT: Ashgate, 2003]); Mohammad Ali Amir-Moezzi, *The Spirituality of Islam: Beliefs and Practices* (London: I. B. Tauris, 2011), 216; Matti Moosa, *Extremist Shiites: The Ghulat Sects* (Syracuse, NY: Syracuse University Press, 1988).
83. Sūrat al-Nisāʾ (4):171 (translation mine). Compare Sūrat al-Māʾida (5):77.
84. The most extensive investigation of the historicity of the Ibn Sabaʾ legend has recently been provided by Sean Anthony, *The Caliph and the Heretic: Ibn Saba' and the Origins of Shī'ism,* (Leiden: Brill, 2012).
85. See *al-Irshād,* 2:171, 308 (403, 504, respectively); *Iʿlām,* 287–294, 402–403; *Manāqib,* 1:239, 323–326, 2:334–339, 364, 375, 3:287, 295, 301, 4:228, 238–239; al-Fattāl, *Rawḍat,* 269; al-Ḥarrānī, *Tuhaf al-ʿuqūl* (Eng: 114–115, 189–190).
86. See *al-Irshād,* 2:190–209 (Eng: 417–430); *Iʿlām,* 284–287.
87. *Al-Irshād,* 2:206–207 (Eng: 429–430); *Iʿlām,* 289–290. See also Qadi, "al-Sayyid al-Ḥimyārī," EI[2].
88. *Al-Irshād,* 2:171 (Eng: 403).

89. *Manāqib,* 3:334–335.
90. Jonathan Brown, "Even If It's Not True It's True: Using Unreliable Ḥadīths in Sunni Islam," *Islamic Law and Society* 18 (2011): 1–52.
91. *Manāqib,* 3:335.
92. In addition to the sources cited below, see Modarressi's summary of the affair of Ja'far: *Crisis and Consolidation,* 70–86.
93. *Dalā'il,* 111. Compare *Iʿlām,* 398; *Manāqib,* 4:294.
94. Modarressi, *Crisis and Consolidation,* 70–77.
95. *Iʿlām,* 367–368; al-Irbilī, *Kashf,* 4:23, 112–113.
96. *Al-Irshād,* 2:323 (Eng: 514); *Manāqib,* 4:294.
97. *Al-Irshād,* 2:324, 336–337 (Eng: 515, 523); *Iʿlām,* 370–372; *Manāqib,* 4:455; al-Irbilī, *Kashf,* 4:65–68.
98. See *Ithbāt,* 166.
99. See *al-Irshād,* 2:238–239 (Eng: 452–453). Another example of brotherly betrayal would be Musa al-Kāzim's brother, Muḥammad, who was said to have spread doubt about al-Kāzim: *Dalā'il,* 169.
100. *Al-Irshād,* 2:171–174 (Eng: 403–405); Compare *Iʿlām,* 270. In at least one account, Muḥammad al-Ḥanafīya was also portrayed as having been shown the truth; in this case, a rock told him about Imam al-Sajjad's right to the imamate (*Dalā'il,* 84).
101. Modarressi, *Crisis and Consolidation,* 81, 84.
102. *Ithbāt,* 244.
103. *Al-Irshād,* 2:336–337 (Eng: 523); *Iʿlām,* 373–374, 399, 437; Irbilī, *Kashf,* 4:80, 113. See also Etan Kohlberg, "Vision and the Imams," in *Autour du regard: Mélanges Gimaret,* ed. É. Chaumont, with D. Aigle, M. A. Amir-Moezzi, and P. Lory, 125–157 (Paris: Peeters, 2003), 132.

Chapter 4: Vulnerable Bodies and Masculine Ideals

1. While there were early Shiʿa theological debates about the nature and extent of the imams' infallibility, most leaned toward a fairly expansive understanding of it. See Wilferd Madelung, "ʿIṣma," EI². On the early historical debates about the roles of the imams in general, see Hossein Modarressi, *Crisis and Consolidation in the Formative Period of Shiʿite Islam: Abū Jaʿfar ibn Qiba al-Rāzī and His Contribution to Imāmite Shīʿite Thought* (Princeton, NJ: The Darwin Press, 1993), 6–18.
2. On *ʿaṣabīya,* see F. Gabrieli, "ʿAṣabiyya," EI²; Helmut Ritter, "Irrational Solidarity Groups: A Socio-Psychological Study in Connection with Ibn Khaldūn," *Oriens* 1, no. 1 (1948): 1–44; Fuad Khuri, *Imams and Emirs: State, Religion and Sects in Islam* (London: Saqi Books, 1990), 50–56. As Ritter notes, the presence of social solidarity, or *ʿaṣabīya,* can effectively erase questions of right or wrong and create a space where things that would otherwise be prohibited become permissible (7, 8).
3. Nadia Maria El Cheikh, "In Search for the Ideal Spouse," *Journal of the Economic and Social History of the Orient* 45, no. 2 (2002): 194–195.

4. Frequently, the physical attributes of the imams were expressly compared with those of the Prophet. Al-Ḥasan was said to resemble the Prophet from the waist down and al-Ḥusayn was said to resemble the Prophet from the waist up: *al-Irshād*, 2:27 (Eng: 296). Also, on al-Ḥusayn's appearance in *maqātil* literature, see Khalid Sindawi, "The Image of Ḥusayn ibn ʿAlī in *Maqātil* Literature," *Quaderni di Studi Arabi* 20–21 (2002–2003): 83–90. In *Dalāʾil*, Fāṭima is recorded inquiring from the Prophet about the inheritance he would leave for her sons. The Prophet tells her that to al-Ḥasan he has left his prestige and power and to al-Ḥusayn he has left his courage and his generosity (7).
5. See Annemarie Schimmel, *And Muhammad Is His Messenger* (Chapel Hill: University of North Carolina Press, 1985), 32–45; Oleg Grabar, "The Story of Portraits of the Prophet Muhammad," *Studia Islamica* 96 (2003): 19–38.
6. *Iʿlām*, 98 (Eng: 129).
7. Sūrat Yūsuf (12):31. For a discussion of Joseph's beauty in relationship to the religious significance of the female body, see Fedwa Malti-Douglas, "Faces of Sin: Corporal Geographies in Contemporary Islamist Discourse," in *Religious Reflections on the Human Body*, ed. Jane Marie Law (Bloomington: Indiana University Press, 1995), 67–75, esp. 70; Annemarie Schimmel, "'I Take off the Dress of the Body': Eros in Sufi Literature and Life," in *Religion and the Body*, ed. Sarah Coakley (Cambridge: Cambridge University Press, 1997), 280.
8. Examples abound, concerning Fātima bt. Asad: al-Irbilī, *Kashf*, 1:124; Muḥammad: *Ithbāt*, 107; al-Ḥasan: *al-Irshād*, 2:5–7 (Eng: 279–280); al-Ḥusayn: *Iʿlām*, 219; al-Kāẓim: *al-Irshād*, 2:218 (Eng: 438); al-ʿAskarī: *al-Irshād*, 2:321 (Eng: 512). See also Uri Rubin, "Pre-existence and Light: Aspects of the Concept of Nūr Muḥammad," *Israel Oriental Studies* 5 (1975): 83–85; Marion Holmes Katz, *The Birth of the Prophet Muḥammad: Devotional Piety in Sunni Islam* (London: Routledge, 2007), 19–20. For an example of beauty playing a role in the description of a Christian saint, see the "Oration on Habib the Martyr, Composed by Mar Jacob," in *Ancient Syriac Documents Relative to the Earliest Establishment of Christianity in Edessa and the Neighboring Countries,"* ed. and trans. W. Cureton (Eugene, OR: Wipf & Stock, 2004), 86; Earnest A. Wallis Budge, trans., *The Book of the Cave of Treasures: A History of the Patriarchs and the Kings, Their Successors from the Creation to the Crucifixion of Christ* (London: Religious Tract Society, 1927; rep. Kessinger Publishing), 52, 71, 165; Budge, *The Book of the Bee: The Syriac Text* (Oxford: Clarendon Press, 1886; rep. Zuu Books, 2011), 65. For some examples of light imagery used in Christian hagiography, see Cureton, *Ancient Syriac Documents*, 86–96; Sebastian Brock, trans., *The History of the Holy Mar Maʿin, With a Guide to the Persian Martyr Acts* (Piscataway, NJ: Gorgias Press, 2008), 19; Budge, *Book of the Cave of Treasures*, 52, 147; Budge, *Book of the Bee*, 48, 67, 116.
9. *Manāqib*, 4:227.
10. Interestingly, Jo Ann McNamara discusses "profound disturbances in the gender system" in Europe at roughly the same time period in "The *Herrenfrage:* The Restructuring of the Gender System, 1050–1150," in *Medieval Masculinities: Regarding Men in the Middle Ages*, ed. Clare A. Lees, with Thelma Fenster and

Jo Ann McNamara (Minneapolis: University of Minnesota Press, 1994), 3–29. She coins the term *Herrenfrage* (literally, "the man question") in her discussion of the significant changes in how masculinity was conceived at the time.

11. Compare this to the many studies on roughly the same time period in Christian contexts. See John Boswell, *Christianity, Social Tolerance, and Homosexuality: Gay People in Western Europe from the Beginning of the Christian Era to the Fourteenth Century* (Chicago: University of Chicago Press, 1980); Peter Brown, *The Body and Society: Men, Women, and Sexual Renunciation in Early Christianity* (New York: Columbia University Press, 1988); Richard Trexler, ed., *Gender Rhetorics: Postures of Dominance and Submission in History* (Binghamton, NY: Medieval & Renaissance Texts & Studies, 1993); Clare Lees, ed., *Medieval Masculinities: Regarding Men in the Middle Ages,* with Thelma Fenster and Jo Ann McNamara (Minneapolis: University of Minnesota Press, 1994); Jeffrey Jerome Cohen and Bonnie Wheeler, eds., *Becoming Male in the Middle Ages* (New York: Garland Publishing, 1997); William E. Burgwinkle, *Sodomy, Masculinity, and Law in Medieval Literature: France and England, 1050–1230* (Cambridge: Cambridge University Press, 2004); Virginia Burrus, *The Sex Lives of the Saints: An Erotics of Ancient Hagiography* (Philadelphia: University of Pennsylvania Press, 2004); Tison Pugh, *Queering Medieval Genres* (New York: Palgrave Macmillan, 2004); P. H. Cullum and Katherine J. Lewis, *Holiness and Masculinity in the Middle Ages* (Cardiff: University of Wales Press, 2005); Jennifer Thibodeaux, ed., *Negotiating Clerical Identities: Priests, Monks and Masculinity in the Middle Ages* (Hampshire: Palgrave Macmillan, 2010); Cordelia Beattie, *Intersections of Gender, Religion, and Ethnicity in the Middle Ages* (New York: Palgrave Macmillan, 2011); Lynda Coon, *Dark Age Bodies: Gender and Monastic Practice in the Early Medieval West* (Philadelphia: University of Pennsylvania Press, 2011).
12. "*Kāna rajl^{an} badīn^{an}*": *al-Irshād,* 2:161. Howard translates it as "a well-built man" (396).
13. An example of this would be the marking on al-Jawād's body, which al-Mufīd, for one, presents as a proof of al-Jawād's imamate: *al-Irshād,* 2:278 (Eng: 483). Compare to *Ithbāt,* 218. The marking harkens back to the "seal" said to have been on Muḥammad's body. See also Uri Rubin, "Pre-existence and Light: Aspects of the Concept of Nūr Muḥammad." *Israel Oriental Studies* 5 (1975): 104; Victor Turner and Edith Turner, "Bodily Marks," ER2.
14. Similar observations have been made regarding Muslim descriptions of the Prophet's physical beauty. See Annemarie Schimmel, *And Muhammad Is His Messenger* (Chapel Hill: University of North Carolina Press, 1985), 34; Ruth Roded, "Alternate Images of the Prophet Muhammad's Virility," in *Islamic Masculinities,* ed. Lahoucine Ouzgane (London: Zed Books, 2006), 58. Denise Soufi discusses the connection between Fāṭima's beauty and her purity in "The Image of Fāṭimah in Classical Muslim Thought" (PhD diss., Princeton University, 1997), 162–167.
15. On Jābir b. ʿAbd Allāh b. ʿAmr al-Anṣārī, see Ibn Ḥajar, *Tahdhīb al-tahdhīb,* ed. Ibrāhīm al-Zaybaq and ʿĀdil Murshid (Beirut: Muʾassasat al-Risālah, 1996),

2:42–43; al-Ṣafadī, *al-Wāfī,* 11:27–28; Etan Kohlberg, "An Unusual Shīʿī *isnād,*" *Israel Oriental Studies* 5 (1975): 142–149; G. H. A. Juynboll, *Encyclopedia of Canonical Ḥadīth* (Leiden: Brill, 2007), 259–260.

16. *Ithbāt,* 176–177; *Irshād,* 2:158–159 (Eng: 394); *Dalāʾil,* 95; *Manāqib,* 4:212–213; Irbilī, *Kashf,* 3:84. In some reports, Jābir lifts his shirt and the shirt of al-Bāqir and presses their stomachs together: Irbilī, *Kashf,* 3: 86. On kissing in Sufi literature, see Schimmel, "Eros in Sufi Literature and Life," 279–280. Regarding the functions of kissing in religious contexts, see Geoffrey Parrinder, "Touching," ER2; Nicholas J. Perella, *The Kiss Sacred and Profane: An Interpretive History of Kiss Symbolism and Related Religio-Erotic Themes* (Berkeley: University of California Press, 1969). Other instances of kissing the bodies of the imams include ʿAlī kissing the feet of Muḥammad: *al-Irshād,* 1:116 (Eng: 78); *al-Irshād,* 2:321–322 (Eng: 512–513); 2: 353 (Eng: 531–532). One may also recall the modern controversy that surrounded the kissing of Ayyatullāh Khomeini's hands at the height of his popularity in Iran.
17. *Al-Irshād,* 2:166–167 (Eng: 400). Compare on al-Kāẓim: *Ithbāt,* 199; *al-Irshād,* 2:231–235 (Eng: 448–450).
18. On the general importance of this inner grouping of the family, see Diane D'Souza, *Partners of Zaynab: A Gendered Perspective of Shia Muslim Faith* (Columbia: University of South Carolina, 2014), 20–26.
19. On the *ahl al-kisāʾ* tradition, see Farhad Daftary, "Ahl al-Kisāʾ," EI[3].
20. Commenting on the centrality of love for this holy family, Christopher Clohessy notes, "God accomplishes everything, including the whole of creation, through them. They are the *raison d'être* for everything that God does, and the very salvation of humankind depends upon love for them" (*Fatima, Daughter of Muhammad* [Piscataway, NJ: Gorgias Press, 2009], 72).
21. *Al-Irshād,* 2:141 (Eng: 382).
22. Al-Mufīd listed love for the imams as one of the five pillars of Islam in his *Al Amaali,* 327. In *Iʿlām,* the Prophet says, "God loves whoever loves al-Ḥusayn" (224); compare *al-Irshād,* 2:127 (Eng: 374). See also *Ithbāt,* 134; 143; *al-Irshād,* 2:27–28 (Eng: 296); Bursī, *Mashāriq,* 99–102; Majlisī, *Tārīkh,* 290–291, 293. Mahmoud Ayoub also discusses this topic in *Redemptive Suffering in Islam: A Study of the Devotional Aspects of ʿĀshūrāʾ in Twelver Shīʿism* (The Hague: Mouton Publishers, 1978), 79; as does Rubin, "Pre-Existence," 66.
23. *Al-Irshād,* 167 (Eng: 400).
24. On bodily performance, see Marcel Mauss, "Le techniques du corps," *Journal de Psychologie* 32, no. 3–4 (1936): 3–23; Mary Douglas, *Natural Symbols: Explorations in Cosmology* (New York: Pantheon Books, 1982); Byran Turner, *Body and Society: Explorations in Social Theory* (New York: Blackwell, 1984); Scott Kugle, *Sufis & Saints' Bodies: Mysticism, Corporeality and Sacred Power in Islam* (Chapel Hill: University of North Carolina, 2007), 11–16.
25. On al-Bāqir's fearlessness of death, see *al-Irshād,* 2:161–162 (Eng: 396–397); *Manāqib* 4:217. On the heroism of al-Ḥusayn, see Sindawi, "The Image of Ḥusayn," 95–96.
26. For lions in early Christian hagiography, see Alison Goddard Elliott, *Roads to Paradise: Reading the Lives of the Early Saints* (Hanover, NH: Brown University

Press, 1987), 144–167, 193–205; Brock, *History of the Holy Mar Maʿin,* 70. On lions in Islamicate literatures, see Annemarie Schimmel, *Islam and the Wonders of Creation: The Animal Kingdom* (London: Al-Furqān Islamic Heritage Foundation, 1424/2003), 51–52.

27. See Khalid Sindawi, "The Role of the Lion in Miracles Associated with Shīʿite Imāms," *Der Islam* 84, no. 2 (2007): 356–390; D'Souza, *Partners of Zaynab,* 66.
28. *Ithbāt,* 217. There were pre-Islamic scholars who articulated the belief that the male sperm determined the sex of a child, such as Lactantius (d. ca. 320). See Virginia Burrus, *"Begotten, Not Made": Conceiving Manhood in Late Antiquity* (Stanford, CA: Stanford University Press, 2000), 31.
29. *Al-Irshād,* 2:186 (Eng: 406); *Dalāʾil,* 95; *Manāqib,* 3:84–85.
30. David Powers, *Muḥammad Is Not the Father of Any of Your Men* (Philadelphia: University of Pennsylvania Press, 2009), 9.
31. *Ithbāt,* 165. A different story, but one that again has Muḥammad choosing between Ibrāhīm and al-Ḥusayn, is found in *Manāqib,* 4:88–89. This can be contrasted with a narration by Ibn Isḥāq that states that had Ibrahīm lived, he would have been a truthful prophet and freed all of the Coptic slaves. See Aysha Hidayatullah, "Māriyya the Copt: Gender, Sex, and Heritage in the Legacy of Muhammad's *umm walad,*" *Islam and Christian-Muslim Relations* 21, no. 3 (2010): 237.
32. He was the tenth Umayyad caliph, ruling from 105/724 to 125/743. See Gabrieli, "Hishām," EI[2].
33. Other examples of imams displaying their skills with weaponry include al-Kāẓim coming down from the heavens with a lance (*ḥarba*) made of light (*Dalāʾil,* 156) and ʿAlī using a catapult (*Manāqib,* 2:335).
34. *natawāratha al-kamāl wa-al-tamām wa-al-dīn: Dalāʾil,* 104.
35. It is tempting here to suggest the caliph is "feminized" in this portrayal. If the sex/gender system that frames the outlook of the readers has an entirely polarized vision of maleness and femaleness, then would not unmasculine be equal to feminine? Derek Neal, in *The Masculine Self in Late Medieval England* (Chicago: University of Chicago, 2008), suggests this may not be a safe assumption (250). But perhaps, at the very least, trickery (*kayd*) seems to have a decidedly feminine association in the medieval context, which we saw in Chapter 3.
36. There are many examples for comparison where legitimacy/virtue/authenticity is discursively entwined with an attack on an opponent's masculinity. See Jennifer Knust, *Abandoned to Lust: Sexual Slander and Ancient Christianity* (New York: Columbia University Press, 2006); Knust, "Enslaved to Demons: Sex, Violence and the Apologies of Justin Martyr," in *Mapping Gender in Ancient Religious Discourses,* ed. Todd Penner and Caroline Vander Stichele (Leiden: Brill, 2007), 431–455.
37. *Dalāʾil,* 103–104.
38. Michael Cooperson, *Classical Arabic Biography* (Cambridge: Cambridge University Press, 2000), 98–99.
39. On early Muslim burial practices, see Leor Halevi, *Muhammad's Grave: Death Rites and the Making of Islamic Society* (New York: Columbia University Press, 2007).

40. *Dalāʾil,* 105–106.

41. This fits with most Shiʿa records, though whether ʿAlī was permitted to look upon the Prophet's genitals was more controversial among Sunnis. The debate over how the Prophet was prepared for burial overlaps with political controversies (see Wilferd Madelung, *Succession: A Study of the Early Caliphate* [Cambridge: Cambridge University Press, 1997], 356–360), disputes over proper Muslim burial rituals, and other social tensions. See Halevi, *Muhammad's Grave,* 43–51, 269 n. 8. Al-Mufīd also recorded an account of Muḥammad asking ʿAlī to wash his body and cover his nakedness: *al-Irshād,* 1:181–182 (Eng: 128). Compare *Ithbāt,* 125–126; *Iʿlām,* 146–147 (209); *Manāqib,* 1:295–296; Majlisī, *Tārīkh,* 123–124.

42. Compare Stephen D. Moore and Janice Capel Anderson, "Taking It Like a Man: Masculinity in 4 Maccabees," *Journal of Biblical Literature* 117, no. 2 (1998): 249–273.

43. Nimrod Hurvitz, "Biographies and Mild Asceticism: A Study of Islamic Moral Imagination," *Studia Islamica* 85 (1997): 58. The connection between *maghazī* literature and *sīra* literature on the Prophet is closely linked. Consider the number of traditions in Ibn Saʿd's *al-Ṭabaqāt al-kubrá* that describe the Prophet's sexual prowess, discussed by Roded, "Alternate Images," 57–71.

44. Al-Ḥasan b. ʿAlī al-Ḥarrānī, *Tuḥaf al-ʿuqūl ʿan āl al-Rasūl,* ed. ʿAlī Akbar al-Ghaffārī ([Beirut]: Dār al-Qārī, 2005), 351; Irbilī, *Kashf,* 3:81.

45. Generally speaking, the characteristics of "mild asceticism," as described by Hurvitz, apply to most of the descriptions of the imams. See Hurvitz, "Biographies and Mild Asceticism," 41–65.

46. Al-Ḥarrānī, *Tuhaf al-Uqoul: The Masterpieces of the Intellects,* trans. Badr Shahin (Qum: Ansariyan Publications, 2001), 347; Irbilī, *Kashf,* 3:109–110. One of the qualifications of an imam is that he is superior in knowledge to all other candidates for the office. Al-Mufīd discusses this in relation to al-Bāqir (*al-Irshād,* 2:157–158 [393–394]), among other places.

47. *Iʿlām,* 287.

48. This tripartite division of people into three categories—infallibles, followers, and subhumans—as it is found in Shiʿa literature in general, is discussed by M. A. Amir-Moezzi, "Seul l'homme de Dieu est humain: Theologie et anthropologie mystique à travers l'exégèse imamite ancienne (aspects de l'imamologie duodécimaine iv)," *Arabica* 45, no. 2 (1998): 193–214; trans. in *The Spirituality of Shiʿi Islam: Beliefs and Practices* (London: I. B. Tauris, 2011), 277–304. Roy Vilozny's study of al-Barqī's (d. 274/888 or 280/894) *al-Maḥāsin* suggests a twofold division of humanity may have been a common Shiʿa perspective in the eighth and ninth centuries, where the followers are generally grouped with the infallibles in the general category of the Shiʿa /saved/human and the other category was occupied by the non-Shiʿa /damned/subhuman. See "A Ŝīʿī Life Cycle According to al-Barqī's *Kitāb al-Maḥāsin,*" *Arabica* 54, no. 3 (2007): 362–396, esp. 393. Amir-Moezzi also has some comments on this twofold division of humanity, where the believer and imam share ontological similarities (*Spirituality,* 210–212). Judging from his citations, the possibility that this was an earlier Shiʿa perspective is supported. It

does seem that the collective biographies of the imams reflect and reinforce an idea of the imams as representing a distinct category of being, whereas the more juridical-minded collections of hadith do not. In the biographies, the idealization of the imams is more devotionally oriented, whereas in a practical-minded work like *al-Maḥāsin,* there is a greater interest in imitating the imams. Furthermore, the tripartite emphasis may partly be a response to the dilemma Vilozny discovers within *al-Maḥāsin*—how to make sense of those Shiʿa members of the community who do not live up to the expectations of the community. By separating the followers of the infallibles from the infallibles themselves, greater space is provided for coming to terms with the Shiʿa Muslim who commits major sins.

49. In addition to the discussion of these themes in Chapters 2 and 3, see Shona Wardrop's dissertation on the imams al-Jawād and al-Hādī, where this theme is shown to be pervasive: "The Lives of the Imāms, Muḥammad al-Jawād and ʿAlī al-Hādī and the Development of the Shīʿite Organization," (PhD diss., University of Edinburgh, 1988).
50. *Al-Irshād,* 2:167–168 (Eng: 401).
51. For comparison, see Hurvitz's analysis of how developing communal concerns shaped the biographies of Ibn Ḥanbal and the Prophet in "Biographies and Mild Asceticism."
52. See Mohammad Ali Amir-Moezzi, *The Divine Guide in Early Shiʿism: The Sources of Esotericism in Islam,* trans. David Streight (Albany: State University of New York Press, 1994), 91–97; Etan Kohlberg, "Vision and the Imams," in *Autour du regard: Mélanges Gimaret,* ed. É. Chaumont (Paris: Peeters, 2003), 125–157; Judith Loebenstein, "Miracles in Šīʿī Thought: A Case-Study of the Miracles Attributed to Imām Gaʿfar al-Ṣādiq," *Arabica* 50, no. 2 (2003): 199–244; Sindawi, "Role of the Lion," 356–390; Khalid Sindawi, "The Sea in the Miracles of Šīʿite Imams," *Oriente Moderno* 89, no. 2 (2009): 445–471; Amir-Moezzi, *Spirituality.*
53. Interestingly, the term *karāma* rarely appears in Shiʿa writings, and the imams' miracles were typically discussed in terms of *muʿjiza* or *kharq al-ʿāda* ("extraordinary"—a term which can refer to any type of miracle). See A. J. Wensinck, "Muʿdjiza," EI²; L. Gardet, "Karāma," EI²; Martin J. McDermott, *The Theology of al-Shaikh al-Mufid* (Beirut: Dar el-Machreq, 1978), 83–84, 112–114; Loebenstein, "Miracles," 202–211; John Renard, *Friends of God: Islamic Images of Piety, Commitment and Servanthood* (Berkeley: University of California Press, 2008), 91–98; David Thomas, "Miracles in Islam," in *The Cambridge Companion to Miracles,* ed. Graham H. Twelftree (Cambridge: Cambridge University Press, 2011), 199–215.
54. Arie Schippers, "'Tales with a Good Ending' in Arabic Literature: Narrative Art and Theory of the Arabic World," *Quaderni Di Studi Arabi* 4 (1986): 57–70.
55. The imams with the largest number of miracle attributions are the first (ʿAlī) and the sixth (al-Ṣādiq). See Mohammad Ali Amir-Moezzi, "Savior c'est pouvoir. Exegeses et implications du miracle dan l'imamisme ancient (Aspects de l'imamologie duodecimaine, V)," in *Miracle et karama,* ed. Denise Aigle (Turnhout, 2000), 251–286 and 258–259; trans. and repr. in *Spirituality,* 193–229

and 203–204). My research in this section supports the suggestion made by Loebenstein that all of the imams appear to have similar types of miracle accounts. See "Miracles in Šīʿī Thought," 242.

56. Sindawi separates al-Ḥusayn's miracles in *maqātil* literature into (a) those of salvation/deliverance, (b) punishment, and (c) those that take some time to happen ("Image of Ḥusayn," 96–100).

57. See Modarressi, *Crisis and Consolidation,* 3–105.

58. On Hisham b. Salim, see Khalid Sindawi, "Hishām b. Sālim al-Jawālīqī and His Role in Shīʿī Thought in the Second Century AH," *Ancient Near Eastern Studies* 48 (2011): 260–77.

59. See *Ithbāt,* 197–198; *al-Irshād,* 2:221–223 (440–442); *Dalāʾil,* 157; *Iʿlām,* 302–303. Also see the fear that underlies the two stories of ʿAlī b. Yaqtin: *al-Irshād,* 2:225–230 (444–447); *Dalāʾil,* 156–157; *Iʿlām,* 304–305. The student's inability to keep the master's identity secret is reminiscent of several accounts in the Christian gospels, for example, Matthew 16:20. Although there's no reason to suggest a textual reliance in this case, there are some rhetorical similarities.

60. *Iʿlām,* 356; also *Manāqib* 4:440.

61. There are many variations of this hadith. One example is Abū Dāwud, *Sunan* (Beirut: Dar al-Fikr, 2001 [1421]), 860 (#4596). Al-Bursī claimed Muḥammad knew 70,000 languages: *Mashāriq anwār al-yaqīn fī asrār Amīr al-Muʾminīn* (Beirut: Dār al-Andalus, 2001), 63.

62. The idea of talking to birds is particularly prominent in Islamicate literatures. The phrase "speech of the birds" (*manṭiq al-ṭayr*) is found in the Qurʾan (27:16, see discussion of Solomon below) and famously used as a mystical allegory in ʿAṭṭār's Persian classic, *Manṭiq al-ṭayr (Conference of the Birds).* On the topic of birds in relationship to the imams, see Khalid Sindawi, "The Role of Birds in Shiʿite Thought," *Quaderni* 3 (2008): 165–181. Examples of al-Kāẓim speaking with birds include *al-Irshād,* 2:225 (444); *Dalāʿil,* 168, 170; *Manāqib,* 4:329. See also a discussion of it attributed to al-Bāqir: *Manāqib,* 4:211.

63. *Manāqib,* 4:323. Also in *Ithbāt,* 199; *al-Irshād,* 2:224–225 (443–444), *Dala'il,* 166–167; *Iʿlām,* 305–306. In another case, a follower recalls watching al-Kazim speak to a group of thirty Abyssinian slaves in their language: *Dalāʾil,* 167.

64. For a Shiʿa theological discussion of the topic of intercession, see the relevant section in Murteẓa Muṭahharī's *ʿAdl ilāhī,* in *Majmūʿ-e āthār* (Tehran: Intashārāt-i ṣadrā, 1381/1423 [2002]), 1:241–265. Cf. McDermott, *Theology of al-Shaikh al-Mufid,* 251–276; Dakake, *Charismatic Community,* 172; Bayhom-Daou, *Shaykh Mufid,* 108. Knowledge of many / all languages was a common feature of Christian saints as well. There, however, the purpose was framed more frequently as a means to spread the Gospel rather than a proof of their validity. See Cureton, *Ancient Syriac Documents,* 8, 25.

65. *Dalāʾil* records al-Bāqir talking to jinn (100–101).

66. Al-Mufīd records al-Kāẓim talking to a tree: *al-Irshād,* 2:224 (443). Al-Bāqir is recorded speaking to milk and a stick: *Dalāʾil,* 95–96. Other instances of causing inanimate objects to speak are discussed by Loebenstein, "Miracles," 237–239.

67. References to prophets and Sufi saints talking to animals Renard, *Friends of God,* 110–112. Compare Elliott, *Roads to Paradise,* 193–204. There are many Christian examples of this motif in addition to those found in the Hebrew Bible (Genesis 3, Numbers 22, etc.). For ancient Syriac/Persian Christian hagiographical examples, see Brock, *History of the Holy Mar Maʿin,* 48, where the saint gives commands to a lion who obeys; and Budge, *Book of the Cave of Treasures,* 64. There are many interesting motifs that appear to overlap with the famed *Kalīla wa dimna* stories translated by Ibn al-Muqaffaʾ in the eighth century. This is a topic that deserves further study.
68. Sūrat al-naml (27):15–26.
69. Loebenstein, "Miracles," 241–242. See also Kohlberg, "Vision," 125–127; Khalid Sindawi, "The Donkey of the Prophet in the Shīʿite Tradition," *al-Masāq* 18, no. 1 (2006): 87–98, esp. 97–98.
70. Sindawi, "The Sea," 455. Examples of comparison between prophets and imams can be found throughout his article.
71. *Al-Irshād,* 2:219 (439).
72. *Al-Irshād,* 2:229–230 (447); two stories in *Manāqib,* 4:323–324.
73. *Al-Irshād,* 2:225 (444); *Dalāʾil,* 168, 170; *Manāqib,* 4:329. See also Sindawi, "Role of Birds," 165–181. Al-Bāqir also speaks with birds (*Ithbāt,* 177; *Dalāʾil,* 98), as does al-Hādī (*Dalāʾil,* 214).
74. *Al-Irshād,* 2:229–230 (447); *Manāqib,* 4:323. Further comments on the significance of lions are made below.
75. One category of stories that must have provoked much amusement were those that tell of the imams turning people into animals (typically as a punishment) and/or back into humans. See Kohlberg, "Vision," 143–146.
76. *Dalāʾil,* 98–99: al-Bāqir.
77. *Ithbāt,* 177: al-Bāqir.
78. *Al-Irshād,* 1:17 (10): ʿAlī.
79. *Ithbāt,* 180: al-Bāqir. For many more references to donkeys, see Sindawi, "The Donkey."
80. *Al-Irshād,* 1:347–348 (Eng: 263): ʿAlī. In this narrative, many of the fish speak to the imam, but a few remain silent. It turns out that the ones who do not speak to the imam are the ritually impure fish (eels and other scaleless fish *(marmāliq)*).
81. *Dalāʾil,* 98–99: al-Bāqir.
82. See Sindawi, "Role of Birds," 169. Or consider the instance where al-Kāẓim fed a poisoned date to the caliph's dog. Thus the animal world is not a utopia, but a place where the followers of the imams are the majority and the enemies are a minority—the opposite of the world in which the Shiʿa live. Compare *Dalāʾil,* 170.
83. *Manāqib,* 4:94.
84. *Al-Irshād,* 1:17, 319–320 (10, 241–242); *Iʿlām,* 169; *Manāqib,* 4:356.
85. Sindawi, "Role of Birds," 168–176.
86. Another example of animals performing Shiʿa rituals can be found in *Manāqib* 4:211. We could perhaps include here the ram that kills one of the people who hurt the Prophet: *Iʿlām,* 98–99 (Eng: 129).

87. An excellent discussion of this topic with regard to Shiʿa literature in general is provided by Kohlberg, "Vision," 125–157. Compare Renard, *Friends of God,* 112–115. Some specific examples in the case of al-Ṣādiq are listed in Loebenstein, "Miracles," 240.

88. A story of al-Ṣādiq records him rebuking a person for grabbing the breast of one of his slaves while he was away: *Dalāʾil,* 115. The same or a similar story is also told of al-Bāqir: Kohlberg, "Vision," 129.

89. Imams are given a light by which they can see the world in all places and see all actions (Kohlberg, "Vision," 125–126, cites *Basa'ir,* Majlisi, Khasibi's *Hidayat*). This may be the kind of sight given to Abraham in Sūrat al-anʿām (6):75.

90. Al-Bāqir answered the questions of a person before they are asked in *Ithbāt,* 108–109; *Dalāʾil,* 108–109. *Iʿlām* describes al-Ṣādiq performing a similar feat (278–279). Al-Kāẓim does the same: *Dalāʾil,* 157; Al-ʿAskarī: *al-Irshād,* 2:331 (520).

91. ʿAlī has knowledge of events yet to come in his life, death, and the situation of his descendants: *Iʿlām,* 179–184. Al-Bāqir foresees the destruction of a building: *Dalāʾil,* 109; predicts the fate of Zayd b. ʿAlī: *Ithbāt,* 177, 183. Al-Kāẓim: *Ithbāt,* 197; *al-Irshād,* 2:224–225 (443); *Dalāʾil,* 163–164; *Manāqib,* 4:327–328.

92. Al-Sajjād takes a trip up to heaven (for references to this story, see Amir-Moezzi, "Knowledge Is Power," in *Spirituality,* 209). And al-Hādī appears to escort a friend to heaven personally: *al-Irshād,* 2:311 (Eng: 506); though this may simply be a vision of heaven.

93. Another example of this ambiguity is present when al-Ṣādiq appears to see/perceive/know the ritual impurity of one of his followers: *al-Irshād,* 2:185 (Eng: 413).

94. See Kohlberg, "Vision," 149.

95. Al-Bāqir can show people visions of the unseen: *Ithbāt,* 179–180; *Manāqib* 4:199–200. We will also note in Chapter 5 the accounts of various forms of light that people witness in the imams, especially at their births.

96. Multiple references for this can be found in Amir-Moezzi, *Spirituality,* 207; Kohlberg, "Vision," 132.

97. Like the other items passed down to the imams, the rod remains today with al-Mahdī. In a miracle attributed to Imam al-Bāqir, the imam strikes the rod of Moses against a rock to draw water from it: *Dalaʾil,* 97—clearly mirroring the famous story of Moses in the Hebrew Bible (Numbers 20:1–13), which has featured prominently in Christian literature as well. Note also that al-Sharīf al-Raḍī uses *qaḍīb* and mantle (*burd*) as symbols of the Prophet's authority (see quote provided by Suzanne Stetkevych, "Al-Sharīf al-Raḍī and the Poetics of ʿAlid Legitimacy Elegy for al-Ḥusayn ibn ʿAlī on ʿĀshūrāʾ, 391 A.H.," *Journal of Arabic Literature* 38 [2007]: 295–296). Christian hagiography sometimes mentioned the passing down of Moses's rod, for example, Budge, *Cave of Treasures,* 166.

98. On Jibt and Ṭāghūt, see Maria Dakake, "Hiding in Plain Sight: The Practical and Doctrinal Significance of Secrecy in Shi'ite Islam," *Journal of the American Academy of Religion* 74, no. 2 (2006): 344–345. Compare Sūrat al-nisāʾ (4):51.

99. This is a reference to those who met at Saqīfa Banī Sāʿida to choose Muḥammad's successor while ʿAlī was away. This is discussed in Chapter 3, but for general references, see G. Lecomte, "Saḳīfa," EI²; Madelung, *Succession*, 28–45.
100. Nāfiʿ b. al-Azraq (d. 65/685) was an early leader of the Azāriqa Kharijite group. See Keith Lewinstein, "Azāriqa," EI³.
101. Abū Sufyān b. Ḥarb and Marwān b. al-Ḥakam represent the two royal lineages of the Umayyad Kingdom
102. *Ithbāt*, 195–196.
103. *Al-Irshād*, 2:225–227 (444–445); *Dalāʾil*, 156–157; *Iʿlām*, 304. For similar accounts, compare another story involving al-Kāẓim and ʿAlī b. Yaqṭīn (*al-Irshād*, 2:227–230, [445–447]; *Iʿlām*, 304–305).
104. Loebenstein chose to mark knowledge-related miracles as one of the categories of al-Ṣādiq's miracles. The other categories used by Loebenstein were those that concerned life and death and those that were nature related. See Loebenstein, "Miracles in Shīʿī Thought." This highlights the abovementioned difficulty of typologizing the imams' miracles. In this section, however, I follow Amir-Moezzi's lead in seeing knowledge as a critical aspect of most of the miracle accounts. See Amir-Moezzi, *Divine Guide*, 69–79; Amir-Moezzi, "Knowledge," in *Spirituality*, esp. 199–200.
105. As a child, al-Kāẓim is shown to be superior to Abū Ḥanīfa (*Ithbāt*, 191–192; *Dalāʾil*, 159), the eponymous founder of the Ḥanafī school of law. Another account demonstrates his superiority over Abū Yūsuf (Bāqir Sharīf Qarashī, *The Fourteen Infallibles in the History of Islam* (Qum: Ansariyan, 1999–2010), 9:197–198), another key figure in the development of Ḥanafī law. Al-Mufid records that al-Kāẓim invalidated the teachings of the jurists of Medina: *al-Irshād*, 2:223 (Eng: 443). Al-Ṣādiq said: "We are the interpreters (*tarājima*) of God's revelation; we are the reservoir of God's knowledge; we are the infallibles. God has commanded obedience to us and forbidden disobedience. We are the profound proof (*al-ḥujja al-bāligha*) for everyone between heaven and earth" (*Iʿlām*, 287).
106. This tension is explored by Hamid Dabashi : *Religion of Protest* (Cambridge, MA: Belknap Press, 2011).
107. Quoted in Renard, *Friends of God*, 266.
108. See Sindawi, "Role of the Lion," esp. 378–384. In one account, the lion from a curtain jumped out at the imam's command (*Manāqib* 4:323–324). In another instance, al-ʿAskarī was thrown to the wild animals to be eaten, but instead the lions joined the imam in prayer: *al-Irshād*, 2:334–335 (522). Shiʿa writers have often claimed that no wild beast would ever eat a descendent of the prophet: Sindawi, "Role of the Lion," 385–388. Ibn ʿAbd al-Waḥḥāb recorded a lion bowing down to Imam ʿAlī in *Uyūn al-muʿjizāt* (Beirut: Muʾassasat al-Aʿlamī lil-Maṭbūʿāt, 2004), 25; 73). This can be contrasted with famous Christian martyrs who, though they were sometimes saved (e.g., Daniel, in the Hebrew tradition), they were often devoured by lions (Saint Ignatius comes to mind). Further, the legendary *Abū Muslim Nāma* contained a physical battle between Abū Muslim and a tiger, a scene that I have not found replicated among the biographies of the imams. See Kathryn

Babayan, *Mystics, Monarchs, and Messiahs: Cultural Landscapes of Early Modern Iran* (Cambridge, MA: Harvard University Press, 2002), 129. A shift in how lions figured in Christian hagiography was occurring around this same time, changing from an animal to which martyrs were fed to an animal that aided the saint. See Elliott, *Roads to Paradise,* 193–204.

109. Examples of the imams transporting their bodies across great distances or through barriers include *Ithbāt,* 196–197, 215–216; and *Dalāʾil,* 133 (where Imam al-Ṣādiq sailed with a companion out to a place where the prophet and previous imams lived in tents). Compare *Dalāʾil,* 139–140. Loebenstein lists some examples of al-Ṣādiq's travels in "Miracles," 240. Amir-Moezzi cites examples in several sources for numerous imams: *Spirituality,* 204–208. The imams were also able to transport the bodies of other people (see the example of Aḥmad al-Tabbān below) and other objects (al-Kāẓim, for example, twice caused a special book to return to him from another location: *Dalāʾil,* 169–170; *Manāqib,* 4:328–329). For this theme in other types of hagiographies, see Renard, *Friends of God,* 115–116.

110. In the latter case, the imam typically returns himself to the place of captivity once his task is finished. This is the case in the story of al-Kāẓim recorded by al-Ṭabrisī (*Iʿlām,* 306). In this account, Abū al-Khālid al-Zabbālī recalls his distress when he saw that the Caliph al-Mahdī had Imam al-Kāẓim in his control and was transferring him to another location. But the imam told Abū al-Khālid to meet him at a specific place on a certain day. Abū al-Khālid faithfully went to the location specified by the imam and awaited his coming. The devoted follower was rewarded when, late in the day, the imam arrived on a mule. When the imam called to him, Abū al-Khālid exclaimed, "Here I am, oh son of the Prophet! Praise God that he saved you from their grip!" But the imam ironically responded, "Abū al-Khālid, I will return to them; I have not escaped [permanently] from them." Interestingly, this is one of the uncommon instances where al-Ṭabrisī adds material not found in al-Mufīd's *al-Irshād.* Within this narrative alone, it is unclear whether al-Kāẓim's movement was miraculous or under the caliph's permission. The same story is found in the *Ithbāt* (196–197), but in the *Ithbāt* the narrator claims God tricked the caliph into giving the imam permission to leave (*ṣarafa Allāh kaydahi ʿanhu*). In either case, the nature of the story fits a general pattern of similar stories about the imams' temporary escapes that make the miraculous nature of the event clearer. This particular story is useful in pointing again to the devotional and didactic purposes of these stories. In this case, the imam's forced departure from the placed inhabited by Abū al-Khālid parallels the forced departure of the twelfth imam, al-Mahdī. In both cases, the followers are informed that the imam will return. And in the case of Abū al-Khālid, his obedience and patience, despite the late hour of the imam's return, was rewarded. As seen already in Chapter 3, the captivity that many of the imams endured during their lifetimes provided fertile ground for the cultivation of religious imagery that can meaningfully speak to a community awaiting the return of al-Mahdī. As the faithful await their imam, they can trust that the imams will protect them. Repeatedly we see that, without trying to forcefully control the flow of history—a history that is destined to

persecute, and eventually murder, them—the imams step outside that natural history to attend to the needs of those who love them.

111. The text here seems to indicate the importance of the Mosque of Kūfa having something to do with a bronze basin (*ṭast*) that is there, but I have yet to identify the significance of this reference.

112. Here the imam displays his ability to control the movement of celestial bodies, particularly the sun.

113. *Dalāʾil*, 170–171.

114. Of course, this also creates a delightful ambiguity as to whether the whole event was just a dream. Nothing in the language suggests this to be the case, but the fact that the narrator was sleeping when the story started and sleeping when it ended certainly leaves open that possibility. Other stories of the imams transporting themselves (with or without others) are less ambiguous, however, and were clearly understood to be real events.

115. Of course, Fāṭima is not a daughter of an imam, but the daughter of the Prophet. But the category of the imams overlaps with that of the Prophet to such a degree that the effect remains the same. See more on Fāṭima below.

116. On Zaynab, see Tahera Qutbuddin, "Zaynab bint ʿAli," ER2; D'Souza, *Partners of Zaynab*, 20–54. Among the biographies of the imams, *Ithbāt* and *Dalāʾil* have very little on Zaynab, but *al-Irshād* (esp. 2:115–120 [Eng: 365–369]) has influential stories about Zaynab that are then found partially in *Iʿlām*, *Manāqib*, and subsequent biographies.

117. On Zaynab's legacy in relationship to Karbala, see Kamran Scot Aghaie, *The Martyrs of Karbala* (Seattle: University of Washington Press, 2004), 9, 118, 136–137; Aghaie, ed., *The Women of Karbala: Ritual Performance and Symbolic Discourses in Modern Shiʿi Islam* (Austin: University of Texas Press, 2005) (esp. chaps. by Ingvild Flaskerud, Faegheh Shirazi, Syed Akbar Hyder, and Lara Z. Deeb); Lara Deeb, *An Enchanted Modern: Gender and Public Piety in Shiʿi Lebanon* (Princeton, NJ: Princeton University Press, 2006), 148ff; D'Souza, *Partners of Zaynab*, 40–54.

118. *Al-Irshād*, 2:115–116 (Eng: 365); *Iʿlām*, 257.

119. *Al-Irshād*, 2:116–117 (Eng: 366); *Iʿlām*, 257. In another case, Zaynab tends to the ill imam: *al-Irshād*, 2:93 (Eng: 348).

120. *Al-Irshād*, 2:121 (369); *Iʿlām*, 258.

121. *Dalāʾil*, 205, 264–265; *al-Iʿlām*, 408; *Manāqib*, 4:411, 426–427, 474; Abū al-Ḥasan al-Irbilī, *Kashf al-ghumma fī maʿrifat al-aʾimma*, ed. ʿAlī al-Fāḍilī ([Iran]: Markaz al-Ṭibāʿa wa-al-Nashr lil-Majmaʿ al-ʿĀlamī li-Ahl al-Bayt, 1426 [2005–2006]), 3:143, 237–238, 241, 274.

122. Ḥāzim al-Khāqānī, *Ummuhāt al-aʾimma* (Beirut: Dār al-Ḥaqq, 1995), 191. She is also the wife of Imam al-Sajjād and mother of Imam al-Bāqir, thus uniting the Ḥasanid and Ḥusaynid lines of the family.

123. *Ithbāt*, 167.

124. *Ithbāt*, 217–218; *Dalāʾil*, 197.

125. Neal, *The Masculine Self*, 252.

126. *Manāqib*, 3:407.

127. Cited by Soufi, "The Image," 169.
128. See Ibn ʿAbd al-Wahhāb, *ʿUyūn,* 140–141; *Iʿlām,* 161–162. See also Soufi, "The Image," 68.
129. Ibn ʿAbd al-Wahhāb, *ʿUyūn,* 135–136, 143–145; *Manāqib,* 3:372. See also the references in Chapter 5; Clohessy, *Fatima,* 70–78.
130. *Dalāʾil,* 12; Ibn ʿAbd al-Wahhāb, *ʿUyūn,* 139. See also Soufi, "The Image," 75; Clohessy, *Fatima,* 82–86.
131. *Iʿlām,* 162–165; *Manāqib,* 3:380, passim. See also Clohessy, *Fatima,* 67–68.
132. *Dalāʾil,* 56–57. See also Soufi, "The Image," 77; Clohessy, *Fatima,* 98–99.
133. *Ithbāt,* 168–169; *al-Irshād,* 2:159, 186 (Eng: 395, 414); *Iʿlām,* 287–288. See Khalid Sindawi, "'Fāṭima's Book': A Shiʿite Qurʾan," *Rivista degli studi orientali* 78, no. 1 (2007): 57–70.
134. For example, she knows of al-Ḥusayn's future painful martyrdom (Soufi, "The Image," 63–4). See also Ibn ʿAbd al-Wahhāb, *ʿUyūn,* 144.
135. She prays so much, for instance, that her feet swell (*Dalāʾil,* 56; Irbilī, *Kashf,* 2:181). See also Soufi, "The Image," 74.
136. See references in Soufi, "The Image," 100–106. This is typically understood to refer primarily to the piece of land called Faḍak, but, as Margoliouth has pointed out, the earliest sources are not always clear about the content of Fāṭima's inheritance, and it occasionally overlaps with her protest over Abū Bakr's claim to the caliphate: David Samuel Margoliouth, "The Last Days of Fatimah," in *Mélanges Hartwig Derenbourg, 1844–1908: Recueil de travaux d'érudition dédiés à la mémoire d'Hartwig Derenbourg par ses amis et ses élèves* (Paris: E. Leroux, 1909), 279–286. The possibility that Fāṭima may have been intended to inherit the caliphate itself is hinted at by Wilferd Madelung, "Introduction," in *The Study of Shiʿi Islam: History, Theology, and Law,* edited by Farhad Daftary and Gurdofarid Miskinzoda (New York: I. B. Tauris, 2014), 3–16. Fāṭima is, of course, denied this inheritance and is thus effectively subjected to betrayal by the Prophet's companions. For more on the betrayal suffered by each of the imams, see Chapter 3.
137. See references in Soufi, "The Image," 109–110, 120.
138. Soufi, "The Image," 119. For more on the topic of martyrdom of the imams, see Chapters 2 and 3.
139. See Soufi, "The Image," 181–195.
140. Quoted from *Bihār al-anwār* by Clohessy, *Fatima,* 67; he gives other references there as well, along with other ways in which her unique status was commented upon.
141. This journey has typically been linked to the *isrāʾ*: Sūrat al-Isrāʾ (17):1. For an overview of this topic, see B. Schrieke [J. Horovitz], "Miʿrādj: In Islamic Exegesis," EI^2; J. E. Bencheikh, "Miʿrādj: In Arabic Literature," EI^2. For the problems that this creates for dating the birth of Fāṭima, see Clohessy, *Fatima,* 16–20.
142. *Iʿlām,* 164. See also Ibn ʿAbd al-Wahhāb, *ʿUyūn,* 137–139; *Manāqib,* 3:383.
143. On the motif of wifely jealousy, see Chapter 3.
144. *Iʿlām,* 164. See also Ibn ʿAbd al-Wahhāb, *ʿUyūn,* 137–139; *Manāqib,* 3:383.
145. Ibid.; Soufi, "The Image," 163–165; Clohessy, *Fatima,* 68–69, 78–84.
146. *Manāqib,* 3:382. See also al-Irbilī, *Kashf,* 2:179.

147. Ibn ʿAbd al-Wahhāb, *ʿUyūn,* 140; *Iʿlām,* 162; *Manāqib,* 3:391; References in Soufi, "The Image," 74.
148. *Manāqib,* 3:406. See also: Soufi, "The Image," 69; Clohessy, *Fatima,* 65.
149. Al-Irbilī, *Kashf,* 2:250–260. Interestingly, this tradition is mostly found among Sunni sources. See Soufi, "The Image," 121–122, n. 168.
150. Ibn ʿAbd al-Wahhāb, *ʿUyūn,* 145–146; *Iʿlām,* 165. On the legal and cultural debates over the merits of a husband washing the body of his deceased wife, see Halevi, *Muhammad's Grave,* 43–83, esp. 59–62, where the example of ʿAlī washing the body of Fāṭima plays a role in how Shiʿa scholars articulated their position on this topic. See also Soufi, "The Image," 121–124.
151. *Iʿlām,* 165.
152. *Manāqib,* 3:405. Cf. *Dalāʾil,* 55–56; Ibn ʿAbd al-Wahhāb, *ʿUyūn,* 145–146. See also Soufi, "The Image," 162.
153. *Manāqib,* III: 405.
154. Soufi, "The Image," 163. On the *ḥūrīya,* see A. J. Wensinck [Ch. Pellat], "Ḥūr," EI^2.
155. *Dalāʾil,* 54–55; Ibn ʿAbd al-Wahhāb, *ʿUyūn,* 140; Soufi, "The Image," 162–164; Karen Ruffle, "May Fatimah Gather Our Tears: The Mystical and Intercessory Powers of Fatimah al-Zahra in Indo-Persian, Shiʿi Devotional Literature and Performance," *Comparative Studies of South Asia, Africa, and the Middle East* 30, no. 3 (2010): 397.
156. See the sources listed in Soufi, "The Image," 158–166; Clohessy, *Fatima,* 94–99; Ruffle, "May Fatimah Gather," 386–389.
157. *Dalāʾil,* 13. See also Soufi, "The Image," 159.
158. For an interesting example, see Fedwa Malti-Douglas's discussion of Shahrazad in *Woman's Body, Woman's Word: Gender and Discourse in Arabo-Islamic Writing* (Princeton, NJ: Princeton University Press, 1991), 11–28.
159. Ruth Mazo Karras, "Active/Passive, Acts/Passions: Greek and Roman Sexualities," *The American Historical Review* 105, no. 4 (2000): 1250–1265.
160. Cited in Soufi, "The Image," 162.
161. Babayan, *Mystics, Monarchs, and Messiahs,* 128. Or consider the vision attributed to al-Shāfiʿī's mother, who compared giving birth to seeing Jupiter rise "from her womb" (*min farjihā*): mentioned by Kecia Ali, *Imam Shafiʿi: Scholar and Saint* (Oxford: Oneworld, 2011), 111.
162. Babayan, *Mystics, Monarchs, and Messiahs,* 128–134.
163. *Ithbāt,* 163–164; Ibn ʿAbd al-Wahhāb, *ʿUyūn,* 140; *Iʿlām,* 161–162. See also Clohessy, *Fatima,* 111–115.
164. *Ithbāt,* 163–164.
165. Ibn ʿAbd al-Wahhab, *ʿUyūn,* 61–62; Soufi, "The Image," 173ff; Clohessy, *Fatima,* 111–115.
166. Jennifer Glancy, *Corporeal Knowledge: Early Christian Bodies* (Oxford: Oxford University Press, 2010), 81–136.
167. *Dalāʾil,* 55. See also Irbilī, *Kashf,* 2:173. On her virginity, see Soufi, "The Image," 167–180; Clohessy, *Fatima,* 103–133. Of course, this clearly relates to the theoretical rivalry between the Virgin Mary and Fāṭima. I discuss this more below. But we

also see here the way in which the category of daughters is regarded with great esteem (albeit derived from their fathers).

168. *Manāqib,* 3:407. Within this accusation is another example of the thorough dehumanization of non-Shiʿa (per the previous discussion in this chapter). It is not a coincidence that the slander is used here in reference to the abuse received by the very woman who never menstruated. See also Etan Kohlberg, "The Position of the 'walad zinā' in Imāmī Shīʿism," *BSOAS* 48, no. 2 (1985): 239; Soufi, "The Image," 113–114.

169. *Manāqib,* 3:383, 409; al-Irbilī, *Kashf,* 2:180. Here again, Fāṭima is being put into implicit comparison with Mary, who is described in the Qurʾan as having "kept her vagina chaste" (Sūrat al-Taḥrīm [66]:12).

170. Within the broader Islamic tradition, medieval Muslim scholars have sometimes compared the merits of women such as Āsīya, Mary, Khadīja, Fāṭima, and ʿĀʾisha. See Denise Spellberg, *Politics, Gender, and the Islamic Past: The Legacy of ʿAʾisha bint Abi Bakr* (New York: Columbia University Press, 1994), esp. 151–190. For most Shiʿa, ʿĀʾisha does not belong in this discussion and is often derided explicitly (see Chapter 3). The biographies used in this study are most commonly interested in the comparisons between Mary and Fāṭima. On this topic, see Mary F. Thurlkill, *Chosen Among Women: Mary and Fatima in Medieval Christianity and Shiʿite Islam* (Notre Dame, IN: Notre Dame University Press, 2007). Ibn Shahrāshūb gives an extensive comparison of the two (3:407–410), and the other biographers of Fāṭima tend to draw comparisons as well (see *Dalāʾil,* 54–57; Ibn ʿAbd al-Wahhāb, *ʿUyūn,* 141–143; *Iʿlām,* 163). Some of the names and qualities of Fāṭima appear to be in direct relationship to Mary, perhaps as an attempt to make sure Fāṭima measures well in the comparison. The attribution of "the virgin" (*al-batūl*) is particularly pertinent in this regard, and the title of "the greater Mary" (*Marīyam al-kubrá*) is even more telling. In all cases, Fāṭima is considered by the Shiʿa biographers to be the greatest of these women, and they crown her with the title "queen of women" (*sayyidat al-nisaʾ*). See also Soufi, "The Image," 167–198; Verena Klemm, "Image Formation of an Islamic Legend: Fāṭima, the Daughter of the Prophet Muḥammad," in *Ideas, Images, and Methods of Portrayal,* ed. S. Günther (Leiden: Brill, 2005), 193–195; Clohessy, *Fatima,* 53–66, 193–223.

171. This has been particularly well explained by Jamal Elias in "Female and Feminine in Islamic Mysticism," *Muslim World* 77, nos. 3–4 (1988): 209–224. On this observation in relationship to Fāṭima, see Soufi, "The Image," 166–167, 196–197; Ruffle, "May Fatimah," esp. 396–397. An even more spiritualized version of the feminine ideal—which is mostly foreign to the biographies used in this study, but interesting for comparative purposes—is described by Henry Corbin, *Spiritual Body and Celestial Earth: From Mazdean Iran to Shīʿite Iran,* trans. Nancy Pearson (Princeton, NJ: Princeton University Press, 1977), esp. 51–73. Barbara Stowasser has described how the wives of the Prophet form a type of feminine ideal in many Sunni literatures: "The Mothers of the Believers in the Ḥadīth," *The Muslim World* 82, nos. 1–2 (1992): 33–35.

172. Soufi, "The Image," 207.

173. See Ruffle, "May Fatimah;" Klemm, "Image Formation." For examples of how the legacies of Fāṭima and Zaynab have recently been used to justify women's participation in public affairs, see Lara Deeb, "From Mourning to Activism: Sayyedeh Zaynab, Lebanese Shi'i Women, and the Transformation of Ashura," in *Women of Karbala*, ed. K. Aghaie (Austin: University of Texas Press, 2005), 241–266; Lara Deeb, "Doing Good, Like Sayyida Zaynab': Lebanese Shi'i Women's Participation in the Public Sphere," in *Religion, Social Practice, and Contested Hegemonies: Reconstructing the Public Sphere in Muslim Majority Societies*, ed. Armando Salvatore and Mark LeVine (New York: Palgrave, 2005), 85–107; Matthew Pierce, "Remembering Fāṭima: New Means of Legitimizing Female Authority in Contemporary Shīʿī Discourse," in *Women, Leadership, and Mosques: Changes in Contemporary Islamic Authority*, ed. Masooda Bano and Hilary Kalmbach (Leiden: Brill, 2012), 345–362; D'Souza, *Partners of Zaynab;* Thurlkill, *Chosen Among Women.*

174. Consider, for instance, the verse that Ibn Shahrāshūb includes, which is attributed to Fāṭima:

> There remains only one measure [of barley]:
> My hand bled despite my arm.
>
> And I have not veil [to wear] on my head
> Except a cloak whose fabric is worn out.
>
> By God, my sons are starving!
> O lord, don't leave them wretched!
>
> Their father is committed to good
> With stout arms and strong hands.

In this verse, Fāṭima faces great difficulties, but she endures them in a model fashion and praises her husband in conclusion (this translation is taken from Soufi, "The Image," 62–63).

175. Soufi, "The Image," 70–71.

176. Irbilī, *Kashf,* 2:267. See further references in Soufi, "The Image," 180–195. See also Muḥammad b. Muḥammad b. al-Nuʿmanī Mufid, *al-Amālī* (Najaf: al-Maṭbaʿat al-Haydariyah, 1962), translated by Asgharali M. M. Jaffer, *Al Amaali* (Middlesex: World Federation, 1998), 133. In a powerful narrative, Imam ʿAlī prays over Muḥammad's grave, saying, "Your daughter will inform you of your community's collaboration in oppressing her, so ask her about what happened!" (Soufi, "The Image," 124; see references to Ibn Abī Ḥadīd, Kulaynī, and al-Mufīd). See also Clohessy, *Fatima,* 163–192.

177. "Whenever one of the fatiyān from anywhere seeks me out, I sense the light of his intention in my inner soul until he arrives. If I am successful in serving him and fulfilling his needs, that light becomes fully mine, but if I cut short my service to him the light goes out": Abū ʿAbd al-Raḥmān Sulamī, *Early Sufi Women: Dhikr an-niswa al-muta ʿabbidāt aṣ-ṣūfiyyāt,* trans. Rkia E. Cornell (Louisville, KY: Fons Vitae, 1999), 196–197.

178. *Manāqib,* 3:410. I have here borrowed Soufi's translation (117–118). This is also found in *Dalāʾil.*
179. See Chapter 2 for a more complete discussion of how the elegies modeled an appropriate manner of coping with the betrayal of the imams. Mourning poetry (*rithāʾ*) was often composed by women in pre-Islamic Arabic and continued to have feminine connotations into the medieval period.
180. See Soufi, "The Image," 119; Klemm, "Image Formation," 204; Clohessy, *Fatima,* 48–66, 135–162; Ruffle, "May Fatimah," 386.
181. D'Souza notes this phenomenon playing out in contemporary ritual practices (*Partners of Zaynab,* 53).
182. I have touched on this topic elsewhere: Pierce, "Loving Fatima: Gender, Religious Devotion, and Islamic Sectarianism" (lecture, Ali Vural Ak Center for Global Islamic Studies, George Mason University, Fairfax, VA, October 29, 2013), http://islamicstudiescenter.gmu.edu/articles/6207.
183. On this, see *Dalāʾil,* 15–18; Ibn ʿAbd al-Wahhāb, *ʿUyūn,* 136; *Iʿlām,* 164–165; *Manāqib,* 3:393–405; Soufi, "The Image," 38–50; Khalid Sindawi, "Legends Concerning the Wedding of Fāṭima al-Zahrāʾ as Reflected in Early Shīʿite Literature," *Orientalia Suecana* 56 (2007): 181–191.
184. Amir-Moezzi has noted that the earliest Shiʿa sources do not typically list miracles being performed by Fāṭima at all: "Knowledge," in *Spirituality,* 203 n. 31.
185. In some ways, the very act of conquering bodily deficiencies makes Fāṭima more relevant to men as well. The imams, of course, have completely perfect bodies but also have the power to completely transcend their confines and limitations. Normal men, however, are less perfect manifestations of humanity and thus the process of emulating the imams includes attempting to overcome their own individual bodily shortcomings (even if they are not inherent to their masculinity). Fāṭima's overcoming of her bodily deficiencies ironically becomes a more achievable goal for men.
186. Kugle, *Sufis & Saints' Bodies,* 78.
187. Schimmel has noted the tendency to associate the feminine with the material world and the masculine with the spiritual world in much of the contemporaneous Sufi literature: "Eros in Sufi Literature,'" 268–283.
188. In this regard, I find Athalya Brenner's critique of Danial Boyarin and Howard Eilberg-Schwartz to be a helpful one: "Mat[t]er, Dichotomy: Some Images of Female and Male Bodies in the Hebrew Bible," in *Begin with the Body,* ed. J. Bekkenkamp and M. De Haardt (Leuven: Peeters, 1998), 201–214. Brenner argues that while the Hebrew Bible may not have as severe a mind-body dualism as would develop in the Christian tradition, the mere fact that gender is both binary and hierarchical inevitably leads to a type of body-nonbody dualism as well. Similarly, though many Islamicate literatures avoid a full denial of the body (as might be readily found in many early Christian literatures, for instance), corporeal functions are not imbued with the same level of religious significance as the noncorporeal.
189. Caroline Walker Bynum, "Why All the Fuss about the Body? A Medievalist Perspective," *Critical Inquiry* 22, no. 1 (1995): 33.

Chapter 5: Entering the Cosmos

1. *Manāqib,* 1:53. This poem about Muḥammad was attributed to al-ʿAbbās b. ʿAbd al-Muṭṭalib. My translation here is only a slight adjustment from the translation provided by Uri Rubin, "Pre-existence and Light: Aspects of the Concept of Nūr Muḥammad." *Israel Oriental Studies* 5 (1975): 90.
2. Additionally, Āghā Buzurg al-Ṭihrānī attributed a work to al-Mufīd, which appears to be devoted to the birth narratives of the imams and the pre-Islamic *awṣiyāʾ*, entitled, *Mawlid al-nabī wa-al-aṣfiyāʾ wa-al-awṣiyāʾ*. The work was also mentioned by Marion Holmes Katz in *The Birth of the Prophet Muḥammad: Devotional Piety in Sunni Islam* (London: Routledge, 2007), 7, 222. This work is lost to us, however, and Martin J. McDermott does not mention it among his list of al-Mufīd's books: *The Theology of al-Shaikh al-Mufīd* (Beirut: Dar el-Machreq, 1978), 25–45. Katz also notes several early works written on the births of Muḥammad, Fāṭima, or one of the first three imams (6–7). Several later works described the births and deaths of the imams, for example, Ibn Khashshāb al-Baghdādī (d. 567–568/1171–1173), *Tārīkh mawālīd al-aʾimmah wa wafīyātihim,* in *Majmūʿah nafīsah fī tārīkh al-aʾimmah: min āthār al-qudamāʾ min ʿulamāʾ al-imāmīyah al-thuqāh,* ed. Maḥmūd al-Ḥusaynī al-Marʿashī (Beirut: Dār al-Qāriʾ, 2002), 119–150. See also Mahmoud Ayoub, *Redemptive Suffering in Islam: A Study of the Devotional Aspects of ʿĀshūrāʾ in Twelver Shīʿism* (The Hague: Mouton Publishers, 1978), 50–54, 70–85.
3. Farīd al-Dīn ʿAṭṭār, *Taẕkirat al-awlīyāʾ*, ed. Muḥammad Istīʿlāmī (Tehran: Intishārāt-i Zuvvār, 1366 [1987–1988]). An English translation of most of the work has been provided by Paul Losensky, *Farid ad-Din ʿAttār's Memorial of God's Friends: Lives and Sayings of Sufis,* in *The Classics of Western Spirituality* (New York: Paulist Press, 2009).
4. ʿAṭṭār, *Taẕkirat al-awlīyāʾ*, 12; trans. Losensky, *Memorial of God's Friends,* 46. We can also take note here of ʿAṭṭār's impression that the qualities of the imams are essentially interchangeable. He follows the above quote by saying, "When he is remembered, it is the remembrance of them all. . . . In other words, the one is twelve, and the twelve are one" (12; Eng: 46).
5. Katz, *Birth of the Prophet,* 7–8.
6. On speech act theory, see J. L. Austin, *How to Do Things with Words* (Oxford: Oxford University Press, 1962); J. Searle, *Speech Acts: An Essay in the Philosophy of Language* (Cambridge: Cambridge University Press, 1969). An application of speech act theory to Persian historiography has been explored by Marilyn Robinson Waldman, *Toward a Theory of Historical Narrative: A Test Case Study in Perso-Islamicate Historiography* (Columbus: Ohio State University Press, 1980).
7. Some of the biographers, such as Ibn Shahrāshūb (and to a lesser extent, al-Mufīd and al-Ṭabrisī) were quite detailed in their notes about how old each imam was when their father died, how old at the death of each ruling king/caliph, how old at the birth of the next imam, and how old at their deaths.

8. Katz, *Birth of the Prophet,* 142. For Katz's discussion of how a community garners blessing through remembrance of Muhammad's birthday, see 143–168. See also McDermott, *Theology of al-Shaikh al-Mufīd,* 113–114.
9. This is seen in al-Fattāl al-Nīsābūrī's (d. 508/1114–1115) popular collection of lectures, *Garden of the Preachers* (*Rawdat al-waʿizin*) (Beirut: Muʾassasat al-Aʿlamī lil-Maṭbūʿāt, 1986), which included a session on this topic (87–93). Most biographers after the twelfth century also utilized several narratives of this sort. See al-Bursī, *Mashāriq anwār al-yaqīn fī asrār Amīr al-Muʾminīn* (Beirut: Dār al-Andalus, 2001), 58–63; Muḥammad Bāqir b. Muḥammad Taqī Majlisī, *Jalāʾ al-ʿuyūn: tārīkh-i chahārdah maʿṣūm,* ed. Sayyid ʿAlī Imāmiyān (Qum: Surūr, 1387 [2008–2009]), 289–294; al-Baḥrānī, *Ḥiliyat al-abrār fī aḥwāl Muḥammad wa-Ālihi al-aṭhār, ʿalayhim al-salām,* ed. Ghulām Riḍā Mawlānā al-Burūjirdī (Qum: Muʾassasat al-Maʿārif al-Islāmīyah, 1411– [1990 or 1991–]), 1:9–19, 2:9–13; al-Baḥrānī, *Madīna maʿājiz: al-aʾimmah al-ithnay ʿashar wa-dalāʾil al-ḥujaj ʿalá al-bashar,* ed. ʿIzzat Allāh al-Mawlāʾī al-Hamdānī (Qum: Muʾassasat al-Maʿārif al-Islāmīyah, 1413–1416 [1992 or 1993–1995]), 1:45–56; Muḥammad Muḥammadī Ishtihārdī, *Sīrat al-maʿṣūmīn al-arbaʿat ʿashar: al-musammá bi-Muntaqá al-durar: dirāsah mūjazah wa-muyassarah wa-hādifah ʿan ḥayat al-maʿṣūmīn al-arbaʿah ʿashar* (Beirut: Muʾassasat al-Balāgh, 2008), 1:35.
10. Rubin, "Pre-existence," 62. See also Uri Rubin, "Prophets and Progenitors in the Early Shīʿa Tradition," *JSAI* 1 (1979): 41–65; Mohammad Ali Amir-Moezzi, *The Divine Guide in Early Shiʿism: The Sources of Esotericism in Islam,* trans. David Streight (Albany: State University of New York Press, 1994), esp. 29–59; Denise Soufi, "The Image of Fāṭima in Classical Muslim Thought" (PhD diss., Princeton University, 1997), 155–165; Uri Rubin, "Islamic Retelling of Biblical History," in *Adaptions and Innovations: Studies on the Interaction between Jewish and Islamic Thought and Literature from the Early Middle Ages to the Late Twentieth Century, Dedicated to Joel Kraemer,* ed. Y. Tzvi Langermann and Josef Stern (Paris: Peeters, 2007), 299–313; Christopher Clohessy, *Fatima, Daughter of Muhammad* (Piscataway, NJ: Gorgias Press, 2009), 74–81.
11. For many references, see Rubin, "Pre-existence."
12. Ibn Isḥaq, *The Life of Muhammad: A Translation of Isḥāq's* Sīrat Rasūl Allāh, intro. and trans. A. Guillaume (Oxford: Oxford University Press, 1955), 69, 72. Ibn Saʿd and al-Ṭabarī had similar narratives; see Rubin, "Pre-existence," 67.
13. This concept is referred to in the Qurʾan, Sūrat Āl ʿImrān (3):81, among other places. See also Bosworth, "Mīthāḳ," EI²; Amir-Moezzi, *Divine Guide,* 33–37.
14. Rubin, "Pre-existence," 67–92. See also Amir-Moezzi, *Divine Guide,* 29–37; Amir-Moezzi, "Savoir c'est pouvoir. Exegeses et implications du miracle dan l'imamisme ancient (Aspects de l'imamologie duodecimaine, V)," in *Miracle et karama,* ed. Denise Aigle (Turnhout, 2000), 262–263. An English translation is provided in *Spirituality,* 193–229.
15. Rubin suggests the term *nūr Allāh* was a different substance, which was only passed on from prophet to prophet, not through all of the ancestors; whereas *nūr Muḥammad* passed, via procreation, through all of the ancestors: "Prophets and Progenitors," 44–45. I am not fully convinced the distinction can be drawn so

cleanly. See also Amir-Moezzi, *Divine Guide,* 38–42; Amir-Moezzi, "Savior c'est pouvoir," 256–258; Ayoub, *Redemptive Suffering,* 54–57.

16. *Ithbāt,* 133. See also Abū al-Ḥasan, ʿAlī b. ʿĪsá b. Abī al-Fatḥ al-Irbilī, *Kashf al-ghumma fī maʿrifat al-aʾimma,* ed. ʿAlī al-Fāḍilī ([Iran]: Markaz al-Ṭibāʿa wa-al-Nashr lil-Majmaʿ al-ʿĀlamī li-Ahl al-Bayt, 1426 [2005–2006]), 1:518–519; al-Bursī, *Mashāriq,* 99; al-Baḥrānī, *Madīna maʿājiz,* 1:53.
17. The examples are far too numerous to warrant listing. It may be noted, however, that al-Mufīd's *al-Irshād* (and subsequently al-Ṭabrisī's *Iʿlām*) made little use of light imagery. His birth narratives were, in general, much more streamlined than the others, but never absent entirely. Al-Ṭabrisī expanded the birth narratives to some extent in his *Iʿlām.* These two works stand out as unique in this regard (the lack of extensive light imagery) among the biographies of the imams in this formative period and among later works.
18. John Renard, *Friends of God: Islamic Images of Piety, Commitment and Servanthood* (Berkeley: University of California Press, 2008), 15–30. On these motifs in early Christian hagiography, see Allison Goddard Elliott, *Roads to Paradise: Reading the Lives of the Early Saints* (Hanover, NH: Brown University Press, 1987), 77–81.
19. For the author of *Ithbāt,* there had been an unbroken chain of *awṣīyāʾ,* which included all the known prophets of history, from Adam to the Shiʿa imams. In this paradigm, which was common among Twelver Shiʿa scholars, all prophets were also *awṣīyāʾ.* The prophets were a distinct type of *waṣī,* one that brought a new message from God, but they were *awṣīyāʾ* just the same.
20. For a discussion of *Ithbāt* in this regard, see Rubin, "Pre-existence," 92–99; Amir-Moezzi, *Divine Guide,* 41–42.
21. *Manāqib,* 1:48–69, 2:196–200.
22. *Manāqib,* 3:311. See also al-Bursī, *Mashāriq,* 99; Majlisī, *Jalāʾ al-ʿuyūn,* 289–290; al-Baḥrānī, *Ḥilyat al-abrār,* 1:9–19; al-Baḥrānī, *Madīna maʿājiz,* 1:53. Although al-Mufīd did not indulge in extensive use of light imagery, the connection between Muḥammad's essence and that of ʿAlī's was made explicit by citing the Prophet's words that he and ʿAlī were made from the same clay (1:43–44 [Eng: 27]; see also *Iʿlām,* 172; Majlisī, *Tārīkh,* 293–294). Furthermore, *Iʿlām,* which drew primarily from al-Mufīd's *al-Irshād,* used some light imagery in the section on Muḥammad's birth (25). Al-Mufīd's work began with ʿAlī.
23. *Dalāʾil,* 59–60; al-Irbilī, *Kashf,* 2:164–165, 173–174; Majlisī, *Jalāʾ al-ʿuyūn,* 292
24. al-Bursī, *Mashāriq,* 63; Majlisī, *Jalāʾ al-ʿuyūn,* 310; Al-Baḥrānī, *Ḥilyat al-abrār,* 1:9–19). See also Clohessy, *Fatima,* 68–72.
25. *Manāqib,* 1:58. See also *Ithbāt,* 133; al-Faṭṭāl, *Rawḍat al-wāʿizīn,* 92.
26. On Jābir b. ʿAbd Allāh b. ʿAmr al-Anṣārī, see Ibn Ḥajar al-ʿAsqalānī, *Tahdhīb al-tahdhīb,* ed. Ibrāhīm al-Zaybaq and ʿĀdil Murshid (Beirut: Muʾassasat al-Risālah, 1996), 2:42–43; Khalīl ibn Aybak al-Ṣafadī, *Kitāb al-Wāfī bi-al-Wafayāt,* ed. Muḥammad Ḥujayrī, Otfried Weintritt, Māhir Zuhayr Jarrār, and Benjamin Jokisch (Leipzig: Deutsche Morgenländische Gesellschaft, in Kommission bei F. A. Brockhaus, 1931), 11:27–28; Etan Kohlberg, "An Unusual Shīʿī *isnād,*" *Israel Oriental Studies* 5 (1975): 142–149; G. H. A. Juynboll, *Encyclopedia of Canonical Ḥadīth* (Leiden: Brill, 2007), 259–260.

27. In addition to the comments in Chapter 4, see below for comments on kissing.
28. *Manāqib,* 2:197.
29. Ibid., 197–198.
30. Ibid., 198. Versions of this account are also found in al-Fattāl, *Rawḍat,* 88–92; Majlisī, *Jalāʾ al-ʿuyūn,* 294–300. Smaller portions of the account can be found in al-Irbilī, *Kashf,* 1:125–127; Al-Baḥrānī, *Ḥilyat al-abrār,* 2:20–24; Al-Baḥrānī, *Madīna maʿājiz,* 1:45–56; ʿAlī Muḥammad ʿAlī Dukhayyil, *A'immatunā* (Beirut: Dār al-Murtaḍá, 1982), 2:356–357; Ishtihārdī, *Sirāt al-maʿṣūmīn,* 1:146–147.
31. *Manāqib,* 2:196–197; Al-Baḥrānī, *Ḥilyat al-abrār,* 2:19–20.
32. The *Ithbāt, al-Irshād,* and *Dalāʾil* all appear to have had more restrictive parameters of interpretation than *Iʿlām, Manāqib,* and most subsequent biographers, such as al-Irbilī, Al-Baḥrānī, and Majlisī.
33. *Al-Irshād,* 1:5 (Eng: 1). See also *Ithbāt,* 133; al-Fattāl, *Rawḍat,* 87; al-Rāwandī, *Kharāʾij wa-al-jarāyih* (Qum: Instishārāt Muṣṭafawī, 1399 H [1979–]), 1:171; *Manāqib,* 2:196–198; al-Irbilī, *Kashf,* 1:125–127; Majlisī, *Jalāʾ al-ʿuyūn,* 300–301; Al-Baḥrānī, *Ḥilyat al-abrār,* 2:19–26; Al-Baḥrānī, *Ghāyat al-marām wa-ḥujjat al-khiṣām fī taʿyīn al-Imām min ṭarīq al-khāṣṣ wa-al-ʿāmm,* ed. ʿAlī ʿĀshūr (Beirut: Muʾassasat al-Tārīkh al-ʿArabī, 2001), 1:50–54.
34. See Ibn Taymīya, *Kitab iqtidaʾ al-ṣirāt al-mustaqīm mukhālafat aṣḥāb al-jaḥīm,* trans. Muhammad Umar Memon, in *Ibn Taimīya's Struggle Against Popular Religion* (The Hague: Mouton, 1976), 258, 302, 363 n. 320. See also Renard, *Friends of God,* 279–281.
35. McDermott, *Theology of al-Shaikh al-Mufīd,* 113–114.
36. On the significance of the Kaʿba, see A. J. Wensinck, "Kaʿba," EI[2]; Uri Rubin, "The Kaʿba: Aspects of Its Ritual Functions," *JSAI* 8 (1986): 97–131; Beverly White Spicer, *The Ka'bah: Rhythms of Culture, Faith, and Physiology* (Lanham, MD: University Press of America, 2003); Robert Bianchi, *Guests of God: Pilgrimage and Politics in the Islamic World* (New York: Oxford University Press, 2004), 23–36.
37. Al-Rāwandī, *Kharāʾij wa-al-jarāyih,* 1:171; al-Irbilī, *Kashf,* 1:125–127.
38. *Manāqib* 2:196, 197; Majlisī, *Jalāʾ al-ʿuyūn,* 302, 305. In another example of prebirth speech, Fāṭima al-Zahrāʾ was said to have talked to her mother, Khadīja, while still in the womb: see Clohessy, *Fatima,* 78–86.
39. Mohammad Ali Amir-Moezzi argues that this claim has its roots in the pro-Persian *shuʿūbīya* movement of the early ninth century: "Shahrbānū, Dame du pays d'Iran et mère des Imams: entre l'Iran préislamique et le Shiisme Imamite," *JSAI* 27 (2002): 497–549; Amir-Moezzi, "Ŝahrbānu," EIr.
40. More often, it was Shahrbānū who was named as wife of al-Ḥusayn and mother of the fourth imam. In the account found in *Dalāʾil,* ʿAlī asked her name, and when she said "Shāhzanān" (meaning, "queen of women"), ʿAlī informed her that this title was reserved for the daughter of the Prophet and that she should be called "Shahrbānawayh" (meaning, "lady of the land"): *Dalāʾil,* 81–82. See also *al-Irshād,* 2:137 (Eng: 380); *Iʿlām,* 259; *Manāqib,* 4:189; Al-Baḥrānī, *Ḥilyat al-abrār,* 3:229–230. Other names are occasionally given as well. Mary Boyce discusses some of the elements of this tradition as well: "Bībī Shahrbānū and the Lady of Pārs," *BSOAS* 30, no. 1 (1967): 30–44. This account of Shahrbānū and Jahānshāh shares

notable parallels with the accounts of Arnawaz and Shahrnaz in Firdowsi's *Shāhnāmeh.*

41. *Ithbāt,* 170. Majlisī added to this line of ʿAlī, saying, "This is a mother of the *awṣiyāʾ* and of my good seed": *Jalāʾ al-ʿuyūn,* 833.
42. Majlisī, *Jalāʾ al-ʿuyūn,* 850. See also *Ithbāt,* 176; *al-Irshād,* 2:155–157 (Eng: 391–393); *Dalāʾil,* 95; *Iʿlām, 268;* Ḥāzim al-Khāqānī, *Ummuhāt al-aʾimma* (Beirut: Dār al-Ḥaqq, 1995), 191.
43. *Ithbāt,* 182; *al-Irshād,* 2:137, 176, 180 (Eng: 380, 406, 409); *Dalāʾil,* 111; *Iʿlām,* 275.
44. *Ithbāt,* 189–191; *al-Irshād,* 2:209, 215 (Eng: 430, 436); *Dalāʾil,* 144–147; *Iʿlām,* 297, 310–311; *Manāqib,* 4:349.
45. Aysha Hidayatullah provides some references on this topic; see "Māriyya the Copt: Gender, Sex and Heritage in the Legacy of Muhammad's *umm walad,*" *Islam and Christian-Muslim Relations* 21, no. 3 (2010): 224–225. Hidayatullah describes the ambiguous social position of the *umm walad* as "somewhere below that of a married woman but above that of an ordinary slave": 225.
46. *Iʿlām,* 310.
47. *Iʿlām,* 310. Al-Ṭabrisī disagreed with al-Mufīd, whom al-Ṭabrisī realized had a very similar account about the mother of Imam al-Riḍā (310–311). See also *al-Irshād,* 2:254–255 (Eng: 465–466); *Ithbāt,* 201–202; *Manāqib,* 4:392.
48. See al-Khāqānī, *Ummuhāt al-aʾimma.*
49. *Ithbāt,* 257. For discussion of the sexuality of the imams, see Chapter 4.
50. For a discussion of the presumed integrity of the imams' daughters, see Chapter 4.
51. *Iʿlām,* 408–409.
52. This conforms to a motif mentioned earlier and also found in stories about Muhammad's birth: Renard, *Friends of God,* 18.
53. In the *Ithbāt* account, the wording says they were overcome with lethargy (*subāt*): 258.
54. *Iʿlām,* 408–409.
55. *Iʿlām,* 408–409. Very similar stories were found in *Ithbāt* (257–261) and *Dalāʾil* (264–265), though with different lines of transmission. The section on al-Mahdī is missing from extant manuscripts of *Manāqib* (see Chapter 1) so we cannot compare Ibn Shahrāshūb's account. Compare Ibn ʿAbd al-Wahhāb, *ʿUyūn al-muʿjizāt,* (Beirut: Muʾassasat al-Aʿlamī lil-Maṭbūʿāt, 2004), 373–378; al-Rāwandī, *al-Kharāʾij wa-al-jarāʾiḥ,* 1:455–456. Although al-Mufīd did not have an elaborate birth narrative, he mentioned that Ḥakīma witnessed al-Mahdī's birth: *al-Irshād,* 2:351 (Eng: 530–531). Most later biographers included one or more of these accounts: see al-Irbilī, *Kashf,* 4:237–238; Al-Baḥrānī, *Madīna maʿājiz,* 8:1–43; ʿAbbās b. Muḥammad Riḍā Qummī, *Muntahá al-āmāl* (Qum: Intishārāt-i Nigāh-i Āshnā, 1388 [2009 or 2010]), 2:495–499; Ishtihārdī, *Sīrat al-maʿṣūmīn,* 3:358–361.
56. This was suggested to me by Omid Safi, a conference panel respondent at the "Rethinking History, Reimagining Community" American Academy of Religion Conference (Atlanta: October 30, 2010).
57. Thus although a miraculous event was occurring through the imam's mother and aunt, the imam functioned as their guide and assumed the source of agency. This again demonstrates the gendered patterns of miracles observed in the Chapter 4.

58. Renard, *Friends of God,* 13–22.

59. Majlisī, *Jalāʾ al-ʿuyūn,* 850. *Ithbāt,* 163–164; *Dalāʾil,* 144–155; Ibn ʿAbd al-Wahhāb, *ʿUyūn,* 62–63. See also Amir-Moezzi, *Divine Guide,* 56–59. Sneezing often accompanied the births of the imams, especially in the *Ithbāt,* Ibn ʿAbd al-Wahhāb's *ʿUyūn,* and Majlisī's *Jalāʾ al-ʿuyūn.* In the Hebrew Bible, 2 Kings 4:34–35, a child revived by the Prophet Elijah sneezed seven times before coming back to life.

60. See *Ithbāt,* 144, 158; Majlisī, *Jalāʾ al-ʿuyūn,* 304; Al-Baḥrānī, *Ḥilyat al-abrār,* 2:28–31. One might contrast the Qurʾanic accounts of Mary and the mother of Moses, in which the role of the mother was generally emphasized.

61. Other examples of this included infant Fāṭima (*Iʿlām,* 164; see Chapter 4); infant ʿAlī (al-Rāwandi, *al-Kharāʾij,* 1:171; *Manāqib,* 2:199; Majlisī, *Jalāʾ al-ʿuyūn,* 303; Al-Baḥrānī, *Madīnat al-maʿājiz,* 1:49); infant ʿAlī b. al-Ḥusayn al-Akbar (this is al-Ḥusayn's older son—not Imam al-Sajjād—who died soon after this, as mentioned by Khalid Sindawi, "The Image of Ḥusayn in *Maqātil* Literature," *Quaderni di Studi Arabi* 20–21 [2002–2003]: 97–98); infant al-Mahdī (*Ithbāt,* 259; *Dalāʾil,* 265).

62. Scott Kugle, *Sufis & Saints' Bodies: Mysticism, Corporeality and Sacred Power in Islam* (Chapel Hill: University of North Carolina Press, 2007), 110, 195; Amir-Moezzi, "Knowledge," in *Spirituality,* 200–201; Amir-Moezzi, *Spirituality,* 44 n. 125; Annemarie Schimmel notes that Greek and Roman poets sometimes used a kiss to symbolize the exchange of souls between two people in "'I Take off the Dress of the Body': Eros in Sufi Literature and Life," in *Religion and the Body,* ed. Sarah Coakley (Cambridge: Cambridge University Press, 1997), 279. In the Christian Gospel of Mark, the saliva of Jesus appears to have had healing powers (8:22–26). Some early Christian thinkers, such as St. Augustine, also believed Jesus transmitted the Holy Spirit to his disciples through a mouth-to-mouth kiss: Nicholas J. Perella, *The Kiss Sacred and Profane: An Interpretive History of Kiss Symbolism and Related Religio-Erotic Themes* (Berkeley: University of California Press, 1969), 18–23. For a detailed discussion of the tradition of kissing among Christians, see Michael Philip Penn, *Kissing Christians: Ritual and Community in the Late Ancient Church* (Philadelphia: University of Pennsylvania Press, 2005). See also Annmari Ronnberg, "Spittle and Spitting," ER2. The transmission of spittle from teacher to student in Morocco has been recorded by Edward Westermarck, *Ritual and Belief in Morocco* (London: Macmilllan, 1926), 1:41. Compare Leor Halevi, *Muhammad's Grave: Death Rites and the Making of Islamic Society* (New York: Columbia University Press, 2007), 49.

63. *Manāqib,* 2:199; Majlisī, *Jalāʾ al-ʿuyūn,* 303–304. Rūmī was said to have breastfed his son; and Abraham received milk from his own fingertips (both in Aflākī [d. 761/1360]): Renard, *Friends of God,* 97.

64. On breastfeeding and nursing in Arabic literature, see Avner Giladi, *Infants, Parents and Wet Nurses: Medieval Islamic Views on Breastfeeding and Their Social Implications* (Leiden: Brill, 1999). On the connection between breast milk and womb blood, see Kugle, *Sufis & Saints' Bodies,* 93–98. The exchange of saliva is also reminiscent of an initiatory rite in some *futūwa* circles, where a saltwater drinking ritual was sometimes replaced with milk; see Lloyd Ridgeon, *Morals and Mysti-*

cism in Persian Sufism: A History of Sufi-futuwwat in Iran (London: Routledge, 2010), 76.

65. This quote, attributed to the Prophet, came after he finished telling ʿAlī that they were made from one piece of clay—as quoted earlier in the chapter—wherein he continued, "part of [the clay] was left over and from that God created our Shīʿa": *al-Irshād,* 1:44 (Eng: 27). See also *Iʿlām,* 172.
66. Cited by Etan Kohlberg, "The Position of the 'walad zinā' in Imāmī Shīʿism," *BSOAS* 48, no. 2 (1985): 241.
67. Kohlberg, "Position of the 'walad zinā'," 240–242. The idea here was that since non-Shiʿa did not pay *khums* (obligatory alms in Shiʿa law), any dowry that a groom used to contract a marriage would be forbidden money on account of his failure to first pay *khums.* Without a legal dowry, the marriage would be considered defective, and the child of such an encounter would be considered *mimzīr.* Within Shiʿa legal thought, the *mimzīr* was distinct from, but similar to, the *walad zinā*—the former retaining slightly less severe social ramifications while carrying many of the same connotations. *Mimzīr* appears to have been heavily influenced by the Jewish halakhic idea of *mamzer.* For discussions of *mamzer* in rabbinic literature, see Shaye Cohen, "The Origins of the Matrilineal Principle in Rabbinic Law," *AJS Review* 10, no. 1 (Spring 1985): 33; Michael L. Satlow, *Tasting the Dish: Rabbinic Rhetoric of Sexuality* (Atlanta: Scholars Press, 1995), 56–59, 84–94; Menahem Elon, "Mamzer," in *The Encyclopaedia Judaica,* 2nd ed. (New York: Thomson Gale, 2007), 13:444; Herbert W. Basser and Simcha Fishbane, "Mamzer," in *The Encyclopaedia of Judaism, Second Edition,* ed. Neusner, Avery-Peck, and Green (Leiden: Brill, 2005), 3:1625–1631; Simcha Fishbane, "The Case of the Modified *Mamzer* in Early Rabbinic Texts," in *Deviancy in Early Rabbinic Literature: A Collection of Socio-Anthropological Essays* (Leiden: Brill, 2007), 4–15.
68. Katz notes that most of the widespread birth narratives of the Prophet were also told in his mother's voice: *Birth of the Prophet,* 32.
69. Most of these have been collected by al-Khāqānī, *Ummuhāt.* Occasionally miracles were attributed to the mothers as well: see *Ithbāt,* 176; *Dalāʾil,* 95.
70. Within the *Ithbāt,* the pre-childbirth experiences and visions of ʿAlī's mother, Fāṭima bt. Asad, played the central role in the conveyance of ʿAlī's cosmic significance. In fact, the extended narratives told from her perspective were arguably the theological apex of the entire book, transitioning the divine history of the *waṣīya* (spiritual inheritance) from its pre-Islamic to its post-Islamic contexts (see Chapter 1). Fāṭima bt. Asad is portrayed as elderly and barren (*mamnūʿa min al-walad*), and making solemn vows (*tandhuru li-dhālik al-nudhūr*) in hopes of conceiving a child. She was regularly told by a sage or priest (*kāhin aw ḥabr*) that she would conceive a child, but she was forced to endure a long period of waiting (*Ithbāt,* 135). When the moment of ʿAlī's birth arrives, Fatima says,

> I dreamed that an iron column emerged from my head and beamed into the sky until it reached the highest heavens and then it returned to me and stayed for a moment, then went out from my feet. I asked, "What is this?" It was said, "This is the killer of the unbelievers (*qātil ahl al-kufr*), head of the covenant of victory.

His courage is strong and the armies break apart in fear of him. He is the assistance of God to his Prophet and his support against his enemies. And by his love the victorious achieve victory and the joyful receive their joy." (*Ithbāt,* 143)

In this narrative, ʿAlī's connection to the Prophet was asserted, the signs of divine mission (e.g., the vision of a column) were provided, and salvation for the community was tied to him. For a discussion of columns of light/iron emanating from bodies, see Amir-Moezzi, *Divine Guide,* 58; Rubin, "Pre-existence," 62–117. Some other examples include Muḥammad (*I'lām,* 25); Fāṭima (al-Burṣī, *Mashāriq,* 133); ʿAlī (Majlisī, *Jalāʾ al-ʿuyūn,* 295); al-Ḥasan (*Dalāʾil,* 60); al-Bāqir (*Ithbāt,* 180–181); al-Kāẓim (*al-Irshād,* 2:218 [Eng: 438]; *Dalāʾil,* 144–145); al-Jawād (Majlisī, *Jalāʾ al-ʿuyūn,* 960); all the imams together (*Dalāʾil,* 59–60; Al-Baḥrānī, *Ḥiiyat al-abrār,* 1:9–19; Majlisī, *Jalāʾ al-ʿuyūn,* 850).

71. Some examples include that Muḥammad's mother claimed knowledge that he would be the head of the people and that he was the one anticipated by the world (*Iʿlām,* 25). Fāṭima bt. Asad was told of ʿAlī's mission by a soothsayer (*Ithbāt,* 135). Fāṭima bt. Muḥammad was told about al-Ḥusayn (*Ithbāt,* 163). The mother of al-Riḍā was told, while still in possession of a slave trader, that she would give birth to "a son such as has not been born in the east or west" (*al-Irshād,* 2:254–255 [Eng: 466]).
72. Cited in Rubin's "Pre-existence," 73. The quote went on to say, "the nations have never ceased to transmit me from father to son, till I emerged from the best two Arab clans—Hāshim and Zuhra." The term for "whore" here, *baghī,* was the same that was used to falsely slander Mary, and the one used by al-Bāqir to describe the mothers of all non-Shiʿa (quoted above).
73. Cited and translated by A. A. Seyed-Gohrab, *Laylī and Majnūn: Love, Madness, and Mystic Longing in Niẓāmī's Epic Romance* (Leiden: Brill, 2003), 239.
74. *Al-Irshād,* 2:16 (Eng: 287). On the issue of wives and poisoning, see Chapter 3.
75. "Most deserving" is one of the common descriptions of the mothers. See *Ithbāt,* 176, 182, 216; *Dalāʾil,* 95. See also Rubin, "Pre-existence," 92–93, 96.
76. Another example, beyond those already listed, is al-Kāẓim (*Dala'il,* 145).
77. On the topic of physical beauty, see Chapter 4.
78. *Ithbāt,* 259–260. See also al-Irbilī, *Kashf,* 4:241–242.
79. The edition of *Ithbāt* that I am using has "Jumāna" here for the mother's name, but this was likely a publisher's typo or scribal error since all other sources have Sumāna.
80. *Ithbāt,* 228.
81. *Ithbāt,* 228. Cf. Ishtihārdī, *Sīrat al-maʿṣūmīn,* 3:131; Bāqir Sharīf Qarashī, *The Fourteen Infallibles in the History of Islam* (Qum: Ansariyan, 1999–2010), 12:27. As we saw in Chapter 4, the image of the imams was entwined with assumptions of masculinity related to valor, weaponry, and heroism, whereas the feminine was characterized by physical comforts.
82. Like his father, al-Hādī inherited the full position of imam at a very young age. When this occurred during the childhood of his father, some of the imam's

followers had concerns about the ability of a child to lead the community. There is reason to assume, therefore, that some of the stories of al-Jawād's youth were circulated specifically to assure those who doubted the child's religious knowledge. By the time of al-Hādī's imamate, however, the issue of a child-imam carried less urgency, and the stories of al-Hādī's youth are no more elaborate or extensive than what is found in the accounts of the other eleven imams.

83. *Dalāʾil,* 214. This story also appeared in *Ithbāt,* 230; Ibn ʿAbd al-Wahhāb, *ʿUyūn,* 337; al-Irbilī, *Kashf,* 4:22. The story of al-Hādī knowing the moment of his father's death was also told in other ways, from different perspectives. See *Ithbāt,* 229–230; *Dalāʾil,* 215; Majlisī, *Jalāʾ al-ʿuyūn,* 970; Al-Baḥrānī, *Madīna al-maʿājiz,* 7:445–446; Ishtihārdī, *Sīrat al-maʿṣūmīn,* 3:136–137.
84. *Ithbāt,* 230–231; Ishtihārdī, *Sīrat al-maʿṣūmīn,* 3:137–138.
85. The early community of followers of the imams was known to have argued over whether the imams were born with their full intellectual capacities or whether they needed to learn. The Zaydis, for instance, largely concurred that the imams had to obtain their knowledge through learning, but the Twelver Shiʿa typically held that the imams were born with most, if not all, of their knowledge.
86. *Al-Irshād,* 1:305–306 (Eng: 229–230).
87. Psalm 8:2, New King James Version.
88. Matthew 21:16.
89. Sūrat al-ʿimrān (3):46. Trans.: Qarai.
90. *Al-Irshād,* 1:305 (Eng: 229). See also *al-Irshād,* 2:274–275, 340–341 (Eng: 480–481, 524); *Iʿlām,* 408; as well as McDermott, *Theology of al-Shaikh al-Mufid,* 85.
91. Divine protection of a pure lineage is, of course, a common theme in biblical literatures. In addition to examples within the Hebrew Bible, see Earnest A. Wallis Budge, trans., *The Book of the Cave of Treasures: A History of the Patriarchs and the Kings, Their Successors from the Creation to the Crucifixion of Christ* (London: Religious Tract Society, 1927; rep. Kessinger Publishing); Budge, *The Book of the Bee: The Syriac Text* (Oxford: Clarendon Press, 1886; rep. Zuu Books, 2011), 110.

Epilogue

1. Robert Bellah, R. Madsen, W. Sullivan, A. Swindler, and S. M. Tipton, *Habits of the Heart: Individualism and Commitment in American Life* (Berkeley: University of California Press, 1985), 153.
2. This is an easily observable reality, a truism within the field. Marshall Hodgson discusses it briefly in *The Venture of Islam* (Chicago: University of Chicago Press, 1974), 1:39–40. See also Wilferd Madelung, "Introduction," in *The Study of Shiʿi Islam: History, Theology and Law,* ed. Farhad Daftary and Gurdofarid Miskinzoda (New York: I. B. Tauris, 2014), 3–4. A simple survey of the works of some of the major scholars of Islam in the twentieth century, such as Goldziher, Caetani, and Watt, verifies the matter.
3. See Etan Kohlberg, "Western Studies of Shi'a Islam," in *Shi'ism, Resistance, and Revolution,* ed. Martin Kramer (Boulder, CO: Westview Press, 1987), 31–44;

Hodgson, *Venture of Islam,* 1:39–40; Madelung, "Introduction," in Daftary and Miskinzoda, *Study of Shiʿi Islam,* 3–4.

4. The Pew Forum on Religion and Public Life, "Mapping the Global Muslim Population: A Report on the Size and Distribution of the World's Muslim Population" (Washington, DC: Pew Research Center, October 2009), 7–8.
5. One of the most popular overviews of the topic in English is Moojan Momen's *An Introduction to Shiʿi Islam.* The author suggests that Sunni and Shiʿa Muslims do not differ significantly in ritual or doctrine, and that the primary difference is attributable to the dispute over succession: Momen, *An Introduction to Shiʿi Islam: The History and Doctrines of Twelver Shiʿism* (New Haven, CT: Yale University Press, 1985), xiii. A similar approach was taken by S. H. M. Jafri in his *Origins and Early Development of Shiʿa Islam* (London: Longman, 1979).
6. See, for example, Asma Afsaruddin, *Excellence and Precedence: Medieval Islamic Discourse on Legitimate Leadership* (Leiden: Brill, 2002), 271–280.
7. Consider Wilfred Cantwell Smith's remarkable statement in *Modern Islam in India:* "We have not given the Shi'ah group separate treatment in this study of the changes wrought in Islam by modern social processes because there is nothing in the differences between Sunni and Shi'ah fundamentally relevant to those processes. The two groups diverge over what answers are to be given to questions which today do not arise." Quoted by Keith Hjortshoj in "Shi'i Identity and Muharram in India," in *Shi'ism, Resistance, and Revolution,* ed. Martin Kramer (Boulder, CO: Westview Press, 1987), 290.
8. Wilferd Madelung, in his *Succession to Muḥammad: A Study of the Early Caliphate* (Cambridge: Cambridge University Press, 1997), put forth one of the most substantive arguments for taking seriously historical dispute over Muhammad's rightful succession. See also his short but informative piece, "Shīʿism in the Age of the Rightly-Guided Caliphs," in *Shīʿite Heritage: Essays on Classical and Modern Traditions,* ed. and trans. L. Clarke (Binghamton, NY: Global Publications, 2001), 9–18. See also Madelung, "Shiism: An Overview," ER2. This may seem like a modest achievement, but many Western scholars continue to take for granted Sunni accounts of the affair and treat Shiʿa claims about the crisis as anachronistic projections. Shiʿa scholars are often very aware of this tendency. Sayyid Muhammad Rizvi collects a few examples of this tendency with regard to the *ghadīr khumm* (see Chapter 3) accounts: *Shīʿism: Imāmate and Wilāyat,* (Canada: Al-Maʿarif Books, 1999), chap. 3. http://www.al-islam.org/shiism-imamate-and-wilayat-sayyid-muhammad-rizvi.
9. Marshall Hodgson, "How Did the Early Shi'a Become Sectarian?" *JAOS* 75, no. 1 (1955): 9–13.
10. Etan Kohlberg, "From Imāmiyya to Ithnā-ʿashariyya," *BSOAS* 39, no. 3 (1976): 521–534.
11. For example, while conceding that doctrines of the imamate were still in formation well after the occultation of the twelfth imam, Hossein Modarressi places the teachings of the imams and their followers at the center of *Crisis and Consolidation in the Formative Period of Shiʿite Islam: Abū Jaʿfar ibn Qiba al-Rāzī and His*

Contribution to Imāmite Shīʿite Thought (Princeton, NJ: The Darwin Press, 1993), a work that has done much to advance understandings of the development of Shiʿism. Modarressi's perspective on early Shiʿa beliefs is contested by some, most notably Mohammad Amir-Moezzi. The latter's *The Divine Guide in Early Shiʿism: The Sources of Esotericism in Islam,* trans. David Streight (Albany: State University of New York Press, 1994) highlights a different selection of teachings attributed to the imams in many eighth- and ninth-century sources. This illuminating work on early Shiʿa esoteric beliefs—specifically in relationship to the imamate—has been followed by a number of excellent articles. Several of them have been recently translated and collected into one invaluable volume: *The Spirituality of Shiʿi Islam: Beliefs and Practices* (London: I. B. Tauris, 2011). The stark contrasts—though not necessarily contradictions—in the presentations of Modaressi and Amir-Moezzi have unnecessarily polarized scholarly research on early Shiʿism. Regardless of their differences, both are similar to Hodgson and Kohlberg in that they conceptualize Shiʿism as a set of (evolving) religious beliefs.

12. See H. Laoust, "Les Agitations Religieuses à Baghdād aux IVᵉ et Vᵉ siècles de l'Hégire," in *Islamic Civilization, 950–1150: Papers on Islamic History III,* ed. D. S. Richards (London: William Clowes & Sons Limited, 1973), 169–186.
13. This perspective is not without historical merit. It is well documented that a group of "penitents" (*tawwābūn*) in the late seventh century were so moved with remorse over having not helped al-Ḥusayn's party that they took up arms against the ruling Umayyad authorities in the face of insurmountable odds. These early Shiʿa—or "proto-Shiʿa"—martyrs helped inspire generations of resistance in the name of the Prophet's family against injustice. Within a century of al-Ḥusayn's death, a revolution had toppled the Umayyad Empire based in Syria. And though the triumph of the ʿAbbasids eventually came to be regarded as a betrayal of Twelver Shiʿa aspirations rather than a fulfillment of them, it allowed new public commemorations and religious observances to flourish. See Mahmoud Ayoub, *Redemptive Suffering: A Study of the Devotional Aspects of ʿĀshūrāʾ in Twelver Shīʿism* (The Hague: Mouton Publishers, 1978), 153–154. Some scholars hold that these rituals mark Shiʿism's debut. Muḥarram rituals are at the foreground of David Pinault's book *The Shiites,* which has served as a major reference in the field in the two decades since its writing. See *The Shiites: Ritual and Popular Piety in a Muslim Community* (New York: St. Martin's Press, 1992), 3–5. This approach is also evident in another popular survey, Heinz Halm's *Shiʿa Islam: From Religion to Revolution,* trans. Allison Brown (Princeton, NJ: Markus Wiener Publishers, 1997). Halm refers to the passion-play rituals in Muḥarram as "the true core of religious observance of Twelver Shi'ism" (x). The updated and expanded edition of this work is titled *The Shiites: A Short History,* trans. Allison Brown (Princeton: Markus Wiener Publishers, 2007). The insightful works of Mahmoud Ayoub and Hamid Dabashi also follow this general trend. Ayoub's *Redemptive Suffering in Islam,* cited above, helpfully conveys the general mood of sorrow and consolation that permeates the literature of the present study. For Dabashi, see especially his book *Shi'ism: A Religion of Protest* (Cambridge, MA: Belknap Press, 2011), where

he reads the history of Shiʿism through what he calls the "Karbala complex." Both Ayoub and Dabashi approach Shiʿism in a way that has deep consonance with the present study. My own difference with their descriptions, besides attempting to limit my discussion to a slightly more confined context (both temporally and textually), is that I would contend that they put too much emphasis on stories of al-Ḥusayn and ʿĀshūrāʾ (see Chapter 3).

14. The question of succession is deceptively complex, and the historical record does not fit neatly into later conceptions of Sunni and Shiʿa Islam. There were many opinions on the matter in the seventh and eighth centuries, and not all of those who believed ʿAlī was the preferred candidate can sensibly be called "Shiʿa"—at least not in the way the term is commonly used today. The conviction that leadership rightfully belonged to someone in the Prophet's family was a sentiment that extended far beyond the bounds of Shiʿism. See I. Goldziher, C. van Arendonk, and A. S. Tritton, "Ahl al-Bayt," EI[2]; C. van Arendonk and W. A. Graham, "Sharīf," EI[2]; Kazuo Morimoto, ed., *Sayyids and Sharifs in Muslim Societies: The Living Links to the Prophet* (London: Routledge, 2012). The success of the ʿAbbāsid revolution is further testament to this reality.

The doctrinal approach is hindered by the fact that the teachings of the scholar-imams Muḥammad al-Bāqir (the fifth) and Jaʿfar al-Ṣādiq (the sixth) are an unverifiable basis for the distinctiveness of Shiʿism. There are major historical uncertainties about what these imams taught in their lifetimes, and much of what they are reported to have said is not at odds with the four major Sunni schools of law. Al-Bāqir is considered a thoroughly reliable transmitter of hadith in most Sunni works (W. Madelung, "Bāqer, Abū Jaʿfar Moḥammad," EIr). And al-Ṣādiq is known to have been a teacher of major Sunni scholars like Abū Ḥanīfa, Mālik b. Anas, and Wāṣil b. ʿAṭāʾ (M. Hodgson, "Djaʿfar al-Ṣādiḳ," EI[2]). Furthermore, as Devin Stewart has demonstrated, there is a history of Shiʿi scholars practicing Sunni schools of law (particularly the Shāfiʿī school). See Stewart, *Islamic Legal Orthodoxy: Twelver Shiite Responses to the Sunni Legal System* (Salt Lake City: University of Utah Press), 1998.

Tracing the Sunni- Shiʿa divide to commemorations of al-Ḥusayn's death also has limitations, for the mourning of his martyrdom (particularly in medieval contexts) was not confined to groups that could be called Shiʿa. The dramatic slaughter of the Prophet's grandson at Karbalāʾ was a gross injustice in the eyes of a wide range of Muslims, and for centuries the event inspired Sunni as well as Shiʿa rituals. See Mohammad-Djaʿfar Mahdjoub, "The Evolution of Popular Eulogy of the Imams among the Shiʿa," in *Authority and Political Culture in Shiʿism,* ed. S. Arjomand, trans. and adapt. John R. Perry (Albany: State University of New York Press, 1988), 65–67; Ali J. Hussain, "The Mourning of History and the History of Mourning: The Evolution of Ritual Commemoration of the Battle of Karbala," *Comparative Studies of South Asia, Africa and the Middle East* 25, no. 1 (2005): 85; Megan Reid, "ʿĀshūrāʾ: Sunnism," EI[3]. The tragedy of ʿĀshūrāʾ is not the property of the Shiʿa alone, though its commemoration did increasingly become so over many centuries: Kamran Aghaie, "ʿĀshūrāʾ (Shīʿism)," EI[3].

15. It should also be noted that a few unique works do not fit nicely into the broad approaches that I have outlined here. Of particular note is Najam Haider's *The Origins of the Shīʿa: Identity, Ritual, and Sacred Space in Eighth-Century Kūfah* (Cambridge: Cambridge University Press, 2011). Here Haider explores early Shiʿa communal boundaries through the lens of specific ritual practices other than the ʿĀshūrāʾ commemorations.
16. Eric Hobsbawm, "The Social Function of the Past: Some Questions," *Past and Present* 55 (1972): 3.
17. Some others who have pointed to this dynamic between Sunni and Shiʿa include Christopher Melchert, "Imāmīs between Rationalism and Traditionalism," in *Shīʿite Heritage: Essays on Classical and Modern Traditions,* ed. and trans. L. Clarke (Binghamton, NY: Global Publications, 2001), 282–283; Afsaruddin, *Excellence and Precedence,* 3–4. An interesting example of this can also be seen in Sean Anthony's attempt to trace the development of early narratives of Ibn Saba' in *The Caliph and the Heretic: Ibn Sabaʾ and the Origins of Shīʿism* (Leiden: Brill, 2012). In the process of exploring some particular Sunni accounts of how Shiʿism developed, he provides insights into how Sunni identity itself was evolving (100–103).
18. However, some recent comments on this question should be noted, especially Abbas Barzegar, "Remembering Community: Historical Narrative in the Formation of Sunni Islam" (PhD diss., Emory University, 2010). See also Patricia Crone's comments in "Uthmāaniyya," EI^2; D. W. Brown, "Sunna," EI^2; Afsaruddin, *Excellence and Precedence,* 20.
19. Bellah et al., *Habits of the Heart,* 153.

Appendix 1

1. The secondary literature on Muḥammad is vast. For general overviews, see F. Buhl and A. T. Welch, "Muḥammad: The Prophet's Life and Career," EI^2; Mahmoud Ayoub, "Muhammad the Prophet," *ALC,* 268–287.
2. See L. Veccia Vaglieri "Fāṭima," EI^2; Jean Calmard and M. A. Amir-Moezzi, "Fāṭema," EIr; Denise Soufi "The Image of Fāṭimah in Classical Muslim Thought" (PhD diss., Princeton University, 1997); Hossein Modarressi, *Tradition and Survival: A Bibliographical Survey of Early Shi'ite Literature* (Oxford: Oneworld, 2003), 1:17–22; Christopher P. Clohessy, *Fatima, Daughter of Muhammad* (Piscataway, NJ: Gorgias Press, 2009); L. V. Vaglieri, "Fāṭima bt. Muḥammad," EI^3.
3. See Dwight M. Donaldson, *The Shi'ite Religion: A History of Islam in Persia and Irak* (London: Luzac & Company, 1933), 27–53; S. H. M. Jafri, *Origins and Early Development of Shiʿa Islam* (London: Longman, 1979), 58–129; Wilferd Madelung, *Succession to Muḥammad: A Study of the Early Caliphate* (Cambridge: Cambridge University Press, 1997); [multiple authors], "ʿAlī b. Abī Ṭālib," *DMBI* [Trans. in *Encyclopedia Islamica,* 3:477–583]; E. Kohlberg and I. K. Poonawala, "ʿAlī b. Abī Ṭāleb," EIr; Robert Gleave, "ʿAlī b. Abī Ṭālib," EI^3; B. Tahera Qutbuddin, "ʿAli ibn Abi Talib," *ALC,* 68–76; Modarressi, *Tradition and Survival,* 1:1–17.

4. See Donaldson, *Shi'ite Religion,* 66–78; Jafri, *Origins,* 130–173; L. Veccia Vaglieri, "(al-) Ḥasan b. ʿAlī b. Abī Ṭālib," EI[2]; W. Madelung, "Ḥasan b. ʿAlī b. Abī Ṭāleb," EIr.
5. See Donaldson, *Shi'ite Religion,* 79–87; Jafri, *Origins,* 174–221; L. Veccia Vaglieri, "(al-) Ḥusayn b. ʿAlī b. Abī Ṭālib," EI[2]; W. Madelung, "Ḥosayn b. ʿAlī: Life and Significance in Shiʿism," EIr.
6. Sometimes Abū al-Ḥasan; see *al-Irshād,* 2:137 (Eng: 380); *Iʿlām,* 260; *Manāqib,* 4:189.
7. See Donaldson, *Shi'ite Religion,* 101–111; Jafri, *Origins,* 239–247; W. Madelung, "ʿAlī b. Ḥosayn," EIr; E. Kohlberg, "Zayn al-ʿĀbidīn," EI[2]; Modarressi, *Tradition and Survival,* 1:33–36.
8. Numerous other dates are also given in various sources, ranging from 114/732 to 118/736. See Kohlberg, "Muḥammad b. ʿAlī b. Zayn al-ʿĀbidīn," EI[2]; Modarressi, *Tradition and Survival,* I: 37–38.
9. See Donaldson, *Shi'ite Religion,* 112–119; Jafri, *Origins,* 247–255; E. Kohlberg, "Muḥammad b. ʿAlī b. Zayn al-ʿĀbidīn," EI[2]; Arzina R. Lalani, *Early Shīʿī Thought: The Teachings of Imam Muḥammad al-Bāqir* (London: I. B. Tauris, 2000); W. Madelung, "Bāqer, Abū Jaʿfar Moḥammad," EIr.
10. See Donaldson, *Shi'ite Religion,* 129–141; Jafri, *Origins,* 259–288; M. Hodgson, "*Djaʿfar* al-Ṣādiḳ," EI[2]; Robert Gleaves, "Jaʿfar al-Ṣādeq: i. Life ii. Teachings," EIr; Omid Safi, "Jaʿfar al-Sadiq," *ALC,* 225–230.
11. Abū Ibrāhīm also appears sometimes. Examples: *Ithbāt,* 189; *Manāqib,* 4:307, 312.
12. See Donaldson, *Shi'ite Religion,* 152–160; E. Kohlberg, "Mūsā al-Kāẓim," EI[2]; Hamid Algar, "Imam Musa al-Kazim and Sufi Tradition," *Islamic Culture* 64 (1990): 1–14.
13. See Donaldson, *Shi'ite Religion,* 161–169; Michael Cooperson, *Classical Arabic Biography* (Cambridge: Cambridge University Press, 2000), 70–106; Deborah G. Tor, "An Historiographical Re-examination of the Appointment and Death of ʿAlī al-Riḍā," *Der Islam* 78 (2001): 103–128; Wilferd Madelung, "ʿAlī al-Reżā," EIr; Tamima Bayhom-Daou, "ʿAlī al-Riḍā," EI[3].
14. See Donaldson, *Shi'ite Religion,* 188–197; Wilferd Madelung, "Muḥammad b. ʿAlī al-Riḍā," EI[2]; Shona Wardrop, "The Lives of the Imāms, Muḥammad al-Jawād and ʿAlī al-Hādī and the Development of the Shīʿite Organization" (PhD diss., University of Edinburgh, 1988).
15. See Donaldson, *Shi'ite Religion,* 209–216; Wardrop, "The Lives of the Imāms;" W. Madelung, "ʿAlī al-Hādī," EIr.
16. See Donaldson, *Shi'ite Religion,* 217–225; J. Eliash, "Ḥasan al-ʿAskarī," EI[2]; H. Halm, "Askarī," EIr.
17. It is customary among the Shiʿa to avoid using the *kunya* or the *ism* of the twelfth imam when referring to him—typically, only a *laqab* is used. Numerous sources do not list his *kunya,* and those that do typically just say that it is the same as the Prophet's *kunya* (e.g., *Iʿlām,* 407). Using the Prophet's *ism* and *kunya* is generally understood by Sunni and Shiʿa Muslims to be otherwise prohibited. The ascription of this *ism* and *kunya* to the twelfth imam, therefore, accentuates the apocalyptic expectations surrounding his character.

18. See Donaldson, *Shi'ite Religion,* 226–241; J. M. Hussain, *The Occultation of the Twelfth Imam: A Historical Background* (London: The Muhammadi Trust, 1982); J. G. J. ter Haar, "Muḥammad al-Ḳāʾim," EI².

Appendix 2

1. It would be worthwhile to give some attention to non-Twelver works that overlap with this genre or are very similar in nature. It would be particularly interesting to look at *al-Hidāyat al-kubrá,* written by the tenth century Nusayrī, al-Khasībī (d. 346/957). And the same could be said for Sibṭ ibn al-Jawzī's (d. 654/1256) *Tadhkirat al-khawāṣṣ,* and Ibn al-Ṣabbāgh's (d. 855/1451–1452) *al-Fuṣūl al-muhimma fī maʿrifat al-aʾimma,* written by a Hanafi and Malaki, respectively. Finally, Zaydī and Ismaʿīlī Shiʿa also wrote on the lives of their imams—though to a lesser extent than Twelvers—and these works might provide helpful contrasts with the Twelver perspectives. In this regard, the Zaydī *al-Ifāda fī tārīkh al-a'imma al-sāda* by al-Nāṭiq bi'l-Ḥaqq (d. 424/1032–1033) may be a place to begin.
2. Abū Bakr, Muḥammad b. Aḥmad b. Muḥammad b. ʿAbd Allāh b. Ismāʿīl, al-Baghdādī, known as Ibn Abī al-Thalj: al-Najāshī, *Rijāl,* 2:299–300, #1038, al-Ṭihrānī, *al-Dharīʿa,* 3:218, #806; Kaḥḥāla, *Muʿjam,* 3:102, #12003; Aḥmad Pākatchī, "Ibn Abī al-Thalj (2)," *DMBI,* 2:633–634. Ibn Abī al-Thalj, *Tārīkh al-a'imma,* in *Majmūʿa nafīsa fī tārīkh al-aʾimma: min āthār al-qudamāʾ min ʿulamāʾ al-imāmīya al-thuqāh,* ed. Maḥmūd al-Ḥusaynī al-Marʿashī (Beirut: Dār al-Qāriʾ, 2002), 9–27.
3. Abū Muḥammad, ʿAbd Allāh b. Aḥmad b. Aḥmad b. Aḥmad b. ʿAbd Allāh b. Naṣr, al-Baghdādī, known as Ibn Khashshāb: al-Ṭihrānī, *al-Dharīʿa,* 3:217–218, #805; Kaḥḥāla, *Muʿjam,* 2:221, #7771; Muḥammad Fāḍilī, "Ibn Khashāb, Abū Muḥammad," *DMBI,* 3:419–420. This work is also known as *Tārīkh al-aʾimma.* Ibn Khashshāb, *Tārīkh mawālīd al-aʾimma wa wafīyātihim,* in *Majmūʿa nafīsa,* ed. al-Marʿashī (Beirut: Dār al-Qāriʾ, 2002), 119–150.
4. Al-Ṭihrānī, *al-Dharīʿa,* 3:209, #772. Al-Ṭabrisī, *Tāj al-mawālīd,* in *Majmūʿa nafīsa,* ed. al-Marʿashī, 65–117.
5. Al-Ḥusayn b. ʿAbd al-Wahhāb: al-ʿĀmilī, 346, 350; al-Ṭihrānī, *al-Dharīʿa,* 15:383–385; # 2390; Kaḥḥāla, *Muʿjam,* 1:621, #4680.
6. Saʿīd b. ʿAbd Allāh b. al-Ḥusayn b. Ḥubba Allāh b. al-Ḥasan al-Rāwandī (Quṭb al-Dīn): *GAL* S 1:710; al-ʿĀmilī, 35:16, 24; al-Ṭihrānī, *al-Dharīʿa,* 7:145–146, #802; Kaḥḥāla, 1:765, #5695; E. Kohlberg, "Rāvandī, Qoṭb-al-dīn," EIr.
7. Abū Muḥammad, al-Ḥasan b. ʿAlī b. al-Ḥusayn b. Shuʿba, al-Ḥarrānī al-Ḥalabī: al-ʿĀmilī, *Aʿyān,* 22:318–321, #4326; al-Ṭihrānī, *al-Dharīʿa,* 3:400, #1435; Kaḥḥāla, 1:567, #4258. Al-Ḥarrānī, *Tuḥaf al-ʿuqūl* (Eng: *Tuhaf al-Uqoul: The Masterpieces of the Intellects*).
8. The title is also known as *Tārīkh āl al-Rasūl.* Jahḍamī, *Tārīkh ahl al-bayt: naql^{an} ʿan al-aʾimma al-Bāqir wa-al-Ṣādiq wa-al-Riḍā wa-al-ʿAskarī ʿan ābāʾihim* (Qum: Dalīl Mā, 1426 [2005 or 2006]).
9. Abū Mansūr, Aḥmad b. ʿAlī b. Abī Talib al-Ṭabrisī: *GAL* S 1:709; al-Ṭihrānī, *al-Dharīʿa,* 1:281–282, #1472; Kaḥḥāla, *Muʿjam,* 1:203, #1509; E. Kohlberg,

"al-Ṭabrisī (Ṭabarsī), Abū Mansūr," EI². Al-Ṭabrisī, *al-Iḥtijāj*, ed. Muḥammad Bāqir al-Kharasān, 2 volumes ([Najaf]: Dār al-Nuʿmān, 1966).

10. Abū ʿAlī, Muḥammad b. al-Ḥasan b. ʿAlī b. Aḥmad b. ʿAlī al-Fattāl, al-Nisābūrī (al-Fārisī): *GAL* 1:513; al-Ṭihrānī, *al-Dharīʿa*, 11:305, #1815; Kaḥḥāla, *Muʿjam*, 3:225, #12821. al-Fattāl, *Rawḍat al-wāʿizīn* (Beirut: Muʾassasat al-Aʿlamī lil-Maṭbūʿāt, 1986).
11. These two works are also of importance in this study since the two authors were both teachers of Ibn Shahrāshūb.
12. Abū Sālim, Muḥammad b. Ṭalḥa b. Muḥammad b. Ḥasan ʿAdawī, Kamāl al-Dīn, al-Nasībī: ʿAbd al-ʿAzīz Ṭabāṭabāʾī, "Ibn Ṭalḥa, Abū Sālim," *DMBI*, 4:144–145.
13. Abū al-Ḥasan, ʿAlī b. ʿĪsá b. Abī al-Fatḥ al-Irbilī, Bahāʾ al-Dīn: *GAL* S 1:713; al-Ṭihrānī, *al-Dharīʿa*, 18:47–48, #619; Kaḥḥāla, *Muʿjam*, 2:484, #9805; Jaʿfarīyān, Muḥammad Riḍā Nājī, "Irbilī," *DMBI*, 7:431–434.
14. Abū Saʿīd (or Abū ʿAlī), al-Ḥasan b. al-Ḥusayn (or b. Muḥammad) al-Bayhaqī, al-Sabzavārī: al-Ṭihrānī, *al-Dharīʿa*, 10:55, #14; al-ʿĀmilī, *Aʿyān*, 21:202–204, #4085. This is one of the earliest extant works of this genre written originally in Persian. Shīʿī Sabzavārī, *Rāḥat al-arvāḥ: dar sharḥ-i zindagī, faẓāʾil va muʿajazzāt-i aʾimma-i Athār* (Tehran: Ahl-i Qalam: Daftar-i Nashr-i Mīrāṣ̱-i Maktūb, 1375 [1996 or 1997]).
15. Rajab b. Muḥammad b. Rajab, al-Bursī al-Ḥillī, al-Shaykh al-Ajl al-Ḥāfiẓ, Raḍī al-Dīn: *GAL* S 2:204, 661; al-Ṭihrānī, *al-Dharīʿa*, 21: 34, #3826; "Bursī," *DMBI*, 11:713–715.
16. Abū Muḥammad, ʿAlī b. Muḥammad b. ʿAlī b. Muḥammad b. Yūnus, al-Bayādī al-Nibāṭī al-ʿĀmilī, Zayn al-Dīn: al-ʿĀmilī, *Aʿyān*, 42:31–31; al-Ṭihrānī, *al-Dharīʿa*, 15:36–37, #219; Kaḥḥāla, *Muʿjam*, II: 519, #10061; Muḥammad Kāẓim ʿAlavī, "Bayāḍī, Zayn al-Dīn," *DMBI*, 13:243–244. Al-Bayāḍī, *al-Ṣirāṭ al-mustaqīm ilá mustahiqqī al-taqdīm*, ed. Muḥammad Bāqir al-Buhbūdī ([Tehran]: al-Maktabah al-Murtadawīyah, 1384– [1964 or 1965–]).
17. Ḥusayn b. ʿAlī Kāshifī, Kamāl al-Dīn, al-Vāʿiẓ ("the preacher"): al-Ṭihrānī, *al-Dharīʿa*, 11:294–295, #1775; G̲holam Hosein Yousofi, "Kāshifī," EI². This work breaks with the general conventions of the genre in several ways—and is of questionable inclusion—but its general influence on popular Shiʿa expressions of piety and the fact that most of the narratives within it concern the Shiʿa imams, makes it worth considering alongside the other works of this analysis. See P. Chelkowski, "Rawḍa-k̲h̲wānī," EI². Kāshifī, *Rawẓat al-shuhadāʾ*, ed. Muḥammad Riẓā Iftikhārzādah (Tehran: Intishārāt-i Mudabbir, 1384 [2005]).
18. Muḥammad b. Ḥusayn b. ʿAbd al-Samad al-ʿĀmilī, Bahāʾ al-Dīn: *GAL* 2:414, 415 and S 2:595–597; al-ʿĀmilī, *Aʾyan*, 44: 216–257; al-Ṭihrānī, al-Dharīʿa, 4:498, #2232; Kaḥḥāla, *Muʿjam*, 3:251, #12998; C. E. Bosworth, *Bahaʾ al-Din al-ʿĀmilī and his Literary Anthologies* (Manchester: University of Manchester, 1989); E. Kohlberg, "Bahāʾ-al-Dīn ʿĀmelī," EIr; C. E. Bosworth, "al-ʿĀmilī," *EAL*. Al-ʿĀmilī, *Tawḍīḥ al-maqāṣid*, in *Majmūʿa nafīsa*, ed. al-Marʿashī, 355–371.
19. Hāshim b. Sulaymān b. Ismāʿīl b. ʿAbd al-Jawād al-Ḥusaynī, al-Bahrānī: *GAL* S 2:506, 533; Kaḥḥāla, *Muʿjam*, 4:51, #17789; W. Madelung, "Bahrānī, Hāŝem," EIr; Mahdī Maṭīʿ, "Bahrānī, Hāshim b. Sulaymān," *DMBI*, 11:386–387.

20. Muḥammad Bāqir b. Muḥammad Taqī, Majlisī al-Thānī: *GAL* S 2:572–574; al-ʿĀmilī, *Aʾyan,* 44:96–101; Kaḥḥāla, *Muʿjam,* 3:154, 155, #12349; Abdul-Hadi Hairi, "Madjlisī, Mullā Muḥammad Bākir," EI[2]; J. Cooper, "al-Majlisī," *EAL;* Colin P. Turner, "The Rise of Twelver Shiʾite Externalism in Safavid Iran and its Consolidation under ʿAllāma Muḥammad Bāqir Majlisī" (PhD diss., University of Durham, 1989).
21. Al-Baḥrānī, *Ghāyat al-marām wa-ḥujjat al-khiṣām fī taʿyīn al-Imām min ṭarīq al-khāṣṣ wa-al-ʿāmm.* See al-Ṭihrānī, *al-Dharīʿa,* 16:21–22; #76.
22. Al-Baḥrānī, *Ḥilyat al-abrār fī aḥwāl Muḥammad wa-ālihi al-aṭhār.* See al-Ṭihrānī, *al-Dharīʿa,* V7:79–80, #424.
23. Al-Baḥrānī, *Madīnat maʿājiz.* See al-Ṭihrānī, *al-Dharīʿa,* 22:253–254, #2834.
24. Majlisī, *Biḥār al-anwār al-jāmiʿa li-durar akhbār al-aʾimma al-aṭhār,* 44 vols., ed. Maḥmūd Duryāb Najafī and Jalāl al-Dīn ʿAlī Ṣaghīr (Beirut: Dār al-Taʿārif lil-Maṭbūʿāt, 2001). See al-Ṭihrānī, *al-Dharīʿa,* 3:16–27, #43.
25. Majlisī, *Jalāʾ al-ʿuyūn.* See al-Ṭihrānī, *al-Dharīʿa,* 5:124–125, #512. This was translated into Arabic about a century later: al-Ṭihrānī, *al-Dharīʿa,* 5:125, #513.
26. Muḥammad Ḥusayn Ṭabāṭabāʾī, *Shīʿeh dar Islām* (Qum: Daftar-i Tablīghāt-i Islāmī, 1348 [1969]), 109–154. English trans.: *Shiʿite Islam,* trans. Seyyed Hossein Nasr (Albany: State University of New York Press, 1975), 173–214.
27. Sharīf al-Jawāhir, *Muthīr al-aḥzān fī aḥwāl al-aʾimma al-ithnā ʿashar* (Najaf: al-Maṭbaʿa al-Ḥaydarīyah, 1966).
28. Hāshim Maʿrūf Ḥasanī, *Ṣīrāṭ al-aʾimma al-ithnā ʿashar,* 2 vols. (Beirut: Dār al-Taʿāruf, 1977.)
29. Mahmood Davari, *Taṣvīr-i khānavādeh-i Payāmbar dar Dāʾirat al-maʿārif-i Islām: tarjumeh va naqd* (Qum: Intishārāt-i Shīʿah'shināsī, 1385 [2006]).

Select Bibliography

Abdel-Meguid, A. "A Survey of the Terms Used in Arabic for 'Narrative' and 'Story.'" *IQ* 1, no. 4 (1954): 195–204.

Abdul, Musa O. A. "The *Majmaʿ al-Bayān* of Ṭabarsī." *IQ* 15 (1971): 106–120.

———. *The Qurʾan: Shaykh Tabarsi's Commentary.* Lahore: Hafeez Press, 1977.

———. "The Unnoticed *Mufassir* Shaykh Ṭabarsī." *IQ* 15 (1971): 96–105.

Afsaruddin, Asma. *Excellence and Precedence: Medieval Islamic Discourse on Legitimate Leadership.* Leiden: Brill, 2002.

———. "In Praise of the Caliphs: Re-Creating History from the *Manāqib* Literature." *IJMES* 31, no. 3 (1999): 329–350.

Aghaie, Kamran. *The Martyrs of Karbala.* Seattle: University of Washington Press, 2004.

———. "The Origins of the Sunnite-Shiʿite Divide and the Emergence of the Taʿziyeh Tradition." *The Drama Review* 49, no. 4 (2005): 42–47.

———, ed. *The Women of Karbala: Ritual Performance and Symbolic Discourses in Modern Shiʿi Islam.* Austin: University of Texas Press, 2005.

Ahmad, S. Maqbul. "Al-Masʿūdī's Contribution to Medieval Arab Geography." *Islamic Culture* 27 (1953): 61–77; and 28 (1954): 275–286.

———. "Travels of Abū al-Ḥasan ʿAlī ibn al-Ḥusayn al-Masʿūdī." *Islamic Culture* 28 (1954): 509–524.

Ahmad, S. Maqbul, and A. Rahman, eds. *Al-Masʿūdī Millenary Commemoration Volume.* Aligarh: Indian Society for the History of Science, 1960.

Ahmed, Sara. *The Cultural Politics of Emotion.* New York: Routledge, 2004.

Akhtar, S. Waheed. *The Early Imāmiyyah Shīʿite Thinkers.* New Delhi: Ashish Publishing House, 1988.

Algar, Hamid. "Imam Musa al-Kazim and Sufi Tradition." *Islamic Culture* 64 (1990): 1–14.

Al-ʿĀmilī, Muḥammad b. al-Husayn b. ʿAbd al-Ṣamad al-Ḥārithī. *Tawḍīḥ al-maqāṣid.* In *Majmūʿa nafīsah fī tārīkh al-aʾimmah: min āthār al-qudamāʾ min ʿulamāʾ*

al-imāmīya al-thuqāh Edited by Maḥmūd al-Ḥusaynī al-Marʿashī, 355–371. Beirut: Dār al-Qāriʾ, 2002.

Al-ʿĀmilī, Muḥsin al-Ḥusaynī. *Aʿyān al-Shīʿa*. 56 vols. Damascus: Maṭbaʿat Ibn Zaydūn, 1353–1379 [1935–1959].

Amir-Moezzi, Mohammad Ali. *The Divine Guide in Early Shiʿism: The Sources of Esotericism in Islam*. Translated by David Streight. Albany: State University of New York Press, 1994.

———. "Knowledge Is Power: Interpretations and Implications of the Miracle in Early Imamism." In *The Spirituality of Shiʿi Islam*, 193–230. London: I. B. Tauris, 2011.

———. "Savior c'est pouvoir. Exegeses et implications du miracle dan l'imamisme ancient (Aspects de l'imamologie duodecimaine, V)." In *Miracle et karama*. Edited by Denise Aigle, 251–286. Turnhout, 2000. Translated and reprinted in *The Spirituality of Shiʿi Islam: Beliefs and Practices*, 193–229. London: I. B. Tauris, 2011.

———. "Seul l'homme de Dieu est humain: Theologie et anthropologie mystique à travers l'exégèse imamite ancienne (aspects de l'imamologie duodécimaine iv)." *Arabica* 45, no. 2 (1998): 193–214. Translated and reprinted in *The Spirituality of Shiʿi Islam: Beliefs and Practices*, 277–304. London: I. B. Tauris, 2011.

———. "Shahrbānū, Dame du pays d'Iran et mère des Imams: entre l'Iran préislamique et le Shiisme Imamite." *JSAI* 27 (2002): 497–549.

———. *The Spirituality of Shiʿi Islam: Beliefs and Practices*. London: I. B. Tauris, 2011.

Anthony, Sean. *The Caliph and the Heretic: Ibn Sabaʾ and the Origins of Shīʿism*. Leiden: Brill, 2012.

Assmann, Jan. "Collective Memory and Cultural Identity." Translated by John Czaplicka, *New German Critique* 65 (Spring-Summer 1995): 125–133. Originally published as "Kollectives Gedachtnis und kulturelle Identitat." In *Kultur und Gedachtnis*. Edited by Jan Assmann and Tonio Holscher, 9–19. Frankfurt am Main, 1988.

———. *Religion and Cultural Memory: Ten Studies*. Translated by Rodney Livingston. Stanford, CA: Stanford University Press, 2006.

Al-ʿAsqalānī, Ibn Ḥajar. *Lisān al-Mīzān*. 6 vols. Ḥaydarābād al-Dakkan, Maṭbaʿat Majlis Dāʾirat al-Maʿārif al-Niẓāmīyah, 1331–1339 [1911–1913].

Athanasiou, Athena, Pothiti Hantzaroula, and Kostas Yannakopoulous. "Towards a New Epistemology: The 'Affective Turn.'" *Historein* 8 (2008): 5–16.

ʿAṭṭār, Farīd al-Dīn.*Taẕkirat al-awlīyāʾ*. Edited by Muḥammad Istīʿlāmī. Tehran: Intishārāt-i Zuvvār, 1366 [1987–1988].

Auchterlonie, Paul. *Arabic Biographical Dictionaries: A Summary Guide and Bibliography*. Durham, NC: Middle East Libraries Committee, 1987.

Ayoub, Mahmoud. *Redemptive Suffering in Islam: A Study of the Devotional Aspects of ʿĀshūrāʾ in Twelver Shīʿism*. The Hague: Mouton Publishers, 1978.

Babayan, Kathryn. *Mystics, Monarchs, and Messiahs: Cultural Landscapes of Early Modern Iran*. Cambridge, MA: Harvard University Press, 2002.

Al-Baghdādī, Abū Bakr Aḥmad ibn ʿAlī, al-Khaṭīb. *Tārīkh Madīnat al-Salām wa-akhbār muḥaddithīhā wa-dhikr quṭṭānihā al-ʿulamāʾ min ghayr ahlihā wa-wāridīhā*. 17 vols. Edited by Bashshār ʿAwwād Maʿrūf. Beirut: Dār al-Gharb al-Islāmī, 2001.

Al-Baḥrānī, Hishām b. Sulayman. *Ghāyat al-marām wa-ḥujjat al-khiṣām fī taʿyīn al-Imām min ṭarīq al-khāṣṣ wa-al-ʿāmm.* 7 vols. Edited by ʿAlī ʿĀshūr. Beirut: Muʾassasat al-Tārīkh al-ʿArabī, 2001.

———. *Ḥilyat al-abrār fī aḥwāl Muḥammad wa-Ālihi al-aṭhār, ʿalayhim al-salām.* 4 vols. Edited by Ghulām Riḍā Mawlānā al-Burūjirdī. Qum: Muʾassasat al-Maʿārif al-Islāmīyah, 1411– [1990 or 1991–].

———. *Madīna maʿājiz: al-aʾimmah al-ithnay ʿashar wa-dalāʾil al-ḥujaj ʿalá al-bashar.* 8 vols. Edited by ʿIzzat Allāh al-Mawlāʾī al-Hamdānī. Qum: Muʾassasat al-Maʿārif al-Islāmīyah, 1413–1416 [1992 or 1993–1995].

Barton, Carlin A. "Savage Miracles: The Redemption of Lost Honor in Roman Society and the Sacrament of the Gladiator and the Martyr." *Representations* 45 (Winter 1994): 41–71.

Barzegar, Abbas. "Remembering Community: Historical Narrative in the Formation of Sunni Islam." PhD diss., Emory University, 2010.

Bayhom-Daou, Tamima. *Shaykh Mufid.* Oxford: Oneworld, 2005.

Bellah, Robert, R. Madsen, W. Sullivan, A. Swindler, and S. M. Tipton. *Habits of the Heart: Individualism and Commitment in American Life.* Berkeley: University of California Press, 1985.

Berkey, Jonathan P. *The Formation of Islam: Religion and Society in the Near East, 600–1800.* Cambridge: Cambridge University Press, 2003.

———. *Popular Preaching & Religious Authority in the Medieval Islamic Near East.* Seattle: University of Washington Press, 2001.

Bernheimer, Teresa. *The ʿAlids: The First Family of Islam, 750–1200.* Edinburgh: Edinburgh University Press, 2013.

Boyarin, Daniel. *Dying for God: Martyrdom and the Making of Christianity and Judaism.* Stanford, CA: Stanford University Press, 1999.

Brock, Sebastian P., trans. *The History of the Holy Mar Maʿin, with a Guide to the Persian Martyr Acts.* Piscataway, NJ: Gorgias Press, 2008.

Brooks, Peter. *Reading for the Plot: Design and Intention in Narrative.* New York: Alfred A. Knopf, 1984.

Brown, Jonathan A. C. "Did the Prophet Say It or Not? The Literal, Historical, and Effective Truth of *Hadiths* in Early Sunnism." *JAOS* 129, no. 2 (2009): 259–285.

———. "Even If It's Not True It's True: Using Unreliable Ḥadīths in Sunni Islam." *Islamic Law and Society* 18 (2011): 1–52.

Brown, Peter. *The Body and Society: Men, Women, and Sexual Renunciation in Early Christianity.* New York: Columbia University Press, 1988.

———. "The Rise and Function of the Holy Man in Late Antiquity." *The Journal of Roman Studies* 61 (1971).

Browne, Edward G. *A Literary History of Persia.* Vol. 1, *From the Earliest Times until Firdawsī.* Cambridge: Cambridge University Press, 1956.

Buckley, Ron. P. "The Early Shiite Ghulāh." *Journal of Semitic Studies* 42, no. 2 (1997): 324–325.

———. "The Morphology and Significance of Some Imāmī Shīʿite Traditions." *Journal of Semitic Studies* 52, no. 2 (Autumn, 2007): 301–334.

Budge, Earnest A. Wallis, trans. *The Book of the Bee: The Syriac Text.* Oxford: Clarendon Press, 1886. Reprint, Zuu Books, 2011.

———, trans. *The Book of the Cave of Treasures: A History of the Patriarchs and the Kings, Their Successors from the Creation to the Crucifixion of Christ.* London: Religious Tract Society, 1927. Reprint, Whitefish, MT: Kessinger Publishing, 2010.

Bulliet, Richard. *Islam: The View from the Edge.* New York: Columbia University Press, 1994.

Burke, Peter. "History as Social Memory." In *Memory: History, Culture and the Mind.* Edited by Thomas Butler, 97–113. Oxford: Basil Blackwell, 1989.

———. *Varieties of Cultural History.* Ithaca, NY: Cornell University Press, 1997.

Burrus, Virgina. *"Begotten, Not Made": Conceiving Manhood in Late Antiquity.* Stanford, CA: Stanford University Press, 2000.

———. *The Sex Lives of the Saints: An Erotics of Ancient Hagiography.* Philadelphia: University of Pennsylvania Press, 2004.

Al-Bursī, *Mashāriq anwār al-yaqīn fī asrār Amīr al-Mu'minīn.* Beirut: Dār al-Andalus, 2001.

Buyukkara, M. Ali. "The Schism in the Party of Mūsā al-Kāẓim and the Emergence of the Wāqifa." *Arabica* 47, no. 1 (2000): 78–99.

Bynum, Caroline Walker. "Why All the Fuss about the Body? A Medievalist Perspective." *Critical Inquiry* 22, no. 1 (1995): 1–33.

Cameron, Averil. *Christianity and the Rhetoric of Empire: The Development of Christian Discourse.* Berkeley: University of California Press, 1991.

Castelli, Elizabeth. *Martyrdom and Memory: Early Christian Culture Making.* New York: Columbia University Press, 2004.

Clark, Elizabeth A. *History, Theory, Text: Historians and the Linguistic Turn.* Cambridge, MA: Harvard University Press, 2004.

Clarke, L., ed. and trans. *Shīʿite Heritage: Essays on Classical and Modern Traditions.* Binghamton, NY: Global Publications, 2001.

Climo, Jacob, and Maria Cattell, eds. *Social Memory and History: Anthropological Perspectives.* Walnut Creek, CA: AltaMira Press, 2002.

Clohessy, Christopher P. *Fatima, Daughter of Muhammad.* Piscataway, NJ: Gorgias Press, 2009.

Confino, Alon. "Collective Memory and Cultural History: Problems of Method." *American Historical Review* 102 (1997): 1386–1403.

Cook, David. *Martyrdom in Islam.* Cambridge: Cambridge University Press, 2007.

Coon, Lynda. *Dark Age Bodies: Gender and Monastic Practice in the Early Medieval West.* Philadelphia: University of Pennsylvania Press, 2011.

Cooperson, Michael. *Classical Arabic Biography.* Cambridge: Cambridge University Press, 2000.

———. *al-Ma'mun.* Oxford: Oneworld, 2005.

Corbin, Henry. "De la philosophie prophétique en Islam Shî'ite." *Eranos Jahrbuch* 31 (1962): 49–116.

———. *Spiritual Body and Celestial Earth: From Mazdean Iran to Shīʿite Iran.* Translated by Nancy Pearson. Princeton, NJ: Princeton University Press, 1977.

Crone, Patricia. "On the Meaning of the ʿAbbāsid call to al-Riḍā." In *The Islamic World: From Classical to Modern Times (Essays in Honor of Bernard Lewis)*. Edited by Clifford Edmund Bosworth, et al., 95–111. Princeton, NJ: Princeton University Press, 1989.

Crow, Douglas Karim. "The Death of al-Ḥusayn b. ʿAli and Early Shiʿi Views of the Imamate." *al-Serat* 12 (1986): 71–116. Reprinted in *Shiʿism*. Edited by Etan Kohlberg, 41–86. Burlington, VT: Ashgate, 2003.

Cullum, P. H., and Katherine J. Lewis. *Holiness and Masculinity in the Middle Ages*. Cardiff: University of Wales Press, 2005.

Cureton, W., ed. and trans. *Ancient Syriac Documents Relative to the Earliest Establishment of Christianity in Edessa and the Neighboring Countries*. Eugene, OR: Wipf & Stock Publishers, 2004.

Dabashi, Hamid. *Shi'ism: A Religion of Protest*. Cambridge, MA: Belknap Press, 2011.

Daftary, Farhad, and Gurdofarid Miskinzoda, eds. *The Study of Shiʿi Islam: History, Theology and Law*. New York: I. B. Tauris, 2014.

Dakake, Maria Massi. *The Charismatic Community: Shiʿite Identity in Early Islam*. Albany: State University of New York Press, 2007.

———. "Hiding in Plain Sight: The Practical and Doctrinal Significance of Secrecy in Shiʿite Islam." *Journal of the American Academy of Religion* 74, no. 2 (2006): 324–355.

Davari, Mahmood. *Taṣvīr-i khānavādeh-i Payāmbar dar Dāʾirat al-maʿārif-i Islām: tarjumeh va naqd*. Qum: Intishārāt-i Shīʿah'shināsī, 1385 [2006].

Deeb, Lara. "Doing Good, Like Sayyida Zaynab': Lebanese Shiʿi Women's Participation in the Public Sphere." In *Religion, Social Practice, and Contested Hegemonies: Reconstructing the Public Sphere in Muslim Majority Societies*. Edited by Armando Salvatore and Mark LeVine, 85–107. New York: Palgrave, 2005.

———. *An Enchanted Modern: Gender and Public Piety in Shiʿi Lebanon*. Princeton, NJ: Princeton University Press, 2006.

———. "From Mourning to Activism: Sayyedeh Zaynab, Lebanese Shiʿi Women, and the Transformation of Ashura." In *Women of Karbala*. Edited by K. Aghaie, 241–266. Austin: University of Texas Press, 2005.

Al-Dhahabī, Muḥammad ibn Aḥmad. *al-ʿIbar fī khabar man ghabar*. 5 vols. Kuwait: Dār al-Maṭbuʿat wa-al-nash, 1960.

———. *Tārīkh al-Islām wa-wafayāt al-mashāhīr wa-al-aʿlām*. Edited by ʿUmar ʿAbd al-Salām Tadmurī. Beirut: Dār al-Kitāb al-ʿArabī, 1989–.

Donaldson, Dwight M. *The Shi'ite Religion: A History of Islam in Persia and Irak*. London: Luzac & Company, 1933.

Donohue, John J. *The Buwayhid Dynasty in Iraq, 334H./945 to 403H./1012: Shaping Institutions for the Future*. Leiden: Brill, 2003.

D'Souza, Diane. *Partners of Zaynab: A Gendered Perspective of Shia Muslim Faith*. Columbia: University of South Carolina, 2014.

Dukhayyil, ʿAlī Muḥammad ʿAlī. *Aʾimmatunā*. 2 vols. Beirut: Dār al-Murtaḍá, 1982.

Dūrī, ʿAbd al-Azīz. *The Rise of Historical Writing Among the Arabs*. Edited and translated by Lawrence I. Conrad. Introduction by Fred Donner. Princeton, NJ: Princeton University Press, 1983.

El Cheikh, Nadia Maria. "The Gendering of 'Death' in *Kitāb al-ʿIqd al-Farīd.*" *Al-Qantara* 31, no. 2 (2010): 411–436.

———. "Mourning and the Role of the *Nāʾiḥa.*" *Estudios onomástico-biográficos de Al-Andalus* 13 (2003): 395–412.

———. "In Search for the Ideal Spouse." *Journal of the Economic and Social History of the Orient* 45, no. 2 (2002): 179–196.

Elias, Jamal. "Female and Feminine in Islamic Mysticism." *Muslim World* 77, nos. 3–4 (1988): 209–224.

Elliott, Alison Goddard. *Roads to Paradise: Reading the Lives of the Early Saints.* Hanover, NH: Brown University Press, 1987.

Ernst, Carl, and Richard Martin, eds. *Rethinking Islamic Studies: From Orientalism to Cosmopolitanism.* Columbia: University of South Carolina, 2010.

Fariq, K. A. "al-Khansāʾ and her Poetry." *Islamic Culture* 37 (1957): 209–219.

Faruqi, Maysam J. "Is There a Shīʿa Philosophy of History? The Case of Masʿūdī." *Journal of Religion* 86, no. 1 (2006): 23–54.

Al-Faṭṭāl, Abū ʿAlī, Muḥammad b. al-Ḥasan b. ʿAlī b. Aḥmad b. ʿAlī. *Rawḍat al-wāʿizīn.* Beirut: Muʾassasat al-Aʿlamī lil-Maṭbūʿāt, 1986.

Fentress, James, and Chris Wickham. *Social Memory.* Cambridge: Blackwell, 1992.

Friedman, Mordechai A. "Tamar, A Symbol of Life: The 'Killer Wife' Superstition in the Bible and Jewish Tradition." *AJS Review* 15, no. 1 (Spring 1990): 23–61.

Fudge, Bruce. *Qurʾānic Hermeneutics: al-Ṭabrisī and the Craft of Commentary.* New York: Routledge, 2011.

Furūshānī, Niʿmat Āllāh Ṣafarī. "*al-Irshād* wa-tārīkh nigārī zindagānī-yi aʾimmah." *A Quarterly for Shiʿite Studies* 6, no. 2 (2008): 37–76.

———. "Shaykh Mufīd va-tārīkh nigārī-yi ou dar *Kitāb al-irshād.*" *A Quarterly for Shiʿite Studies* 5, no. 2 (2007): 7–36.

Gana, Nouri. *Signifying Loss: Toward a Poetics of Narrative Mourning.* Lewisburg, PA: Bucknell University Press, 2011.

Giladi, Avner. *Infants, Parents and Wet Nurses: Medieval Islamic Views on Breastfeeding and Their Social Implications.* Leiden: Brill, 1999.

Glancy, Jennifer. *Corporeal Knowledge: Early Christian Bodies.* Oxford: Oxford University Press, 2010.

Gleave, Robert. *Scripturalist Islam.* Leiden: Brill, 2007.

Grabar, Oleg. "The Story of Portraits of the Prophet Muhammad." *Studia Islamica* 96 (2003): 19–38.

Gruber, Ernst August. *Verdienst und Rang: Die Faḍāʾil als literarisches und gesellschaftliches Problem im Islam.* Freiburg im Breisgau: K. Schwarz, 1975.

Gutas, Dimitri. *Greek Thought, Arabic Culture: The Graeco-Arabic Translation Movement in Baghdad and Early ʿAbbāsid Society (2nd–4th / 8th–10th centuries).* New York: Routledge, 1998.

Hadas, Moses, and Morton Smith. *Heroes and Gods: Spiritual Biographies in Antiquity.* Freeport, NY: Books for Library Press, 1965.

Haider, Najam. *The Origins of the Shīʿa: Identity, Ritual, and Sacred Space in Eighth-Century Kūfah.* Cambridge: Cambridge University Press, 2011.

———. *Shīʿī Islam: An Introduction.* Cambridge: Cambridge University Press, 2014.

Halevi, Leor. *Muhammad's Grave: Death Rites and the Making of Islamic Society.* New York: Columbia University Press, 2007.

Halm, Heinz. *Shiʿa Islam: From Religion to Revolution.* Translated by Allison Brown. Princeton, NJ: Markus Wiener Publishers, 1997.

———. *The Shiites: A Short History.* Translated by Allison Brown. Princeton. NJ: Markus Wiener Publishers, 2007.

Hammond, Marlè. *Beyond Elegy: Classical Arabic Women's Poetry in Context.* Oxford: Oxford University Press, 2010.

———, ed. *Transforming Loss into Beauty: Essays on Arabic Literature and Culture in Honor of Magda Al-Nowaihi.* Cairo: American University Press, 2008.

Al-Ḥarrānī, al-Ḥasan b. ʿAlī. *Tuḥaf al-ʿuqūl ʿan āl al-Rasūl.* Edited by ʿAlī Akbar al-Ghaffārī. [Beirut]: Dār al-Qārī, 2005. English translation: *Tuhaf al-Uqoul: The Masterpieces of the Intellects.* Translated by Badr Shahin. Qum: Ansariyan Publications, 2001.

Ḥasanī, Hāshim Maʿrūf. *Ṣīrāṭ al-aʾimma al-ithnā ʿashar.* 2 vols. Beirut: Dār al-Taʿāruf, 1977.

Heffernan, Thomas J. *Sacred Biography: Saints and Their Biographers in the Middle Ages.* Oxford: Oxford University Press, 1988.

Herman, David. *Basic Elements of Narrative.* West Sussex, UK: Wiley-Blackwell, 2009.

———, ed. *Cambridge Companion to Narrative.* Cambridge: Cambridge University Press, 2007.

Hidayatullah, Aysha. "Māriyya the Copt: Gender, Sex and Heritage in the Legacy of Muhammad's *umm walad.*" *Islam and Christian-Muslim Relations* 21, no. 3 (2010): 221–243.

Hinds, Martin. *Studies in Early Islamic History.* Princeton, NJ: Darwin Press, 1996.

Hjortshoj, Keith. "Shi'i Identity and Muharram in India." In *Shi'ism, Resistance, and Revolution.* Edited by Martin Kramer, 289–307. Boulder, CO: Westview Press, 1987.

Hobsbawm, Eric. "The Social Function of the Past: Some Questions." *Past and Present* 55 (1972): 3–17.

Hodgson, Marshall. "How Did the Early Shi'a Become Sectarian?" *JAOS* 75, no. 1 (1955): 1–13. Reprinted in *Shīʿism.* Edited by Etan Kohlberg, 3–16. Burlington, VT: Ashgate, 2003.

———. *The Venture of Islam.* 3 vols. Chicago: University of Chicago Press, 1974.

Horovitz, Josef. *The Earliest Biographies of the Prophet and Their Authors.* Princeton, NJ: Darwin Press, 2002.

Hurvitz, Nimrod. "Biographies and Mild Asceticism: A Study of Islamic Moral Imagination." *Studia Islamica* 85 (1997): 41–65.

Hussain, Ali J. "The Mourning of History and the History of Mourning: The Evolution of Ritual Commemoration of the Battle of Karbala." *Comparative Studies of South Asia, Africa and the Middle East* 25, no. 1 (2005): 78–88.

Hussain, J. M. *The Occultation of the Twelfth Imam: A Historical Background.* London: The Muhammadi Trust, 1982.

Hylén, Torsten. "Ḥusayn, the Mediator: A Structural Analysis of the Karbalāʾ Drama according to Abū Jaʿfar Muḥammad b. Jarīr al-Ṭabarī (d. 310/923)." PhD diss., Uppsala Universitet, 2007.

Ibn ʿAbd al-Wahhāb. *ʿUyūn al-muʿjizāt*. Beirut: Muʾassasat al-Aʿlamī lil-Maṭbūʿāt, 2004.

Ibn Abī al-Thalj. *Tārīkh al-aʾimma*. In *Majmūʿa nafīsa fī tārīkh al-aʾimma: min āthār al-qudamāʾ min ʿulamāʾ al-imāmīya al-thuqāh*. Edited by Maḥmūd al-Ḥusaynī al-Marʿashī. Beirut: Dār al-Qāriʾ, 2002.

Ibn al-Athīr, ʿIzz al-Dīn ʿAlī b. Muḥammad. *al-Kāmil fī al-taʾrīkh*. 11 vols. Edited by ʿUmar ʿAbd al-Salām Tadmurī. Beirut: Dār al-Kitāb al-ʿArabī, 1997.

Ibn Bābawayh al-Qummī, Muḥammad b. ʿAlī. *Iʿtiqādat al-imāmiyah*. In *Muṣannafāt li-Shaykh al-Mufīd*, vol. 5. Qum: al-Muʾtamir al-ʿĀlimī li-Alafīyah al-Shaykh al-Mufīd, 1413 [1992]. English translation: *Shiʿite Creed*. 3rd edition. Translated by Asaf A. A. Fyzee. Tehran: World Organization for Islamic Services, 1999.

Ibn Ḥajar al-ʿAsqalānī, Aḥmad b. ʿAlī. *Tahdhīb al-tahdhīb*. 4 vols. Edited by Ibrāhīm al-Zaybaq and ʿĀdil Murshid. Beirut: Muʾassasat al-Risālah, 1996.

Ibn Isḥaq. *The Life of Muhammad: A Translation of Isḥāq's* Sīrat Rasūl Allāh. Introduction and translation by A. Guillaume. Oxford: Oxford University Press, 1955.

Ibn al-Jawzī, ʿAbd al-Raḥmān b. ʿAlī. *al-Muntaẓam fī tārīkh al-mulūk wa-al-umam*. 19 vols. Edited by Muḥammad ʿAbd al-Qādir ʿAṭā, Muṣṭafá ʿAbd al-Qādir ʿAṭā, and Naʿīm Zarzūrmuntazam. Beirut: Dār al-Kutub al-ʿIlmīyah, 1992.

Ibn Khaldūn. *Tārīkh Ibn Khaldūn: al-Muqaddima*. Beirut: Dār al-Kitāb al-Lubnānī, 1961.

Ibn Khallikān. *Wafayāt al-aʿyān*. 8 vols. Edited by Iḥsān ʿAbbās. Beirut: Dar Assakafa, [1968?–1972?].

Ibn Khashshāb. *Tārīkh mawālīd al-aʾimma wa wafīyātihim*. In *Majmūʿa nafīsa fī tārīkh al-aʾimma: min āthār al-qudamāʾ min ʿulamāʾ al-imāmīya al-thuqāh*. Edited by Maḥmūd al-Ḥusaynī al-Marʿashī, 119–150. Beirut: Dār al-Qāriʾ, 2002.

Ibn Nadīm, *al-Fihrist*. Edited by Yūsuf ʿAlī Ṭawīl. Beirut: Dār al-Kutub al-ʿIlmīyah, 2002. English translation: *The Fihrist of Ibn al-Nadīm: A Tenth-Century Survey of Muslim Culture*. 2 vols. Translated by Bayard Dodge. New York: Columbia University Press, 1970.

Ibn Rāshid, Maʿmar. *The Expeditions: An Early Biography of Muḥammad*. Edited and Translated by Sean W. Anthony. Foreword by M. A. S. Abdel Haleem. New York: New York University Press, 2014.

Ibn Shahrāshūb, Muḥammad b. ʿAlī. *Kitāb maʿālim al-ʿulamāʾ fī fihrist kutub al-muṣannifīn minhum qadīman wa-ḥadīthan*. Edited by ʿAbbās Iqbal. Tehran: Maṭba Faradīn, 1353 [1934].

Ibn Taymīya. *Kitab iqtidaʾ al-ṣirāt al-mustaqīm mukhālafat aṣḥāb al-jaḥīm*. Translated by Muhammad Umar Memon. In *Ibn Taimīya's Struggle Against Popular Religion*. The Hague: Mouton, 1976.

Al-Irbilī, Abū al-Ḥasan, ʿAlī b. ʿĪsá b. Abī al-Fatḥ. *Kashf al-ghumma fī maʿrifat al-aʾimma*. Edited by ʿAlī al-Fāḍilī. 4 vols. [Iran]: Markaz al-Ṭibāʿa wa-al-Nashr lil-Majmaʿ al-ʿĀlamī li-Ahl al-Bayt, 1426 [2005–2006].

Irwin, Robert. "'Futuwwa': Chivalry and Gangsterism in Medieval Cairo." *Muqarnas* 21, Essays in Honor of J. M. Rogers (2004): 161–170.

Al-Iṣbahānī, Mirzā ʿAbd Allāh Afandī, *Rīyāḍ al-ʿulamāʾ wa-ḥīyāḍ al-fuḍalāʾ*. 6 vols. Qum: Maṭbaʿat al-khayyām, 1401 [1980].

Al-Isfahānī, Abū al-Faraj. *Maqātil al-ṭālibyīn*. Edited by Aḥmad Ṣaqr. Cairo: Dār Iḥyā' al-Kutub al-ʿArabīya, 1368 [1949].

Ishtihārdī, Muḥammad Muḥammadī. *Maṣā'ib Āl Muḥammad: fī bayān ḥayāt wa-al-maṣā'ib al-mu'limah lil-maʿṣūmīn al-arbaʿat ʿashar wa-shuhadā' wa-sabāyā Karbalā' maʿa marāthīhim*. Beirut: Dār al-Kātib al-ʿArabī, 2002.

———. *Sīrat al-maʿṣūmīn al-arbaʿat ʿashar: al-musammá bi-Muntaqá al-durar: dirāsah mūjazah wa-muyassarah wa-hādifah ʿan ḥayat al-maʿṣūmīn al-arbaʿah ʿashar*. 3 vols. Beirut: Mu'assasat al-Balāgh, 2008.

Al-Ithnāʿasharī, ʿAbd al-Mahdī. "Mashyakha Ibn Shahrāshūb (1)." *Turāthunā* 24, no. 93/94 (1429 [2008]): 11–95.

———. "Mashyakha Ibn Shahrāshūb (2)." *Turāthūna* 24, no. 95/97 (1429 [2008]): 7–95.

Jaʿfar, Mahdī Khalīl. *al-Mawsūʿah al-kubrá li- Ahl al-Bayt*. 16 vols. Beirut: Markaz al-Sharq al-Awsaṭ al-Thaqāfī, 2009.

Jafri, S. H. M. *Origins and Early Development of Shiʿa Islam*. London: Longman, 1979.

Jahḍamī, Naṣr b. ʿAlī. *Tārīkh ahl al-bayt: naqlʿan al-a'imma al-Bāqir wa-al-Ṣādiq wa-al-Riḍā wa-al-ʿAskarī ʿan ābā'ihim*. Qum: Dalīl Mā, 1426 [2005 or 2006].

Jaques, R. Kevin. "Arabic Islamic Prosopography: The Tabaqat Genre." In *Prosopography Approaches and Applications: A Handbook*, ed. K. S. B. Keats-Rohan, 387–414. Oxford: University of Oxford, 2007.

Al-Jawāhir, [Sharīf]. *Muthīr al-aḥzān fī aḥwāl al-a'imma al-ithnā ʿashar*. Najaf: al-Maṭbaʿah al-Ḥaydarīyah, 1966.

Juynboll, G. H. A. *Encyclopedia of Canonical Ḥadīth*. Leiden: Brill, 2007.

Kaḥḥāla, ʿUmar Riḍā. *Muʿjam al-mu'allifīn: tarājim muṣannifī al-kutub al-ʿArabīyah*. 4 vols. Beirut: Mu'assasat al-Risālah, 1993.

Karīmān, Ḥusayn. *Ṭabrisī va Majmaʿ al-bayān*. 2 vols. Tehran: Dānishgāh-i Tihrān, 1340–1341 [1961–1962].

Kāshifī, Ḥusayn b. ʿAlī. *Rawẓat al-shuhadā'*. Edited by Muḥammad Riẓā Iftikhārzādah. Tehran: Intishārāt-i Mudabbir, 1384 [2005].

Katz, Marion Holmes. *The Birth of the Prophet Muḥammad: Devotional Piety in Sunni Islam*. London: Routledge, 2007.

Khalidi, Tarif. "Islamic Biographical Dictionaries: A Preliminary Assessment." *Muslim World* 63 (1973): 53–65.

———. *Islamic Historiography: The Histories of Masʿūdī*. Albany: State University of New York Press, 1975.

———. "Masʿūdī's Lost Works: A Reconstruction of Their Content." *JAOS* 94, no. 1 (1974): 35–41.

Khānjānī, Qāsim. "Mudawwanāt al-Shaykh al-Mufīd wa-qarā'ituhu al-kalāmīya lil-tārīkh." *Turāthunā* 25, no. 97/98 (1430 [2009]): 87–198.

Al-Khāqānī, Ḥāzim. *Ummuhāt al-a'imma*. Beirut: Dār al-Ḥaqq, 1995.

Khuri, Fuad. *Imams and Emirs: State, Religion and Sects in Islam*. London: Saqi Books, 1990.

Klemm, Verena. "Image Formation of an Islamic Legend: Fāṭima, the Daughter of the Prophet Muḥammad." In *Ideas, Images, and Methods of Portrayal*. Edited by S. Günther, 181–208. Leiden: Brill, 2005.

Knust, Jennifer. *Abandoned to Lust: Sexual Slander and Ancient Christianity.* New York: Columbia University Press, 2006.

———. "Enslaved to Demons: Sex, Violence and the Apologies of Justin Martyr." In *Mapping Gender in Ancient Religious Discourses.* Edited by Todd Penner and Caroline Vander Stichele, 431–455. Leiden: Brill, 2007.

Kohlberg, Etan. "From Imāmiyya to Ithnā-ʿashariyya." *BSOAS* 39, no. 3 (1976): 521–534.

———. *Medieval Muslim Scholar at Work: Ibn Ṭāwūs and His Library.* Leiden: Brill, 1992.

———. "The Position of the 'walad zinā' in Imāmī Shīʿism." *BSOAS* 48, no. 2 (1985): 237–266.

———. "Some Imāmī-shīʿī Views on *Taqiyya.*" *JAOS* 95, no. 3 (Jul.–Sep. 1975): 395–402.

———. "An Unusual Shīʿī *isnād.*" *Israel Oriental Studies* 5 (1975): 142–149.

———. "Vision and the Imams." In *Autour du regard: Mélanges Gimaret.* Edited by É. Chaumont, with D. Aigle, M. A. Amir-Moezzi, and P. Lory, 125–157. Paris: Peeters, 2003.

———. "Western Studies of Shi'a Islam." In *Shi'ism, Resistance, and Revolution,* ed. Martin Kramer, 31–44. Boulder, CO: Westview Press, 1987.

Kugle, Scott. *Sufis & Saints' Bodies: Mysticism, Corporeality and Sacred Power in Islam.* Chapel Hill: University of North Carolina Press, 2007.

Lalani, Arzina R. *Early Shīʿī Thought: The Teachings of Imam Muḥammad al-Bāqir.* London: I. B. Tauris, 2000.

Laoust, H. "Les Agitations Religieuses à Baghdād aux IVe et Ve siècles de l'Hégire." In *Islamic Civilization, 950–1150: Papers on Islamic History III.* Edited by D. S. Richards, 169–186. London: William Clowes & Sons Limited, 1973.

Lassner, Jacob. *Islamic Revolution and Historical Memory: An Inquiry into the Art of ʿAbbāsid Apologetics.* New Haven, CT: American Oriental Society, 1986.

Lees, Clare, ed. *Medieval Masculinities: Regarding Men in the Middle Ages.* With assistance from Thelma Fenster and Jo Ann McNamara. Minneapolis: University of Minnesota Press, 1994.

Lifshitz, Felice. "Beyond Positivism and Genre: 'Hagiographical' Texts as Historical Narrative." *Viator* 25 (1994): 95–113.

Loebenstein, Judith. "Miracles in Šīʿī Thought: A Case-Study of the Miracles Attributed to Imām Gaʿfar al-Ṣādiq." *Arabica* 50, no. 2 (2003): 199–244.

Losensky, Paul. *Farid ad-Din ʿAttār's Memorial of God's Friends: Lives and Sayings of Sufis.* New York: Paulist Press, 2009.

Mack, Burton. "A Radically Social Theory of Religion." In *Secular Theories of Religion: Current Perspectives.* Edited by Tim Jensen and Mikael Rothstein, 123–136. Copenhagen: Museum Tusculanum Press, 2000.

Madelung, Wilferd. "Imāmism and Muʿtazilite Theology." In *Le Shiʿisme imamate.* Edited by T. Fahd, 13–29. Paris: Presses Universitaires, 1970.

———. *Succession to Muḥammad: A Study of the Early Caliphate.* Cambridge: Cambridge University Press, 1997.

Mahdjoub, Mohammad-Djaʿfar. "The Evolution of Popular Eulogy of the Imams among the Shiʿa." In *Authority and Political Culture in Shiʿism.* Edited by

S. Arjomand, 54–79. Translated and adapted by John R. Perry. Albany: State University of New York Press, 1988.
Majlisī, Muḥammad Bāqir b. Muḥammad Taqī. *Jalāʾ al-ʿuyūn: tārīkh-i chahārdah maʿṣūm*. Edited by Sayyid ʿAlī Imāmiyān. Qum: Surūr, 1387 [2008–2009].
Makdisi, George. "The Sunni Revival." In *Islamic Civilization, 950–1150*. Edited by D. S. Richards, 155–168. Oxford: Cassirer, 1973.
Malti-Douglas, Fedwa. "Controversy and Its Effects in the Biographical Tradition of al-Khaṭīb al-Baghdādī." *Studia Islamica* 46 (1977): 115–131.
———. "Dreams, the Blind, and the Semiotics of the Biographical Notice." *Studia Islamica* 51 (1980): 137–162.
———. "Faces of Sin: Corporal Geographies in Contemporary Islamist Discourse." In *Religious Reflections on the Human Body*. Edited by Jane Marie Law, 67–75. Bloomington: Indiana University Press, 1995.
———. *Woman's Body, Woman's Word: Gender and Discourse in Arabo-Islamic Writing*. Princeton, NJ: Princeton University Press, 1991.
Al-Marʿashī, Maḥmūd al-Ḥusaynī. *Majmūʿa nafīsa fī tārīkh al-aʾimma: min āthār al-qudamāʾ min ʿulamāʾ al-imāmīya al-thuqāh*. Beirut: Dār al-Qāriʾ, 2002.
Martin, Dale, and Patricia Cox Miller, eds. *The Cultural Turn in Late Ancient Studies: Gender, Asceticism, and Historiography*. Durham, NC: Duke University Press, 2005.
Al-Masʿūdī. *Murūj al-dhahab wa-maʿādin al-jawhar*. 7 vols. Edited by Charles Pellat. Beirut: Publications de l'Universite Libanaise, 1965–1979. French translation: *Les prairies d'or*. 5 vols. Translated by Charles Pellat. Paris: Société asiatique, 1962–1997.
———. *Tanbīh wa-al-ishrāf*. Edited by Michael Jan de Goeje. Beirut: Maktabat Khayyāṭ, 1965.
McDermott, Martin J. *The Theology of al-Shaikh al-Mufīd*. Beirut: Dar el-Machreq, 1978.
Meisami, Julie Scott. "Masʿūdī on Love and the Fall of the Barmakids." *Journal of the Royal Asiatic Society of Great Britain and Ireland* 2 (1989): 252–277.
———. "Masʿūdī and the Reign of al-Amīn: Narrative and Meaning in Medieval Muslim Historiography." In *On Fiction and* Adab *in Medieval Arabic Literature*. Edited by Philip F. Kennedy, 149–176. Wiesbaden: Harrassowitz, 2005.
Melchert, Christopher. *The Formation of the Sunni Schools of Law: 9th–10th Centuries C.E.* Leiden: Brill, 1997.
Miller, Patricia Cox. *Biography in Late Antiquity: A Quest for the Holy Man*. Berkeley: University of California Press, 1983.
Mills, Margaret A. "The Gender of the Trick: Female Tricksters and Male Narrators." *Asian Folklore Studies* 60, no. 2 (2001): 237–258.
———. "Whose Best Tricks? Makr-i zan as a Topos in Persian Oral Literature." *Iranian Studies* 32, no. 2 (1999): 261–270.
Modarressi, Hossein. *Crisis and Consolidation in the Formative Period of Shiʿite Islam: Abū Jaʿfar ibn Qiba al-Rāzī and His Contribution to Imāmite Shīʿite Thought*. Princeton, NJ: The Darwin Press, 1993.
———. *Tradition and Survival: A Bibliographical Survey of Early Shiʿite Literature*. Vol. 1. Oxford: Oneworld, 2003.
Moin, A. Azfar. "Partisan Dreams and Prophetic Visions: Shīʿī Critique in al-Masʿūdī's History of the Abbasids." *JAOS* 127, no. 4 (2007): 415–427.

Momen, Moojan. *An Introduction to Shi'i Islam: The History and Doctrines of Twelver Shi'ism.* New Haven, CT: Yale University Press, 1985.

Moosa, Matti. *Extremist Shiites: The Ghulat Sects.* Syracuse, NY: Syracuse University Press, 1988.

Morimoto, Kazuo, ed. *Sayyids and Sharifs in Muslim Societies: The Living Links to the Prophet.* London: Routledge, 2012.

Al-Mufīd, Muḥammad b. Muḥammad b. al-Nuʿmanī. *al-Amālī.* Najaf: al-Maṭbaʿat al-Haydariyah, 1962. Translation: *Al Amaali.* Translated by Asgharali M. M. Jaffer. Middlesex: World Federation, 1998.

Muḥammadī, Muḥammad Raḥīm Bayg. *Ibn Shahrāshūb: dar ḥarīm-i vilāyat.* n.p.: Markaz-i Chāp va Nashr-i Sāzmān-i Ṭablīghāt-i Islāmī, 1374 (Shamsī) [1996].

Al-Najashi. *Rijāl al-Najāshī.* 2 vols. Edited by Muḥammad Jawād al-Nāʾinī. Beirut: Dār al-Adwāʾ, 1988.

Najmabadi, Afsaneh. "Reading: And Enjoying: 'Wiles of Women' Stories as a Feminist." *Iranian Studies* 32, no. 2 (Spring 1999): 203–222.

———. "Reading 'Wiles of Women' Stories as Fictions of Masculinity." In *Imagined Masculinities: Male Identity and Culture in the Modern Middle East.* Edited by Mai Ghoussoub and Emma Sinclair-Webb, 147–168. London: Saqi Books, 2000.

Nakash, Yitzhak. "An Attempt to Trace the Origin of the Rituals of ʿĀshūrāʾ." *Die Welt des Islams,* n.s. 33, no. 2 (1993): 161–181.

Neal, Derek. *The Masculine Self in Late Medieval England.* Chicago: University of Chicago Press, 2008.

Newman, Andrew. *The Formative Period of Twelver Shiʿism: Ḥadīth as Discourse between Qum and Baghdad.* Richmond, UK: Curzon, 2000.

Olick, Jeffrey K., and Joyce Robbins. "Social Memory Studies: From 'Collective Memory' to the Historical Sociology of Mnemonic Practices." *Annual Review of Sociology* 24 (1998): 105–140.

Passerini, Luisa. "Connecting Emotions: Contributions from Cultural History." *Historein* 8 (2008): 117–127.

[Peer Mohamed Ebrahim Trust]. *Biography of Imam Taqi (A. S.).* Karachi: Peer Mohamed Ebrahim Trust, 1975.

Pellat, Charles. "Masʿūdī et l'Imāmisme." In *Le Shîʿisme imâmite: Colloque de Strasbourg (6–9 mai 1968),* 69–90. Paris: Presses Universitaires de France, 1970.

Perella, Nicholas J. *The Kiss Sacred and Profane: An Interpretive History of Kiss Symbolism and Related Religio-Erotic Themes.* Berkeley: University of California Press, 1969.

Perkins, Judith. *The Suffering Self: Pain and Narrative Representation in the Early Christian Era.* New York: Routledge, 1995.

Pierce, Matthew. "Ibn Shahrashub and Shiʿa Rhetorical Strategies in the 6th/12th Century." *Journal of Shiʿa Islamic Studies* 5, no. 4 (Autumn 2012): 441–454.

———. "Remembering Fāṭima: New Means of Legitimizing Female Authority in Contemporary Shīʿī Discourse." In *Women, Leadership, and Mosques: Changes in Contemporary Islamic Authority.* Edited by Masooda Bano and Hilary Kalmbach, 345–362. Leiden: Brill, 2012.

Pinault, David. *The Shiites: Ritual and Popular Piety in a Muslim Community.* New York: St. Martin's Press, 1992.

Pīshvā'ī, Mahdī. *Sīrah-i pīshvāyān: nigarishī bar zindagānī-i ijtimāʿī, siyāsī va farhangī-i imāmān-i maʿṣūm ʿalayhum al-salām*. Qum: Mu'assasah-i Imām Ṣādiq, 1388 [2009].

Powers, David. *Muḥammad Is Not the Father of Any of Your Men*. Philadelphia: University of Pennsylvania Press, 2009.

Al-Qāḍī, Wadād. "Biographical Dictionaries: Inner Structure and Cultural Significance." In *The Book in the Islamic World*. Edited by George N. Atiyeh, 93–122. Albany: State University of New York Press, 1995.

———. "Biographical Dictionaries as the Scholars' Alternative History of the Muslim Community." In *Organizing Knowledge: Encyclopædic Activities in the Pre-Eighteenth Century Islamic World*. Edited by Gerhard Endress, 23–75. Leiden: Brill, 2006.

———. "The Development of the Term *ghulāt* in Muslim Literature with Special Reference to the Kaysāniyya." In *Akten des VII Kongresses für Arabistik und Islamwissenschaft*. Edited by Albert Dietrich, 86–99. Göttingen: Vandenhoeck & Ruprecht, 1976. Reprinted in *Shīʿism*, edited by Etan Kohlberg, 169–194. Burlington, VT: Ashgate, 2003.

———. "In the Footsteps of Arabic Biographical Literature: A Journey, Unfinished, in the Company of Knowledge." *Journal of Near Eastern Studies* 68, no. 4 (2009): 241–252.

Qummī, ʿAbbās b. Muḥammad Riḍā. *Muntahá al-āmāl*. 2 vols. Qum: Intishārāt-i Nigāh-i Āshnā, 1388 [2009 or 2010].

Qurashī, Bāqir Sharīf. *The Fourteen Infallibles in the History of Islam*. 14 vols. Qum: Ansariyan, 1999–2010.

Al-Rāwandī. *Kharā'ij wa-al-jarāyih*. Qum: Intishārāt Muṣṭafawī, 1399 H [1979–].

Renard, John. *Friends of God: Islamic Images of Piety, Commitment and Servanthood*. Berkeley: University of California Press, 2008.

Reynolds, Dwight, ed. *Interpreting the Self: Autobiography in the Arabic Literary Tradition*. Berkeley: University of California Press, 2001.

Ridgeon, Lloyd. *Morals and Mysticism in Persian Sufism: A History of Sufi-futuwwat in Iran*. London: Routledge, 2010.

Al-Rifāʿī, ʿAbd al-Jabbār. *Muʿjam mā kutiba ʿan al-Rasūl wa-ahl al-bayt, ṣalawāt ʿalayhim Allāh*. 12 vols. Tehran: Sāzmān-i Chāp va Intishārāt-i Vizārat-i Farhang va Irshād-i Islāmī, 1371– [1992–].

Ritter, Helmut. "Irrational Solidarity Groups: A Socio-Psychological Study in Connection with Ibn Khaldūn." *Oriens* 1, no. 1 (1948): 1–44.

Robinson, Chase F. *Islamic Historiography*. Cambridge: Cambridge University Press, 2003.

Roded, Ruth. "Alternate Images of the Prophet Muhammad's Virility." In *Islamic Masculinities*. Edited by Lahoucine Ouzgane, 57–71. London: Zed Books, 2006.

———. *Women in Islamic Biographical Collections*. Boulder, CO: Lynne Rienner Publishers, 1994.

Rosenthal, Franz. *Four Essays on Art and Literature in Islam*. Leiden: Brill, 1971.

Rubin, Uri. "Islamic Retelling of Biblical History." In *Adaptions and Innovations: Studies on the Interaction between Jewish and Islamic Thought and Literature from the Early Middle Ages to the Late Twentieth Century, Dedicated to Joel Kraemer*. Edited by Y. Tzvi Langermann and Josef Stern, 299–313. Paris: Peeters, 2007.

———. "The Ka'ba: Aspects of Its Ritual Functions." *JSAI* 8 (1986): 97–131.
———. "Pre-existence and Light: Aspects of the Concept of Nūr Muḥammad." *Israel Oriental Studies* 5 (1975): 62–119.
———. "Prophets and Progenitors in the Early Shī'a Tradition." *JSAI* 1 (1979): 41–65.
Ruffle, Karen. "May Fatimah Gather Our Tears: The Mystical and Intercessory Powers of Fatimah al-Zahra in Indo-Persian, Shi'i Devotional Literature and Performance." *Comparative Studies of South Asia, Africa, and the Middle East* 30, no. 3 (2010): 386–397.
Sabzavārī, [Shī'ī]. *Rāḥat al-arvāḥ: dar sharḥ-i zindagī, faẓā'il va mu'ajazzāt-i a'imma-i Aṭhār.* Tehran: Ahl-i Qalam: Daftar-i Nashr-i Mīrāṣ-i Maktūb, 1375 [1996 or 1997].
Ṣafadī, Khalīl ibn Aybak. *Kitāb al-Wāfī bi-al-Wafayāt.* 30 vols. Edited by Muḥammad Ḥujayrī, Otfried Weintritt, Māhir Zuhayr Jarrār, and Benjamin Jokisch. Leipzig: Deutsche Morgenländische Gesellschaft, in Kommission bei F. A. Brockhaus, 1931.
Savant, Sarah Bowen. *The New Muslims of Post-Conquest Iran: Tradition, Memory, and Conversion.* Cambridge: Cambridge University Press, 2013.
Schimmel, Annemarie. *And Muhammad Is His Messenger.* Chapel Hill: University of North Carolina Press, 1985.
———. "'I Take off the Dress of the Body': Eros in Sufi Literature and Life." In *Religion and the Body.* Edited by Sarah Coakley, 262–288. Cambridge: Cambridge University Press, 1997.
———. *Islam and the Wonders of Creation: The Animal Kingdom.* London: Al-Furqān Islamic Heritage Foundation, 1424/2003.
Schippers, Arie. "'Tales with a Good Ending' in Arabic Literature: Narrative Art and Theory of the Arabic World." *Quaderni Di Studi Arabi* 4 (1986): 57–70.
Schoeler, Gregor. *The Genesis of Literature in Islam: From the Aural to the Read.* Revised edition in collaboration with and translated by Shawkat M. Toorawa. Edinburgh: Edinburgh University Press, 2002.
———. *The Oral and the Written in Early Islam.* London: Routledge, 2006.
Searle, J. *Speech Acts: An Essay in the Philosophy of Language.* Cambridge: Cambridge University Press, 1969.
Shaban, M. A. *The Abbasid Revolution.* Cambridge: Cambridge University Press, 1970.
Sharon, Moshe. *Black Banners from the East: The Establishment of the 'Abbāsid State: Incubation of a Revolt.* Leiden: Brill, 1983.
Shboul, Ahmad M. H. *Al-Mas'ūdī and His World: A Muslim Humanist and His Interest in Non-Muslims.* London: Ithaca Press, 1979.
Sibṭ b. al-Jawzī, Yūsuf ibn Qizughlī. *Tadhkirat al-khawāṣ.* Qum: Manshūrāt Dhuwī al-Qurbī, 1427.
Sindawi, Khalid. "The Donkey of the Prophet in the Shī'ite Tradition." *al-Masāq* 18, no. 1 (2006): 87–98.
———. "'Fāṭima's Book': A Shi'ite Qur'an." *Rivista degli studi orientali* 78, no. 1 (2007): 57–70.
———. "Hishām b. Sālim al-Jawālīqī and His Role in Shī'ī Thought in the Second Century AH." *Ancient Near Eastern Studies* 48 (2011): 260–277.

———. "Al-Ḥusain ibn ʿAlî and Yaḥyâ ibn Zakariyyâ in the Shîʿite sources: a comparative study." *Islamic Culture* 78, no. 3 (2004): 37–53.

———. "The Image of Ḥusayn ibn ʿAlī in *Maqātil* Literature." *Quaderni di Studi Arabi* 20–21 (2002–2003): 79–104.

———. "Jesus and Ḥusayn Ibn ʿAlī Ibn ʾAbū Ṭālib: A Comparative Study." *Ancient Near Eastern Studies* 44 (2007): 50–65.

———. "Legends Concerning the Wedding of Fāṭima al-Zahrāʾ as Reflected in Early Shīʿite Literature." *Orientalia Suecana* 56 (2007): 181–191.

———. "Link between Joshua Bin Nun and ʿAlī Ibn Abū Ṭālib." *Ancient Near Eastern Studies* 47 (2010): 305–321.

———. "*Al-Mustabṣirūn,* 'Those Who Are Able to See the Light': Sunnī Conversion to Twelver Shīʿism in Modern Times." *Die Welt des Islams* 51 (2011): 210–234.

———. "Noah and Noah's Ark as the Primordial Model of Shiʿism in Shiʿite Literature." *Quaderni di Studi Arabi nuova serie* 1 (2006): 29–48.

———. "The Role of Birds in Shiʿite Thought." *Quaderni* 3 (2008): 165–181.

———. "The Role of the Lion in Miracles Associated with Shīʿite Imāms." *Der Islam* 84, no. 2 (2007): 356–390.

———. "The Sea in the Miracles of Šīʿite Imams." *Oriente Moderno* 89, no. 2 (2009): 445–471.

———. "Visit to the Tomb of al-Ḥusayn b. ʿAlī in Shiite Poetry: First to Fifth Centuries AH (8th–11th Centuries CE)." *Journal of Arabic Literature* 37, no. 2 (2006): 230–258.

Soufi, Denise. "The Image of Fāṭimah in Classical Muslim Thought." PhD diss., Princeton University, 1997.

Spellberg, Denise. *Politics, Gender, and the Islamic Past: The Legacy of ʿAʾisha bint Abi Bakr.* New York: Columbia University Press, 1994.

Stetkevych, Suzanne. "The Generous Eye/I and the Poetics of Redemption: An Elegy by al-Fāriʿah b. Shaddād al-Murriyah." In *Literary Heritage of Classical Islam: Arabic and Islamic Studies in Honor of James Bellamy.* Edited by M. Mir, 85–105. Princeton, NJ: The Darwin Press, 1993.

———. "Obligations and Poetics of Gender: Women's Elegy and Blood Vengeance." In *The Immortals Speak: Pre-Islamic Poetry and the Poetics of Ritual,* 161–205. Ithaca, NY: Cornell University Press, 1993.

———. "Al-Sharīf al-Raḍī and the Poetics of ʿAlid Legitimacy Elegy for al-Ḥusayn ibn ʿAlī on ʿĀshūrāʾ, 391 A.H." *Journal of Arabic Literature* 38 (2007): 293–323.

Stewart, Devin. *Islamic Legal Orthodoxy: Twelver Shiite Responses to the Sunni Legal System.* Salt Lake City: University of Utah Press, 1998.

Stowasser, Barbara. "The Mothers of the Believers in the Ḥadīth." *The Muslim World* 82, nos. 1–2 (1992): 1–36.

Sulamī, Abū ʿAbd al-Raḥmān. *Early Sufi Women: Dhikr an-niswa al-muta ʿabbidāt aṣ-ṣūfiyyāt.* Translated by Rkia E. Cornell. Louisville, KY: Fons Vitae, 1999.

Swartz, Merlin. *Ibn al-Jawzī's* Kitāb al-Quṣṣāṣ wa-al-Mudhakkirīn. Beirut: Dar el-Machreq Éditeurs, 1971.

Al-Ṭabarī, Muḥammad b. Jarīr b. Yazīd. *The History of al-Ṭabarī: An Annotated Translation.* 40 vols. Edited by Ehsan Yar-Shater. Albany: State University of New York Press, ca. 1985–2007.

Ṭabāṭabā'ī, Muḥammad Ḥusayn. *Shī'eh dar Islām.* Qum: Daftar-i Tablīghāt-i Islāmī, 1348 [1969]. English translation: *Shi'ite Islam.* Translated by Seyyed Hossein Nasr. Albany: State University of New York Press, 1975.

Al-Ṭabrisī, Abū Manṣūr. *al-Iḥtijāj.* Edited by Muḥammad Bāqir al-Kharasān. 2 vols. [Najaf]: Dār al-Nu'mān, 1966.

Al-Ṭabrisī, Faḍl b. al-Ḥasan. *Tāj al-mawālīd.* In *Majmū'a nafīsa fī tārīkh al-a'imma: min āthār al-qudamā' min 'ulamā' al-imāmīya al-thuqāh.* Edited by Maḥmūd al-Ḥusaynī al-Mar'ashī, 65–117. Beirut: Dār al-Qāri', 2002.

Taylor, Anna. "Hagiography and Early Medieval History." *Religion Compass* 7, no. 1 (2013).

Al-Tha'labī, *'Arā'is al-majālis fī qiṣaṣ al-anbiyā.* Annotated, translated, and introduced by William M. Brinner. Leiden: Brill, 2002.

Thurlkill, Mary F. *Chosen Among Women: Mary and Fatima in Medieval Christianity and Shi'ite Islam.* Notre Dame, IN: University of Notre Dame Press, 2007.

Al-Ṭihrānī, Muḥammad Muḥsin Āghā Buzurg. *al-Dharī'ah ilá taṣānif al-Shī'ah.* 26 vols. Najaf: Maṭba'at al-Qaḍā, 1936–.

Tor, Deborah G. "An Historiographical Re-examination of the Appointment and Death of 'Alī al-Riḍā," *Der Islam* 78 (2001): 103–128.

Al-Ṭūsī, Muḥammad b. al-Ḥasan. *Fihrist kutub al-Shi'ah wa uṣūlahum wa-asm al-muṣan-fīn wa-aṣḥāb al-uṣūl.* Edited by 'Abd al-Azīz Ṭabāṭabā'ī. Qum: Maktabat al-Muḥaqiq al-Ṭabāṭabā'ī, 1420 [1999–2000].

Vilozny, Roy. "A Šī'ī Life Cycle According to al-Barqī's *Kitāb al-Maḥāsin.*" *Arabica* 54, no. 3 (2007): 362–396.

Waldman, Marilyn Robinson. *Toward a Theory of Historical Narrative: A Test Case Study in Perso-Islamicate Historiography.* Columbus: Ohio State University Press, 1980.

Wardrop, Shona. "The Lives of the Imāms, Muḥammad al-Jawād and 'Alī al-Hādī and the Development of the Shī'ite Organization." PhD diss., University of Edinburgh, 1988.

Williams, Michael Stuart. *Authorized Lives in Early Christian Biography: Between Eusebius and Augustine.* Cambridge: Cambridge University Press, 2008.

[World Organization for Islamic Sciences] (WOFIS). *A Brief History of the Fourteen Infallibles.* Tehran: World Organization for Islamic Sciences, 1984.

Acknowledgments

I could not possibly list all the people who have influenced this project, which has taken many years to complete. Innumerable conversations, some of them merely in passing, have impacted the ways my research developed. Many of those conversations were with people with whom I have lost touch or whose names I no longer remember. My time studying in Iran was formative, however, and I will never forget the generosity and assistance provided to me by the Imam Khomeini Education and Research Institute in its partnership with the Mennonite Central Committee. I am especially indebted to the many kindnesses of Muhammad Legenhausen, Heidi Javandil, Abolhasan Haghani, Hussein Tofighi, Mohammad Nateq, Mohammad Fanaie Eshkevari, Evie Shellenberger, Wally Shellenberger, and Ed Martin.

I am also indebted to many at Boston University who invested significant time in helping me along, including Scott Michael Girdner, Karen Nardella, Deeana Klepper, Herbert Mason, Houchang Chehabi, and Merlin Swartz. Jennifer Knust played a particularly formative role in shaping my understanding of gender theory and the gendered dynamics in religious texts. The many hours she spent reading and discussing theory with me and Courtney Wilson VanVeller are among my fondest memories from my time at BU. Perhaps the most fortuitous event of my academic career, however, was coming under the guidance of Kecia Ali. Her insights have impacted my work at all levels, and her generosity in reading drafts of this project, talking through ideas, and providing counseling of all types can never be repaid. She has been a model advisor and is a valued friend. Others in the Boston area whose time with me influenced my work, though they may not realize it, include Leila Ahmed, Roy Mottahedeh, and the late Wolfhart Heinrichs. The Institute for the Study of Muslim Societies & Civilizations made my study at Boston University possible.

In recent years, I have greatly benefited from the supportive community at Centre College, including the financial contributions the college has provided to assist me in my research. I am especially grateful to my colleagues in the Religion Program: C. Thomas

McCollough, Beth Glazier-McDonald, Rick Axtell, W. David Hall, Lee Jefferson, and Christian Haskett. Also, many thanks to the "Lounge Lunch" crew for the comic relief that has made every trial in recent years less burdensome. I am also grateful to my students at Centre College who read portions of the manuscript and offered feedback, including Wood Smith, who helped me find thematic analogues in early Christian writings. A portion of my research on Fatima was presented in a talk at George Mason University's Ali Vural Ak Center for Global Islamic Studies, and conversations there helped me refine my arguments.

Sharmila Sen at Harvard University Press has provided insightful advice along the path toward publishing this book, and I am grateful for her belief in this project. It has been wonderful to work with her and with Heather Hughes to bring this research into fruition. I am also indebted to the anonymous readers whose insights and suggestions improved the manuscript. Andrew Newman provided many instructive comments on an earlier draft of the manuscript, for which I am deeply appreciative.

My friendships with Ata Anzali, Sean Anthony, Catherine Bronson, and Micah Lott extend far beyond our professional activities, and they have shaped me as a person even as they have sharpened my academic endeavors. Their companionship has meant much over many years. I am grateful to my family, especially to my two daughters, to whom I dedicate this book, and to my mother, Janet Pierce. Finally, my wife, Laurie, has been an emotional support through many stages of life, my unwavering ally, my most critical editor, and my closest friend. Thank you.

Index

For the purposes of alphabetizing this index, I ignore Arabic's definite article (*al-*), as well as the letters *ʿayn* (ʿ) and *hamza* (ʾ).